The Irish Labour Party in transition

Michael Gallagher

The
Irish Labour Party
in transition
1957–82

Manchester University Press

Gill and Macmillan

Copyright © Michael Gallagher 1982

Published by
Manchester University Press
Oxford Road, Manchester M13 9PL

British Library cataloguing in publication data
Gallagher, Michael
   The Irish Labour Party in transition 1957–82.
   1. Irish Labour Party – History
   I. Title
   324.2417′074   JN1571

   ISBN 0–7190–0866–2

Published in Ireland by
Gill and Macmillan Ltd
Goldenbridge
Dublin 8

7171 1250 0

Photoset in Plantin
by Northern Phototypesetting Company, Bolton
Printed and bound in Great Britain by
Biddles Ltd, Guildford and King's Lynn

Contents

List of tables

Preface

It is customary for authors of books and theses to begin by attempting to establish the crucial importance of the tiny area of human activity with which they are concerned, and then to proceed to berate the rest of the academic world for having 'totally ignored' it in the past. While it is true that modern (i.e. post-1922) Irish political history still seems a relatively neglected area, partly because of the reluctance of politicians to commit their experiences to paper, the terrain is far less uncharted than was the case only ten years ago. Moreover the Labour Party has probably received an above-average share of attention, perhaps because to non-Irish writers it is the only party to come from a familiar mould, and because, in the past at least, it has seemed the most open and willing to help researchers. Even so, much work remains for political cartographers, and a study of the Irish Labour Party between 1957 and 1982 need not be prefaced by an apology for going over well-trodden ground.

This book is a much modified version of a PhD thesis on 'The Irish Labour Party in Transition, 1957–1973' submitted to the University of Strathclyde, Glasgow, in 1979, and takes account of developments up to the defeat of the fourth coalition government in February 1982. Many individuals and institutions were of assistance in various ways during the preparation of thesis and book. I should like to thank my thesis supervisor, Tom Mackie, and Professor Richard Rose, both of the University of Strathclyde; Professor Basil Chubb and Michael Marsh of Trinity College, Dublin; Brian Farrell and Tom Garvin of University College, Dublin; John Whyte, Professor Cornelius O'Leary and the late Professor Rodney Green of Queen's University, Belfast; and Owen Dudley Edwards of the University of Edinburgh.

I should also like to thank those present or former Irish politicians and trade unionists, listed in the bibliography, who agreed to be interviewed. Since they were being asked about matters which were still politically sensitive, some were reluctant to talk freely, but most were fairly open, and some, who would no doubt prefer not to be singled out, were very helpful indeed. Since interviewees were promised confidentiality, they are not quoted by name in the text. Labour's Head Office willingly provided documents, records and information, and I should like particularly to thank Seamus Scally, general secretary. In addition, several party members and others not actually interviewed have also been of help.

The resources of a number of libraries have been drawn on. I am grateful for the facilities offered by the National Library of Ireland, Dublin, and the libraries of Trinity College, Dublin, University College, Dublin, Queen's University of Belfast and the University of Strathclyde, as well as the Mitchell Library, Glasgow. Financial support was provided initially by the Social Science Research Council of the United Kingdom, and subsequently by a research fellowship at the Institute of Irish Studies, Queen's University, Belfast.

The tasks of typing the manuscript, proof-reading and indexing were speedily and efficiently carried out by myself.

Abbreviations used

AC	Administrative Council
ATGWU	Amalgamated Transport and General Workers' Union
CIU	Congress of Irish Unions
DD	Dáil Debates
FF	Fianna Fáil
FG	Fine Gael
FWUI	Federated Workers' Union of Ireland
ICTU	Irish Congress of Trade Unions
I Ind	Irish Independent
ILP	Irish Labour Party
IP	Irish Press
IPOOA	Irish Post Office Officials' Association
IRA	Irish Republican Army
IT	Irish Times
ITGWU	Irish Transport and General Workers' Union
ITUC	Irish Trades Union Congress
LCLL	Liaison Committee of the Labour Left
NILP	Northern Ireland Labour Party
NPD	National Progressive Democrats
PLP	Parliamentary Labour Party
POWU	Post Office Workers' Union
PR	Proportional Representation; the name by which the Irish electoral system is generally known in Ireland
RLP	Republican Labour Party
RTE	Radio Telefís Eireann
SD	Seanad Debates
SDLP	Social Democratic and Labour Party
S Ind	Sunday Independent

SLP	Socialist Labour Party
SP	Sunday Press
STV	Single transferable vote
TCD	Trinity College Dublin
TD	Teachta Dála (Dáil deputy)
UCD	University College Dublin
WUI	Workers' Union of Ireland

Glossary of Irish terms

Ard-Fheis	Term used for annual conferences of several political parties
Ceann Comhairle	Speaker or chairman of Dáil
Dáil	Lower house of parliament
Oireachtas	Parliament
Seanad	Senate, upper house of parliament
Tánaiste	Deputy Prime Minister
Taoiseach	Prime Minister

1
Background and context

The Irish Labour Party has been described as 'perhaps the most difficult of the Irish parties to understand'.[1] The general weakness of the Irish left, and the picture, accurate until the 1960s, of a conservative Labour Party with sometimes not a single parliamentary seat in the industrial centre of the country, and with the support of only a small minority of trade union members, have all seemed puzzling to some. This book examines the party over the period 1957 to 1982, one of transition for it during which some, but not all, of the anomalies were resolved.

The electoral potential of any party is determined to some extent by the nature of the party system within which it operates, by its own background, and by the political culture and social structure of the society in which it exists. In the case of the Irish Labour Party, it can be argued, each of these factors is inimical to its prospects. The cleavage which generated the largest two parties in the State is none of those employed by Lipset and Rokkan to explain the development of European party systems: centre versus periphery, landed interests versus industrialists, Church versus State and employers versus workers.[2] Ireland's by-passing of the first two of these conflicts was due mainly to its status as a part of the United Kingdom until 1922, and the breaking away of the Irish Free State in that year, which has led to suggestions that its political system is 'best viewed' as an example of decolonialising political systems.[3]

Instead, modern politics in the Republic of Ireland can be said to date from December 1921, when the Anglo-Irish Treaty, establishing the Irish Free State, was signed.[4] A sizeable minority in both the Dáil (the lower house of the Oireachtas, the parliament) and the country opposed it, and the then-dominant Sinn Féin party split irrevocably over the question of whether it should be accepted. The pro-Treaty TDs (Dáil deputies) formed themselves into the Cumann na nGaedheal party, which in 1933 merged with two smaller groups to form Fine Gael. The anti-Treaty TDs at first refused to recognise the legitimacy of the Dáil, but in 1927 those who had followed Eamon de Valera into the Fianna Fáil party, which he had founded in the previous year, took their seats.

These two parties have always been the largest in the State. Cumann na nGaedheal was in power from 1922 to 1932, but Fianna Fáil then embarked on an unbroken run of sixteen years in office. Coalition governments were in power between 1948 and 1951, and between 1954 and 1957. In its early years Fianna Fáil probably drew its support mainly from small farmers, the lower middle class and the working class, and appeared vaguely radical by the standards of Irish politics, while Fine Gael appealed to the wealthier sections of Irish society and was very conservative. From the 1940s to 1957, however, there was little socio-economic difference between the parties, both having a centre-right outlook. The only significant difference was that Fianna Fáil cultivated an image of being slightly more nationalistic, and attached more importance to the revival of the Irish language.[5]

Such a cleavage is not, obviously, one ripe for exploitation by a Labour party. The polarisation of the electorate in the 1920s around a subject far removed from the traditional socio-economic concerns of Labour parties left the ILP out in the cold, arguing that voters had chosen the wrong issue over which to divide. Most Labour members have always tended to believe that, with respect to the issues most important to themselves, the two major parties are little different, and that in reality the fundamental cleavage in Irish politics runs between their party on the one hand and Fianna Fáil and Fine Gael on the other. Their failure to attract the support of more than a fifth of the Irish electorate to their side can be attributed partly to the image which the party presented to the electorate up to 1957.

1.1 The Irish Labour Party from its foundation to 1957

The circumstances surrounding the formation of the Irish Labour Party had a strong impact on its subsequent development. The general point is put forcefully by Duverger: 'Just as men bear all their lives the mark of their childhood, so parties are profoundly influenced by their origins . . . It is the whole life of the party which bears the mark of its origin.'[6] The ILP was founded by the Irish Trade Union Congress (ITUC), but the year of its foundation is a matter for debate. The party itself commemorates 1912, when the ITUC, meeting in Clonmel, passed a motion to the effect that it establish its own party. Little, if any, action ensued, so a slightly stronger case could be made for 1914, when the ITUC added 'and Labour Party' to its name. However, apart from a Dublin by-election in 1915, the party did not enter the electoral arena until the 1920 local elections, and did not contest a general election until 1922. It did not attain an independent existence until 1930, when the ITUC and the Labour Party separated.[7]

At the 1922 election Labour won 21·3 per cent of the votes cast, its highest ever strength, and saw seventeen of its eighteen candidates elected, but by 1933 it was reduced to 5·7 per cent of the votes and eight TDs in the 153-member Dáil. Its fortunes then improved slightly, and it rose to seventeen seats in 1943, but its advance was checked by an internal rift which led to the establishment of a break-away National Labour Party (see below); the two parties re-merged in June 1950.[8] Labour first tasted power in 1948, when it took part in a coalition government, the first Inter-Party government, which lasted until 1951, and it was also part of the 1954–1957 second Inter-Party government.

Throughout this period, Labour's outlook was such as to lead to its being described as 'the most opportunistically conservative Labour Party anywhere in the known world' and as 'not recognizable as a Labour Party on the normal social democratic pattern'.[9] It was almost entirely reformist and did not in any way favour a socialist reconstruction of society; instead, it called for reductions in the taxes on food, or for ultra-incrementalist measures such as an 'extra half-ounce of tea for all bog workers'.[10] Most of its TDs were assiduous workers for their constituents, but did not make any national impact. Nor, on the whole, did its leaders, of whom there were only three between 1922 and 1960. The first, Thomas Johnson, was a thoughtful, hard-working man and an excellent parliamentarian, but he lost his seat in September 1927. His successor, T. J. O'Connell, has been described as being 'in the Johnson mould . . . a careful, cautious leader of great dedication and integrity, but with little popular appeal'.[11] He lost his Dáil seat in 1932, and was succeeded by William Norton, whose career is assessed in Chapter 2.4 below. The leadership of these three men has been described as 'usually competent [but] rarely . . . inspired', 'indifferent' and 'not outstanding'.[12]

Labour's foundation by the trade union movement was of paramount importance. Before 1930 it was unashamedly 'a party of trade unionists for trade unionists';[13] after 1930 it remained so in spirit. Up to 1930 it regarded itself as simply the political arm of the trade union movement. Originally membership was limited to affiliated trade unions and trade councils; moves to broaden the membership were defeated at the 1914, 1918 and 1924 Congresses, and although provision had been made for trade unionists to join as individual members, very few did so.[14] The 1914 Congress, concerned to 'prevent the politicians from worming their way into the new Party', also ordained that any Labour candidate for a public body must be a trade union member.[15] After 1930 only the formal position changed. The party remained 'trade unionist in personnel and mentality'[16] and seemed to see its function as 'the defence or promotion of trades union interests in the Dáil'.[17] Exactly half the individuals who were Labour TDs between 1922 and 1948 were trade union officials, as were twenty-seven of the forty-four candidates at the June 1927 general election, and most of the party's leading figures were 'first and foremost trade union officials'.[18] They possessed neither the inclination to seek new bases of support nor much idea of how they might go about looking for it. Labour neither attracted, nor really tried to attract, many farmers, professional people or 'intellectuals' to its ranks. Conor Cruise O'Brien's 1966 description of it as having been 'dominated for years by dismal poltroons, on the lines of O'Casey's Uncle Payther',[19] unfair as it may be, probably encapsulates fairly accurately the appearance it had in the eyes of the intelligentsia. In Mitchell's words, the ITUC–Labour Party relationship was simply one in which 'the over-possessive parent stunted its child's growth'.[20]

Consequently the party suffered in the eyes of non-trade unionists from appearing to be little more than an appendage of the trade union movement. This close identification might not have posed a problem had it actually got the electoral support of most trade unionists, but instead it was the victim of an unfortunate irony whereby non-unionists regarded it as a trade union party while only a minority of union members thought of it as their party. Even at one of Labour's strongest moments, in 1969, a Gallup survey found that only 37 per cent of working-class trade union members were Labour supporters.[21] It may be that, nurtured so closely by the ITUC as it was, the party has always been identified in the eyes of many workers with the trade union establishment and bureaucracy rather than with the ordinary trade unionist, and certainly it has tended to be wary about involving itself in matters which Congress regards as falling within its own sphere.

Another disadvantage of the close relationship between the two bodies was that, on two occasions, disputes within the trade union substructure adversely affected the political party superstructure. In 1923 a split within the Irish Transport and General Workers' Union (ITGWU), at that time the core of the ITUC and hence of the Labour Party, led to the establishment by James Larkin of a new union, the Workers' Union of Ireland (WUI). Larkin stood on five occasions in Dublin constituencies as an Independent Labour candidate, three times against official Labour candidates, and was twice elected. The second dispute, in many ways a continuation of the first, erupted in 1944, by which time Larkin had been re-admitted to the Labour Party. The ITGWU, whose general secretary, William O'Brien, nurtured a vindictive dislike of Larkin, failed to have him and his son expelled from the party, and disaffiliated in pique. Of the seventeen Labour TDs, eight were ITGWU members, and five of these now broke away to form the National Labour Party, which, with the encouragement of the ITGWU, devoted most of its energies to attacking Labour.[22]

Rivalry between Larkinites and the Labour Party severely damaged the latter in Dublin for many years,[23] and goes a long way towards explaining why Labour was a mainly rural force for so long. It is noticeable that at the 1922 election Labour's average strength at the two Dublin City constituencies it contested was not much below its national average, but at the 1923 election, after the ITGWU split had taken place, its share of the votes in Dublin City had slumped to 2·5 per cent as against 11·5 per cent in the rest of Ireland. This remained the pattern until 1943, the first election at which both the Larkinites and the ITGWU threw their weight behind the Labour Party, and at which for the first time the party's strength in Dublin City (16·8 per cent) actually exceeded its strength in the rest of Ireland (15·5 per cent). Subsequently Labour was adversely affected in Dublin by the 1944 split, and by competition for the left-of-centre vote from Clann na Poblachta (see note 1, Chapter 2) and some left-leaning Independents.

An advantage of the union connection, however, was that money from the unions for long constituted the most important source of income for the party; it was paid in the form of affiliation fees by affiliated unions,[24] and of support for union members standing for

Labour at elections. Moreover, it would be little exaggeration to say that at times, when Labour was weak and its parliamentary party consisted mainly of people largely uninterested in matters beyond their own constituency boundaries, the trade union base was all that kept it together and gave it any sense of purpose.

While Labour's development from the womb of the unions was, at times, only too obvious, the impact of James Connolly and James Larkin, generally regarded as its two most prominent founders, seemed for many years to be negligible. Connolly, who proposed the key resolution at the Clonmel Congress, has been described as 'possibly the most significant contributor to left-wing political theory to be produced by the British Isles in the past hundred years'.[25] He was a Marxist who had worked in the USA with Daniel De Leon's Socialist Labor Party and the syndicalist Industrial Workers of the World. He returned to Ireland in 1910 to work for the tiny Socialist Party of Ireland and the ITGWU, and became leader of the Irish Citizen Army, a small body of armed workers, and took part in the Easter Rising of 1916. He was one of the seven signatories of the insurgents' Proclamation and commanded the insurrectionary forces in Dublin. He was executed by the British in May 1916.[26]

Larkin, born and raised in Liverpool, entered Ireland in 1907, and can take principal credit for introducing the 'new unionism', with its emphasis on militant action and the sympathetic strike, to the country. An activist rather than a writer, he spoke in favour of the Clonmel resolution, founded the ITGWU, and led the great Dublin strike of 1913, which was defeated by an employers' lock-out. He spent the years 1914 to 1923 in the USA, and never regained the powerful position he had enjoyed before his departure. It was his attempt, upon his return, to re-forge his links with the rank and file of the ITGWU, and to by-pass and displace the leadership group which had built up the union in his absence, that caused the 1923 dispute.[27]

These brief backgrounds raise an obvious question: if Connolly and Larkin founded the Irish Labour Party, why was it such a reformist, timid, non-socialist and anti-communist party from 1922 to the 1960s? Thornley, attempting to answer a similar question – 'How did the militant Marxist movement of Connolly and Larkin become the gradualist and scarcely socialist party of today?' – maintains that the reason lay in Labour's failure to be sufficiently nationalist, but *en route* to this dubious conclusion[28] he acknowledges a point which may be more valid when he concedes that 'the revolutionary fervour of

Connolly and Larkin was never fully representative of the movement as a whole'.[29]

The truth is that their revolutionary fervour was never representative of the movement at all. Few of the contemporaries of Connolly and Larkin in the labour movement shared their Marxism, and Emmet Larkin maintains, probably correctly, that they 'had captured the Irish Labour movement more because of their integrity and abilities than their devotion to an ideology'.[30] Thornley acknowledges that Connolly's Citizen Army was very small even at the peak of its strength, and that Larkin's authority even over his union was limited outside Dublin.[31] Connolly died before Labour had to face the reality of contesting elections in an Irish State, and it is doubtful whether he could have maintained, or would have wanted to maintain, a leading position within the party while continuing to expound his political beliefs. He had little electoral success, and never won an election for a public office despite a number of attempts, whereas most other leaders of the labour movement had done so by the time of his death. It is hard to imagine Connolly finding himself in harmony with the people who constituted the Parliamentary Labour Party for many years after 1922, or feeling comfortable in a party which passed resolutions condemning 'Godless Communism', and it is fanciful to imagine that he could single-handedly have steered Labour onto a different path. Had he lived, he would quite probably have fallen out with the party in the same way as Larkin and P. T. Daly.

It is being argued, then, that the question of why the 'militant Marxist movement' of Connolly and Larkin became the reformist party of the post-1922 period does not really require an answer, because Labour was never in fact imbued with the political philosophy of Connolly and Larkin. Much of the mystery disappears if it is accepted that, despite the resolutions of the 1912 and 1914 Congresses, a 'Labour Party' existed only on paper until the 1922 general election campaign. Mitchell in fact admits that in 1922 Labour was 'still largely a paper organization', and he also points out that candidate selection was done by local conferences of trade unions and trade councils, since there was 'no separate political structure'.[32] The party was really only called into life by the 1922 campaign, and its manifesto was entirely reformist.[33] The seventeen Labour TDs elected then were in the mould of, and in several cases were, the men who were to dominate the party for the next forty years. By 1922, moreover, the trade union movement was no longer a crusade against social injustice but an increasingly cautious and bureaucratic organisation which often seemed more concerned with the size of its funds than with, say, the fate of the unemployed. In other words, there is no question of a radical Labour Party of 1912–22 subsequently becoming timid and reformist. In reality there was no Labour Party before 1922, and although there were radicals before that date, they were not the ones who actually created the party. This task fell to ordinary trade unionists, who thought of politics in specific bread-and-butter terms rather than in ideological terms, as Connolly had.

Party members of the most conservative opinions regularly asserted that they believed in 'the principles of James Connolly', but the principles themselves were distorted beyond recognition and effectively forgotten. The reverence for Connolly sprang from respect for his memory, and from his participation in the labour struggles of the 1910s and in the Easter Rising, as well as the callousness of his execution, rather than from any sympathy with his rarely-read writings. William O'Brien, for example, seems to have considered himself 'unswervingly loyal' to Connolly's teachings, without being aware of any incongruity in his behaviour, while conducting the 1944 campaign alleging that Labour had been taken over by communists.[34] Connolly remained a revered (and useful) symbol for the party, but his impact on its direction was negligible.

1.2 The political culture of the Irish Republic

The manner in which Labour was founded, and the influences most powerful at the time of its birth, go some way towards explaining its limited appeal over the years, but for a fuller explanation it is necessary to look also at its political context. A country's political culture, which may be defined as 'the emotional and attitudinal environment within which the political system operates' or 'the overall distribution of citizens' orientations to political objects',[35] has many components, and no attempt will be made here to paint a full picture of Irish political culture. Instead, some of those aspects which have particular significance for Labour will be examined, before their impact is assessed in Chapter 1.3 below.

1.2.1   *The conservative nature of political attitudes*
It has sometimes been asserted that the Irish are suspicious of left-wing political philosophies. Mansergh, for example, writes that one of

Labour's problems has been 'the Irishman's distaste for the rigidity of a Socialist system', and Judge believes that the party has been handicapped by 'the shadowy background of some form of Socialism'.[36]

The view that Irish political and social attitudes are particularly conservative is true in some respects, but open to question in others. In social matters the Republic has been notoriously illiberal by the standards of the rest of the world. The Constitution prohibits the enactment of any law allowing for the provision of divorce, and the sale of contraceptives, even to married people, was illegal until 1979. Censorship in the past was so strict that almost every international writer of merit had works banned, although there has been a liberalisation since the mid-1960s. Here the impact of the strength of the Catholic Church is obvious.

Politically, too, attitudes are in some ways conservative. The Constitution itself declares that the State 'acknowledges' that man has 'the natural right' to the private ownership of goods, and guarantees that it will pass no law attempting to abolish this right. The State also undertakes to 'favour and, where necessary, supplement private initiative in industry and commerce'.[37]

A survey of 2,300 Dubliners carried out in 1972 and 1973 by Mac Gréil found that, of seventy 'stimulus categories', Communists were sixty-ninth in order of popularity, ahead only of 'Drug Pushers' and below both wings of the IRA, 'Criminals' and 'Drug Addicts'.[38] Only 22·9 per cent of those surveyed were prepared to accept a communist into their family, and 27·2 per cent favoured their expulsion from Ireland. 'Socialists' finished in forty-fourth position, one place above 'Heavy Drinkers', while Labour Party members emerged as the thirtieth most popular, with 76·3 per cent of respondents willing to marry one or admit one to their family; only 1·6 per cent favoured the deportation of Labour members. A majority of respondents agreed that 'Communism should be outlawed in Ireland', a hostility based mainly on political rather than religious grounds. Communists, like socialists and Labour Party members, were regarded least favourably by women, the old, those with least education, those in unskilled or semi-skilled manual employment, and those raised in rural areas.[39] It must be borne in mind that the survey covered only residents of Dublin, and that attitudes are probably less liberal in the rest of Ireland.

Certainly, organised communism has always been pitifully weak in

Ireland. Its only electoral success came in September 1927, when James Larkin won election to the Dáil, although he was unable to take his seat because he was an undischarged bankrupt. At the time he was a candidate member of the executive committee of the Communist International, of which his Irish Workers' League was the Irish section.[40] It need hardly be said that his election was due to his personal appeal rather than to enthusiasm in North Dublin for the Comintern.

What evidence there is does indeed suggest that the attitudes of the Irish are relatively conservative. Surveys carried out by Inglehart and Klingemann in the nine European Community countries in September 1973 asked respondents to place their political views somewhere on a scale running from 1 (extreme left) to 10 (extreme right), and the average for each country was calculated, the 'centre' position being 5·5. The Irish figure of 6·30 was by some distance the closest to the right-wing end of the scale; the Netherlands' figure of 5·80 was the second highest. In Ireland 61 per cent of respondents placed their views somewhere to the right of centre, again by far the highest proportion. Moreover, whereas in every other country the most popular points on the scale were 5 or 6, i.e. slightly to the left or the right of centre, in Ireland more people (16·8 per cent) opted for 10, the extreme right-wing position, than for any other point on the scale.[41] When the figures were broken down to distinguish between identifiers with the different parties the same pattern emerged. Labour supporters were only slightly to the left of centre, their average of 5·03 being to the right of every other socialist or social democratic party. Fine Gael's and Fianna Fáil's figures (6·68 and 6·59 respectively) were both among the fourteen highest (i.e. most right-wing) of the forty-five parties covered.[42]

At the same time, there are few voices raised in favour of a stridently right-wing approach to politics, and whereas social attitudes have tended to be illiberal, economic attitudes have been pragmatic. Successive governments, while expressing a preference for private enterprise, have been prepared to extend the level of State activity in the economy where glaring needs have existed and the private sector has failed to meet them. Although no Irish government has embarked on nationalisation on ideological grounds, none has been unwilling to create nationalised industries – always called 'semi-State industries' or 'State-sponsored bodies' – if this can be justified on pragmatic grounds. The two major parties profess not an explicit conservatism but a dislike of 'isms', and claim to be non-doctrinaire parties without ideological obsessions. According to them, class conflict is not endemic in society; society is essentially in harmony, and the interests of all groups are complementary rather than antagonistic, so that those who take a contrary view are acting against the national interest, by attempting to foment class conflict and set section against section. The only acceptable -ism is pragmatism.

Indeed, Inglehart and Klingemann conclude that the reason why Ireland emerged from their study as a 'persistent deviant case', with apparently unusually right-wing attitudes, is simply that 'the left–right dimension is less meaningful in Ireland than in most other Western countries'.[43] No Irish party accepts the label 'conservative', and none calls itself 'right-wing'. As Sartori points out, referring to the 'evaluative imbalance between left and right', 'left' possesses an 'ever-growing evaluative positiveness' and has become 'the most coveted and crucial word in the war of words with which political battles are fought.'[44] Almost all Irish politicians are at pains to stress that they are slightly left of centre, although their definitions of the term are sometimes idiosyncratic. For example, Paddy Donegan TD, a former Fine Gael Minister and wealthy businessman, who in a non-Irish context would be regarded as an archetypal right-winger, once stated:[45]

Lots of people might possibly think of me as a conservative. But I am not a conservative at all and never was. I define myself completely and absolutely as a little bit left of centre because everyone who knows me realizes that I am a bit of a believer in the calculated risk both in business and politics.

Similarly, a very wealthy Fianna Fáil TD once indicated that, while he would gladly accept a definition of himself as a socialist, he was opposed to 'doctrinaire socialism', which involved such things as the introduction of a wealth tax and 'talking about wealth, capital, millionaires, downtrodden workers'.[46] The Fianna Fáil Taoiseach (Prime Minister) Seán Lemass, a strong believer in private enterprise, frequently accused the Labour Party of being 'conservative', and the Fianna Fáil Minister Erskine Childers often described his party, with evident sincerity, as 'a radical, left of centre, free enterprise party'. In a series of debates in the early 1960s, TDs of each party claimed that their party was to the left of their opponent's (see Chapter 3.1 below). Garvin, from research in a Dublin constituency in 1972–73, found that activists of each party believed, or professed to believe, that their rivals were further to the right than they were.[47]

1.2.2   *The position of the Roman Catholic Church*

According to the most recent census, 93·9 per cent of the population of the Irish Republic in 1971 were Catholics.[48] Most of these were practising Catholics. A survey conducted in 1973 and 1974 found that 91 per cent of Catholic respondents claimed to attend Mass at least once weekly, and 97 per cent claimed to pray at least once daily.[49] A combination of the overwhelming proportion of Catholics, the hierarchical nature of the Catholic Church, and the authoritarianism which is another feature of Irish political culture, all combine to give the Church a powerful place in Irish society. The 1937 Constitution 'recognised' the 'special position' of the Catholic Church, along with the existence of other Churches, in two sub-sections of an Article which were deleted by referendum in 1972.[50] In the past the Hierarchy, as the Catholic bishops collectively are known, issued pronouncements *ex cathedra* on many subjects and expected governments to heed its 'advice', leading to a belief that it wielded considerable political power.[51]

The Irish Catholic Church has traditionally been very conservative by European standards, especially but not exclusively in matters of sexual morality.[52] Until recently it was obsessively anti-communist and was deeply suspicious of State involvement in the economy and many other areas of societal activity. It was hostile to the early efforts of Connolly and Larkin to improve the lot of the urban working class, partly because most priests tended to be sons of farmers rather than of labourers,[53] and partly because Catholic social teaching at the time was inspired by Pope Leo XIII's 1891 encyclical *Rerum Novarum*. This advocated, rather vaguely, 'class harmony' rather than 'class warfare', asserted man's 'right' to private property, and was regarded as a refutation of the arguments of socialists.[54] Neither Connolly nor Larkin was anti-clerical, Connolly maintaining that socialists should not embroil themselves in conflict with the Church, which would rapidly 'adjust to the new order' if socialism were ever established.[55]

The only hint of conflict between Labour and the Church arose in the late 1930s, when the party adopted a new constitution. This included a declaration that Labour's aim was 'the establishment in Ireland of a Workers' Republic', that it believed in 'a system of government which is based upon the public ownership by the people of all essential sources of wealth', and that one of its objects was 'to win for the people of Ireland, collectively, the ownership and control of the whole produce of their labour [and] to secure the democratic management of all industries and services by the whole body of citizens'.[56]

However, some members were disturbed by such sentiments. The Irish National Teachers' Organisation, a union affiliated to the party, was worried that, taken out of context, they might lead to a suspicion that 'the aims of the Labour Party were socialistic',[57] and consequently it asked the Hierarchy to pass an opinion on them. The Hierarchy duly obliged by declaring them 'contrary to Catholic social teaching', which put the ball back in Labour's court. The leadership felt that, under the circumstances, it had no option but to remove the contentious phrases. At the 1939 conference William Norton denied that the use of 'Workers' Republic' meant that Labour wanted to establish a political system like the Soviet Union's, or that the constitution made inadequate provision for the safeguarding of private property, but, he added fatalistically, to refuse to make changes would put weapons into the hands of Labour's enemies.[58] The conference voted by eighty-nine votes to twenty-five to allow the Administrative Council to amend the constitution, and the AC did so in April 1940. Of the three troublesome phrases, the third was simply dropped, and the first two were so rewritten as to make them wholly platitudinous. Among other changes, the words 'Workers' Republic' were removed from the first – they were not reinstated until 1972 – and the second now declared that Labour recognised 'the rights of private property'.[59]

To some extent, then, it is possible to see this incident as an example of fear of the Church preventing Labour from moving to the left, although the picture is not quite so simple. For one thing, it is not certain that Labour really was attempting to move to the left. At the 1935 conference one delegate claimed that the phrase 'Workers' Republic' had been included only because it was associated with Connolly, and in the hope of giving a radical veneer to an otherwise innocuous document. Connolly, he said, had been a 'revolutionary socialist' rather than a 'mere Reformist', and the new constitution differed greatly from what he stood for. It was even more 'wishy-washy' than the old one; that had been 'pale pink' and the new one was 'pale white'.[60]

It is important also to note that the Hierarchy was merely called upon as an ally by the more conservative sections of the party, and did not offer its opinion unbidden. In the main, Labour was almost as conservative as any other section of Irish society. Moss quotes the Dean of Ossory as saying in 1927 that socialism was 'in conflict with the fundamental principles of Christianity',[61] but it would be wrong to overlook the fact that many Labour members would have agreed with this view. For example, at a mass meeting in Limerick in 1936, Michael Keyes, the Labour TD for the constituency, proposed a motion to the effect[62]

> That we pledge our support to the Irish Christian Front in its efforts to bring into existence in this country a social and economic system based on the Christian ideals of life, as expressed in the Papal Encyclicals, and thereby to overcome the evils of Communism and Socialism, which are altogether contrary to Christian principles.

Labour's 1934 conference enthusiastically passed a motion declaring the party committed to the aim of 'a just Social Order based on Christian teaching' and opposed to 'any attempt to introduce anti-Christian communistic doctrines into the movement'.[63] When, at the 1938 conference, the youthful Conor Cruise O'Brien criticised the Spanish Nationalists while proposing a motion against fascism, William Norton intervened to state that the reference was irrelevant, and another TD, Gerrard McGowan, said that as a Catholic he must protest: 'With respect to everybody's religious beliefs, he said, they were Catholics first and politicians afterwards.'[64]

Despite all this, Labour found itself accused of communism in 1944, when the National Labour Party was formed. Although, of course, the power struggle within the union movement was at the root of the split, National Labour claimed that it had broken away because Labour had been taken over by communists, and it was supported by the Catholic paper *The Standard*.[65] National Labour's 1944 election manifesto stated that the party was pledged 'to strive by all legitimate means for the attainment of the ideal of social justice in accord with Christian beliefs and principles', adding that its candidates would face 'the fury of elements whose underground designs they have exposed and defeated. They stand neither for Moscow nor London'.[66] The party leader, James Everett, alleged that Labour had 'become infested by Communists' as a result of 'the underground designs of Moscow, London and Belfast [and] the wilful, underhand and equally culpable acquiescence of responsible persons in the Labour Party'. He contrasted this with National Labour's position: 'I am proud that the fundamental purpose of the party I represent is definitely and irrevocably committed to the Papal Encyclicals [and] to a declaration of resolve to implement the Christian philosophy of social justice enshrined therein'.[67] The two Labour parties re-merged amicably in

1950, and in fact, despite the fusillade launched by National Labour and the *Standard*, it is unlikely that their accusations were taken very seriously by many, or indeed believed by most of those who laid them so vigorously.

When the question of Church–State relations was raised dramatically by the Mother and Child episode in 1951, Labour kept largely out of the discussion. The incident arose when a health scheme, proposed by Dr Noel Browne, the Minister for Health, was pronounced contrary to Catholic social teaching by the Hierarchy. Browne refused, despite the insistence of all his Cabinet colleagues, to withdraw the scheme, and his resignation was requested and tendered in April 1951.[68] When the Dáil debated the affair, the only Labour TD to speak was the party leader, who criticised Browne's lack of judgement and suggested that he had actually been seeking a 'head-on collision' with the Church.[69] Then, addressing himself to the suggestion that the real issue was whether the government or the Hierarchy ruled the country, he declared that 'that issue is not going to arise in this country'. He went on:[70]

I say the Government will not allow that situation to arise, that there will be no flouting of the authority of the Bishops in the matter of Catholic social or Catholic moral teaching and if anybody imagines that defiance of the Bishops in this matter is to give liberty to the masses of the people then let him look at other countries where the moral law and Catholic social teaching has been defied and there he will find that the workers or the masses of the people have got very little liberty, very little of the liberty that was promised them when they abandoned adherence to, or recognition of, the moral law.

In short, there is little or no truth in the view, sometimes expressed since the mid-1960s, that Labour before then was a secretly or potentially radical party frustrated or held in check by a conservative Church. Such a view uses the power of the clergy as an excuse for the conservatism of the Labour Party. Until the mid-1960s very few politicians suggested or, quite probably, believed that the Church had too much power. One of the exceptions was James Larkin junior, who conducted an anti-clerical campaign when running as a communist in Dublin South in 1932. He was, notes Lysaght, 'lucky to lose only his deposit'.[71]

In the late 1950s the Church was still as conservative as ever. Clergy insisted, in the face of all the evidence, that communism was the most serious danger facing the country. One priest alleged that there were 700 or 800 Communist Party members in Dublin, led by men trained in Moscow and Leningrad, and that in some homes, presumably those owned by communists not yet familiar with Khrushchev's speech to the CPSU's twentieth congress, pictures of the sacred heart had been replaced by pictures of Stalin.[72] Persecution of religious bodies was regarded as an intrinsic feature of communism. The ludicrous fear that Ireland was in imminent danger of becoming a communist country was not confined to the clergy, of course. In 1961 a newspaper urged its readers to vote in the general election lest Ireland's fate be that of Eastern Europe:[73]

Do not think that such a thing is impossible as far as Catholic Ireland is concerned. It happened in Catholic Poland, and remember that one of the chief aims of Communism is world domination and this policy has plans to incorporate Ireland as well. There is a hard core of active communists in the country just biding their time until their chance comes. They are ever watchful and waiting just to pounce.

With the benefit of hindsight such diatribes may be seen as symptoms of a society riddled with self-doubt, but at the time there were few to take issue with them.

Nevertheless, change was taking place, and in the late 1950s the Church's traditional attitudes faced increasing resistance.[74] *Rerum Novarum* had been followed in 1931 by *Quadragesimo Anno*, in which Pius XI advocated corporatism and vocationalism, but Pope John XXIII's 1961 encyclical *Mater et Magistra* was much less hostile to socialism, to some extent welcoming State involvement in the running of society.[75] All the same, the pace of change in Ireland during the 1960s proved painfully slow, and even in 1976 Smith suggested that the relationship between religion and politics in Ireland was virtually unique. In most countries, he wrote, religion becomes separated from politics via a two-stage process. First, it moves from being a political issue to being merely a passive determinant of voting behaviour, and then it ceases to be even that. In Ireland, he observed, the relationship was still in a 'pre-primary stage', as religion had scarcely even been raised as a political issue; the State and society were permeated by religious values.[76]

1.2.3 *Individualism and conformism*
Individualism, by which is meant a preference for individual action as opposed to co-operation, is another significant feature of Irish political culture. Its most obvious political manifestation is the prevalence of 'broker politics', a well documented aspect of the political process. The essence of brokerage is that Irish politicians, in order to gain and retain

support, must build up a personal clientele of voters. This is achieved by acting as a broker between individual constituents on the one hand and the State or a private company on the other, i.e. by assisting, or appearing to assist, constituents to procure various benefits. Because of the need to act as brokers, backbench TDs spend a much greater proportion of their time engaged in work on behalf of their constituents than in participating actively in the legislative process. It is not uncommon for TDs to receive 200 letters a week, while some research suggests that British MPs, serving much larger constituencies, may expect to receive only about twenty-five.[77]

One cause of this phenomenon is the electoral system, the single transferable vote in multi-member constituencies. Because voters are able to give preference votes to candidates in any order they choose, each candidate is in competition with all other candidates, even – sometimes especially – those from her own party. A candidate cannot, as a rule, distance herself greatly from her running mates on policy matters, so she must employ another method of giving herself an edge over them. Usually, she will try to appear a more assiduous and more successful servant of her constituents,[78] to which end she must deal sympathetically with all requests for assistance, even if she feels she cannot be of any real help to the constituent or if she would prefer to be devoting her time to legislative matters. Another cause is the absence of alternative mechanisms for citizens to use if they are uncertain as to how they should apply for an allowance or a grant or wish to pursue a grievance against the civil service. A third explanation is that TDs are responding to Parkinson's Law, and engage in brokerage partly because the pitiful weakness of the Dáil *vis à vis* government means that they have no useful parliamentary role to play and therefore may as well spend their time dealing with constituents' problems as dissipating their energies delivering, or listening to others deliver, pre-written rhetorical speeches in the Dáil chamber. The strength of Catholicism may also be relevant. It has been pointed out that Catholicism involves a 'range of benevolent patron saints intermediate between God and favour-seeking, dependent humans', and brokerage might be seen as a secular equivalent of this.[79]

In addition, it seems that many constituents approach TDs for assistance because they believe, rightly or wrongly, that TDs have 'pull' and can obtain for them things which they could not obtain for themselves. This attitude is sometimes seen as a continuation of the pre-1922 perception of the central administration as an alien and

malign entity, best approached through an intermediary.[80] Whether a
TD really can pull strings on which constituents cannot get their
hands is an open question. Two studies conducted at opposite ends of
Ireland came to very different conclusions. Bax, who studied machine
politics in County Cork, suggests that politicians often do have
significant influence with public officials, while Sacks, who worked in
County Donegal, concludes that politicians are for the most part
deceiving their constituents by exercising what he terms 'imaginary
patronage'.[81] In many ways the question of whether the public believes
that a broker's efforts can influence events is as important as the
objective reality, and there is no doubt that most politicians encourage
the belief that their services are worth utilising. Some eminent ones,
indeed, have spoken openly in favour of the use of political patronage.
In 1967 the Minister for Education declared that he had 'no
hesitation, all things being equal, in supporting people who support me
or us'.[82] Four years later the Taoiseach said that it had always been the
case that most government briefs went to 'the barristers who are
disposed favourably to the party in power'.[83] In 1965 a Fine Gael TD
declared himself 'a great believer in putting a friend into a good job',
and added that if he ever attained a position of influence in the
country, he would offer no apology for 'filling every post I can, subject
to qualifications and ability, with my own friends and political
supporters'.[84] During the *cause célèbre* which became known as the
'Battle of Baltinglass' it was revealed that five TDs and two Senators
had made representations to the relevant Minister on behalf of the
successful applicant for the position of a sub-postmaster.[85]

Clearly, broker politics encourage individualism. Jobs and money
are both in limited supply, so that individuals know that their demand
can be met only if someone else's is not. It is in an individual's interests
to ensure that his case for a grant, or for a job in a factory whose owner
is a friend of a TD, is better presented than those of other individuals,
who are in effect his competitors. Brokerage produces vertical
associations, from the TD down to the individual constituent, rather
than horizontal associations of people in a similar situation – the
unemployed, for example – acting together. Two surveys, one
conducted in 1967 and the other around 1970, found that a majority of
respondents who felt that national or local government was intending
to do something unjust, and who wanted to try to prevent it, would act
as individuals rather than in a group.[86]

The same attitude can be detected from studies of Irish rural life.

The limited degree of co-operation involved in the practice of 'cooring'[87] has largely died out, and 'mutual aid has made way for an ethic of independence'.[88] Chubb's description of smallholders and their families as 'conservative, unimaginative, shrewd in the short run and individualistic'[89] is borne out by incidents cited by Brody. In one case, for example, some farmers were asked to give their consent to a county council scheme to improve a road servicing their farms. A majority refused because, Brody suggests, they feared they would be giving more benefit to others than they would receive themselves, and they preferred to put up with the existing cart track than to 'run the risks they felt must come from too much co-operating'.[90] Co-operative schemes in rural Ireland have experienced difficulty in getting off the ground, and even the founder of the most famous one has admitted that one of the main problems faced by his scheme over the years has been 'lack of co-operation from the majority of the people'.[91]

The large number of interest groups in the Republic, it is true, testifies to a willingness to co-operate for some purposes. Among these groups are trade unions, whose total membership encompasses slightly more than half of all wage and salary earners.[92] Even here, however, a lack of preparedness to sink differences in the interests of co-operation is shown by the proliferation of unions, most of which are craft unions with a membership of fewer than 1,500. In 1973 a comparative survey described the number of trade unions in the Republic as 'astonishingly large' by European standards; in 1979 there were eighty-five for fewer than half a million unionised workers.[93]

Moreover, individualism has not been associated with individuality. The emphasis on self-reliance and the reluctance to co-operate too closely with others have been accompanied not by a lively diversity of opinions or a pluralist society but by a narrow consensus and, until recently, a dull conformity with respect to most important subjects. Little imaginative or inquiring thinking took place, and creative artists have not found the intellectual climate a sympathetic one. The pressure for conformity is, not surprisingly, greatest in small rural communities where everybody knows everybody else's business.[94] Political attitudes, like all others, are liable to be subject to communal pressure. Studies carried out in County Clare in the 1930s, and on one of the Aran Islands in the 1960s, have described pressures brought to bear on people to support Fianna Fáil.[95] An additional source of pressure comes from the fact that election results, although officially published only on a constituency basis, are known in practice to the party 'tallymen' and others for much smaller areas, to a degree which sometimes comes close to violating the secrecy of the ballot. For example, in 1969 a newspaper reported that, of the fifteen papers in the ballot box from a small island in the South Kerry constituency, fourteen contained a first preference for one of the two Fianna Fáil candidates and the fifteenth had a first preference for the other, a significant deviation in the circumstances then obtaining in the constituency.[96] In short, a variety of local pressures combine to keep each individual's political opinions and voting behaviour in line with the majority's.

1.2.4 *Social structure and the weakness of class cleavages*

By modern European standards the outstanding feature of Ireland's social structure is the strength of the agricultural sector; in 1971 about 25·8 per cent of the population fell into the agricultural socio-economic groups.[97] From the same census the following breakdown can be obtained.[98] Farmers constituted 22·2 per cent of the population; higher and lower professionals, employers and managers and salaried employees made up 15 per cent; intermediate and other non-manual workers (mainly service workers) were 24 per cent; manual workers (including agricultural workers) were 38 per cent. If intermediate non-manual workers are taken as belonging to the middle class, but other non-manual workers are regarded as working-class, then middle-class strength is 28·2 per cent and working-class strength 49·6 per cent. Of the respondents to a 1969 Gallup survey, 22 per cent were farmers (social groups F1 and F2), while 30 per cent can be regarded as middle-class (social groups AB and C1) and 47 per cent as working-class (social groups C2 and DE).[99]

Three other points are worth making. The first is that employees constitute a relatively low proportion of the labour force; the 1964 figure has been estimated at 58 per cent, as against 90 per cent in Britain.[100] The second is that most farms are small; according to the 1971 census, 35·1 per cent of farmers owned less than thirty acres, and 61·2 per cent owned less than fifty acres.[101] The third, which demonstrates the still basically rural nature of Ireland, is that in 1971 only 52·2 per cent of the population lived in towns of 1,500 or more people.[102]

These objectively derived figures are instructive, but those derived from people's subjective assessments of their own position are also important, for it appears that many of those who are 'objectively' (i.e.

according to their occupation) members of the working class actually considered themselves middle-class. Of the respondents to the 1969 survey, 56 per cent said that they regarded themselves as upper, upper-middle, middle or lower-middle class, and only 36 per cent saw themselves as working-class. More than five times as many farmers placed themselves in one of the four higher categories as in the working class.[103] In contrast, when Butler and Stokes asked their British respondents in 1963 and 1970 for a subjective assessment, eleven-twelfths accepted or offered a categorisation of themselves, and of these 67 per cent (in 1963) and 63 per cent (in 1970) said that they were working-class.[104]

Ireland also differs from Britain and most other countries in that class cleavages appear to be weakly perceived – admittedly, the evidence on this point is only impressionistic – and in that class is not an important determinant of voting behaviour, even though no other factor is any more significant. Tree (AID) analyses performed by Whyte, running in succession each of the three main parties against the other two, found that the greatest degree of variance explained on any run was 14·8 per cent.[105] In so far as social class was a factor, it appeared, according to the 1969 survey, that Fianna Fáil drew support fairly evenly from all classes, while Fine Gael was strongest among the middle class and large farmers. Labour's support stood at about 14 per cent of the middle class, 28 per cent of the working class and only 3 per cent of farmers. Surveys conducted in 1976 and 1977 painted a similar picture.[106] Ecological analysis suggests that Labour has never attracted much support from farmers, and that up to the mid-1960s farm labourers were the backbone of its support.[107] The 1969 survey found that 73 per cent of Labour's supporters were members of the working class, and two later polls conducted by Irish Marketing Surveys, one in May 1970 and one in February 1973, found that 84·1 per cent and 76·5 per cent respectively of the party's supporters were working-class. Since only about 50 per cent of the respondents to each survey were working-class, the Irish Labour Party can be regarded as cohesive with respect to class according to the criteria of Rose and Urwin, and their conclusion that all the Irish parties are 'heterogeneous' in terms of their support is no longer valid.[108]

The use of Alford's 'index of class voting' confirms that social class has an unusually low impact on voting behaviour in the Republic. The measure is calculated by the simple expedient of subtracting the percentage of persons in non-manual occupations voting for 'Left parties' from the percentage of persons in manual occupations voting for the same parties.[109] Taking only Labour as a 'Left party', and excluding farmers, as Alford does, the value of the index according to the 1969 survey is +14.[110] The indices obtained from analysis of the 1970 and 1973 surveys are +14 and +10 respectively. Each of these figures is lower than the index of class voting in any of the ten countries considered by Lijphart, where the indices ranged from +53 to +15.[111]

1.2.5   Emigration

Ever since the 1840s Ireland has suffered from a very high level of emigration. Between 1926 and 1971, it is estimated, over a million people emigrated from the Republic, while the population remained fairly stable at around three million.[112] For many, emigration has been a simple matter of economic necessity rather than a conscious decision to take the 'exit' option instead of remaining to 'voice' protest. Many farms, especially in the western counties, where emigration has been highest, are too small to support more than one family or to be subdivided. Consequently they are handed on from father to one son, and the other children have little choice but to move out.[113] The low level of employment opportunities in Ireland in the past meant that many left not just their own locality but the country itself. Emigration seems to have been regarded fatalistically, as the natural sequel to leaving school rather than as something to provoke resentment, and was encouraged by the success stories reported by earlier emigrants.[114] The proximity of Britain, the Irish communities there and in the USA, and the absence of language problems, combined to make it less traumatic than it might have been, a relatively low-cost option.

Emigration has helped sustain the conservatism of Irish society and politics. It helps to preserve the society left behind in that money sent home from abroad helps to prop up the uneconomic small farms which the emigrants were forced to leave.[115] Moreover, emigration has often been seen as a 'safety valve' or an outlet siphoning off the vigorous and discontented, who might otherwise have been a force for radical social and political change.[116] The many creative writers and other artists who left the country can be cited as examples. Indeed, a Fine Gael Parliamentary Secretary once admitted that emigration 'does help in the problem of creating full employment'.[117]

During the 1950s the average annual rate of emigration was fourteen per thousand of the population, and at one stage it was almost as high as the birth rate. This led to serious suggestions that the country was 'teetering perilously on the brink of near extinction', that 'the Irish race' was vanishing, and that the emigration figures were a sign of 'inevitable doom'.[118] The belief that the country was 'finished' led even some of those who had secure jobs to leave them and emigrate to countries which could offer them and their families a future.[119] However, the worst forebodings were not fulfilled. Emigration fell to an average figure of below six per thousand in the early 1960s and below four per thousand in the late 1960s. Whether it will resume again on a large scale if employment prospects in the other EEC countries and in the USA seem markedly brighter than those in Ireland remains to be seen.

1.3 The Irish Labour Party in comparative perspective

Irish politics, Irish political parties and the strength of the Irish left are all unusual by Western democratic standards. Irish politics are unusual in that the most basic cleavage, that between Fianna Fáil and Fine Gael, springs from a split in a nationalist party early in the century. Politics do not rotate around class divisions, religious divisions, regional divisions, communal divisions, or a clerical versus anti-clerical division. Some of these divisions are absent from Irish society; the rest have, as yet, had only a limited impact on politics. In so far as Irish politics rotate at all, they tend to be focused on personalities, on short-lived emotive 'issues' such as an unpopular government decision, or on the parties' ill-defined 'records' or 'traditions'. In 1964 David Thornley observed that Ireland had conducted its politics since 1922 'almost without controversy upon those issues of social and economic policy which are the theme of politics elsewhere'.[120]

The parties, too, are not easily compared with parties in other countries. By the late 1960s Labour was recognisably a social democratic party, but there is little agreement on how to categorise Fianna Fáil or Fine Gael. Blondel treats one – wisely, he does not say which – as 'Liberal/Radical' and the other as 'Conservative'.[121] Henig and Pinder have called Fianna Fáil 'Agrarian' and Fine Gael 'Conservative'.[122] Smith calls Fianna Fáil 'Centre/Agrarian' and Fine Gael 'Liberal–Conservative', while elsewhere in his book Fianna Fáil is described as 'Left Centre' and Fine Gael as 'Conservative'.[123] Little trouble is taken to justify these labels, particularly the positioning of Fianna Fáil to the left of Fine Gael. The parties were compelled to categorise themselves when their representatives took their places in the Consultative Assembly of the Council of Europe in the mid-1960s. Labour joined the Socialist group and Fine Gael the Christian Democrats. Fianna Fáil's representatives were at first placed, to their chagrin, with a heterogeneous group which included the Italian neo-fascists, and eventually joined with the Gaullists to form the 'European Democrats for Progress'.

The most unusual feature of the Irish left is simply its weakness. Of nineteen Western democracies surveyed by Blondel in the late 1960s, thirteen had medium or large socialist parties.[124] In three of the others a small or a small to medium-sized socialist party co-existed with a small to medium or a medium-sized communist party, so that the total left-wing vote was fairly strong. A fourth exception was the United States, without even a small left-wing party. The only two countries which possessed a small socialist party while lacking a communist party of more than negligible strength were Canada and the Irish Republic. Similarly, Epstein notes that, of the twenty countries he covers, only the USA, Canada and the Irish Republic lack a large socialist working-class party.[125]

Many features of Irish politics, then, are unusual, but they do not defy explanation. As Whyte points out, the unique nature of Irish politics derives from the simple fact that the context from which they spring is also unique.[126] Epstein, when considering the causes of the different strengths of socialist parties, has written that 'Ireland can be disregarded because of its size and small industrial base or treated as a special case for historical reasons'.[127] This sentence, although sometimes cited by Irish political scientists to illustrate what they regard as the insultingly cursory treatment Ireland usually receives in comparative studies, is in fact not entirely unreasonable.

The weakness of the Irish Labour Party becomes a mystery only if a monocausal explanation is demanded. Many strong socialist parties have to face one or other of the obstacles which the ILP has to face; none has to face them all. The political and social environment described above, in which the Irish Labour Party has to operate, is not one conducive to the emergence of a strong socialist party.

First, the fact that the State was created in such dramatic circumstances led inevitably to the downplaying of social and economic issues in its early years. Ironically, since in most cases unity produces strength, it may well be that the two wings of Sinn Féin, by splitting apart and fighting a civil war on such an emotive issue as 'majority rule on the one hand' or 'the inalienability of the national sovereignty on the other',[128] assured themselves of more support in later elections than they would have won had they remained a single party or drifted apart over some less stark issue. The loyalties created in 1922, and by the civil war of 1922–23, transcended class divisions, and have been transmitted to succeeding generations. In addition, Fianna Fáil, which was weak in Dublin during the 1920s and early 1930s, and seems not to have won much support from the industrial working class during that period,[129] assured itself of lasting support from this sector by its policy of building protectionist walls behind which Irish industries developed during the 1930s. Even though for many Ministers this policy was probably motivated more by the dream of autarky than by the desire to provide full employment, it gave Fianna Fáil, especially in Dublin, the image of 'the party of the working man' or 'the party which provided the jobs', an image which was to persist despite its closeness to big business during the 1960s.

Secondly, political attitudes too have militated against the emergence of a strong left-wing party. The absurd fear of communism, which in reality never had enough strength in Ireland even to muster a convincing spectre, meant that Labour always felt it necessary to avoid doing anything which could be construed as a move towards communism. Since the distinction between socialism and communism is by no means clear in the minds of all voters, even the allegation that it was socialist was one it feared. Even though, until the 1960s, the powerful and conservative Catholic Church consistently identified communism as the greatest threat to Irish society, it may seem with the benefit of hindsight that Labour was unnecessarily timid. Arguably the approach it took, namely to join in the denunciations of communism and even occasionally of socialism, was ill advised and only played into its opponents' hands. The former Fianna Fáil Minister James Ryan once described Labour as 'frightened of socialism and nationalisation', and added that 'if they were more Labour they might not go far at once but they could be seen as a different kind of party and gain ultimate strength'.[130] Such suggestions must, of course, be balanced against the view that Labour has in the past been too far to the left for its own good.[131]

Thirdly, the absence of a tradition of serious political debate, and the major parties' anti-ideological position, means that a party adopting a coherent socialist policy will rarely elicit a coherent capitalist response. Labour has faced the problem that its opponents have refused to argue with it on its own terms. Fianna Fáil, for example, rarely issues an election manifesto. Ayearst's comment that Labour has always been 'fighting an uphill battle against general indifference'[132] is very apposite. A self-professed left-wing party fighting against two larger parties which deny that terms like 'left' and 'right' have any meaning in the context of the society in which they operate, while occasionally describing themselves as 'if anything, slightly left of centre', is in an unenviable position. It must first establish the primacy of the divisions and issues *it* regards as important – in other words, win the battle over the 'language of politics' – before it can hope to attract widespread support on the basis of the position it takes on these issues. Labour has thus faced the problem of trying to appear significantly to the left of the two major parties without laying itself open to the charge of being 'doctrinaire' or 'dogmatic'.

Individualism is clearly more compatible with the spirit of capitalism than with socialism. A reluctance to co-operate too closely with others, and a tendency to approach the central administration via an intermediary, are stumbling blocks to a socialist party wishing to increase State intervention in the economy and society. In 1969 a provincial newspaper commented that it would take Labour very many years to gain much strength in parts of rural Ireland, 'where the notion of co-operation, not to mind socialism, is not yet readily accepted'.[133] Moreover, if people see the solution to their system-caused problems in individualistic terms, then Labour TDs and county councillors have little option but to respond to this perception. A public representative who works hard for his constituents on an individual basis – helping one to find a job, another to find a house, and so on – will be regarded as doing much more than one who refuses to deal with individual problems and instead works, through speeches and writings, to transform the structure of society. A socialist public representative can continue to make socialist speeches, but he is likely to be re-elected only if he deals with the symptoms of a disease he believes to be endemic in the system. Similarly, a belief that self-reliance is a virtue is a handicap to a party which favours increasing taxes in order to divert more resources to the underprivileged. Moreover, the pressures for conformity exerted by rural Irish society also increase the likelihood that a small party will remain small. In much the same way, candidates of a small party, usually out of power, will probably have fewer brokerage resources at their disposal than TDs and candidates of larger parties.

Most important, the social structure of the Irish Republic could not be expected to generate a strong socialist party. The objectively defined working class is not large by the standards of modern industrial societies, and the subjectively defined working class is even smaller. The deep sense of working-class consciousness prevalent in most European countries, especially during, but by no means confined to, the period when the party system was taking shape, has never been present in Ireland, north or south. Moreover, even many of those who do regard themselves as working-class do not regard voting Labour as an automatic political expression of this social identity, as they would in Britain. The reluctance of survey respondents to consider themselves working-class may be an illustration of the 'rural and small-town petty snobbery' cited by Murphy as one of the barriers faced by Labour. In addition, as Mac Gréil has pointed out, if it is true that most people believe the Republic has a society in which vertical social mobility is high, then this militates against a socialist party by leading to those in the lower strata blaming themselves rather than the organisation of society for their failure to 'get on'.[134]

One of Labour's main problems has always been the strength of the agricultural sector, the rural ethos of Irish society outside three or four major cities, and the antipathy of Irish farmers to the party. It is true that a form of socialism has flourished in agricultural countries like China and Cuba,[135] but it must be borne in mind that before their revolutions these countries were landlord–tenant societies rather than smallholding societies. It is also true that the Norwegian Labour Party wins substantial support from farmers,[136] but here too there are significant differences from the ILP's position. One of the most important is that there were no events comparable to the Irish nationalist struggle to cement farmers' loyalties to other parties, and the description of the peaceful termination of the union with Sweden as 'another fortunate occurrence' for Norwegian Labour[137] may be a considerable understatement. In general, small farmers do not support socialist parties, and by European standards it is the Norwegian party, not the Irish party, which is the deviant. Huntington comments that 'no social group is more conservative than a landowning peasantry'.[138]

If the Irish Labour Party had been able to play some part in winning the smallholders the ownership of their land it might have established a link with them, but in fact ownership was decided by Land Acts of the late nineteenth century, and much of rural Ireland was a society of small, independent proprietors by the time Labour was created. In the twentieth century rural society has on the whole lacked any of the traditional sources of agrarian discontent.[139] It has been suggested that Labour could have gained support from small farmers by taking up the land annuities issue during the 1920s,[140] but this is doubtful. Any attempt by Labour, still a part of the union movement, to exploit small farmers' grievances would have seemed as incongruous as, say, a statement from the Farmers' Party calling for higher wages for Dublin dock workers. There was hardly any overlap between the interests of the farmers and of Labour's supporters. Labour had very little to offer Irish farmers, and they in turn have never been noted as a class for their concern for the conditions of the urban and rural working class. If Labour had by some miracle attracted farmers into membership on a large scale, its whole nature would have changed, and it would no longer have been the political instrument of the people for whom it had been created.

Finally, the ever-open option of emigration deprives any country of those who are likely to be its most disaffected citizens. Labour has suffered particularly from this in Ireland, since it has made it much harder for it to win over Fianna Fáil's working-class supporters. In the past, when the economy was prospering they saw no need to vote against the *status quo*, while when it was in recession those with least commitment to the country were as likely to emigrate as to change their voting behaviour. The weight of emigration during the first half of the twentieth century resulted in an ageing population – between 1926 and 1961 the proportion of the population in the fifteen to twenty-nine age group fell from 25·0 per cent to 19·1 per cent, while the proportion of those over forty-five rose from 28·0 per cent to 32·5 per cent[141] – and, as a delegate to Labour's 1972 annual conference was to observe, 'people tottering on the brink of the grave are not the most receptive to radical socialist policies'.

All in all, then, it was not really surprising that there was no strong left-wing party in Ireland in 1957. The nature of the main political cleavage, the country's social structure and political culture, and its own ridiculous history, combined to ensure that the Irish Labour Party remained weak for the first thirty-five years of the State. The 1960s and 1970s were in many ways decades of change, however, and at times during this period there were grounds for believing that the party's prospects were improving.

2

The aftermath of the second coalition, 1957–61

2.1 The 1957 general election

At the beginning of 1957 the second coalition, or Inter-Party, government was in power. It was dominated by Fine Gael, which had nine of the fourteen Ministries, Labour having four and Clann na Talmhan the other. The government was in a precarious position in the Dáil, where it relied on the three seats of Clann na Poblachta, which was giving it external support, for an overall majority.[1] It was even weaker in the country as a whole. The six by-elections held in 1956 all produced large gains for Fianna Fáil. The economy was in a deep recession, and to cope with a serious balance of payments deficit packages of austerity measures had been introduced in February and July 1956, including large increases in import levies and a cut-back in public expenditure.[2] Gross national output was actually shrinking, and total industrial output fell by eleven per cent between 1955 and 1958.[3]

Most disturbingly for Labour, there were nearly 95,000 people on the live unemployment register in January 1957, the highest January figure since 1942.[4] The tone of the government's economic policies was set primarily by the Minister for Finance, the Fine Gael TD Gerard Sweetman, who was on the right wing of his party. After the austerity measures were introduced, criticism of the general drift of the government's economic policies began to emanate with increasing loudness from both the trade union movement and the Labour Party itself. At meetings of the Dublin Trades Council, Labour's participation in the 'anti-working class' government was criticised, and there were calls for it to withdraw.[5] The ITGWU official newspaper accused Labour of having 'drifted into the rut of conservatism'.[6]

In an attempt to rebuild the shattered morale of the government parties, a special meeting of their parliamentary representatives was convened to hear an address by the Taoiseach, who outlined a rather vague 'plan' to boost the economy.[7] It received a fairly warm welcome from its audience, but failed to deflect Labour criticisms. Far from involving more State activity, it promised less, one of its principles being 'to favour and encourage private investment to supplement and relieve public investment'. The backbench Labour TD James Larkin, a leading member of the WUI founded by his father and a persistent critic of government policy, argued that it did nothing to alleviate the immediate unemployment problem,[8] a view shared by Labour's national executive, the Administrative Council.[9] Another Labour TD told a meeting in his constituency that the government was not doing enough to combat unemployment.[10]

Labour wanted an immediate reflation of the economy, an end to the credit squeeze and a reduction of the import levies, but its position as a member of the coalition prevented the leadership from expressing its views openly, which gave ordinary members the erroneous impression that it was content with the situation. Its discontent was finally revealed in the Dáil in a speech by the deputy leader, Dan Desmond, who made it clear that Labour might withdraw from the government unless changes were made. Part of the problem, he said, was that the government was pursuing austere policies of the sort adopted by Fianna Fáil in 1952, which Labour had opposed vigorously. He hoped that the government would realise that this approach, in Labour's eyes, 'would of necessity be wrong and could not have our support if it were to continue in the 1957–58 period'.[11] Labour, he said, realised that on many occasions the two major parties were 'expressing exactly the same conservative views in relation to finance'.[12]

The government's problems were exacerbated when the IRA began a campaign of violence against selected targets in the north in December 1956. The Clann na Poblachta leadership, which for some time had been expressing reservations about the government's handling of economic policy,[13] now came under strong rank-and-file pressure to withdraw its support entirely from the government unless it ended its policy of 'repression against Republicans' and released all republican prisoners.[14] A combination of these factors led to the party announcing at the end of January 1957 that it would be tabling a motion of no confidence in the government when the Dáil reconvened.

Most of the reasons given for the Clann's withdrawal of support related to failures in the sphere of economic activity, although it was stated that many of these failures were due partly to a lack of government policy on 'ending partition'.[15]

The precise Dáil position at this stage was that the voting strength of the government amounted to seventy TDs,[16] as did the combined strengths of Fianna Fáil and Clann na Poblachta, which left the five independents holding the balance of power. Of these, two, the Byrne brothers, were consistent Fine Gael supporters, while Ben Maguire was Fianna Fáil in all but name. The position of the other two Independents was uncertain, but, given that the Ceann Comhairle would almost certainly have given his casting vote against the motion in the event of a tie, the government would have survived unless they had both voted with the opposition. However, although on paper it had a chance of defeating the motion, it does not appear that it even thought seriously about fighting it.[17] The truth seems to be that the government had more or less lost confidence in itself, and was relieved at the prospect of leaving office.[18] It obtained a dissolution from President O'Kelly, and the election was called for 5 March.

The election campaign[19] was notable mainly for the reluctance of Fine Gael and Labour to say whether they were campaigning for the return of the government, and for talk of the possibility of a 'national', all-party government (see Chapter 8.2 below). It also revealed Labour's lack of a distinctive outlook, for, while its manifesto was solid, it contained few firm proposals and could not be described as either inspiring or radical.[20] Of its Ministers, only the Minister for Social Welfare, Brendan Corish, laid any stress on the separate identity of the Labour Party.[21] The only ideological speech made by the Justice Minister, James Everett, was one in which he attacked communism.[22] The party leader, William Norton, uttered only vague defences of the government's record, laid no emphasis on any special Labour contribution to it, and produced a list of platitudes when invited to give reasons why Labour merited support.[23] Unlike the other party leaders, he did not go on a speaking tour of the country, and his constituency advertisements, portraying him as a kind of benevolent uncle, minimised his party affiliation to such an extent as to be worth quoting *in extenso:*[24]

William Norton, The People's Friend, Champion of Every Good Cause. William Norton respectfully solicits your No. 1 Vote at the General Election. William Norton has been your Deputy over 25 years. He has rendered splendid service to his constituents, irrespective of their political views. He serves everybody; he imposes no political tests. He is the friend of all who need assistance or advice; he deals with all letters promptly; he is always available to his constituents; he befriends the weak and helpless; he champions every good cause; whether as a Deputy or as a Minister; he looks after the County Kildare as nobody else does. Vote No. 1 Norton, The Labour Candidate.

All in all, Labour's campaign was lacklustre and even half-hearted, since many Labour supporters were uncertain as to whether they actually wanted the government returned. Its low expectations were summed up by a commentator who wrote that 'the Labour Party hopes for the traditional vote, without being over-sanguine'.[25]

The results showed that its pessimism was entirely justified, for it fell back from eighteen seats at the dissolution to only twelve (see Appendix 1), its lowest number since 1944. Fianna Fáil, with a then-record seventy-eight seats, was assured of a comfortable majority in the Dáil. Labour's TDs included only one newcomer, and most owed their election to a sizeable personal vote. The weakness of Labour, *qua* Labour, was emphasised by its dismal performance in the Dublin region, where it won only one seat out of thirty, and where an unemployed carpenter, Jack Murphy, standing on an 'Unemployed Workers' platform, won the seat vacated by James Larkin.

2.2 The aftermath of the election

In the aftermath of the election Labour was in perhaps as weak a position as it had ever been. Like the country as a whole, it was dispirited, demoralised and uncertain of its future. It was having difficulty in retaining its members and in generating enthusiasm among those who remained; party organisation in 1956–57 'did not make the progress which had been expected' and the 1957 national collection 'did not come up to expectations'.[26] The party was in a position of intellectual and theoretical, as well as electoral, weakness. It had been unable to formulate any coherent alternative to the economic strategy pursued by Sweetman, and in particular it never used the word 'socialism'. An article in the then lay Catholic periodical *Hibernia* posed the question of whether a Catholic could be a socialist and concluded, perhaps with relief, that the question did not arise in Ireland, since the Labour Party made no pretence of being socialist.[27]

Labour had an opportunity for stocktaking at two conferences which took place within an eight-month period. At the postponed 1957 annual conference, one delegate admitted that the party had never been so weak; the party chairman, James Tully, suggested that it was at a crossroads and that the conference was consequently the most important in its history.[28] However, apart from taking a significant decision on coalition (see Chapter 8.3 below), it produced no evidence that any fresh thinking was in progress.

A remarkably honest appraisal of the party's record was made by William Norton at a special consultative conference held in February 1958.[29] They had reached, he said, endorsing Tully's comments, 'a cross-roads in the progress and development of the Labour Party, and it is up to us to take now the decisions that will determine the strength or weakness of Labour for a long time ahead'. The 'broad economic and social programme' which the party had adopted in the past had been satisfactory in as far as it related to people's immediate needs, but 'as a long-term policy it has been inadequate'. Labour had 'tended to treat the symptoms rather than the disease', and 'must abandon methods that have yielded such dismal results'. If the party had the courage to devise a policy to meet contemporary needs, it could 'attract the support of all those progressive elements in the community who desire a forward policy that will end stagnation and frustration'. However, apart from some thoughts on Northern Ireland (see Chapter 7.3 below), Norton was unable to offer, as a contrast to the party's inadequate past programme, a clear and inspiring vision of what its future approach should be, and it was not until the change of leadership two years later that genuine attempts were made to attract 'progressive elements'.

At around the same time Labour was making efforts to establish closer relations with the trade union movement, which had been conspicuously absent from the 1957 election campaign and had indeed previously criticised the Inter-Party government and endorsed Fianna Fáil's economic programme.[30] The two union congresses which had been in existence since the 1945 split reached agreement in October 1957 on a new united authority, the Irish Congress of Trade Unions (ICTU), which came into existence in February 1959. Although Labour constantly urged the unions to become more active politically, pointing out that some of their aims were political rather than industrial so that they needed the political muscle of a strong Labour party,[31] there was little sign of any political involvement until the proportional representation campaign later in 1959. There can be little doubt that most union members were supporters of other parties

– in the late 1950s there were about 327,000 trade unionists in the Republic,[32] while Labour received only 112,000 votes at the 1957 general election – and thus had no desire to see the movement become tied to Labour. Moreover, even many of those who did wish to see the unions work for a radical change in Irish society were unconvinced that the Labour Party was a suitable vehicle to use for this purpose, because of its electoral weakness and the poverty of its ideas.

An ideological initiative which was eventually to affect Labour came from an organisation called the 1913 Club, which was formed in February 1958[33] and derived its name from its members' belief that 1913 was the most recent year in which the two ideas of national independence and social justice had been in harmony. Those associated with it included the TDs Noel Browne and Jack McQuillan, the future TD David Thornley, the future Labour vice-chairman Proinsias Mac Aonghusa, the radical Senator Owen Sheehy-Skeffington, and the historians Owen Dudley Edwards and Desmond Ryan. At one of its early meetings Sheehy-Skeffington, who had been expelled from Labour in the early 1940s, said that the party had failed, and called for the emergence of a movement which would work for a planned economy and would not be afraid to call itself socialist.[34]

In May 1958 the formation of the National Progressive Democrats (NPD) was announced by Browne and McQuillan. Both men were Independent TDs who had first entered the Dáil in 1948 as Clann na Poblachta TDs; both had left that party during the Mother and Child affair. Both were later to join Labour, and to fall out with it. In view of the radical opinions which had been aired at 1913 Club meetings, the NPD's programme at its foundation was disappointingly tame.[35] Its main proposal was for the retirement from politics of men whose record went back to the civil war, so as to 'leave the political arena to younger men who are free of their hatreds and obsessions', a proposal reminiscent of, and as unrealistic as, one made by the National League during its short existence in the 1920s. In addition, it described the policy of compulsory Irish in the schools as 'insanity', though on the curious ground that, because so many people emigrated, Irish would give them no advantage in the countries where they would eventually work. Finally, it advocated a reduction of spending on the presidency, the army and foreign embassies.

Although the programme seemed fairly harmless, it was soon attacked as being sinister. A Parliamentary Secretary warned against 'Communist groups' whose aim was to undermine the institutions of the State; they often began, he said, by alleging that the presidency cost too much.[36] Browne had earlier expressed his belief in a 'socialist solution' to Ireland's problems,[37] but later in 1958 he delivered a fierce attack of his own on communism. Ireland, he said, had a devout and zealous communist underground, whose members had infiltrated the trade union movement, the press, the civil service and the political parties. If the economic situation in Ireland and Britain worsened, the communists would be presented with an opportunity to take over the country, as they had taken over Poland.[38]

The NPD's first electoral test came in a by-election in Dublin in June 1958. Its candidate lost his deposit, which led to an internal dispute, with a minority group leaving after alleging that the party was being run undemocratically by Dr Browne.[39] The by-election had some significance because it seemed to show that a unified left-wing party might be successful. Fianna Fáil and Fine Gael together won only 52 per cent of the votes, with the rest divided fairly equally among Labour, the NPD and Clann na Poblachta. Since each of these parties had vaguely 'radical' overtones, it seemed that if Labour could broaden its appeal to attract those who had voted for the two smaller parties it could become a major force. During and after the campaign Labour's election director, Donal Nevin, spoke of the need for 'progressively-minded people' to unite,[40] and the same thought underlay many of Brendan Corish's actions after he became leader. Later in 1958 the NPD issued a full policy statement' more coherent than its original programme and more radical than Labour's aims. It argued that private enterprise had failed, so that there was a need for greater State involvement in the economy, and called for a large expansion of the social welfare services, including a free national health service and unlimited educational opportunities for all.[41]

2.3 The PR referendum campaign, 1959

Fianna Fáil's proposal to hold a referendum to decide whether to replace the existing electoral system, the single transferable vote in multi-member constituencies (known simply as 'PR' in Ireland), by the single non-transferable vote in single-member constituencies, as used in Britain, found no support from any of the opposition parties.[42] Labour reacted with hostility, arguing that the change was 'designed to wipe out the representation of minorities',[43] and mounted a determined pro-PR campaign, which involved issuing 90,000 posters and 500,000 handbills.[44] Labour's instinctive opposition to the proposal, based on a feeling that it depended for its continued existence as a parliamentary force on the retention of PR, drew criticism from Seán Lemass, who argued that it showed that the party was fundamentally timid. A change to single-member constituencies, he said, would produce a two-party system, and Labour, even though it was weaker than Fine Gael, would be more likely to emerge as Fianna Fáil's rival because, 'however incoherent and mealy-mouthed they are on occasions about their policy, [they] have a distinct character [and] could represent an economic or a social conception which would be peculiar to themselves'.[45]

In theory, of course, a change might have benefited Labour. It might have led to a two-party system,[46] which might have been a left–right system, with Labour as the party of the left. However, to assume that a two-party system in Ireland would necessarily be a left–right one in the classical British mould greatly overvalues the political effect of the existing electoral system and undervalues the other reasons for Ireland's particular political system. Moreover, even if a two-party system did ensue, Labour, as the smaller party, would have been more likely to disappear than Fine Gael, as it would have been the victim of the familiar 'wasted vote' consideration. There is no doubt that the present system has enabled Labour to capture seats in fairly close proportion to its votes,[47] and although some academics have argued that this has deprived it of an incentive to try to broaden its appeal and has encouraged it to settle for a safe third-party role,[48] the party can hardly be blamed for preferring the option which at least guaranteed survival.

Perhaps because the government's case seemed to be prevailing, the vigour of Labour's attacks increased as the campaign went on. One speaker suggested that Fianna Fáil might intend to put its opponents into concentration camps,[49] while a Senator warned that Labour might be forced to forsake the democratic processes and go 'underground' if the proposal went through.[50] The argument advanced by the party's deputy leader, Dan Desmond, was possibly the most interesting, because of what it revealed about the attitude of the speaker, and no doubt of other rural TDs (Desmond represented Cork South), towards the possibility of political change. He warned that the abolition of PR would introduce a 'new, deadly dangerous factor', namely the possible entry into the Dáil of 'anything from 20 to 40 members of a Party whose sheer determination would be to carry out a policy in accordance with the dictates of a foreign Eastern power'. It would raise 'the possibility of the introduction of people and of members of a Party who, thanks be to God, were never able to show any strength up to the present owing to the fact that we had PR to protect us'. He added:[51]

There is another danger and that is the tendency on the part of some of the younger members – but the men who would probably control the destinies of a Party and of a Government – to swing towards liberalism ... I have no hesitation in saying that I am prepared to go under direction to cast my vote which, in its own small way, will be a clear indication that, as a representative of a rural constituency, I am not prepared to be a party to the passing of a motion which can give us liberalism, Communism and a removal of the true Christian principle of Government that we have had, whether it was a Fianna Fáil government, a Cumann na nGaedheal government or an Inter-Party government.

Such a speech goes some way towards explaining why Labour had no great appeal in the eyes of middle-class liberals or the intelligentsia before the 1960s.

The proposal to abolish PR was defeated narrowly, by just over 33,000 votes in a poll of over 900,000.[52] The outcome could be said to have been decided in Dublin, where a majority of 45,762 against change overturned an anti-PR majority of 12,095 in the rest of the country. Although Labour took some of the credit for the defeat of the proposal, it was still in a very weak position. When three by-elections arose in July 1959 it was able to nominate candidates in only two. Although its vote in Meath rose significantly, in Dublin South West it won only about 11 per cent of the votes cast, an improvement on its 1957 performance but still extremely low for a Labour party in the industrial centre of the country. It had been unable to nominate a candidate in Clare because there was no organisation there,[53] and organisation throughout the country remained unsatisfactory; few new branches were being formed, and old ones were lapsing because members were emigrating as a result of being unemployed.[54] Whereas in most countries a high unemployment rate would boost the fortunes of a Labour party in opposition, the proximity of the British labour market has meant that such a situation can pose more problems to the Irish Labour Party than it raises opportunities.

The only sign of hope for the party was the increase in the political activity of the trade unions. Two leading members of the union movement had been members of a Labour committee set up to defeat the proposed change in the electoral system,[55] and the ICTU had entered the referendum campaign aggressively in its final stages. One of Labour's radio broadcasts was shared between William Norton and an ICTU member. In December 1959 ICTU set up a high-powered sub-committee 'to study the problem of effective political organization to ensure the implementation of resolutions which are sent to the government',[56] a move seen as a sign of ICTU's increasing interest in strengthening the Labour Party.

2.4 Changes in party leadership 1959–60

All three main parties acquired new leaders in a nine-month period in 1959–60. Eamon de Valera became President in June 1959 and was succeeded as Taoiseach and Fianna Fáil leader by Seán Lemass, a move which signified the triumph of Fianna Fáil's pragmatic, modernising wing over its traditional, autarkic and neo-Gaelic wing. Lemass's main objectives were to raise the Republic's gross national product and its standard of living, whereas for de Valera ending partition and reviving the Irish language had been more important. Whereas de Valera and other traditionalists continued to raise the issues of the 1920s at every general election,[57] Lemass seemed more interested in contemporary problems than in raking over past disputes.

Fine Gael was also undergoing its first taste of division between a traditionalist old guard and a forward-looking younger group. For a while after the 1957 election nothing happened to modify its very conservative image. Its parliamentary leader called frequently for a reduction in taxation and the removals of the 'shackles' from private enterprise,[58] and its TDs continued to warn that under-cover agents were preparing a communist assault on Ireland,[59] and to claim that communism had infiltrated into every level of society and was the country's greatest enemy.[60] Its image as a party of wealthy amateurs was reinforced when it opposed a proposal to raise TDs' meagre salaries, apparently on the ground that most TDs had other sources of income.[61]

Nevertheless, behind the ultra-conservative appearance some changes were taking place. The journal *National Observer*, edited jointly by Declan Costello and Alexis FitzGerald, reflected the views of a group of 'young tigers'. The most dramatic development came in May 1959 when Costello, a TD since 1951 and the son of the former Taoiseach, made a speech which set the tone for a conflict that continued within Fine Gael for many years and whose key paragraph read:[62]

I would suggest that we should not be afraid to use techniques that are traditionally associated with parties of the left, and that we should be prepared to jettison notions and concepts which belong to the heyday of nineteenth century liberalism; that we should accept the necessity for the state to plan economic development; to undertake capital investment on a large scale for the purpose of increasing national wealth; that the school-leaving age should be increased; that banking techniques be altered so that the state could directly alter the level of credit in the country; that we try to bring about conditions where there is genuine equality for all, irrespective of the level of society in which they have been born ... With regard to the political party of which I am a member, I believe that Fine Gael should move openly and firmly to the left.

He urged that social welfare payments should be raised, with taxation being increased to cover the cost. James Dillon, a leading Fine Gael right-winger, expressed his complete lack of sympathy with Costello's suggestion that the party should move to the left; it should move, he said with a characteristic distaste for labels, neither to the left nor to the right but 'straight ahead'.[63]

Dillon became leader of Fine Gael in October 1959, after a contest with the former Foreign Minister Liam Cosgrave, when the party president, i.e. the leader outside the Dáil, Richard Mulcahy, resigned his position, and the parliamentary leader, John Costello, also stood down rather than abandon his law practice.[64] The change seemed likely to make Fine Gael more active; Costello had tended to regard politics as a part-time occupation, while Mulcahy had not been an inspiring leader, the *National Observer* commenting that he 'could rarely express his vision with the clarity with which he saw it'.[65] Dillon was the president of the Ancient Order of Hibernians, a Catholic body dedicated to ending partition and opposing communism, and frequently expressed clearly his vision, which was of a new 'Commonwealth of Nations', comprising the white nations of the British Commonwealth, Ireland and the USA.[66] It seemed likely that under his leadership Fine Gael would become more vigorous, but no less conservative. Seán Lemass, however, having earlier suggested that it was Labour rather than Fine Gael which had a 'distinct character', now maintained that Fine Gael could become the sole opposition party, representing the outlook of the old Irish Parliamentary Party, which Dillon's father had led. Labour, being a 'class party', was now dismissed as obsolete, and compared to an old railway engine lacking the power to get up steam again,[67] an analysis which, however inaccurate, at least demonstrates the prevailing lack of certainty as to how the political system might develop.

Labour acquired a new leader on 2 March 1960, when Brendan Corish was selected to replace William Norton, who had resigned a week earlier.[68] Norton had been leader since 1932, but although the party, which had then seemed on the verge of extinction, had advanced to a position of strength in 1943, it did not advance any further, and from then on Norton could not be said to have been a very successful leader. The Labour Party seemed to rank only third in his affections, behind both his union and his constituency. He was general secretary of the Post Office Workers' Union between 1924 and 1957, and devoted at least as much time to this job as to the Labour leadership. He also nursed his Kildare constituency assiduously, and rarely strayed from it during election campaigns.

By 1960 there was a feeling throughout the party that the time had come for a change of leadership. The left wing, which wanted a distinctive Labour image asserted, had had little confidence in Norton for many years, and its hostility was made clear at the 1959 annual conference, when a long-standing ideological and personal antipathy between Norton and James Larkin had erupted. Larkin was one of the most thoughtful people high in the Labour hierarchy, and he was concerned that the party was in danger of becoming a mere collection of individuals motivated more by self-interest than by a commitment to any distinct ideological outlook. At the conference he suggested that Norton's recent acceptance of a directorship of the Irish subsidiary of the General Electric Company was incompatible with his leadership of Labour, and Norton's response, a vigorous attack on Larkin in which he referred to the latter's past membership of the Communist Party, backfired, producing shouts of disapproval and some foot-stamping.

Norton also lacked support from the right wing of the party, which in any case had always regarded him with more respect than affection. A highly intelligent man, with a great interest in, though little sympathy for, left-wing parties and socialist thought in many countries, he became increasingly cynical towards the end of his life, and his attitude towards some of the less articulate Labour TDs bordered on open contempt. Even those TDs who shared his indifference to subjects like the formulation of fresh policies and the development of university branches had an uneasy feeling that changes were necessary if the party was to make any progress. Norton appeared to have run out of ideas and energy, and to have little faith in Labour's future. By 1960 he had become the symbol of defeat and of the demoralising experience of the second coalition; a national newspaper probably summed up the views of many party members when it described the change of leadership as the shaking off of his 'colourless hegemony'.[69]

Despite the general dissatisfaction with his leadership, Norton stepped down of his own accord and could probably have retained the position had he wanted. The Labour leader was, and still is, elected by the party's TDs, and it is unlikely that the TDs of 1960 would have got round to mustering the collective will to remove him. As far back as the 1940s there had been rumours that he wanted to relinquish the leadership,[70] and it seems that his long-standing lack of enthusiasm for the position became a positive aversion after the criticism he received at the 1959 conference. Leadership of the party at that time, especially to one with as gloomy a view of its future as Norton had, seemed a thankless task. The party leader had to be an active parliamentarian and keep himself well briefed on all aspects of government activity. He could expect little help from the Labour TDs, most of whom were too busy attending to their constituency business, and the party had no back-up or research facilities. Moreover, because Labour had declared itself against further coalitions, the leadership did not encompass the prospect of a place in government in the foreseeable future.

Nevertheless, there was a minor competition for the leadership after Norton resigned. Apart from Corish, the aspirants, perhaps no more than half-hearted ones, were Dan Desmond, the deputy leader, and Sean Casey, a TD from Cork City. Both men, however, lacked any governmental experience and were often in poor health. Apart from Corish and Norton, the only Labour TD to have been a Minister was James Everett, whose age ruled him out of contention. Corish had the support both of Norton, who seems to have regarded him as something of a protégé, and of James Larkin, who although not a member of the Parliamentary Labour Party appears to have played the role of kingmaker in the leadership change. When it became obvious that Corish had the support of a majority of TDs his potential rivals withdrew and he was selected unanimously.

Corish was a largely unknown quantity at the time, for although he had generally been more assertive of a distinctive Labour image than Norton had, in other respects his record was not encouraging from the viewpoint of those who hoped to see the party move to the left. In 1953 he had revealed the 'special position' the Catholic Church occupied in his heart:[71]

I am an Irishman second; I am a Catholic first . . . If the Hierarchy gives me any direction with regard to Catholic social teaching or Catholic moral teaching, I accept without qualification in all respects the teaching of the Hierarchy and the Church to which I belong.

In 1957 he had seemed to align himself with conservative religious attitudes during the 'Fethard-on-Sea boycott', an affair in which Catholics in this town in his Wexford constituency had conducted a boycott of local Protestants after the Protestant partner in a mixed marriage had left the town with her children, leaving her husband behind. Corish took issue with the Taoiseach's condemnation of the boycott, and asked him to ensure that 'certain people will not conspire . . . to kidnap Catholic children'.[72] For a while, too, he had apparently been a member of the Knights of St Columbanus, a very conservative all-male lay Catholic organisation.[73]

His background was a typical one for a rural TD and did not suggest any outstanding qualities. He had played Gaelic football for his county, a strong boost then as now for any aspiring TD, and had originally inherited his seat at a by-election in 1945 caused by the death of his father, a TD since 1921. Corish was aged forty-one when he became leader, and perhaps symbolically he was 'lean and hungry' in appearance, whereas Norton looked overweight and complacent. Interestingly, although Corish moved his work into the party leader's room in Leinster House, the seat of the Oireachtas, Norton did not move out, and he continued to use the room until his death in 1963.

2.5 Labour's attempts to create 'progressive unity'

It soon became clear that the leadership change had amounted to more than just a change of personalities, and that Corish intended to lead the party in a new direction. Speaking in Trinity College, Dublin – addressing a university audience was very much a new departure for a Labour leader – he stressed that the ILP should not be regarded as a party for trade unionists only.[74] The first positive fruit of the new approach came in September 1960, when the AC published a document urging the 'unity of progressive forces'.[75] It proposed 'the emergence, after the next election, of a progressive bloc of deputies of sufficient strength, and with sufficient clarity of purpose, to be able, from a position of independence, strongly to influence whatever government the election throws up', and said that 'the future demands the unity of progressive forces accepting the constitution, if power is to be wrested from the parties of reaction'.

This was clearly a call for a closer liaison, and perhaps ultimately formal unity, between Labour, Clann na Poblachta and the NPD; the reference to 'forces accepting the constitution' made it clear that Sinn Féin was not included. It marked probably the first occasion on which the Labour Party had stated that it wished to become a broadly supported 'progressive' party, rather than just a parliamentary pressure group acting as the political voice of the trade unions or a loosely linked collection of individuals. Auguring well for it was the fact that Seán MacBride, at his party's Ard-Fheis three months earlier, had advocated the construction of a 'third force' in Irish politics, a Republican–Labour party which he implied could be formed by a merger between Labour, Clann na Poblachta and Sinn Féin.[76] When addressing a meeting of the 1913 Club he again spoke of the need for a third force, although this time he suggested that Labour, the Clann and the NPD would be its main components.[77]

The AC's document was debated for four hours at Labour's 1960 annual conference, and was finally passed by the narrow margin of seventy-nine votes to sixty-one.[78] In his opening address the party chairman, James Tully, recommended its acceptance; its purpose was to unite the whole left in the Labour Party, so that trade unionists, small farmers and the self-employed, as well as 'intelligent people in other walks of life', could work together and 'build up a tremendous political force'. It ran into some opposition, however. James Larkin suggested that the AC take it back for review; instead of making the mistake of aligning itself with other parties, Labour should formulate a clear statement of its own principles and proceed on that basis. William Norton maintained that it had 'caused confusion' among party members and could be interpreted as a call for a 'united front', which had worked to the disadvantage of labour movements in other countries. Another speaker expressed suspicion of the phrase 'progressive forces' and said he was opposed to the idea of Labour 'veering' to the left or the right.

It seems that four main concerns were felt by those who voted against the document. The first was a fear on the part of the conservative section of the party that its adoption would mean that Labour was moving to the left. The second, shared by Larkin and others, was the belief that Labour could ultimately advance only by growing organically from a firm trade union base, and that attempts to expand by grafting a few personalities on to the PLP would only produce problems and retard the party's growth in the long term. The third was a suspicion that, underneath all the rhetoric, the document might be intended mainly to make possible another coalition with Fine Gael. Finally, some members of all ideological positions did not entirely like or trust some of those with whom Labour would be uniting, particularly Noel Browne and Seán MacBride. In his reply to the debate Corish attempted, successfully as far as most delegates were concerned, to dispel these fears. The aim outlined by the document, he said, was simply to unite all those whom they in the Labour Party regarded as progressive. Although there had been talk of a 'third force' in Irish politics, what was needed was a second force, an opposition to the two conservative parties. He emphasised that there was no question of Labour's either growing away from the unions or compromising its basic principles, let alone of its entering another Inter-Party government.

Clann na Poblachta reacted enthusiastically to the document, issuing a statement which laid stress on the priority it attached to economic issues and the need for 'comprehensive economic planning', and which indicated that it was willing to co-operate with Labour on the terms outlined in the document. As a result, there were talks on a possible union between the two parties, but despite optimistic newspaper reports[79] they did not reach a very advanced stage. The Clann held out for a merger to form a new party, with a name such as 'Labour-Clann', with Corish as leader and MacBride as deputy leader. Labour, however, because it had 12 TDs as against the Clann's one, and because it felt it had a bright future whereas the Clann was on its last legs, insisted that Clann na Poblachta dissolve itself and join the Labour Party. The talks were never of primary importance for Labour, and never came close to producing an agreement, although their final breakdown was not noted until March 1962.[80]

The new vigour injected into the party by the change of leadership continued to manifest itself, although there were no signs of dramatic policy changes. In an interview late in 1960 Corish did not answer directly a question as to whether Labour was a socialist party, but after outlining a few of its policies he admitted cautiously that its outlook could be called 'a form of Christian Socialism'.[81] In March 1961 it was announced that Labour TDs would be asked to concentrate their

attention on a particular area of governmental activity.[82] Although it
was to be another four years before party spokespersons in particular
fields were appointed, this move served notice to Labour TDs that in
future membership of the PLP would be expected to involve some
interest in national affairs as well as constituency issues. In the same
month, following ICTU's establishment in 1959 of a sub-committee to
examine the question of political activity, it was stated that a 'Joint
Committee', comprising members of ICTU's Economic Committee
and 'trade union members of the Labour Party', would hold monthly
meetings to discuss, among other things, matters due to be debated in
the Dáil.[83] However, this development proved to have as little impact
as most of the other steps designed to strengthen the links between
Labour and the unions. Far from meeting monthly, the Joint
Committee seems to have met on only about a dozen occasions over the
next six years.[84] In 1967 the Labour leader described it as 'a rather
loose sort of arrangement',[85] and it was superseded by an equally
ineffective 'Joint Council'. Nevertheless, calls continued throughout
1961, from Corish and from leading unionists like James Larkin and
John Conroy, for greater union support for Labour.[86]

The future shape of the party system remained uncertain. Fine Gael
under James Dillon became no less conservative and no more vigorous.
When Dillon made major speeches it was usually to argue that Ireland
should depend for economic growth on private enterprise, and that its
economy should be linked more closely to that of Britain.[87] In 1961
John Costello was reported as suggesting the possibility of sections of
the two major parties breaking away to join Labour.[88] To add to the
feeling that a major change was imminent, Seán Lemass, whose
opinions of the relative prospects of the opposition parties seemed to
change annually, argued that Fine Gael was a 'superfluous party'.
Democracy worked best with only two parties, so one of the opposition
parties must be redundant, and Fine Gael was the more likely to
disappear because, unlike Labour, it did not represent any view or
interest not otherwise represented in the Dáil.[89] For Labour's part, a
Senator expressed the hope that Fianna Fáil and Fine Gael would soon
merge to form a Conservative government.[90] There was activity at the
minor party level, too. The leadership of Clann na Talmhan passed
into the hands of a seven-man committee, which, in an attempt to shed
the 'stigma' of having been in the last coalition, considered changing
the party's name to the 'National Farmers' Party' or creating a new
'National Rural Party',[91] but no action was taken. Some talks took

place between some Independents and members of Clann na Talmhan and Clann na Poblachta on the possibility of establishing a new western-based party or alliance,[92] but again there was no tangible outcome.

On the eve of the 1961 general election there was a feeling that Irish politics were about to enter a transitional period from which something very different would emerge. Some believed, and more hoped, that Fianna Fáil and Fine Gael would merge to form one large party, or that they would each break in two, with 'right' and 'left' wings going their separate ways, or that Fine Gael would simply disappear. Even though Labour was weak in electoral terms, time seemed to be on its side, in view of the general assumption that socio-economic issues, with which Labour seemed well equipped to deal, would dominate Irish politics in the future. Nevertheless, despite the feeling that change was in the air, there were few signs of fresh political thinking, with the possible exception of Declan Costello's 1959 speech, and the two-man NPD was the liveliest party in the Dáil.

2.6 **The 1961 general election**

The 1961 general election, held on 4 October, was widely agreed to be one of the dullest ever,[93] was reported by newspapers on the inside pages, and was overshadowed by the deaths of Irish troops in the Congo. Labour issued a 4,000 word manifesto advocating more public ownership, the establishment of a planning board to formulate a plan for greater capital investment, the creation of a national health service to apply to all employees and small farmers, free secondary and vocational education, and automatic increases in welfare payments and pensions in line with increases in the national income.[94] Like most of Labour's previous manifestoes, it was solid and well-meaning but contained no dramatic proposals and was obviously not going to be implemented after the election. Labour nominated only thirty-five candidates, five more than in 1957, although this time they gave the impression of conducting a more serious and co-ordinated campaign. They stressed the need for economic planning and an expansion of the public sector, called both Fianna Fáil and Fine Gael 'conservative', and reiterated Labour's opposition to coalition.

The manifesto was accompanied by a supporting statement from the ICTU, the first such statement, it was said, since the party and the Congress separated in 1930. The ICTU established a 'Labour

Legislative Fund', as it had at previous elections, which was 'used to publicize the economic, social and legislative policies of Congress and to promote trade union support for Labour in the General Election'. The fund was in fact a very thinly disguised way of enabling some public service unions, prohibited by law from giving direct financial support to any party, to contribute to Labour's campaign expenses. Similar funds set up at the 1957 and 1965 elections raised about £1,100.[95]

The main issue of the campaign, in as far as there was one, was that of compulsory Irish in the schools. James Dillon's suggestion that pupils who failed only an Irish examination should not be deemed to have failed in all subjects was described by one Minister as 'an act of national treachery which brought Ireland back a century in the national advance',[96] and a provincial paper expressed the view that 'the records of Irish history will be searched in vain for a parallel for such loathsome intrigue'.[97] Dillon also stressed that Fine Gael was 'the party of free enterprise, Liberal in the Gladstonian sense' – a pointed rebuttal of Declan Costello's 1959 speech – and said that if he became Taoiseach he would set up a special department 'to hasten the end of partition'.[98] Fianna Fáil fought the campaign on its 'record of economic progress' and held out the prospect of further advancement if Ireland joined the EEC. The minor parties made very little impact. Sinn Féin made only a token effort to defend its four seats, and the two Clanns nominated only eleven candidates between them. The NPD, which never had nor aspired to a mass membership and consisted only of its two TDs and their supporters, ran only one other candidate, a Carlow county councillor who asked if she could campaign on the NPD label. None of the merger talks had produced any result, and although a prominent Limerick Clann na Poblachta member, Stephen Coughlan, joined Labour on the eve of the election with the whole of the local Clann organisation, this was entirely the result of an approach at local level.

The main features of the results were a decline in support for Fianna Fáil and a gain for Fine Gael (see Appendix 1). Fianna Fáil's losses left it three seats short of an overall Dáil majority, creating the expectation that there would soon be another general election; its share of the votes dropped by over 4 per cent. Fine Gael gained over 5 per cent in votes, reaching its greatest strength since 1938, and picked up seven seats. For Labour the results were a modest success, although it could hardly have failed to improve on its dismal 1957 performance. A British newspaper concluded that the electorate's indifference to Sinn Féin, 'coupled with the quickening interest in Labour, may prove in perspective to have marked a decisive turning point in the progress of the Republic'.[99]

It rose from twelve to sixteen seats. Eleven of its TDs had been outgoing TDs, and the election of three of the others – a son of a former TD in Carlow-Kilkenny, Coughlan in East Limerick, and a former TD in Meath – could be explained largely in personal terms. A gain in South Tipperary gave the party two seats in the county for the first time since 1927, and in Dublin North West a leading member of the ITGWU, Michael Mullen, gained a seat, although this was offset by the defeat in Dublin North East of Denis Larkin of the WUI. In terms of votes, Labour rose to 11·6 per cent, about the same level as in 1951 and 1954 (see Appendix 2). Most of its extra 24,000 votes were picked up in Munster, and it performed very disappointingly in Dublin, where its percentage scarcely increased, whereas Fine Gael's share rose by over 5 per cent. Labour still had only one seat in the whole of Dublin, and was weaker there than Independent candidates, who polled 4,000 more votes and won three seats.

3

The move to socialism, 1961–67

3.1 Labour and Irish politics in the early 1960s

On the whole, Labour was reasonably satisfied with the results of the 1961 election, and when the Dáil reassembled there were signs of broader support for the party. Four TDs outside the PLP indicated their support for the nomination of Corish as Taoiseach: the two NPD TDs, Sean Dunne, a former Labour TD now sitting as an Independent because he had not been selected as a Labour candidate, and the entertainingly eccentric Independent Joseph Leneghan.[1] The most significant feature of the debate was perhaps an allegation by James Dillon that Labour was being used by Marxists, presumably an allusion to Noel Browne's promise of support, and his challenge to any secret Marxists to reveal themselves.[2] To Corish's denial that he knew to whom Dillon's remarks referred, Dillon replied that 'they will take damn good care you will not find out'. Labour's policy, said Corish, was based not on 'rip-roaring Marxism' but on 'Christian socialism'.[3] This rather bizarre exchange terminated in the following manner:[4]

Mr Corish: We in the Labour Party propose – and this is a definite proposal – that where it is shown, and it has been shown recently, that private enterprise, either foreign or in this country, fails to establish industry to absorb our unemployed, then we believe it is the responsibility of the State to extend the activities of the State bodies and semi-State industries in an effort to absorb the unemployed. I do not know whether anybody calls that Marxism or not.
Mr Dillon: It is enshrined in the policy of Fine Gael.
Mr Corish: It is enshrined in the recent Encyclical of Pope John XXIII.

This incident, minor in itself, showed that in 1961 Labour's immediate reaction to any suggestion that it was deviating much from the traditional pattern of Irish political thought was a very defensive and timid one.

The economic advances in the late 1950s and early 1960s, and the consequential attitudinal changes, seemed likely to prove to Labour's advantage. Partly as a result of the First Economic Programme, and partly as a result of an upturn in world trade leading to a greatly increased demand for Irish exports, the economy, and especially the industrial sector, began to expand rapidly. Between 1958 and 1963 national output, which had not grown at all between 1952 and 1958, rose by 23 per cent, while the volume of national investment almost doubled, the purchasing power of wages rose by a fifth and unemployment fell by a third.[5] It became clear that the Irish Republic was not, after all, doomed to die of a complete loss of confidence in itself. There is general agreement among the authors of a number of books published in the late 1960s that the country passed a turning point in the late 1950s,[6] and that its people became more self-confident and optimistic about the future. It seemed reasonable to expect that this new mood would have a political impact, and that the Irish would become less firmly attached to the conservatism of the past, more ready to look with interest at political ideas popular in other countries, and less inclined to react with fear and suspicion to ideas new to Ireland.

Politics in the early 1960s were still in a very amorphous state, with no clear issues around which debate could focus. During 1962 the question of whether Ireland should join the European Economic Community identified a difference between Fianna Fáil and Fine Gael, on the one hand, and Labour and the NPD on the other. The two major parties favoured joining, but the consensus of opinion at Labour's 1962 conference seemed to be that Ireland should do whatever Britain did, because such a high proportion of Irish exports went to the British market.[7] After the NPD advocated seeking only associate membership, which would allow for a much longer adjustment period, Brendan Corish suggested that more thought should be given to this option.[8] In the event, when Britain's application for membership was turned down in January 1963 Ireland's was allowed to 'wither on the vine'.

The relative positions of the two major parties on a left–right spectrum remained unclear, although some insight into each party's self-image was provided by a series of discussions staged early in 1963.[9] It transpired, perhaps inevitably, that each person taking part saw his own party as 'left of centre' or 'progressive'. To a Fianna Fáil TD, Fine Gael was 'ultra-conservative', while to a Fine Gael TD Fianna Fáil was 'a most conservative Tory Party'. Fine Gael politicians had kind words for Labour, but one Fianna Fáil TD said that his party was 'the real Labour Party' and that Labour was irrelevant, while another said that, while his party believed that the whole community should work together, behind the words of his Labour opponent could be seen 'the imported idea of the class struggle, which divides and stratifies the community'.

In fact around this time Fianna Fáil was beginning to acquire a rather right-wing image. At its 1962 Ard-Fheis a delegate referred to the danger posed by the number of communists in Dublin,[10] and in the Dail Fianna Fáil TDs made increasing use of the allegation that their opponents were communists; Noel Browne, in particular, often found that his questions were met with the suggestion that he 'ask Khrushchev'.[11] This image was dented for a while by a comment made by Seán Lemass during the Budget debates in April 1963, when he said he believed 'the time has come when national policy should take a shift to the left', by which he meant that the State should be more involved in guiding the economy.[12] He followed this up by telling American businessmen that 'we have no Communist Party, and of the three parties we have, the one that calls itself the Labour Party is the most conservative in the country'.[13] A month later he accused Labour of timidity, saying that it aspired to the heights but lacked the nerve for the journey.[14]

Lemass's reference to a 'shift to the left' was taken with surprising seriousness by some commentators, and led to suggestions that Fianna Fáil would become the left-wing party in an entirely new alignment.[15] This and his frequent descriptions of Labour as 'conservative' can only be understood, however, if viewed in the context of his overall philosophy. Lemass could be considered a 'radical Conservative', in that he was a dynamic and energetic Minister, prepared to experiment with new policies in order to stimulate economic growth, while believing firmly in the merits of private enterprise, supplemented 'where necessary' by State enterprise. His description of the other parties as 'conservative' meant that they seemed slow-moving, devoid of ideas and negative.

His favourite phrase was said to be 'A rising tide lifts all boats', by which he meant that if the gross national income rose, all would benefit, so that Labour appeared 'conservative' to him because it attached at least as high a priority to the distribution of wealth as to its creation. It was for this reason, too, that he would have regarded himself as 'left of centre', since for him, as for many others in the Republic, the phrase denoted dynamism and adventurousness rather than a belief in equality.[16] His 'shift to the left' speech had no tangible consequences in political terms, but the immense significance attached to it in some quarters shows how fluid and uncertain the political picture was at that period.

3.2 The expansion of the Parliamentary Labour Party, 1963

The year 1963 was one of growth for the Labour Party in several respects. In a by-election in Dublin North East its vote more than doubled in a smaller poll, and the 18·5 per cent of the votes it won represented its highest percentage in any Dublin City constituency since a by-election in December 1945. Its annual report spoke of 'an increasing number of applications to join the Party', including 'a good sprinkling of applicants from the professional classes',[17] suggesting that Corish's attempts to broaden its appeal were bearing fruit. Nevertheless it was still the case, especially in Dublin, that many branches of the party were simply branches of trade unions, and non-unionists joining Labour sometimes found that their interest was treated with considerable surprise, if not indeed suspicion.[18]

Three new TDs joined the PLP in November 1963. Shortly after the defeat of a no confidence motion arising out of the heated 'turnover tax' debate, Seán Dunne was readmitted to the fold.[19] More significantly, the two National Progressive Democrat TDs joined the PLP at the end of the month, a move which was no great surprise in view of the developments of the previous two years.[20] The NPD TDs announced that their party was to be disbanded, and issued a statement saying that they had accepted an invitation to join Labour because Irish politics were 'at last narrowing down to the natural division between conservative and progressive forces', and the time was right for 'the union of forward-looking forces'.[21]

However, it appears that the initiative came from the NPD rather than from Labour. It seems that in 1961 the two TDs approached Tom Kyne, a senior and respected member of the PLP, and asked him to attempt to secure their admission, giving him a free hand tactically.[22] When the decision to admit them was taken there was no real opposition to McQuillan's application, but four TDs, including Corish and Norton, voted against the admittance of Browne, mainly because they were not convinced of his ability to work amicably within Labour or any other party. Browne had in fact applied to join Labour in 1952 but had not been admitted, mainly because of Norton's opposition.[23]

The significance of the move was that the NPD had seemed, during its five-year existence, to be a radical alternative to the main parties, to the extent that a Parliamentary Secretary had once said that 'if there is any fundamental difference in this House, it is between practically the whole lot of us and Dr Noel Browne'.[24] The NPD, aptly described as 'lively but minuscule',[25] had been prone to employ Dáil tactics which flouted the conventions of a more than averagely conservative parliament. For a period its TDs repeatedly called for a quorum,[26] dragging government TDs from their letter-writing activities several times a day, and in 1958 they questioned the Taoiseach closely about his links with the *Irish Press*.[27] Browne was regarded by many as the leading figure of the Irish left, and he had considerable appeal to the young, especially students, from whom he received assistance during his election campaigns. Consequently Labour now seemed likely to become more left-wing and more attractive to groups like students and the liberal intelligentsia.

The immediate impact, however, was to provoke an attack from the Minister for Health, Seán MacEntee, who made a speech so fiery that on legal advice the newspapers refrained from publishing certain passages of it. He referred to 'the Marxist technique of infiltration', and used the NPD TDs' statement that they had been invited to join Labour as evidence that the latter had 'humbled itself' and begged them to join it.[28] As in 1961, Corish reacted defensively to the charge. There would be 'no change of policy' as a result of the acquisition of the NPD, he said, and added that 'our policy is based on good, sound Christian principles and always will be'.[29]

Symbolically, as Noel Browne entered the Labour Party and shifted its centre of gravity towards the left, William Norton, the most intelligent and articulate member of Labour's right wing, died, on 4 December 1963. His control of his Kildare constituency organisation was demonstrated when his son Patrick was selected to contest the resulting by-election, despite being previously unknown in the constituency and despite his lack of sympathy with many features of the party, which resulted in his resignation four years later. Indeed, even during the by-election campaign he caused Labour some embarrassment by complaining about the unjust treatment of businessmen and attacking compulsory Irish.[30] Both he and Corish appealed for the support of groups like the self-employed, businessmen and non-trade unionists in general,[31] but in the other by-election held in February 1964, in Cork City, where the party had always been very trade unionist, it ran a campaign which could scarcely have attracted the middle class or non-trade unionists. One of its advertisements, for example, read:[32]

Holding clear and definite trade union principles Donal Hurley believes that the future of Ireland and her people depends on a strong trade union movement, working in close co-operation with a vigorous political Labour movement. Workers, vote for your own man. You wouldn't scab on the job. Don't scab at the ballot box!

In the event, Labour's performances at the by-elections were satisfactory but not spectacular, its percentage vote rising slightly in each constituency.

3.3 Fine Gael's move to the left, 1964–65

The long-term significance of the February 1964 by-elections, both of which were won by the government, was that they led to an upheaval within Fine Gael. The party seemed, even to many of its own members, to be devoid of policies and constructive ideas in general, and many of its senior members appeared to devote more of their time to their legal practices or their businesses than to politics. There had been no attempt since the 1961 election to move away from the party's conservative image. James Dillon had been content to hit out at the traditional targets, describing 'communist aggression' as 'the mad dog of world politics today',[33] and in a Dáil debate on capital punishment Fine Gael was the only party to offer any defence of the idea.[34] After some discontent was expressed at parliamentary party meetings, the party spent several months pondering uncertainly on its future.

Its policy vacuum was filled in a surprising manner in May 1964, when it adopted, *mutatis mutandis*, an eight-point programme drafted by Declan Costello. This document advocated, among other things, full economic planning, government control of the banks' credit policies and the introduction of full price control,[35] and all in all was very radical for an apparently conservative party. Some TDs found themselves in general agreement with it, while others, despite their personal reservations, thought that its adoption would benefit Fine Gael electorally. The conservative wing, led by Dillon and Gerard Sweetman, eventually realised that it was outnumbered, and capitulated, and a committee was set up to prepare a full policy document on the basis of a slightly modified version of Costello's original programme.[36] However, the party remained in a state of high internal tension until after the 1965 general election.

Labour reacted with public scepticism to Fine Gael's new programme, although some senior members were privately impressed by Costello's efforts. Corish went so far as to describe it as 'new and radical', but he also alleged that for Fine Gael the purpose of planning was merely to create a favourable climate for private enterprise.[37] By coincidence, leading members of both the major parties made speeches on the same day in June 1964 in which they reaffirmed their faith in market forces. Dillon declared that 'Fine Gael is today, as it has always been, the party of private enterprise', and Sweetman made a similar speech, while Seán Lemass derided the concept of full economic planning, especially in a nation of 'people so individualistic as the Irish', and stated that the freedom of 'free-roving private enterprise' was a central aspect of Fianna Fáil's policy.[38] These speeches, each in its own way an attack on Fine Gael's new programme, enabled James Tully to brand the two major parties as equally conservative; the speeches could have been written by the same hand, 'falling back on the well-worn clichés of the freedom of competition and the supremacy of private enterprise'.[39]

Nevertheless, with both Fianna Fáil, after Lemass's 'shift to the left' comment, and Fine Gael apparently seeking a more left-wing image, Labour was in some danger of being left behind.[40] A major step towards the establishment of a clearer identity was taken in June 1964, when for the first time Corish described Labour in an interview as a socialist party.[41] Instead of repeating his 1960 statement that it could be called 'Christian Socialist', he now maintained that he had used this phrase only to emphasise that, in his view, socialism was a Christian philosophy, and because he thought that there were those who associated socialism and atheism. Asked direct whether Labour's future policies would lay greater emphasis on socialist ideology, he answered, 'All our general and particular policy documents have, in fact, emphasized socialist ideology, and any further policies will certainly continue to do so.' He maintained that Labour's future was steadily growing brighter; in the past 'the politics of nationalism' had predominated, but recently Labour's social and economic policies had captured the public imagination, to the extent that they had 'to some degree been adopted by both Fianna Fáil and Fine Gael'. Labour also received a minor boost when the Workers' Union of Ireland announced that it was to affiliate to the party as from January 1965.[42] The WUI was the country's second largest union, with about 30,000 members, and its affiliation doubled the number of trade unionists affiliated to the party. The WUI had never been affiliated to Labour, but it had grown much closer to the party over the years, with three members of the Larkin family becoming Labour TDs.

At the same time as Labour became slightly more assertive at the national level, however, it was forced on to the defensive in a by-election in Roscommon by a libel case involving its newly acquired TD there, Jack McQuillan. He was suing a local newspaper for reporting a councillor's allegation that he was a communist, and the evidence given in the case, which ended less than a week before the by-election, illustrated the fear of rural Labour members of the consequences if they were called communists. McQuillan said that, as a practising Catholic, communism was to him 'a damnable idea', as it 'denied God'.[43] Both his counsel and one of his witnesses, who declared that any suggestion of communism was 'intolerable' to him, maintained that if such an allegation gained credence McQuillan's whole career might be endangered.[44] This tactic, of linking communism and anti-Catholicism and denying them both, probably did not help Labour, and it was not a great success legally, since although the jury found in McQuillan's favour he was awarded only a halfpenny damages. Labour fared very badly in the by-election and was unable even to attract a candidate in a Galway by-election later in the year, emphasising the point that the road ahead in the west of Ireland remained a very difficult one.

A by-election in Mid-Cork precipitated by the death of Labour's deputy leader Dan Desmond proved more successful from Labour's viewpoint. Its candidate was Desmond's widow, Eileen, who had been active in his constituency work. The Taoiseach hinted before polling day that a general election was likely unless Fianna Fáil won, and when Mrs Desmond took the seat, to give Labour its first by-election victory since 1949, the Dáil was dissolved before she was able to take her seat and the election was announced for 7 April.

3.4 The 1965 general election

The 1965 election campaign provided a marked contrast to that of 1961. The latter had been dull and attracted little public interest, but the 1965 campaign was fought hard by the parties on fairly distinct policies and did capture the attention of the public, despite a British journalist's comment that the electorate was 'seething with apathy'.[45] The eternally optimistic *Irish Times* political correspondent described the campaign as 'the greatest and most objective that Ireland has ever known', seeing in it 'the birth of the new Irish social democracy'.[46] Certainly there can be little doubt that there was more serious debate on social and economic matters than during any previous campaign.

Labour's manifesto, entitled *The Next Five Years*, was an updated version of the 1961 manifesto, with some new points added.[47] In particular it laid a greater emphasis on public enterprise and planning than before, although it did not contain the word 'socialism'. It referred slightingly to 'half-baked versions of Labour's ideas', presumably an allusion to Fine Gael's new programme. Its candidates concentrated their fire on Fianna Fáil and expounded Labour's policies, calling for an improvement in the health service, assistance for small farmers, price control, an extension of the education system, and increased economic activity by the State and full economic planning. Labour nominated forty-four candidates, a number then exceeded only in 1943, and the broadening of its base was shown by the dramatic rise in the proportion from a professional background (see Appendix 4).

Fine Gael's campaign was in many ways a continuation of its internal feud. No policy document had yet emerged from the committee established to produce one, suggesting to one journalist a 'persistence into the Costello era of the old preference for campaigning unencumbered by any coherent policy'.[48] The party hastily issued a thirty-page document entitled *Towards a Just Society*, which embodied the thinking of the left-leaning group rather than of the 'old guard', who were clearly embarrassed by it. Dillon introduced it to the press somewhat whimsically, and stressed throughout the campaign that Fine Gael believed in the virtues of private enterprise. He occasionally directly contradicted the *Just Society* document, for example over profit control and dividend limitation,[49] and on one occasion felt it necessary to deny that his party consisted of 'Bolshevik Revolutionaries'.[50] Fianna Fáil alleged that the manifesto was 'neither available to the general public nor acceptable to their own party',[51] and Seán MacEntee referred to Declan Costello as 'the cherubic Robespierre of the party, sitting tight-lipped' and to Dillon as 'the titular head bombinating about free enterprise'.[52]

Fianna Fáil, as usual, did not issue a manifesto, preferring to stand on its 'record'. Its attacks on Labour took two forms. On the one hand, Lemass adopted his familiar, patronising approach, describing Labour as a 'stick-in-the-mud party' whose members 'have learned nothing and forgotten nothing. The world is moving ahead but the Labour Party is not going with it.' Labour was tied up by antiquated ideas about the world; its members were 'an ineffective group of well-meaning men who would like to do some good but have no very clear notions of how to go about it'.[53] On the other hand, presaging later Fianna Fáil practice, the Minister for Local Government, Neil Blaney, accused it of being too left-wing. He alleged that the 'so-called intellectuals' of Labour were 'tinkering with dangerous public ownership ideas in order to be true to the ideals of the international socialist camp'; while pretending to be liberal socialists, Labour was influenced by and offered a haven to forces whose concept of government was derived from the policies of the extreme socialist camp.[54]

The minor parties made very little impact on the campaign. Clann na Poblachta, which had been dealt a severe blow by the departure from Ireland of Seán MacBride in October 1963, nominated only four candidates. Clann na Talmhan did not nominate any; its local organisations in East Galway and Roscommon joined Fine Gael, and its last TD did not stand for re-election.[55] Only twenty Independents stood, the lowest number since 1938.

In the event, Fianna Fáil won exactly half the 144 seats (see Appendix 1), which amounted to a small overall majority, given the continuation as Ceann Comhairle of Patrick Hogan, a Labour TD. The collapse of the minor-party and Independent vote produced gains for all the main parties. Fianna Fáil added two seats, and its share of the votes rose by almost 4 per cent. Fine Gael's gains were small, but its support base shifted greatly; it lost votes in Dublin but made large gains in the west, partly by absorbing the remnants of Clann na Talmhan.[56] Only two Independents and one minor-party candidate were elected, giving the main parties an unprecedented hegemony.

Labour made the largest gains, of six seats and nearly 4 per cent of the votes. Its capture of twenty-two seats had been equalled once (in June 1927) but never surpassed, and its percentage of the votes had been exceeded only twice (in 1922 and 1943). It gained votes in every province, but its most significant advance came in Dublin City, where its percentage vote more than doubled to 19·5 per cent, the highest level then achieved. This reflected a determined effort by the party, including the establishment of a Dublin City Organisation Committee which was said to have greatly improved the branch structure.[57] The Universities branch, which had received very little attention before 1960, was commended by the AC for its contribution to the campaign.[58]

Moreover, there was some change in the nature of the PLP, although it was much less marked than the change in candidates' backgrounds (see Appendix 5). Two of the new TDs were not entirely in the old mould. One of them, John O'Connell, was a medical doctor – the first ever elected for Labour – while another, Michael O'Leary, was a university-educated research officer with ICTU. The other four were more traditional figures. Three were trade union officials: Frank Cluskey and the former TD Denis Larkin in Dublin, and Henry Byrne in Laois-Offaly. In Kildare, Patrick Norton regained the Labour seat, running as in 1964 on an almost entirely personal platform. In addition to these actual gains, it came close to picking up seats in three constituencies – Kerry South, Dún Laoghaire and Roscommon – in which no Labour candidate had ever been elected. The only disappointment was that both its 1963 recruits from the NPD lost their seats, albeit by modest margins.

Overall, the party regarded these results as highly satisfactory, both in themselves and because they seemed to have broken a pattern. As the party leader noted at the next annual conference, there had been a tendency in the past for an advance at one election to be followed by a retreat at the next, but now the gains made in 1961 had been not only preserved but significantly added to.[59] Consequently, Labour felt that 'one more push' would enable it to pick up the five seats it had come close to winning and would take it up to hitherto unattained heights.

3.5 Electoral tests, 1965–66

No further electoral contests arose until the presidential election of June 1966, which Labour eventually decided not to contest. Although Brendan Corish told the 1965 annual conference that Labour was coming to be regarded as a major force and as more or less on a par with the two major parties,[60] the reality was otherwise, and most members saw little point in expending scarce resources on a doomed campaign for the largely ceremonial office of the presidency. Despite the advocacy by the party vice-chairman Proinsias Mac Aonghusa of the merits of nominating a Labour candidate,[61] Labour finally contented itself with the forlorn suggestion that the main parties support an 'agreed' candidate.[62] Mac Aonghusa later gave implicit advice to Labour supporters to vote for the Fine Gael candidate,[63] although an accusation by the party leader three weeks before the election that both major parties had 'a prior commitment to conservatism' suggested that the leadership had no great interest in the outcome.[64]

Certainly Fine Gael's campaign was better designed to appeal to uncommited voters than Fianna Fáil's, since instead of criticising the outgoing President de Valera, who was seeking re-election, it concentrated exclusively on the merits of its candidate, Tom O'Higgins, as a 'forward-looking' and relatively young person. In consequence, Fianna Fáil was forced to fight a defensive campaign, and several of its leading figures, including Ministers, implied that only illegitimate offspring of the old Royal Irish Constabulary, and those opposed to the idea of Irish independence, would consider voting against de Valera.

O'Higgins did surprisingly well, losing by only 11,000 votes in a total poll of over 1,100,000.[65] The nature of his campaign suggested that the closeness of the result demonstrated not so much a surge in popularity for Fine Gael as a vague and as yet unfocused desire for change. Moreover the pattern of votes for the candidates in 1966 correlated very weakly with the support of the parties at the 1965 election,[66] suggesting that traditional voting allegiances were wavering. The result had no direct significance for Labour, but it was another straw in the wind persuading politicians and commentators that major political change was imminent.

In the build-up to the October 1966 annual conference Labour began preparing the ground for an open declaration that it was a socialist party. At the 1965 conference Corish had described its policies as 'socialistic',[67] and in 1966 he stated that socialism had recently become 'much more fashionable', indicating at the same time that Labour would be nominating many more candidates than usual at the next election.[68] The 1966 conference itself was attended by about 600 delegates, the largest number ever; there had been about 300 delegates in 1964 and 400 in 1965.[69] This expansion reflected the rapid increase in the party's membership (see Appendix 3). For the first time party spokesmen declared openly that Labour was a socialist party, Corish saying that he stood for the establishment of a socialist republic. The conference also acknowledged an affinity with social democratic parties elsewhere by voting, with only one left-wing dissenter, to apply for membership of the Socialist International.[70] However, there were no new policies; the word 'socialism' was not defined, and was in effect merely a label used to describe the same policies as before. Of the national newspapers, only the *Irish Times* attached any great significance to the conference, arguing that it added up to a profound change in Irish political life. It concluded that since both the major parties were 'wedded to private enterprise' Labour, because it advocated 'State interference', was now 'the real opposition'.[71] Whether accurate or not, this was certainly the image Labour now sought to project.

The first electoral test of the new image, if such it was, was provided by two by-elections held in December 1966 in the Kerry South and Waterford constituencies. The two major parties entered these under relatively new leaders. James Dillon had resigned from the Fine Gael leadership at the first parliamentary party meeting after the 1965 general election, and the same meeting, advised by Dillon to select a new leader at once, unanimously supported Gerard Sweetman's proposal that Liam Cosgrave became leader.[72] This manoeuvre seems to have been designed to ensure that the leadership remained in conservative hands, and in particular to minimise the possibility of Declan Costello becoming leader. Although it later emerged that Cosgrave was indeed well on the right of the party, he seemed at the time to be almost a liberal, mainly because at the 1964 party conference he had stated that it was 'a well-known political maxim that a party, to secure and retain public support, should be slightly to the left of centre'.[73] Fianna Fáil gained a new leader in November 1966, when Seán Lemass resigned and, in a two-man contest, Jack Lynch received the votes of fifty-two Fianna Fáil TDs against the nineteen for George Colley.[74] Lynch was known as an easy-going and likable man with no strong ideological outlook, and the electorate thus had no idea whether the government party was likely to move to the right or the left, if either, under his leadership.

Although Corish spoke briefly of 'socialism' at the Waterford candidate selection conference,[75] the word does not seem to have been mentioned much, if at all, during the campaigns, which were fought along traditional lines. Labour's result in each constituency was about the same as in 1965, a disappointment for the party, since it had hoped for a dramatic improvement.[76] Perhaps predictably, it attributed its failure to advance to 'poor organisation'. Michael O'Leary called for a complete overhaul of the party's organisation,[77] but this reaction was largely just a rationalisation of the simple fact that Labour's support had not grown since 1965.

3.6 Relationships with trade unions 1966–67 and the Mac Aonghusa expulsion

As well as a lack of satisfaction with the state of the organisation, there was also some concern, reportedly shared by the party leader, that Labour still had the image of a party for trade unionists only,[78] an image reinforced by the fact that all three of its elected officers were union officials. However, the party was also concerned that the formal links between itself and some of the largest unions were non-existent, so that it was gratified by signs that both the Amalgamated Transport and General Workers' Union (ATGWU) and the ITGWU were taking steps towards affiliation.

The ATGWU, the Irish arm of the British TGWU, had members in both parts of Ireland. It had been affiliated to both the Irish Labour Party and the Northern Ireland Labour Party until the latter split in 1949 over the constitutional question, whereupon it disaffiliated from both parties. In November 1966 Matt Merrigan, the general secretary of the union, circulated to all members a summary of the past relationship between Labour and the union, which stressed the advantages of reaffiliating to the party and pointed out that other unions with a thirty-two-county membership did not seem to have suffered by affiliating. No firm action was taken for another two years, however.

The question of the reaffiliation of the ITGWU to the Labour Party, after the 1943 break, became something of a hardy annual at the union's conferences in the 1960s, with the Drogheda branch making the running. In 1960 it put down a motion urging affiliation but withdrew it at the request of the general president, who said that the National Executive Council (NEC) had set up a working committee to examine the whole question.[79] Nothing having happened in the interim, it tabled a similar motion at the 1962 conference, which was supported by Brendan Corish. However, the president again secured the motion's withdrawal, stating that the matter was receiving attention from the NEC, which would come to Conference for a decision when the working committee's report was completed.[80] Another motion from the Drogheda branch at the 1963 conference was sufficiently vague and innocuous to be accepted.[81]

By 1965 there were still no signs of progress, so, undaunted, the Drogheda branch put down yet another motion calling for affiliation. The NEC was forced to admit that the special working committee still had not reported, owing to pressure of other business, but secured the withdrawal of the motion in return for a promise to make a statement to the 1966 conference.[82] The statement was duly made, by the union's general secretary, Fintan Kennedy, who said that the NEC would table a motion for affiliation at the following year's conference; the reason for the further year's delay was to allow every delegate to ascertain his branch members' views on the subject.[83] Later in the year Kennedy sent a letter to each branch and district council urging them to discuss the question.[84]

The NEC did indeed put a motion to the 1967 conference empowering the union to affiliate to Labour, a course recommended by Kennedy on the ground that many of the union's aims, such as full employment and better health and educational facilities, were essentially political, and could best be secured 'through the political medium of active participation in the Irish Labour Party'.[85] Despite opposition from one delegate who argued that the union would be split if it affiliated to a party, and from another who suggested that Labour was not worth supporting, the conference seemed to agree with the sentiments of a delegate who said that 'the Labour Party may not be perfect but it is the only Labour Party we have', and passed the resolution by 176 votes to fifteen. Three months later it was announced that the union would be affiliating as from 1 January 1968.[86]

The decision was greeted with great enthusiasm by Brendan Corish, who described it as 'the most significant development in Irish politics'.[87] He added:

It means that the Labour Party from now on will more and more have the support of the workers. It means that politics in this country will eventually become polarized into left and right. It means that Labour can look forward to the prospect of forming an alternative government.

The party's official paper called the event 'a watershed in the history of the Labour Party'.[88] Inevitably, such hopes were disappointed. The electoral impact of the affiliation was negligible, and the financial impact was not much greater. Despite some initial assumptions that the whole of the union's political fund, then standing at approximately

£90,000, would at once be handed over to Labour, it soon transpired that apart from the subventions which had always been made anyway the only extra contribution to party funds would be in the form of an annual affiliation fee. In the end, the union affiliated for just two-thirds of its members, 100,000 out of 150,000, and paid only £1,642 to the party in 1968 and 1969.[89]

The inordinate length of time taken for the matter to reach a head made it appear to some that the NEC was employing delaying tactics, but in fact apathy was the main retarding influence, with a wish to be certain that affiliation would not split the union 'from bow to stern', as a delegate to the 1967 conference suggested it would,[90] also a consideration. The impetus, such as it was, came mainly from a few individuals at the top, who were concerned to test and prepare the ground thoroughly in advance to ensure that they were not moving too quickly for the membership's liking. That the attitude of most members was one of supreme indifference was strongly suggested by the speech of a Cork delegate at the 1971 conference. He recalled that in 1967 his branch had gone to great lengths to ascertain its members' wishes, by organising a plebiscite, informing all the members of the arrangements made, and setting aside a full week for voting. At the end of the week only twenty-two of the 1,800 members had bothered to vote.[91] The affiliation's lack of significant impact on either the union or the party suggests that those who were apathetic may have had the most realistic assessment of the importance of the issue.

During the same period the formal links between Labour and ICTU were also becoming closer, while the actual relationship remained unaltered. In 1967 the ICTU annual conference passed a motion establishing a 'Joint Council', comprising representatives of ICTU and the Labour Party, which was 'to meet regularly at stated intervals for consultation and co-ordination of policies and activities'.[92] Seconding the motion, Brendan Corish expressed the hope that it would increase the political awareness of the unions and their support for Labour,[93] and a national newspaper gave the story prominent treatment under the headline 'ICTU Establishes Political Council: Big Boost for Labour'.[94] However, the Council was nothing more than a revamped version of the old Joint Committee, and it proved of no more importance. Only two meetings of the Council appear ever to have taken place,[95] and at Labour's 1969 conference the vice-president of ICTU stated that little had been either attempted or achieved by the Council; in fact, he admitted, 'there has been nothing done'.

The question of Labour's relations with, and possible domination by, the unions was raised dramatically early in 1967 by the expulsion from the party of Proinsias Mac Aonghusa, who had been its vice-chairman between 1964 and 1966. The expulsion was not carried out in a very creditable manner – the AC announced in mid-January that he had been expelled but then waited for three weeks before offering any explanation. The reason eventually given, that he was associated with a publication called *Labour Newsletter* and had sent abusive replies to letters from a party sub-committee investigating this publication,[96] was not very convincing. In the absence of a more plausible explanation, Mac Aonghusa's own claim that he had been expelled because 'his idea of a broadly-based Labour Party free from too much trade union influence was bitterly opposed by a number of important people'[97] and that the incident demonstrated that Labour 'has become far too much dominated by the trade unions, neglects national issues and concentrates solely on bread-and-butter union issues'[98] gained some credibility. One paper concluded that it showed that 'the Labour Party is at least suspicious of intellectuals' and was 'fearful of expanding beyond the reach of the power of the trade unions'.[99]

In fact the trade unions, and Labour's relations with them, had virtually nothing to do with the expulsion. Mac Aonghusa had made many enemies on his way up the party hierarchy. He had alienated some of those who were opposed to the move to the left, and was not popular with many veteran TDs, especially James Tully, the party whip. In 1966 he had written that 'the do-nothing backwoodsmen who personified the Labour Party in many people's eyes in the past no longer hold sway',[100] an obvious reference to some of these TDs. Many party figures regarded him as over-vocal and inclined to give his views as if he were speaking for the whole party. He had been a prominent critic of the Language Freedom Movement, an organisation opposed to compulsory Irish in the educational system, many of whose meetings were broken up by supporters of the *status quo*.

The affair spluttered on until October 1967. It emerged that Brendan Corish had opposed the expulsion, which induced Mac Aonghusa to allege that he had no say in 'the real leadership' of the party,[101] and the only TD to speak directly on the affair initially, Dr John O'Connell, described the charges as 'fictitious' and said that Mac Aonghusa had been 'the only positive activist' in the party.[102] Mac Aonghusa went through the process of applying for readmission, and was allowed to address the October conference to appeal against his expulsion. He rested his case on the manner of his expulsion, without repeating his earlier charges of trade union domination, but the expulsion was upheld by 365 votes to 209.[103]

The affair had no long-term significance, mainly because the tide feared by those instrumental in engineering the expulsion swept in anyway. Indeed, Mac Aonghusa's association with the distinctly illiberal tactics of the opponents of the Language Freedom Movement had made him to some extent a liability to the party. However, the manner of his expulsion – he was not informed in advance that his expulsion was being considered, and was given no opportunity to defend himself against any of the charges made at the meeting – savoured of the Star Chamber, and confirmed the suspicions of those who believed that the party establishment was opposed to the steady move to the left. One journalist stated that Labour had 'disgraced itself', and that it was clearly content to remain an inoffensive minor party,[104] while a national newspaper concluded that the expulsion revealed Labour as a party unable to tolerate 'stormy characters . . . a party without much confidence in itself, a party of safe men', in contrast to the dynamic socialist image it was attempting to project.[105]

4

Into the valley of death, 1967–69

4.1 The New Republic conference

The move to the left proceeded at an accelerating rate throughout 1967, and there was a sign that Labour was acquiring a new professionalism to back up its new image when a political director was appointed in May.[1] The appointee, Brendan Halligan, was a university graduate with a background as an economist and an executive in a semi-State company. He became general secretary of the party the following January, and played an important part in formulating the leadership's strategy over the next ten years. Whereas the outgoing secretary, Senator Mary Davidson, who had been on the Head Office staff since the 1920s, had seemed to see her role as mainly administrative, Halligan sought a more active political role for the office. The previous year he had delivered a lecture in which he accused Labour of having 'lost the people', and argued that 'its role has been minimal in areas beyond its sectional interests and its responses to change in the main have been defensive'.[2]

Upon his appointment he commented that 'it is almost respectable now to be a socialist', and declared that Labour intended to force the two major parties into some kind of merger.[3] Five months later he elaborated his views in a periodical article in which he outlined a number of reasons for believing that Labour's future was bright.[4] These included the failure of the two major parties to move with the times; their lack of distinctive identities or *raisons d'être*; the disappearance of the 'old guard' from the political scene and the electorate; the emergence of new voters without formed voting habits; the growth of Labour branches in the universities; the growing political consciousness of the unions, as evidenced by the increase in affiliations; the votes, money and psychological boost brought by these affiliations; and the new, acceptable image of socialism in Ireland. The cheers that had greeted a remark about 'leaning to the left' at the 1966 conference, he said, had been 'mass recognition of the fact that socialism had arrived, and a vacuum had been filled at last, and an abnormality corrected'. He repeated the myth that before the 1960s Labour had been secretly socialist: 'The conference cheers were born of no small degree of relief that public expression could be given to private beliefs and that a forty-five year wait was over'.

The first electoral test for the new organisation came in the local elections of June 1967. Labour's programme was thorough and well presented, and made much mention of 'socialism'.[5] It nominated 540 candidates – a third of them, it was claimed, in their twenties – for the 796 seats at stake.[6] However, it won only eighty-six and attracted a lower share of votes than it had at the 1965 general election.[7] Its vote in Dublin City rose by 6·6 per cent, taking it to within two seats of Fianna Fáil, and almost quadrupling its strength there at the previous local elections. Outside Dublin, however, it fell back. The next annual report admitted that the results were disappointing – in fact they presaged those of the 1969 general election – and attributed them, as usual, to faults in the organisational machinery.[8]

The balance of power within the party continued to shift to the left. Noel Browne, described by a journalist as 'the most forthright Labour Party member ever to have been a TD',[9] put himself forward for the vice-chairmanship and was returned unopposed at the October conference. Earlier in the year Browne had spoken of Labour's 'dismal record of cowardly compromise' and had accused the party of having led an 'innocuous conservative existence' which had 'offered no threat whatever to established privileged capitalist interests'.[10] Browne also argued that the Church bore a heavy responsibility for 'stolid, decadent' Irish society; politicians, he said, had risked 'political assassination by drowning in holy water' if they probed deeply into the 'scabrous society' created by the Church and the political establishment. The party chairmanship also changed hands. James Tully, who had held the position for thirteen years, stood down and was succeeded by Barry Desmond, a graduate in his early thirties. Labour received the seal of approval of the Socialist International in April 1967, when it was accepted into membership.

Some of the motions put down by Dublin branches for the 1967 conference showed that Browne's rhetoric, inconceivable a few years earlier, now represented the views of quite a few members. One urged the PLP to 'abandon its role as the third Conservative Party in Ireland', and another demanded that elected representatives should abide by party policies as laid down by annual conferences. A third called on the AC to draw up a panel of names from which all parliamentary candidates would have to be drawn; one requirement for inclusion on the panel, it added pointedly, should be a 'basic knowledge of Labour policy'.[11]

The conference itself, attended by about 700 delegates, marked the beginning of Labour's brief golden age, which lasted until the 1969 election results were known. It was dominated by the leader's address, in which the themes of 'Let's Build the New Republic' and 'The Seventies will be Socialist' were unveiled.[12] The Irish people, he maintained, faced a 'crisis of decision' as to whether they would continue to support one of the parties dedicated to maintaining the *status quo*, or Labour, whose task was to provide a socialist alternative. He acknowledged that in the past Labour had often been regarded as 'a rural pressure group or a body of agricultural independents' and had disappointed even its most fervent supporters'. However, he said, Labour was now in a position from where it could, with an effort of unequalled intensity', gain fifty seats and form a government. The party had growing support from the trade union movement, and as a result of its recent gains in Dublin it had support from all sections of the community, but especially from 'the new impatient generation'. In order to meet their expectations it must be prepared to question every aspect of society and proclaim the need for 'deep and fundamental change'.

Almost every delegate made much use of the word 'socialism', but it remained an ill defined term, not backed up by anything tangible, and used almost as a ritual word, as proof of comradeship and as a mark of a distinctive Labour identity. Corish made an attempt to flesh it out; he declared that it meant 'a belief in freedom and in the right of every man to develop as he wishes', 'a belief in equality', the primacy of the community rather than the individual, and a belief in efficiency. This rather tame definition emphasised how sorely Labour needed new policies to underpin the new image it was trying hard to cultivate.

A brief summary of the New Republic speech cannot convey the impact it made on the conference, because of its honest appraisal of Labour's uninspiring record and the confident, assertive tone it struck when looking to the future. One journalist, admittedly a strong sympathiser of the party, described it as 'the most comprehensive, intelligent, most radical statement ever heard from a Labour leader since Connolly'.[13] All three national newspapers gave it considerable prominence, and there was no longer any doubt that Labour wanted to be regarded as a socialist party.

The new image was given its first electoral airing in two by-elections in November 1967, with the Labour campaign highlighting 'socialism'. Its Limerick West candidate, however, had a cautious interpretation of the term: 'I am a socialist in the sense that if private enterprise fails then public enterprise must do the job'.[14] He lost his deposit, and although in Cork City, where the vacancy had been created by the death of Labour's Seán Casey, the party's vote rose from 16·9 to 24·6 per cent, Labour remained in third place. The results of two further by-elections, in March 1968, were also disappointing for Labour. The Wicklow contest resulted from the death of veteran Labour TD James Everett, and the party's candidate, Liam Kavanagh, was his nephew, having been selected at local insistence despite much pressure from the national organisation to secure the selection of Noel Browne. Despite this, and the government's unpopular announcement of another referendum on PR, the Labour vote actually fell, and although it rose in Clare the candidate still lost his deposit. In all four cases the usual rather facile excuse of 'poor organisation' was offered.

Although the electorate did not seem moved one way or the other by Labour's stress on 'socialism', Fianna Fáil's attitude to the party began to change. Until his retirement Seán Lemass's paternalistic attitude had prevailed, and was reiterated in July 1966 in a comment long remembered by Labour, and which rankled with it much more than allegations of communism:[15]

I gather from Deputy Tully that someone accused the Labour Party of going 'Red', which hurt his feelings very much. May I straightaway dissociate myself from any such suggestion? The Labour Party are, and always have been, the most conservative element in our community. Far from the Labour Party going 'Red', they are not going anywhere ... The Labour Party are a nice, respectable, docile, harmless body of men – as harmless a body as ever graced any parliament.

When Jack Lynch became Taoiseach he took the same line at first, speaking of 'the lethargic conservatism of the so-called Labour Party',[16] but as Labour moved further to the left during 1967 Fianna Fáil moved openly to the right. A fund-raising organisation called Taca (the nearest English equivalent is 'Support') was set up late in

1966 and recruited members from wealthy businessmen, allegedly holding dinners at up to £100 per place.[17] Coupled with a Ministerial admission that Fianna Fáil supporters were in turn 'supported' by the government,[18] there was an obvious danger that the party's working-class and small-farmer voters would be alienated, but Taca continued to thrive. In the November 1967 by-elections Lynch implied that Labour was shackled by a 'hidebound ideology', and warned that if it got power 'private enterprise would take second place to nationalization', which would have dire consequences for the country.[19]

4.2 The Norton and McQuillan affairs

The question of whether Labour was indeed veering towards communism was raised suddenly in December 1967, when Patrick Norton TD resigned from the party. He wrote a letter to Corish, sending copies to the media,[20] in which he alleged that 'a small but vocal group of ambitious fellow-travellers have been allowed to take possession of the leadership and the party; and that the party now stands openly for a workers' republic, which is a euphemism for something more extreme'. Whereas earlier in the 1960s Corish had reacted defensively to such charges, seeking to establish that Labour policies were compatible with papal encyclicals, he dismissed Norton's allegations unsympathetically: 'the plain fact is that Deputy Norton is not prepared to accept the new socialist policy of the Labour Party and never was since he came into the Dáil'. This point was borne out by Norton's admission that he had been unable 'to digest the new Left-wing image of the Labour Party', and it had been obvious for some time that he was drifting away. Nor did Labour feel obliged to defend itself against a newspaper's claim that Norton's allegation about fellow-travellers was 'serious and fundamental'.[21] The incident was essentially a minor problem of transition, and did not harm Labour much; the Kildare branches remained loyal, and it seemed to demonstrate that Norton was conservative rather than that it was communist. It may even have been to Labour's advantage, by publicising and establishing the genuineness of its move to the left.

The expulsion of Senator Jack McQuillan from the PLP in April 1968, however, almost certainly did damage the party. McQuillan had been elected to the Dáil for Roscommon at five general elections from 1948, under three different labels, but had lost his seat in 1965, perhaps partly because the Labour label had alienated the small farmers who constituted the bulk of his support. The roots of his expulsion went back to February 1966, when he had become general secretary of a new trade union, the Irish Post Office Officials' Association (IPOOA), a break-away union formed by post office employees dissatisfied with the way the Post Office Workers' Union (POWU) was representing their interests. The general secretary of the POWU, which was naturally opposed to the existence of the new union, stated that he had 'drawn the attention of the Parliamentary Labour Party to the anti-trade union activities of Senator Jack McQuillan',[22] and said there were no excuses for break-away unions.[23] Since the POWU was affiliated to, and was thus a financial supporter of, the Labour Party, it felt that the least Labour could do in return was to refrain from harbouring at its highest level people who were weakening the union. The POWU was also a member of ICTU, which regarded the formation of break-away unions very unfavourably. It made its views known to Labour,[24] and unceremoniously rejected an application for membership from the IPOOA, informing it that it should dissolve itself.[25] Early in the dispute the PLP stated that McQuillan had not consulted it before taking the IPOOA post, and that it did not support the idea of 'splinter unions',[26] and from this point on there was ever-increasing pressure from most PLP members on McQuillan to sever his connection with the IPOOA or face the risk of expulsion.

McQuillan refused to take the first option, stating that 'the issue to me is the right or otherwise of a trade union boss to reach into and dictate to a political party on what it should do in the political sphere'.[27] He drew some public support from the ATGWU general secretary Matt Merrigan, who pointed out that there were many unions in ICTU which were not affiliated to Labour, and asked whether the party had 'taken leave of its senses' for considering expelling McQuillan 'because he chose to earn his livelihood as a professional servant of a trade union not in affiliation with ICTU'.[28] Within the PLP, however, McQuillan was almost isolated, with Dr John O'Connell the only member to support him throughout. Most PLP members were themselves trade unionists, with an almost instinctive hostility to break-away unions. Consequently they needed little prodding to act, and although the threat of disaffiliation by the POWU was in the air, this was not the decisive factor in bringing matters to a head. In-fighting between the unions reached a peak in

1968; the IPOOA began strike action for negotiating rights with the Department of Posts and Telegraphs, and alleged that the Department and the POWU were in a conspiracy to destroy it.[29] Finally, an IPOOA member was dismissed, and McQuillan tabled a Seanad motion condemning the incident despite a warning from the PLP that this would result in his expulsion. The whip was withdrawn on 23 April.[30]

A motion at the POWU's next annual conference proposed that the union cease contributing to Labour funds until McQuillan was expelled from ordinary membership of the party,[31] but it soon became clear that this would not be necessary. After several 'challenges' to Corish to debate the issue with him in Roscommon had gone unanswered, McQuillan convened a meeting of his organisation and announced that he was leaving the Labour Party and retiring from public life. A statement was issued which, despite veering from the third to the first person when referring to McQuillan, conveys the mood of bitterness which, judging by reports, characterised the meeting:[32]

The political organization which supported and elected Jack McQuillan met for the last time last night. The Leader of the Labour Party was condemned in the strongest possible terms for his failure to accept an invitation to come to Roscommon and explain the events which led up to the removal of the Whip from Senator McQuillan.

Senator McQuillan said that personal disillusionment came some time ago as far as the Parliamentary Labour Party is concerned. At Party meetings which he attended regularly he found it was a waste of time urging Mr Corish and company to initiate discussions in Dáil Eireann on the necessity for taking into public ownership the flour milling, distilling and bacon industries. A discussion on co-operative farming sent them running for Holy Water; mention of the West of Ireland sent them scurrying for lunch.

To my dismay, it became clear that Socialism was only a gimmick as far as Mr Corish and his colleagues were concerned. The proof of the matter lies in the fact that Fine Gael are more than willing to join forces with them. A few old bones in the guise of minor Cabinet posts will satisfy the Labour doggies.

The removal of the Whip from me brought matters to a head. The Party stood exposed as a puppet of trade union bosses who pulled the strings in the background. Today it is dependent for its survival on the financial backing of a couple of trade unions.

Although many of his supporters urged him to contest the next election as an Independent, he insisted that he was disillusioned and was 'finished' with public life.[33]

In many ways Labour lost more than it gained by forcing a break with McQuillan. Its reasons for doing so were that otherwise the

POWU might disaffiliate, and other unions considering affiliating might not do so. In addition, most PLP members regarded themselves as members of the trade union movement as well as of the Labour Party, and disapproved of McQuillan's involvement with the IPOOA. If McQuillan had not been expelled, they would have found themselves in increasingly bad standing, at both the formal and the informal level, with the trade union establishment. The withdrawal of the whip was understandable and perhaps inevitable, but it may well have cost Labour support in the west. McQuillan won votes from small farmers, and was one of the few tangible signs of a Labour presence west of the Shannon. Labour had always suffered electorally from a suspicion among many small farmers that it was not really interested in them and was basically a mouthpiece or puppet of the unions. During the 1960s it had made strenuous efforts to throw off this image, but there can be little doubt that it was powerfully reinforced by McQuillan's expulsion.

4.3 The 1968 PR referendum

During 1968 Labour continued gearing itself for the forthcoming general election, with the expansion of its Head Office staff[34] and the holding of a conference at which the policies on which the 1969 election was to be fought were first discussed.[35] At last there was a solid sign of growth in Labour's electoral support; in a by-election in East Limerick its vote rose by about 5,000 and its candidate came within 1,000 votes of winning the seat. The party leader proclaimed that Labour was now 'challenging to be the challengers of the government'.[36]

A full-scale electoral contest occurred later in the year when Fianna Fáil made another attempt to abolish the PR electoral system and replace it by the British one. Both opposition parties campaigned against a change, even though several leading Fine Gael members had expressed reservations about the *status quo*.[37] Labour's AC alleged that the move was intended 'to entrench the new rich in the Fianna Fáil Cabinet in power', and the party held an emergency conference at which Corish declared that it must 'go on a war footing' to overcome the 'crisis'.[38] Using the slogan 'The Straight Vote is Crooked, so Vote No', Labour issued about 900,000 pieces of literature. In fact Labour's response might have been expected to be more mixed than it was, for whereas in 1959 its survival had seemed to depend on the retention of

PR, it was now much more ambitious and maintained that it was on the verge of overtaking Fine Gael. James Tully claimed that Labour supported PR on grounds of democratic principle, and would continue to do so even if it became the largest party in the State.[39] However, the unanimity of Labour's hostility to the proposal suggests that despite its heady rhetoric it still had a minority party mentality.

The campaign lacked the tension of that of 1959, since the government's proposal seemed doomed from the start. Many Fianna Fáil backbenchers did not involve themselves, fearing that under the 'straight vote' they might be swept aside by 'Taca men' imposed centrally; their fears were not assuaged by party advertisements promising that the change would produce 'more effective, hard-working TDs' and would no longer enable a 'weak man' to get elected on a strong one's surplus.[40] Fine Gael's advertisements implied that Fianna Fáil's aim was to set up a Nazi-style dictatorship.[41] More effective was probably a television assessment by academics Basil Chubb and David Thornley, suggesting that Fianna Fáil might win over ninety seats at the next election if it were held under the British system.[42]

The proposal was defeated by a three-to-two margin, with only four of the thirty-eight constituencies voting in favour.[43] Labour's 1965 vote correlated negatively ($r = -0.51$) with the anti-PR vote, as would be expected. Corish claimed that Labour, together with the unions and the organised farmers, had been mainly responsible for the result. He argued that Labour's organisation had gained valuable campaign experience and was now 'battle-hardened'; this had been Labour's 'first real national campaign', and it had at last 'entered' Connacht and Ulster.[44]

However, even while it was basking in the glory of this victory, two clouds were looming on the horizon. The first concerned relationships with the trade unions. Early in 1969 the ATGWU, the country's third largest union, affiliated,[45] but it was gradually becoming apparent that these affiliations were having little practical impact. ICTU had entered the PR campaign in its later stages, but had stressed that this was to defend the principle of PR, which it uses in its internal elections, and not for any 'political party' reasons.[46] A month later ICTU announced that henceforth its officers could not hold executive positions in political parties;[47] at the time, two of Labour's officers were also ICTU officers. Both these decisions were entirely reasonable: it had a natural desire to retain the full-time services of its employees, and the fact that only about a fifth of the unions in ICTU were affiliated to Labour inhibited it from committing itself to that party's pro-PR campaign. Nevertheless, both actions seemed somewhat anti-climactic after the plethora of 'political councils' and union affiliations which were supposed to be bringing the unions and party closer together. Even in financial terms, Corish stated in 1969 that direct union contributions to Labour amounted annually only to £3,500, not even enough to run party headquarters.[48]

Secondly, it was around this time that Labour began to suffer from a credibility problem, as Fine Gael had in 1964–65. A gap was developing between the annual conference and the parliamentary party; the former was committed to an approach which seemed to inspire neither enthusiasm nor interest among many PLP members. David Thornley once spoke of Labour as a combination of a fairly right-wing 'band of hardworking parliamentarians' and 'a fire-breathing party congress, whose ideological purity is in inverse ratio to its political realism',[49] and there was certainly suspicion as to how far the PLP would be willing or even able to implement the bold new policies now being formulated. Noel Browne described the New Republic conference as 'exhilarating but effectively futile', because it had had no impact on the PLP, and concluded that there were now 'two ideologically unconnected Labour parties – the socialist conference party and the conservative parliamentary party'. Labour's new image, he suggested, was intended to win the support of left-wing activists without abandoning 'the traditional extremely right-wing conservatism of the "Irish Labour Party" '.[50]

In a European context there was nothing surprising about the direction in which the party was moving. The late 1960s was a time of radical dissent across the Western world, and with the establishment of a national television service in 1962, and an expanded coverage of foreign news by the Irish newspapers during the 1960s, Ireland was no longer blanketed by Britain from developments in Europe. The impact of these external influences was probably greatest on the young, not yet fully socialised into the traditional patterns of Irish political thought, and those living in Dublin, where all the British television and radio stations can be received. Few European social democratic parties were pulled much to the left by the wave of student protests. Most of them were too much a part of the political establishment to have any appeal to the radicals, and moreover they had too large a membership, and were too well organised, to be easily taken over. Only the Dutch Labour Party, the PvdA, was significantly affected, by the New Left faction which was active between 1966 and 1970.[51] The Irish Labour Party in 1966, in contrast to most social democratic parties, had been out of office for nearly a decade, and was moving to the left already. It had fewer than 5,000 members, most of whom were only too glad to leave policy-making to someone else, and − as yet − no strong central machinery, and consequently attracted an 'anti-system' element which began to drift away after the party changed its attitude to coalition in 1970.

Some TDs welcomed the move to the left, and one veteran rural TD not only declared himself a socialist but added that his policy was 'the policy of Connolly, possibly of Marx and other socialist thinkers', and he did not rule out Mao Tse-Tung as a source of inspiration.[52] Most rural TDs had a very different view. Possessing a Napoleonic contempt for 'ideologues', they regarded many of the vocal new members as people whose knowledge came from books rather than from practical experience of life, and who had little understanding of 'the ordinary people', especially in rural Ireland. They were − and still are − inclined to draw a distinction between 'practical' socialists, who do a 'good turn' for their neighbours every day, and 'theoretical' socialists, who confine their activities to the verbal level and are never seen between annual conferences. They felt that they had carried Labour's flag during the years when it was not a profitable task, and were not pleased to discover that they were regarded by many new members as an anachronism, derided as 'backwoodsmen' or 'satraps' and treated with scarcely concealed contempt because of their lack of a coherent ideology or a university education.

Realising that the tide was flowing against them, most of the TDs in this category kept their powder dry; there was little open criticism of the move to the left until after the 1969 election. Occasionally, though, it could be seen that not every TD was imbued with the new socialist spirit of the party. James Tully asked whether certain remarks of Labour or of Fianna Fáil were 'more like the comments of the red element'.[53] Michael Pat Murphy, far from identifying the class struggle as the basic force underlying change in Irish society, expressed an almost corporatist view of the State:[54]

There appears to be a divisive atmosphere being created in the community. Large blocs of opinion are being compelled to move away into separate and distinct groups. This trend is contrary to the ideals to which we should aspire; it is contrary to the formation of a harmonious society. Undoubtedly it is essential for the development of society that various shades of opinion should thrive, but these disparate opinions should always function towards the ultimate good of the state.

4.4 The 1969 conference and the new policies

For the moment, though, Labour's spirits were high, and they received a further boost in December 1968 when it was announced that Dr Conor Cruise O'Brien had become a member. O'Brien was internationally known as a diplomat, author and academic, and his acquisition was regarded as so significant that a special meeting was held to mark the occasion. Dr O'Brien made a speech – reported in full by the *Irish Times*, which also regarded the event as a major development – in which he argued that Ireland was poised to take a decisive shift to the left, with Fianna Fáil, which had grown tired and conservative in office, giving way to Labour.[55] In the past, he would have doubted whether Labour could have taken advantage of this, since it had seemed content with occasional spells in Fine Gael-dominated coalitions.[56] Moreover, Labour had feared being called communist, but recent fundamental changes in the outlook of the Irish people meant that discussion could now be much more open.

The January 1969 annual conference was the last event marked by the mood of mass euphoria which tended to characterise Labour gatherings in the late 1960s, and yet again the number of delegates (850) was the largest ever. Dublin delegates seemed to make most of the running in the move to the left, because they spoke more often than other delegates. Analysis shows that over half the speakers at the 1971 and 1972 conferences came from Dublin branches, and at the 1974 and 1975 conferences more than half the resolutions were submitted by Dublin branches.[57]

However, the proportion of delegates from Dublin was actually lower than the proportion of Labour's votes at the preceding and succeeding general elections arising there (see Table 4.1). This disparity, very marked in 1969 and at some of the 1970s conferences, led some Dublin delegates to argue that conferences were 'rigged', since in 1969 each Dublin delegate 'represented' 519 Labour voters, while each rural Leinster delegate represented only 203 and each Munster delegate 231. Such claims became heated once a divergence of views developed between Dublin and rural members, and were often accompanied by allegations that the latter were barely genuine delegates at all, in that their 'cards' were 'marked' in advance; they were herded to the conferences in busloads, and then told by the party establishment which motions and which speakers to support, and which to oppose. Certainly, branches in some rural constituencies have a strong air of TDs' supporters' clubs about them. On the other hand, Dublin delegates are probably not representative of the views of Dublin Labour voters; for example, the Dublin membership has always been strongly anti-coalitionist, while the evidence of transfers at elections in the 1970s suggests that Dublin Labour voters supported the idea of coalition. The phenomenon of pragmatic leaders, militant activists and pragmatic voters is, of course, a familiar one to students of political parties, especially left-wing parties,[58] but in the Irish Labour Party's case it seems as yet to hold true only in Dublin.

Table 4.1 *Geographical origin of delegates at Labour's 1969 conference and of Labour votes at the 1965 and 1969 general elections*

| | Delegates to 1969 conference | | Votes at general elections (%) | |
	N	%	1965	1969
Dublin	180	23·8	28·5	41·6
Rest of Leinster	240	31·8	27·2	21·7
Munster	280	37·1	37·8	28·9
Connacht	30	4·0	5·3	5·2
Ulster	25	3·3	1·1	2·6
Total	755	100·0	100·0	100·0

Notes
1. The figures for delegates exclude the ninety-five delegates from affiliated trade unions.
2. A breakdown of conference delegates by province of origin is not available for other years, though the ratios approximate to the breakdown of branches given in Appendix 3.
Source. *Annual Report 1969*, p. 60.

The main work of the conference was to discuss the policies passed at the July 1968 policy conference; all were basically approved. The rhetoric scaled new heights of optimism. Many speakers talked about what 'the Labour government' would do. Brendan Corish declared that if Labour provided the policies and leadership the country lacked, 'I believe that by the time we meet next year in this place, we could be the government of this country . . . We know our place, and our place is in government'. Barry Desmond, the party chairman, stated that when it came to solving the main social evils, 'I don't think we can question the cost and question the impossibility; we've just got to do it'. Noel Browne, presumably referring to the socialist bloc, told the conference that 'one third of the world is already socialist. One third of the world has already found social justice through socialism.'

Other delegates were more cautious. John O'Donovan, a future TD, warned, probably accurately, that Labour would lose votes by advocating the nationalisation of the banks, since voters would believe the inevitable allegations that it would take the people's savings from them. Michael O'Leary acknowledged that some would feel that Labour was 'riding into the valley of death' by associating itself with its policy document on workers' democracy. A cynical, and as it transpired an all too realistic, note was struck by the fraternal delegate from the Israeli Labour Party, who said that he felt delegates had displayed a certain amount of naivety. When Labour got into government its members would inevitably lose some of this, he said, so he would advise them to 'enjoy it while you can'.

The outline policy documents under discussion, covering agriculture, workers' democracy, health, social welfare, education, foreign policy, local government, banking and financial policy, housing, taxation, maritime policy and industrial development, were gathered together and published in a 150 page booklet,[59] and have been collectively known ever since as 'the 1969 policies'.

The longest document was that dealing with agriculture. Labour undertook to promote the farmers' co-operative movement, to which end it would 'transfer many of the activities now being carried out by private enterprise to the State to be held in trust for the emerging co-operative movement'.[60] More Marketing Boards would be set up, and credit to enable farmers to expand would be extended. A Rural Development Corporation would be established, to engage in 'negotiating the take-over of land that is not being worked, or which is being neglected due to lack of ability or lack of interest of the occupier'. It would aim to buy out elderly, inefficient farmers and encourage the earlier transfer of land from father to son.[61] Although the document did not go as far as that of July 1968, which had been described by a Labour Senator as 'political dynamite',[62] it did, then, propose to nationalise some agricultural activities and to allow a State body to take over the land of incompetent and idle farmers.

The document on worker democracy defined its subject as 'full participation by the workers in all decisions involving the utilization of the resources employed by an enterprise or organization'. It spoke contemptuously of 'the frills of profit-sharing' and 'the irrelevancies of works councils', adding, ' "Participation" is often a device to ensure co-operation with managements for the purpose of controlling and exploiting for private profit.'[63] Labour's objective was 'a fundamental change in society', and it would be necessary to create 'new organizational structures in the work place' and to launch 'a massive programme of adult education' as 'an essential complementary programme' to worker democracy.[64]

The educational system would be reorganised, and education would be compulsory up to the age of sixteen and free at all levels.[65] Corporal punishment would be discontinued, and discipline would be partly maintained by the pupils themselves; 'pupil participation', 'schools councils' and 'pupil self-government' would help prepare pupils for their roles in the democratised society.[66] According to the section on foreign policy, Labour would suspend all economic dealings with South Africa, and in general would 'recognize the need for a social revolution on a world scale and oppose the force of counter-revolutionary imperialism and racism'.[67]

The document on banking and financial policy stated that Labour favoured more governmental control over Ireland's financial affairs. It was vague as to whether the commercial banks would be nationalised. On the one hand, it declared that Labour 'stands for public control of all the nation's financial institutions', spelt out that insurance companies would be 'brought under public control' and referred to 'the ultimate goal of bringing the banks under public control'.[68] On the other hand, it said nothing explicit about nationalising the banks, and repeatedly stressed that the Central Bank should have more control over them, implying that they would continue to exist. 'The Labour government' would also weaken the link with the British financial system, by establishing an Irish money market, using fiscal measures to discourage investment in Britain, and encouraging investment in Ireland by the unsocialist device of 'expanding tax reliefs on interest earned'.[69]

To meet the shortage of housing, firms in the building materials industry would be nationalised, as would all building land and building societies, while the estates of 'large landowners' would be 'vest[ed] in the community'.[70] Labour would 'authorise public authorities to designate land for building purposes and all such land will be brought under control at prices to be determined by the previous use of the land in question'.[71] A Physical Planning Authority would be established, and it would formulate a National Development Plan, under which 100,000 houses would be built in five years.

On taxation, Labour would introduce a capital gains tax, an annual wealth tax, a flat-rate tax on company profits, and income tax on farmers whose land had a rateable value of more than £100.[72] As things stood, farmers paid no income tax, and the document acknowledged that this was mainly because of 'the effect it will have on the fortunes of any party who sought to introduce such a form of taxation', a point emphasised at the 1977 general election. The document stressed that most of the income raised by taxation of wealthy farmers would be used to help poorer farmers, but the latter may nonetheless have feared that the measure could be the thin end of a wedge.

One of the most important proposals was for the creation of a department of Economic Development, which would devise and implement a comprehensive National Plan. The department would start by initiating a survey of the nation's resources, and would draw up an inventory of them. It would analyse 'the trends of technological development over the next two to three decades . . . in order to identify possible growth areas for the economy'. This done, the plan ('the optimum strategy for maximizing the use of our resources') would be formulated. It would 'set down the type of industries to be established and the areas in which they will be located'. The plan would cover a period of fifteen or twenty years, and would be 'total, comprehensive, aggressive, imaginative and flexible'.[73]

To find fault with the programme would not be difficult. It appeared to rest on the assumptions that Labour was on the verge of a fifteen-year spell in government, and that it would find unlimited funds at its disposal upon entering office. There was no attempt to cost the various proposals. The suggestion that it would be possible to devise and implement a comprehensive national plan in a country so reliant on imported raw materials and vulnerable to changes in the world economic climate betrayed a rather starry-eyed naivety, as did the idea that capital invested in Britain could be attracted back by minor fiscal manipulation, when in fact a flight of capital from Ireland would have been more likely to follow an election victory for Labour.

Whatever the programme's defects, it is to Labour's credit that it produced it at all. No other party had offered a comparable critique of

Irish society, or had set out its aims and policies at such length and in such detail; it contrasts markedly with Fianna Fáil's failure to issue even an election manifesto between the 1950s and 1977. Its naivety sprang from its creators' genuine concern to improve the quality of life of the Irish people. It represented a rare infusion of idealism into a political system in which voting behaviour was generally assumed to be determined by a combination of inherited allegiances and self-interest. Labour itself felt that criticism would be more justly directed at those parties which did not produce policies than at the admittedly imperfect policies which it had worked hard to produce. Speaking at the 1969 annual conference, Seán Dunne TD pointed out that for a long time Labour had been accused of lacking policies. 'And yet,' he went on plaintively, 'as soon as we produce the proposals every damn thing in the world is wrong with them in certain quarters, and particularly amongst political commentators.'

4.5 The approach to the 1969 general election

Inevitably, the trickle of allegations that Labour was communist now became a flood, many of them based on distortions of the facts. The president of the Federation of Irish Industries, an employers' organisation, discerned something contradictory in what he described as Labour's claim that policies which in Czechoslovakia had caused people to burn themselves alive in the name of freedom would lead to paradise in Ireland.[74] A remark, scarcely more than an *obiter dictum*, made at the conference by Conor Cruise O'Brien, to the effect that Ireland should close its diplomatic mission in Portugal and open one in Cuba instead, proved a rich source of inspiration for the fertile imaginations of Labour's opponents. James Dillon declared that 'Labour has now announced as their ideal for Ireland that we should become the Cuba of the Atlantic, with a Castro to lead us'.[75] In February 1969 Patrick Norton joined Fianna Fáil, alleging that Labour had abandoned practical and progressive policies in favour of 'Cuban socialism'.[76] Erskine Childers stated that some leading Labour personalities 'openly advocate Ireland joining the socialist world of Russia, China and satellites'.[77] Neil Blaney alleged that Labour not only regarded Cuba as a model but would like to invite the Red Army to set up nuclear warheads around the coast.[78]

At the 1969 conference Labour had also approved the idea of making the contraceptive pill more widely available. This drew from the Fine Gael TD Oliver J. Flanagan, well known for his conservative views on matters of sexual morality, the allegation that it was 'a brazen defiance of Catholic teaching', a rebuff to the Hierarchy and a 'slap in the teeth' for the Pope.[79] Labour did not respond, but some of its members feared that it could be seriously harmed by allegations that its new approach was in conflict with Catholic teaching. In the world-wide Catholic Church the papacy of John XXIII, *Mater et Magistra*, and the Second Vatican Council, which deliberated between 1962 and 1965 and encouraged greater discussion within the Church, all had a liberalising influence. These trends were resisted by the Irish Hierarchy. John Charles McQuaid, Archbishop of Dublin between 1940 and 1972, and a long-standing *bête noire* of Irish liberals, returned from the Vatican Council to inform Irish Catholics that the reforms it envisaged would not affect them: 'You may have been worried by much talk of changes to come. Allow me to reassure you. No change will worry the tranquillity of your Christian lives.'[80]

Although the 1960s were in general a period of 'quiescence' in Church–State relations,[81] it seemed that this was not so much because the Church was becoming less conservative as because it was more restrained in its expression of its conservative attitudes. Even before the 1969 campaign got under way, some Labour spokesmen were seeking to head off the charge that socialism and Catholicism were incompatible. Brendan Halligan gave the papal encyclicals, especially those of John XXIII, as authorities for Labour's move to the left; Labour, he said, was in fact the only party making an attempt to implement his teachings, *Mater et Magistra* having been ignored by right-wing Catholics in Ireland and elsewhere.[82] John O'Connell declared that in some respects Labour's policies fell short of the standards of Pope John, and claimed that other Popes had advocated policies like Labour's document on workers' democracy; if Labour was condemned as communist because of the policy document, he said, 'we are content to stand condemned in the company of the great Popes'.[83]

In the main, though, Labour felt supremely confident about its prospects in the forthcoming general election. The other parties seemed to have problems. Fianna Fáil's morale had been dented by the heavy defeat of its proposal to change the electoral system, and its association with Taca seemed likely to cost it support among the working class and small farmers, although Taca's membership fee had been cut from £100 to £5 to placate party critics.[84] Moreover the party seemed to have a leadership problem. Lynch appeared amiable but weak and vacillatory; he was still regarded as a caretaker Taoiseach and as little more than *primus inter pares* in the Cabinet, and Fianna Fáil's lack of a dominant leader in the de Valera or Lemass mould was thought likely to be an electoral handicap.

Fine Gael was still internally divided. Declan Costello announced in 1967 that he was leaving politics because of ill health, and confirmed this two years later, but there is little doubt that the apparently unshakable grip of the conservative wing, headed by Liam Cosgrave and Gerard Sweetman, contributed to his decision.[85] The liberal wing, which at the highest level now consisted only of Tom O'Higgins TD and Senators James Dooge and Garret FitzGerald, tried to assert itself at the 1968 Ard-Fheis, which discussed a proposal that the party change its name to 'Fine Gael – Social Democratic Party'. Dooge described Fine Gael as 'a radical party' and said, 'We are not doctrinaire socialists, but we are not afraid of being selective socialists.' Although most delegates clearly favoured the change, forceful chairmanship by Sweetman, who was called a 'fascist' by some delegates, succeeded in having the matter referred to a postal ballot of all branches, which resulted in a vote of 653 to 81 in favour of the *status quo*.[86] The *Just Society* idea had made some impact on the party, though, even if only on its rhetoric, and it made much use of phrases like 'social reform' and described its policies as 'progressive' and 'forward-looking'. It still studiously refrained from offering or accepting a position on a left–right spectrum, and although in the past labels like 'right' and 'left' had played little part in Irish politics there was a feeling that a British-type two-party system might be emerging. If this happened, it was thought, Fine Gael's fuzzy image might leave the party crushed between Fianna Fáil on the right and Labour on the left.

There were no other active parties in existence. A special Ard-Fheis of Clann na Poblachta held in July 1965 decided to dissolve the party, and a statement was issued explaining that party members had felt there was no point in continuing as a party, since the Clann had very little support and no apparent prospect of regaining any.[87] Sinn Féin still preserved a nominal existence, though it was then in a state of electoral dormancy.

5

The 1969 general election

5.1 Labour's approach to the campaign

The result of the general election held on 18 June 1969 was a
shattering blow to the Labour Party, and caused it to revise
fundamentally its assessment of its own future and the likely
development of Irish politics, leading to a reversal of the 'no coalition'
strategy. To understand why a performance which on paper was
similar to the party's previous results should have had such an impact,
it is necessary to understand the expectations with which Labour
entered the campaign.

The party believed that it was on the verge of a major breakthrough,
and several leading figures made rash predictions to this effect. The
normally shrewd James Tully once suggested that Labour would have
a Dáil majority after the election,[1] and in his constituency
advertisements sought voters' support 'to return a Labour
government'.[2] Many speakers made it clear that they expected Labour
to be at least the second largest party in the new Dáil, and the party
leader once 'promised' that a record number of Labour TDs would be
elected.[3] Even after the polls closed, at a time when he could not have
been trying to create a bandwagon effect, Corish stated that he was
certain Labour had won more seats than Fine Gael.[4] A political
correspondent predicted that Labour would win twenty-eight to thirty
seats, and some provincial newspapers seemed to expect a leap in
Labour's strength.[5]

This optimism was backed up by a campaign costing £25,000,[6] a
large figure by the party's own standards, and by the nomination of
ninety-nine candidates, compared with an average of thirty-seven at
the three previous elections and a peak of seventy in 1943. In only
seven constituencies did Labour nominate just one candidate, and two

of these were cases where outgoing TDs had successfully resisted pressure to take running mates.[7] In nineteen constituencies there were two Labour candidates, ten had three, and in six, all in the Greater Dublin area, there were four; in the Dublin area Labour put up more candidates than Fianna Fáil. There was a difference also in the nature of the Labour candidates (see Table 5.1). Of the 1969 candidates, over a half, as opposed to about a quarter at recent elections, were not members of any elected body, and over two-thirds, as opposed to about a third in the past, were new to Dáil elections. At the start of the campaign it seemed that the freshness of these candidates, unencumbered by association with the party's previous uninspiring record, might be an electoral asset. Moreover, although at previous elections about a third of the Labour candidates had been trade union officials (see Appendix 4), on this occasion just over a fifth were. For the first time ever, there were more candidates in the 'professional' category than in any other, reflecting Labour's success over the past nine years in attracting such people and the appeal it hoped to make to the middle class and the intelligentsia at the election. In 1961 only one of its thirty-five candidates had been a professional. In another respect there was little change, though; only three of the ninety-nine candidates were women.

Some of the 1969 professionals were prominent, highly educated personalities usually referred to, either admiringly or pejoratively, as 'the intellectuals'. Following the acquisition of Conor Cruise O'Brien, who stood in Dublin North East, Justin Keating, a Trinity College lecturer who was well known to farmers because of his work on agricultural programmes on television, was selected as a Labour candidate in North County Dublin; he had joined the party about eighteen months earlier. In May Dr David Thornley announced that he was to stand in Dublin North West, stating that he was satisfied that 'the Norton era' in the party's history was over for good.[8] Thornley too was a lecturer at TCD, and had become nationally known by presenting the popular and often controversial television current affairs programme 'Seven Days'. Three other 'doctors' stood for Labour in Dublin constituencies: Noel Browne and John O'Connell, who were both medical doctors, and John O'Donovan, an economics lecturer at University College, Dublin. Labour had become intellectually respectable.

Moreover the party was fighting on an explicitly socialist platform, described by one newspaper as 'one of the most socialist programmes in

Table 5.1   *Background and fates of Labour candidates, 1969*

	Elected	Eliminated	Lost deposit	Total	%
Region					
Dublin City	8	7	10	25	25·3
Dublin County	2	4	4	10	10·1
Rest of Leinster	4	6	9	19	19·2
Munster	4	9	12	25	25·3
Connacht	0	3	10	13	13·1
Ulster	0	0	7	7	7·1
Occupation					
Manual employee	1	7	7	15	15·2
Trade union official	7	7	7	21	21·2
Non-manual employee	2	4	13	19	19·2
Commercial	2	4	11	17	17·2
Farmer	0	1	4	5	5·1
Professional	6	6	10	22	22·2
(Politician)	7	2	0	9	9·1
Membership of public bodies					
Dáil	11	3	0	14	14·1
Seanad	0	1	1	2	2·0
County council	9	20	15	44	44·4
None	7	9	37	53	53·5
Electoral experience					
Previous Dáil campaigns	14	10	8	32	32·3
No previous Dáil campaigns	4	19	44	67	67·7
Total	18	29	52	99	100·0

Notes. For occupation, the 'Commercial' category includes small businessmen, shopkeepers, publicans, garage proprietors, bookmakers and other self-employed persons. The 'Professional' category includes schoolteachers, solicitors, doctors, university lecturers, journalists and architects. In the case of candidates with more than one occupation, the major occupation has been taken. In the case of candidates who were full-time, or almost full-time, politicians, their other or previous occupation has been used, although the number of full-time politicians is also given.

A member of a 'county council' is a member of one of the twenty-seven county councils or one of the four main city corporations. It must be borne in mind that some Oireachtas members also belonged to county councils.

'Eliminated' candidates are those who neither were elected nor lost their deposits.

Europe'.[9] The manifesto was a condensed version of the 1969 policy documents, with some of the rhetoric moderated, and its introduction captured the optimistic and assertive spirit in which Labour entered the campaign:[10]

The politics of the old Republic are over. The choice is no longer between two identical parties, divided only by the tragedy of history. The choice is now between the old Republic of bitterness, stagnation and failure, represented by the two Civil War Parties, and the New Republic of opportunity, change and hope, represented by the Labour party. Ireland is at a crisis of decision. There is only one way forward – with Labour. But there are many ways backwards. Labour will not retard the growth of the new politics by cynically abandoning its ideals for short term party advantage. The hopes of the future will not be betrayed. This is a time of great national change. The outworn habits of the past are being abandoned. In politics traditions die hard, but change is evident. The Referendum was overwhelmingly defeated by a quarter of a million votes mainly by the young people of Ireland. The two Civil War parties have lost their attraction for the new generation. The politics of the seventies will not be modelled on the forties or the fifties. This is a time for renewal, for new thinking, for fresh ideas. Labour is the party of the future. It has brought in the new politics. The advance of Labour cannot be stopped. Never before has the challenge of Labour been so strong. This time it is time for Labour.

The party also issued a catechismic booklet to canvassers, designed to enable them to deal with voters' questions, which is of help in reconstructing its fears and expectations.[11] Canvassers were to confirm that Labour was a socialist party, but the suggestion that its policies were 'communist inspired' was to be described as 'a stupid statement', since they had been 'written by Irish men and women, based on the inspiration of Connolly's teaching, the Christian outlook, and the demands of the future'. Voters who asked how Labour would finance its policies were to be told that the government would reverse the flow of investment from Ireland to Britain and would use the extra money generated by the expansion of the economy. Canvassers were to inform sceptical voters who asked how Labour could possibly form a government that if the swing away from Fianna Fáil manifested in the PR referendum were repeated, Fianna Fáil would be 'destroyed as a major political party', while Fine Gael was characterised as a party of part-time politicians. The not unreasonable question, 'With only 18 seats in Dáil Eireann, how can the party expect to be taken seriously as

---

Sources. Provincial and national newspapers, trade union publications, campaign literature.

an alternative government?', was to be dismissed cavalierly as 'quite misleading', on the ground that it implied that no small party could ever grow to become a major party. The booklet, then, is useful to the researcher, demonstrating that Labour anticipated the 'red smear' campaign and was aware of a credibility gap between its size and its ambitions; but it was not so useful politically, because although 10,000 copies were printed, only 5,000 were taken up by the constituency organisations.[12]

5.2 The election campaign

Labour's campaign received an early boost when Michael Joe Costello, a widely respected agricultural expert, declared his support for the party's farming policies,[13] and it also emerged that Rickard Deasy, a former president of the National Farmers' Association, was to stand for Labour in North Tipperary. This caused surprise, not least within the constituency, where local resentment was given expression in a statement issued by the two candidates already selected, in which they announced unenthusiastically that, 'putting their own local interests aside', they would 'welcome' his addition.[14] At national level, however, where the intricacies of constituency politics are not always fully understood, it was believed that the capture of Keating, Costello and Deasy could lead to a massive increase in Labour's support among farmers.[15]

Labour candidates took up points from the manifesto, promising that the party in power would provide a free national health service for all, expand the social security system, embark upon a crash house-building programme, and introduce a system of economic planning. The manifesto was even vaguer on the question of whether Labour would nationalise the banks than the policy programme had been, stating that 'Labour will make financial institutions serve the people' and mentioning 'Labour's policy of public control over Irish capital'. Conor Cruise O'Brien took up the sale by the Finance Minister, Charles Haughey, of some land for £204,000, arguing that it was unethical and revealed that self-interest lay behind Fianna Fáil's attachment to the capitalist system.[16] The ICTU president, James Dunne, 'pledged' the 'support' of ICTU for Labour's efforts, and said he looked forward to working with a Labour government.[17] The ITGWU held a press conference for Labour, placed advertisements in the papers urging its members to support the Labour candidates, and spent around £17,000 in support of Labour's campaign, a figure which dwarfed its affiliation fee of £1,642.[18] Other unions placed advertisements in the provincial press in support of individual candidates who were members of the union concerned.

At the national level, Labour ran an energetic advertising campaign, built around the slogans 'Let's Build the New Republic' and 'The Seventies will be Socialist'. At the local level, candidates both expounded party policies and stressed their personal records; an inverse relationship seemed to obtain between a candidate's experience and his appeal for support on the basis of his party affiliation. Whereas new candidates made bold promises and generally lost their deposits, experienced campaigners tended not to emphasise their connection with Labour. The outgoing TD in Cork South West, Michael Pat Murphy, made no secret of his intention not to use any of the centrally prepared literature and to campaign, as always, on his personal record. His local newspaper advertisements detailed this – his efficient and speedy work on behalf of his constituents, his promotion of tourism and industry in the constituency, and so on – at length, and mentioned only twice, unobtrusively, that he was the Labour candidate and had carried out his services to his constituents 'as a Labour TD'.[19] In North Kerry, Dan Spring TD did not mention the Labour Party at all in his advertisements, which merely stated that he had worked for the constituency for twenty-six years and urged, 'He helps you. Now you help him!' The local paper's political correspondent commented that although this was 'a far cry' from 'The New Republic', it was nevertheless 'the very stuff of politics in County Kerry' and was likely to see Spring re-elected,[20] as indeed it did. At a Labour Party public meeting in North Tipperary the two weaker candidates, each of whom lost his deposit, spoke mainly about party policies, including Labour's promise to introduce a free national health service, while the strongest candidate, a county councillor since 1960 and a future TD, unashamedly stressed his personal record, stating that he had 'served the people since 1956 . . . knew the needs of the people . . . and knew they needed more medical cards'.[21]

Fianna Fáil did not issue a manifesto, Charles Haughey, the election director, explaining that 'Manifestoes have a Marxist ring about them'.[22] It fought as usual on its record in office, and advised voters not to jeopardise the progress made. Early in the campaign, seeking to capitalise on the disunity of the opposition, it employed the slogan 'There is no alternative', but when it appeared that voters regarded this as arrogant it revived a phrase which had first appeared at its January 1969 Ard-Fheis: 'Fianna Fáil – the Party of Reality'. Its candidates argued that Labour could make extravagant promises because it knew it would never have to find the money to pay for them. The social conscience of 'The Party of Reality' – or 'the party of stark reality' as one of its candidates described it[23] – was as great as the opposition's, but it would not make irresponsible promises to win support.

Fianna Fáil defended the capitalist system against Labour's criticisms. At the outset of the campaign the Taoiseach stated that the party believed in 'the right of private property, in private initiative and in private enterprise supplemented where necessary by the efforts of the state'.[24] A candidate in Meath declared that 'Fianna Fáil will stand at all times for private enterprise'.[25] The Minister for Education, Brian Lenihan, addressed an appeal to 'common sense people with a stake in the country' and promised them 'security and stability'.[26] Although most Fianna Fáil advertisements bore a picture of the Taoiseach with the suggestion 'Let's Back Jack', Lynch did not play a prominent part in the campaign at national level. Instead of making major speeches at a few large venues, he went on a nation-wide 'meet the people' tour, addressing many small groups of people; convents were said to feature particularly strongly on his itinerary.[27] After the election it was often suggested that Lynch's tour and his personal popularity had been important factors in maintaining Fianna Fáil in office.[28]

Fine Gael again fought the election on a *Just Society* platform; its policies were a diluted version of those subsumed under the same heading in 1965, and in consequence they had the support of the whole party this time. For the first time ever it nominated more candidates than Fianna Fáil, 125 as against 122. Fine Gael claimed that its policies offered a constructive and 'progressive' alternative to the government while avoiding Labour's naive utopianism. Its policies were spelled out in detail, were costed,[29] and involved a shift in government expenditure towards the social and health services. For the first time since 1938 no minor parties nominated candidates.

On the whole, Labour's campaign was fairly covered by the mass media. With 26·5 per cent of the candidates, its campaign speeches were given 25·1 per cent of the column inches devoted by the three national newspapers to speeches.[30] Two of the papers gave more space to Labour than to Fine Gael. Only the *Irish Press* committed itself editorially – to Fianna Fáil, of course – but under a new editor it took a less Manichean view of the contest than it had tended to in the past. Television and radio journalists were in many cases sympathetic to Labour, if only because its campaign seemed to be bringing something fresh to a rather dull political system, and party members were prepared to acknowledge afterwards that RTE's coverage of the election had been, if anything, generous to Labour.

5.3 The 'red smear' campaign

For the most part, Labour was forced on to the defensive by the tactics employed by Fianna Fáil, which can be divided into two categories: allegations that its policies were communist and alien to Ireland, and allegations that they were inconsistent with the principles of Roman Catholicism.

A few days after the campaign began a large Fianna Fáil advertisement described Labour's policies as 'alien doctrines which are foreign to our people's traditions and beliefs',[31] and this set the tone for the rest of the campaign. A Meath candidate said that Labour's ideology was 'foreign and contrary to Irish tradition and heritage', while in Laois a senior member of the party organisation attacked Labour for propounding 'doctrines alien to the Irish people'.[32] Kevin Boland, the Minister for Local Government, alleged that Labour wanted to take away people's land, property and savings, and that its policies had been 'imposed on the reluctant but ultimately compliant old guard' by 'the intellectuals, the doctors, the university dons and the professional agitators'.[33] Michael Moran, the Minister for Justice, described Corish as a mere puppet of 'the modern Marxist élite' and of 'the new left-wing political queers who have taken over the Labour Party from the steps of Trinity College and Telefis Éireann'.[34] Neil Blaney, the Minister for Agriculture, described Labour's membership as ranging from 'capitalists' to 'pseudo-intellectual Marxists, Maoists, Trotskyites and the like who have emerged from the sidelines like carrion birds to pick off the flesh of the Irish people'.[35] Patrick Norton, now standing for Fianna Fáil in Kildare, accused Corish of having been either unable or unwilling to continue his (Norton's) father's refusal to allow 'extremists' to 'infiltrate' the party.[36] Seán MacEntee stated that Labour stood for Lenin, Stalin and 'the red flames of burning homesteads in Meath'.[37] Almost every Fianna Fáil attack included the allegation that Labour wanted to impose 'Cuban socialism' on Ireland, or contained some other allusion to Cuba or to Fidel Castro, who, following O'Brien's comments at the 1969 conference, was said to be the idol of Labour's 'intellectuals'.

Many Fianna Fáil candidates alleged that Labour had plans for widespread nationalisation. In Galway an outgoing TD stated that 'no one in rural Ireland wants the socialistic policies of Labour or the taking over by them of the people's savings over the years'.[38] Bax offers a first-hand account of a Fianna Fáil campaign in County Cork, during which a group of canvassers encountered three elderly people who had inferred from a Labour broadcast that the party would appropriate their life savings, lodged in a bank, if it came to power, a notion of which the canvassers certainly did not disabuse them.[39] Senator Eoin Ryan alleged that Labour intended that every firm, every factory, every job and every farm would be owned and controlled by the government, and a Dublin TD claimed that it would 'confiscate' Guinness's brewery.[40] Jack Lynch asked whether land nationalisation was 'still' among Labour's policies, which he described as essentially the same as those which had been tried and had failed in Eastern Europe.[41] Neil Blaney, too, often alleged that Labour intended to nationalise land.[42]

Some provincial papers expressed similar views. One accused Labour of being 'much closer to a Communist Party' than to a normal Labour party and of 'preaching sedition left, right and centre', and referred scathingly to the party's 'acquisition of some doctrinaire intellectuals'.[43] Another referred to 'Conor Cruise O'Brien and all the other Dublin-based Castros', adding that 'Free Ireland has certainly shown the difference between Christian socialism and the Godless brand which certain elements in our midst would try to have foisted on us'.[44] A third claimed that 'Labour has alienated a number of its followers by its extreme leftist policy which goes as far as nationalizing almost everything except the land, and who knows but that would follow if the opportunity arose'.[45] Two or three other provincial newspapers criticised Labour, and none came out in its support.

Occasionally Fine Gael speakers made similar charges. Professor John Kelly, embarking on a career as the most colourful rhetoretician among Irish politicians, said that he would be wary about joining Labour's 'ship' even if he were invited: 'I want to know where the ship is heading and they won't let me see their navigation instructions. There are a lot of funny noises coming from below and I suspect they have some queer fellows in the engine room.'[46] Liam Cosgrave said of

Labour's policies that 'They are none of them for 1969. The Labour programme is for 1984,' and later described them as 'far too doctrinaire and unrealistic'.[47]

The accusation of communism contained the implicit accusation of atheism and anti-Catholicism, which was also made explicitly, usually in the door-to-door canvass or the after-mass meeting at the chapel gates but occasionally in a prepared speech or a supplied script sent to the newspapers. The Minister for Defence, Michael Hilliard, said that some of those who had 'forced their way into' Labour were not 'believers in the fundamental Christian principles which have activated our people down the centuries'.[48] A successful Fianna Fáil candidate in Mayo, Joseph Leneghan, said that if Labour came to power there would be laws permitting abortion and divorce, and it would be 'great for the fellow who wanted a second wife every night'.[49] Michael Pat Murphy alleged that in his constituency Fianna Fáil had claimed that Labour's policy would be to throw priests into prison and torture them,[50] and a Sligo Labour member spoke of a Fianna Fáil candidate alleging that it was Labour policy to tear down every crucifix in the country.[51] Labour believed that Jack Lynch, in the course of his convent tour, was portraying Labour as a dangerously extremist party, and several Labour TDs have alleged[52] that nuns teaching in convent schools told their pupils to inform their parents that they should not vote Labour. Some priests were said to have warned their parishioners from the pulpit that socialism was the same as communism, or that they should be careful not to vote for a party unless they could be certain that it was not communist. O'Brien gives an account of a priest in County Kerry who informed his parishioners that socialism was even worse than communism, since it was a Protestant version of communism.[53]

Labour reacted to such allegations sometimes by counter-attacking, but more often defensively. At the start of the campaign Brendan Corish said boldly that although some people said Labour's programme was too radical, he had 'seen this happen before', and 'in four or five years' time this policy will be regarded as somewhat conservative'.[54] O'Brien pointed out that the 'red smear' had been tried against some of the Irish patriots of the past, and indeed against Fianna Fáil itself during the 1920s.[55] A Tipperary candidate 'defied' any Irishman to say that 'Tacaism' was more Irish and christian than socialism.[56] A Roscommon-Leitrim candidate refuted allegations that Labour's policies were alien by claiming that historical figures of the stature of Fintan Lalor, Michael Davitt, Patrick Pearse and James Connolly had 'often called for' policies such as those now advocated by Labour, adding that 'the only alien policy we can be accused of adopting is that dictated by the late Pope John'.[57] Noel Browne returned the allegation most vigorously, arguing that the free enterprise conservative political philosophy of the two major parties was derived from British imperialism and was therefore itself alien to Ireland.[58]

On other occasions candidates preferred to deny the charges and to try to distance themselves from the taint of communism. A Kildare candidate said that Labour's policies 'are based on solid Christian concepts of equality and justice and thank God we are not Communists, nor fellow-travellers', and he pointed out that Patrick Norton's allegations had been made against his own father at the time of the National Labour split.[59] John O'Connell TD felt it necessary to assure voters that 'when the Labour movement speaks of socialism, it speaks of a society where personal property exists'.[60] Some candidates went to such lengths to try and dispel any suspicion that their Catholicism might be less than wholehearted as to recall Conor Cruise O'Brien's 1966 characterisation of the party as one whose leaders never mentioned James Connolly's name without 'some allusion establishing the speaker's religious orthodoxy, and if possible Connolly's also'.[61] At the start of the campaign Corish attributed socialism's acceptability to 'a new climate in the world' created by the late Pope John: 'I have taken particular care to read his Encyclicals and reading them one finds that we are much behind the ideas which Pope John propounded'.[62] O'Brien himself, having raised the spectre of Cuba in the first place, sought to banish it by producing a press cutting which showed that eight American Catholic bishops had advocated the lifting of the American trade boycott of Cuba.[63] Even Noel Browne was reported as saying that it was to 'Christian Socialism' that Labour had committed itself.[64]

David Thornley, when his candidacy was announced, took care to emphasise that it was as 'a sincere committed Christian' that he was joining Labour,[65] and the party secretary, Brendan Halligan, advised anyone who thought its policies might be communist to read them, after which it would be obvious that they were in fact based on papal teachings.[66] In Carlow-Kilkenny a candidate said that many of Labour's policies 'followed closely along the lines of the teachings of Pope John XXIII',[67] while a Kildare candidate went one better by stating that Labour wanted to create the kind of society 'envisaged by the late Pope John XXIII and St. Francis Xavier'.[68] In Dublin the party's vice-chairman, Dermot O'Rourke, also sought to establish that the absence of the papal imprimatur on Labour's manifesto was a mere technicality, since it was 'in accordance with the teachings of' Popes John XXIII and Paul VI.[69] In Donegal-Leitrim a candidate declared that 'Socialism is as old as time and Christ its greatest exponent', and pointed out that the Vatican had diplomatic relations with Cuba.[70] A Sligo candidate described Labour's ideals as being 'in line with those of Vatican II and the World Council of Churches', adding with some exaggeration that 'that was why bishops and clergy in Ireland had spoken out in favour of them'.[71]

5.4 The election results

Contrary to almost all expectations, Fianna Fáil emerged from the election with a clear Dáil majority, seventy-five seats out of 144. Fine Gael moved up from forty-seven to fifty seats, while Labour, which had gained twenty-two seats in 1965, now won only eighteen, the number it had had at the dissolution. Only one Independent was elected (see Appendix 1). Fianna Fáil's victory was achieved despite a drop in its share of the votes, mainly by a judicious revision of constituency boundaries, under which its votes produced a high yield in seats.[72] Thus in Dublin City its share of the votes fell from 47 per cent in 1965 to 39 per cent in 1969, but its share of the seats dropped only from 52 to 48 per cent. In the province of Connacht, although its votes rose only from 48 to 51 per cent, its share of the seats went up from 52 to 62 per cent.

Labour, in contrast, made a significant gain in votes but fell back in terms of seats. It won more votes than ever before, and achieved its highest percentage vote since 1922. In Dublin City it overtook Fine Gael for the first time in a general election, and won over nine times as many votes as it had in 1957 (see Appendix 2). In seats, too, its performance here was impressive. Whereas in 1957 and 1961 there had been only one Labour TD in the city, there were now eight, with ten in the whole Greater Dublin area. The upsurge in professional people, which in 1965 had had an impact only at the candidate level, now made itself felt at the PLP level; a third of the Dáil party had a professional background. Eight of the eighteen Labour TDs had university degrees, as opposed to two of those elected in 1965. Its prominent Dublin recruits – Justin Keating, Conor Cruise O'Brien and David Thornley – were all elected comfortably, Thornley becoming the first Labour candidate ever to head the poll in a Dublin constituency, and Noel Browne was elected for the first time as a Labour candidate.

Outside Dublin, however, it fell back. TDs of over twenty years' standing were defeated in Waterford and North East Cork, and a TD who had won over 10,000 votes in 1965 lost her seat in Mid-Cork. Rickard Deasy, whose acquisition had been announced so proudly, received an ignominious 517 votes in North Tipperary and finished bottom of the poll. Altogether it won only eight of a possible 105 seats outside the capital. Despite putting up over twice as many candidates as in 1965, it actually won 6,653 fewer votes outside Dublin. Even within Dublin it could be pointed out that its share of the votes was only 5 per cent above that achieved at the local elections of June 1967. Over the whole country, each candidate won only 2,268 votes, as opposed to 4,482 in 1965; the ratio of votes to candidates fell in every region, even in Dublin, where it dropped from 3,668 to 2,669.

Overall, then, Labour's performance in 1969 differed in degree rather than in kind from many of its previous performances, which might suggest that the electorate had reacted with indifference, rather than enthusiasm or antipathy, to its new approach. If it had been expecting to lose votes, then the results would have been a triumph; since it had expected to win votes and seats on a grand scale, and in view of the resources and enthusiasm it had put into the campaign, they were almost traumatically disappointing. Fully fifty-two of the ninety-nine candidates lost their deposits.[73] Table 5.1 makes it clear that the campaign was a massacre of the innocents. About two-thirds of those who were not members of public bodies or had never before stood for the Dáil lost their deposits, whereas those more familiar to the electorate fared much better. The only newcomers to Dáil elections to win seats were four well-known national figures standing in Dublin constituencies.

The reason most often advanced by Labour members for the party's disappointing performance was Fianna Fáil's 'red smear' campaign, which the next annual report described as 'a calculated national campaign that stepped far beyond the bounds of normal political debate' and had been 'the result of a deliberate and calculated directive issued at national level'.[74] Many Labour candidates made the same allegation at the after-count speeches in their constituencies.[75] Matt

Merrigan, an AC member, suggested that Fianna Fáil's aim had been to equate intellectualism and dissent in politics with homosexuality in sexual behaviour, citing Moran's reference to 'left-wing political queers', so that the electorate's religious and cultural conservatism could be mobilised to contain the Labour threat.[76] A provincial newspaper commented that Labour's policies were 'not fully understood by people in the provinces, and left easy scope for misrepresentation by unscrupulous politicians'.[77]

That a 'smear campaign' was conducted is beyond dispute, and Labour was obviously justified in claiming that Fianna Fáil had made a determined effort to distort its policies and mislead voters about its real intentions. Whether Fianna Fáil was thereby behaving immorally is a question to which there is no objective answer. If all is indeed fair in love, war and politics, then perhaps Labour was naive to complain. It is open to any party to misrepresent another's policies as fundamentally as Fianna Fáil misrepresented Labour's, but the tactic is not usually employed because it is likely to rebound on the party using it. In 1969, however, Labour was vulnerable to it because of its left-wing policies, its inexperienced candidates and its unrealistic predictions of a socialist government. In other words, it could be said that by the approach it adopted Labour handed its opponents a stick with which Fianna Fáil not surprisingly proceeded to beat it.

The precise effect of the smear campaign is also difficult to assess. Labour members themselves at all levels of the party seem still to be divided in their views as to its impact. Some believe that it influenced many voters who might otherwise have supported Labour, while others feel it would be a gross underestimation of the political intelligence of Irish voters to suppose that they really took seriously the allegations that a Labour government would close the churches and torture priests. An allegation which may have influenced some undecided voters was that Labour intended to nationalise land. Although, of course, Labour did not intend to do this, it did make it clear that it did not regard the farmer's title to his land as sacrosanct, since it proposed to allow local authorities to acquire land compulsorily, from farmers if need be, under certain circumstances. A provincial newspaper commented sympathetically that one of Labour's problems was the selfishness of the Irish about their property, especially land, and the fact that 'the suggestion that county councils should acquire land at farm value to make room for the homeless is regarded as the most extreme form of "Cubanism" '. Irish farmers, it added, interpreted Fintan Lalor's dictum as 'the soil of Ireland for the people of Ireland – who can buy or inherit it'.[78]

Labour's immediate inclination to attribute its failure to make a breakthrough entirely to Fianna Fáil's smear campaign sprang partly from a desire to salvage its pride, by identifying another party's 'unfair' tactics as the real cause rather than its own shortcomings. Before long, members were admitting that other factors too had played a part. A Mayo candidate summed up what was to become a widespread feeling by saying that Labour had been trying to do too much too quickly.[79] It had been aiming not, as in 1961 and 1965, for a modest increase in its strength, but for a majority of seats. By speaking about what 'the Labour government' would do, it gave itself an enormous credibility problem. To form a government it needed to gain about sixty new TDs, most of whom would be unknown and inexperienced. Of its ninety-nine candidates, only two had Ministerial experience, and two others, the younger of whom was fifty-eight, had been Parliamentary Secretaries. The very newness of most of the Labour candidates also increased their vulnerability to Fianna Fáil's tactics, which in some constituencies took the form of telling voters that although the local Labour candidates were 'all right', they were 'in with a crowd of communists'. The air of political innocence about many of them did nothing to dispel fears that they might, if elected, become the dupes of the communists said to have taken over the party. Moreover, because so few of Labour's candidates were known nationally, doubtful voters could not be sure that candidates in other constituencies were not really communists. Just as important, even if they were not communists, there was no guarantee that their inexperience would not lead to their behaving impetuously and attempting to implement ill-thought-out policies.

Ideology apart, their inexperience meant that they lacked the 'clienteles' almost essential for success in rural Ireland. They had no personal organisation and in many cases hardly any party organisation either. They sought election on the basis of the Labour manifesto and as much of their personal appeal as they could convey to the electorate in a few weeks, only to discover that this combination, in a country where voters do not read party manifestoes before deciding which way to vote, was not enough to draw many people in rural Ireland away from traditional allegiances. The party itself later acknowledged that the 'weak quality of some candidates' was one cause of its failure to make the anticipated gains, observing that many 'suffered from the disadvantage of being unknown outside of a local base'.[80]

In many ways there are parallels between Labour's 1969 campaign and that of Clann na Poblachta in 1948. The Clann, aiming to overturn the existing political order, entered the campaign with confidence and was widely expected to do very well. It put up ninety-three candidates, the great majority new to political life. Fianna Fáil alleged that it was a communist party and warned that this might be Ireland's last democratic election. The Clann won ten seats, a respectable total for a new party, but a very disappointing one given its high expectations. Forty-seven of its candidates lost their deposits.

Another feature of Labour's candidates was that none of them appeared to be an expert or a specialist in economics or finance, which created the problem that voters were unclear about exactly how its ambitious and attractive proposals would be paid for. It seemed to attach much importance to the five or six hundred million pounds said to have been invested abroad by Irish nationals, and the canvassers' booklet advised them to tell voters that a Labour government 'would encourage them to bring that capital back home and invest it in Ireland'.[81] Most voters must have reacted with scepticism to the idea that Irish capitalists would repatriate their money purely out of an altruistic desire to assist a socialist government.

Labour's chances of winning significant support from farmers were hampered by more than allegations about land nationalisation. Employing farmers were as reluctant as ever to vote for a party they identified with their labourers, and Labour's use of phrases like 'worker democracy' may have given farmers the impression that it was planning to put their workers 'above them'.[82] Among small farmers in the west the memory of the McQuillan expulsion may have lingered on. In addition, its manifesto showed that it still favoured 'pensioning off' elderly farmers, as well as making mention of compulsory land purchase. It had also stated that farmers, albeit only wealthy ones at first, would be brought into the tax net. Finally, Conor Cruise O'Brien's raising of Charles Haughey's land sale may well have cost Labour votes among farmers, for while it helped to identify Fianna Fáil with big business in the eyes of the Dublin working class, the lesson many farmers drew from the episode was that Labour did not believe that an owner of land should be free to sell it to whomsoever he liked, at as high a price as he could obtain.

Although Labour blamed the constituency boundary revisions for its failure to win more seats,[83] this was not a major factor. In many rural constituencies it won only five or ten per cent of the votes, which would not guarantee a seat in anything less than a nine-seat constituency. Labour's accusations that the revision was directed against the party have validity only for Cork. Labour would have regained its seat in the city if this had not been divided up, for the first time, into two three-seaters. The county constituencies were so redrawn that two of its TDs, Eileen Desmond and Patrick McAuliffe, found their main support bases split by the new boundary lines, so that they both had to fight in constituencies to many of whose electors they were unknown, and they both lost their seats.

Labour's exaggerated estimation of its prospects also contributed to the loss of two of its seats. Following a decision of the 1967 conference, the AC had decided that all outgoing TDs should take at least one running mate,[84] which caused resentment among some TDs, especially those from rural constituencies who relied on a large personal vote for re-election. Two, Michael Pat Murphy and Dan Spring, stood alone despite the ruling, while a third, Paddy Tierney in North Tipperary, refused to defend his seat once it became clear to him that he could not defy the edict. The other Labour TDs complied with it, although some of the 'running mates' chosen were clearly makeweights selected because they posed no threat to the incumbent's position.[85] In Mid-Cork and Waterford, however, the second candidate was strong enough to mount a serious campaign, as a result of which the two candidates in each constituency ran virtually separate campaigns. Consequently, when the weaker candidate was eliminated, a relatively low proportion of his transfers, fewer than 60 per cent, went to the stronger, and both Labour TDs, Eileen Desmond and Tom Kyne, lost their seats even though the total Labour vote in each constituency had been enough to win a seat under normal circumstances. Partly because of over-nomination, there was internal rivalry in many constituencies, and the annual report commented that 'good team work ... was remarkable only by its absence in a great many Labour campaigns'.[86] The fate of Desmond and Kyne, and the narrow survival of Murphy and Spring, both of whom might well have lost their seats had they not run alone, led to the repeal of the AC's rule in November 1972.

Labour's disappointment was the consequence of the disparity between its expectations and its achievement, and since its performance was one of its best ever, its disappointment must be attributed mainly to its unrealistic assessment of its prospects. With the benefit of hindsight, many party members came to feel that Labour simply lost touch with the mood of the country in the late 1960s. Fantasies of an irresistible sweep to power were nurtured by the hot-house atmosphere of party conferences and the rapid increase in membership, and Labour hurtled, at ever-increasing speed, to the inevitable mortification of the election results. The evidence from local elections and by-elections, almost all of which showed that there had been little change in Labour's strength outside Dublin since 1965, was dismissed airily. Uninspiring by-election results were put down to organisational shortcomings; the unpalatable conclusion that its support simply was not growing was avoided. The election marked the failure of Labour's attempt to move overnight from minor party to major party, but the enthusiasm of its campaign, and the scale of its commitment, ensured that it was remembered as a glorious failure.

6

The retreat from Havana, 1969–73

6.1 The reaction to the 1969 election

The result of the election was a traumatic blow to the party.[1] It changed dramatically Labour's assessment of its short-term prospects, which led to a change of attitude on coalition and to a tacit setting aside of the 1969 policies. For a while, however, Labour continued to castigate 'the two conservative parties', and the January 1970 annual conference was unrepentant.

In his leader's address Brendan Corish declared his continued faith in each one of the 1969 policy documents, and said that it had been essential for Labour to fight the last election in the manner it did, as part of 'the unceasing political war to make this a socialist state'.[2] Labour had lost a battle but not the war; Irish politics were still in a transitional phase, and Labour must not relax its pressure to create a new political system. There could be no going back to the 'comfortable' days when 'we were pretty vague about our ideals, we were limited in our objectives . . . [and] timid about our policies'.

Attempts to have the 1969 approach abandoned were unsuccessful. The two Tipperary constituency organisations proposed a motion calling on the party to enunciate policies which would be more acceptable to the electorate. The 1969 policies, its supporters said, had not gone down well in rural areas, and Labour's cause here had not been helped by mentions of Cuba at last year's conference or by 'snide remarks' about 'things that are very dear to our Irish people'. What had been built up by men like 'the great Bill Norton' should not now be destroyed by irresponsibility. James Tully moved a similar motion, asking that party policy be referred to the incoming AC for review. He accused some party members of being 'commies', and commented that he was 'sick and tired' of 'smart alecs . . . with sweat dripping on to their school books who talk about the workers of this country', a sentiment which attracted a mixture of disapproval and applause. The policies were defended by Justin Keating, who denied that Labour had suffered a defeat at all in the election and attributed the apparent success of Fianna Fáil's smear campaign to many Labour members' inability to explain the policies clearly, resulting from a failure to familiarise themselves with them. Conor Cruise O'Brien, too, argued that Labour had to clarify and explain its policies, not drop them. If Labour was concerned only to enunciate 'acceptable' policies, it could enunciate Fianna Fáil policies; to pass the Tipperary motion would be to say to the electorate, 'These are our principles, and if you don't like them, we'll change them.' Both motions were heavily defeated.

Despite these fighting words, Labour was losing strength. Individual members in rural areas had begun to vote with their feet almost as soon as the election was over. A defeated candidate in South Tipperary resigned from the party, as did a prominent Limerick member, who expressed his disagreement with 'the socialist republic idea'.[3] The former TD Paddy Tierney also left, stating that for the past two years Labour had been 'going the wrong road, led by people whom I feel will create a greater division between city and rural people'.[4] The steady growth in party membership was reversed in rural areas (see Appendix 3), where those who had been swept into the party on the wave of enthusiasm of the late 1960s began to drift away as the tide ebbed. The lesson that Labour was still only a third party was hammered home at three by-elections early in 1970. In Dublin South West, Labour had won two seats in 1969, but after the death of one of its TDs, Seán Dunne, it had great difficulty in selecting a candidate because of factionalism within the local organisation. The Labour vote fell by over a half, from 44·3 per cent to 21·5 per cent, and this defeat, in probably the most working-class constituency in the country, left no room for doubt that the 1969 election had been the crest of the wave. In Longford-Westmeath the Labour candidate lost his deposit, and a gain in Kildare brought the party only up to its traditional level; here the Labour candidate was, perhaps, helped by Justin Keating's pointing out that he seemed invulnerable to any 'red smear', since he was a GAA member and a Pioneer and had had a Christian Brothers education.[5]

The transition of the previous decade had created a party riddled with internal contradictions, but these had remained largely latent while Labour's fortunes had seemed set for spectacular improvement.

With the 1969 results the bubble had burst, and the internal divisions were exposed for all to see; between 1969 and 1973, indeed, some Labour members made a point of airing them in public. The party as a whole now contained three distinct groups: the traditional rural right, the pro-coalition left and the anti-coalition left. The problems of transition were beginning to manifest themselves. Annual conferences witnessed fierce arguments between pro- and anti-coalitionists. The question of coalition was about the only one not to engender disagreement within the PLP – only Dr Noel Browne opposed it – but on almost every other issue the range of TDs' views was wide. The evenness of the balance within the PLP between right and left made some of the conflicts particularly intense. Of Labour's seventeen TDs in 1970, nine represented Dublin constituencies and eight rural constituencies; eight had university degrees and nine did not; nine had entered the PLP since 1965 and eight became members earlier.

The tension was brought out very clearly by the argument over Stephen Coughlan in 1970. Since the 1969 election Coughlan, the Labour TD for East Limerick, had incurred the disapproval of many Labour members by a number of deeds. He had criticised anti-*apartheid* campaigners,[6] and had warned a left-wing group in Limerick that they should leave the city before they were 'crushed without mercy'.[7] When a shot was later fired at their bookshop he issued a statement condemning not the violence but the bookshop, which he termed 'a deliberate provocation' to the people of Limerick, since the left-wingers were 'completely opposed to our Christian traditions'.[8] Labour's AC, in response to calls from Dublin members for his expulsion, issued its own statement which also seemed more concerned about the existence of the bookshop than the violence used against it, which led to further criticism from Dublin members.[9]

The dispute erupted in April 1970, when Coughlan made a speech to the Credit Union League of Ireland. After praising the role of credit unions because they made reliance on moneylenders unnecessary, he gave his retrospective endorsement to a campaign conducted against Limerick Jews in 1904, and urged people to join a credit union instead of being exploited by 'extortionist warble-fly bloodsuckers'.[10] There was a flood of calls from Dublin branches for his expulsion, and Corish at once repudiated his remarks, stating that anti-semitism was repugnant to the Irish people and to the Labour Party.[11] The PLP voted overwhelmingly against withdrawing the whip from him, and Coughlan, at its instigation, issued an apology in which he stated, 'I sincerely regret the words I used,' and listed favours members of his family had done in the past for the Limerick Jews.[12] The Chief Rabbi of Ireland accepted the apology, while adding that he had been 'distressed by the shocking outburst of anti-Jewish remarks'.[13] Labour's AC was then presented with a motion to expel Coughlan from the party, which it defeated by a narrow margin. After four left-wing members had resigned from the AC and left the meeting, those remaining adopted a statement which endorsed Corish's rejection of 'the recent anti-semitic remarks of Alderman Coughlan TD', implied that only the Chief Rabbi's acceptance of his apology had forestalled stronger measures, and warned that any party members repeating such views would 'incur immediate expulsion'.[14] As well as the four AC members, a Head Office employee and Labour's Financial Secretary resigned their party posts in protest against the failure to expel Coughlan.

The matter was not finally resolved until the next annual conference, in February 1971, which defeated yet another motion calling for Coughlan's expulsion. Those supporting it, who included Conor Cruise O'Brien and Matt Merrigan, one of those who had resigned from the AC the previous year, argued that Labour could not convincingly condemn sectarianism while it continued to harbour Coughlan on its Dáil benches, and that his earlier utterances showed that his comments about the Jews, far from being an emotional outburst as his defenders claimed, sprang from a political outlook completely opposed to Labour's. Those against the motion, including Brendan Corish, Michael O'Leary and David Thornley, argued that Labour should put the matter behind it and concentrate its energies on Fianna Fáil rather than on internal disputes.

Certainly there was a widespread realisation that party unity was in danger; at one point in the initial stage of the affair, indeed, Coughlan threatened that if he were expelled he would form a new version of the National Labour Party, which could have attracted some of Labour's more conservative rural supporters. While a minority would have been glad to see him and those of like mind leave the party, a majority, while not necessarily taking Coughlan's threat seriously, wanted to prevent rather than force a split. The internal pressure for expulsion was less than might have been the case in other left-wing parties, because anti-semitism has generally been tolerated in Ireland, perhaps because, unlike most European countries, it had no anti-semitic movement during the 1930s to give anti-semitism a bad name.[15] The writer of a 'warmly commendatory introduction' to an anti-semitic book published in 1931 later became Archbishop of Dublin;[16] a young deputy who made several anti-semitic speeches in 1943[17] enjoyed great electoral success for the next thirty years and was made a Minister in 1976; the Clann na Talmhan leader stated in 1959 that 'the damn Jews' should not be permitted to live in Ireland,[18] without incurring any criticism. Consequently, while many Labour members were very disturbed when they heard of Coughlan's remarks, there were others who wondered what all the fuss was about.

This not very salubrious incident, as well as bringing into the open the growing rift between Dublin and rural members, demonstrated that the party had become much more cautious. Had the incident occurred before 1969 Coughlan might well have been expelled, but in the wake of the 1969 result Labour had little expectation of making any sort of breakthrough and was concerned above all to preserve its existing forces and to maintain as much internal unity as possible. High principles were now a luxury which could not always be afforded.

6.2 The Arms Crisis and the paralysis of politics

The affair which became known as the Arms Crisis erupted dramatically at 2.50 a.m. on 6 May 1970, when a government statement was issued to the effect that two Ministers, Neil Blaney and Charles Haughey, had been dismissed because they did not subscribe fully to government policy on Northern Ireland and that a third, Kevin Boland, had resigned. The following day it was announced that Blaney and Haughey had been dismissed because they were suspected of involvement in an illegal attempt to import arms for use in the north, and on the same day a Parliamentary Secretary, Paudge Brennan, also resigned. A fourth Minister, Michael Moran, had resigned at the Taoiseach's suggestion three days before the dismissals, on the ground of ill-health. Although for a while this rift, unprecedented in an Irish government, seemed likely to bring about a general election, and although the Fianna Fáil TDs formed into two camps, with the 'dissidents' including at one stage almost a fifth of the Dáil party, in the end the traditional loyalty to the party and its leadership asserted itself. Very few of the dissidents criticised Lynch publicly, and all the Fianna Fáil TDs supported the government in votes of confidence in May and November.

From May 1970 to the time of the 1973 general election, Irish politics were overshadowed first by the Arms Crisis and then by the wider Northern Ireland problem, issues which made normal political fare seem relatively trivial. Consequently, political development seemed to enter a state of paralysis. Both opposition parties took the view, summed up by Justin Keating's comment that 'the unity of Fianna Fáil is their shame',[19] that there was something dishonourable about the government party's concealment of its well-known internal divisions by the adoption of a public facade of unity. Their distaste for Fianna Fáil made a coalition agreement increasingly inevitable, and as a result Labour saw no point in continuing to expound the 1969 policies, let alone trying to formulate new ones. A feeling of frustration set in, and without the soothing balm of either a belief in a better future or a taste of real power, the party's internal contradictions were exacerbated. The PLP in particular often seemed to be in a state of civil war, and even though the topics around which the conflicts revolved were sometimes important ones, the arguments were all too often couched rancorously or in personal terms.

The central figure in many of the disputes was Dr Noel Browne, who in September 1970 began what was to become a habit of making very critical comments about the Labour Party. He accused the other Labour TDs of having espoused 'socialism' at the last election without having either known or cared what it meant, purely because they hoped it would propel them into office. Now, believing it to be electorally unpopular, they were eager to abandon it. He himself, he said, preferred 'Marxist based revolutionary socialism' to 'social democratic reformism'.[20] In a Sunday newspaper article he elaborated his views, advocating the provision of divorce, contraception facilities and 'therapeutic legal abortion' in 'certain cases'. Describing 'all capital or profits' as 'simply unpaid wages', he also said that Labour should favour the nationalisation of banks, insurance companies and the fishing industry, among others.[21] In response to a reply from David Thornley in the following week's issue, he said that no socialist could imagine that Labour would suffer any loss if two of its TDs, Stephen Coughlan and Michael Pat Murphy, left it.

At this point Brendan Corish attempted to stop the rot with a speech in Oughterard, County Galway, in which he stated that the magnitude of Labour's task, which was the construction of a socialist society, demanded dedication and self-discipline. Regrettably, this need had recently been ignored in 'a couple of spectacular instances', which had given the impression that the party was disunited. Before making a public statement members should ask themselves whether it would actually help Labour or would 'simply let Fianna Fáil off the hook'.[22] This appeal to TDs' better nature did not find a matching response, and the rows continued unabated. The two TDs named by Browne urged that he be disciplined, and Browne accused all his fellow Labour TDs of 'complete and wanton irresponsibility'.[23] Matt Merrigan, a long-standing associate of Browne, speaking underneath a portrait of Lenin and addressing a meeting of a group called the Young Socialist Association, then discussing the possibility of forming a break-away Labour Party, alleged that Labour had fallen into the hands of 'intellectual carpet baggers'.[24]

The 1971 annual conference reflected the new, petulant mood of the party. Far from displaying the defiance of the 1970 conference, it spent a lot of time on internal disputes, the tone being set when it began with a thirty-minute row over the agenda.[25] The debate on Coughlan's expulsion divided the conference, and generated further trouble. Two delegates who expressed agreement with Coughlan's original remarks were suspended from party membership for six months,[26] while when David Thornley rose to speak another delegate was rash enough to ask him where his rosary beads were, an allusion to what some considered Thornley's exaggerated profession of his Catholicism. In a *reductio ad absurdum* of Labour's declared opposition to sectarianism, the AC later decided that this comment was 'sectarian', and the unfortunate delegate too was suspended from party membership for six months.[27] The conference came out strongly against Irish membership of the EEC, although not without disagreement as to how it should oppose entry. Suggestions, mainly from Dublin delegates, that it should mount street demonstrations and co-ordinate its campaign with that of 'republicans' were received without enthusiasm by most of those present, as was one delegate's claim that, as EEC entry approached, Labour was 'drawing near the point where a revolutionary situation will be presented to us'. The conference also passed a motion calling for the use of contraceptives to be left to the conscience of each individual, despite opposition from some rural delegates. This liberalising theme was touched upon by the party leader, who stated that the country needed a new constitution which should not contain any 'disabilities for minorities' with respect to issues like divorce and family planning.

The next dispute concerned an organisation called the Socialist Labour Alliance, set up after a 'Socialist-Republican Unity

Conference' held in March 1971. Its most prominent member, Paddy
Healy, a member of Labour's AC, characterised the Labour leadership
as 'a bunch of careerists, time-servers and hacks whose sole remaining
function is to act as an influence of the bosses in the working class,
bandying around the word "socialism" in an attempt to hide their
treachery'.[28] The AC reciprocated by declaring membership of this
body to be incompatible with membership of Labour, and purged itself
of Healy.[29] The new organisation never attracted many members, and
does not seem to have remained in existence for long, although the AC
had to dissolve a branch in June when it refused to expel Healy, which
in turn prompted the resignation of the member who had been co-
opted to replace him on the AC.[30]

This was followed by yet another argument involving Noel Browne,
who in a much publicised speech in Tramore, County Waterford,
delivered a strong attack on the Church, which he described as a
'sectarian and bigoted politically conservative pressure group' and as
'one of the most dedicated, resilient, obscurantist and conservative
political machines in the history of man'.[31] Its record was one of
'chameleon conformism to the demands of social justice'; it changed its
attitude on social questions only when external pressures forced it to,
and never out of sincere conviction. Furthermore, he suggested, many
priests had 'chosen their celibate lives because they find the whole
subject of sex and heterosexual relationships threatening and
embarrassing'.

At any rate, the PLP found Browne threatening and embarrassing,
and hastened to dissociate itself from him, perhaps concluding,
probably correctly, that he was hoping to make the idea of a coalition
with Labour seem less attractive to Fine Gael's conservatives. It issued
a long statement expressing 'regret' for the 'offence' he had caused,
and described his speculations on priests' motives for entering their
profession as 'an insult'.[32] While acknowledging that the Church 'has
been conservative in its attitude on important and controversial
issues', it claimed that in recent years bishops and clergy had shown
great social concern. At the same time, it expressed a less liberal view
on contraception than the 1971 conference, favouring its availability
for married couples only. The statement produced a complaint from
Browne, and expressions of 'shame' and 'disgust' from some of his
supporters.[33]

The topic of contraception provided the focus for the next internal
dispute, when Browne and John O'Connell introduced a private

members' Bill to liberalise the law on the availability of contraceptives and birth control literature. The Bill had run into opposition within the PLP, and in the Dáil it was refused even a first reading, with three Labour TDs, Stephen Coughlan, Michael Pat Murphy and Dan Spring, joining with Fianna Fáil and eight Fine Gael TDs to defeat it by seventy-five votes to forty-four.[34]

However, the 1972 annual conference voted not to discuss an emergency motion to have the three TDs expelled, and in fact delegates left the PLP in no doubt that they were tired of the incessant bickering, which had a bad effect on party morale and was one of the reasons why membership declined to the extent that the number of branches registered in 1972 was actually below the 1967 level (see Appendix 3). The mood of the conference was unquestionably in favour of firmer discipline, a fact acknowledged by Corish in his leader's address.[35] In the past, he said, Labour had in effect been building a new party, a process in which disagreement was inevitable. He had seen his role as bridging the differences between the various tendencies while the change was taking place, but Labour was now at the end of the transition period, so that standards which might have sufficed in the past were no longer acceptable, and he would not continue to lean over backwards to be tolerant towards prominent party members who aired internal disagreements.

It is certainly true that Corish was often criticised in private for not being sufficiently firm in imposing discipline, especially on TDs. To some extent, his non-authoritarian leadership style was a matter of personal preference, and was consistent with his long-term aim of making Labour as broadly based as possible. In addition, the severe disappointment of the 1969 election results had deprived him of some of the forcefulness he had previously displayed. To a greater extent, a liberal attitude was dictated by the absence of a feasible alternative. The leadership was under pressure from each wing to discipline or expel members of the other wing, and there were many who would have welcomed wholesale purges or even a split. Papering over the cracks at least preserved the party more or less intact. Moreover, not all the Labour TDs were entirely amenable to party discipline. Dr Browne regarded himself as a socialist first and a Labour Party member second, and felt that his obligation to continue to enunciate his long-held principles took precedence over considerations of party discipline. In fact his membership of the PLP was tenuous during the year before the 1973 election. He resigned his spokesmanship immediately after the 1972 conference, thus becoming the only Labour TD without a portfolio,[36] and attended PLP meetings only sporadically and not always for their full duration. Not all the new TDs, especially those from academic backgrounds, found the task of dealing with constituents' problems one which occupied many of their mental energies.[37]

The problem of creating unity was caused basically by the fact that the views of TDs alone covered virtually the whole of the political spectrum. At one end, Noel Browne frequently advocated extensive nationalisation, criticised the role of the Church, and spoke in favour of the availability of divorce, contraception and abortion in certain cases. At the other, Michael Pat Murphy appeared to favour the denationalisation of some semi-State bodies,[38] declared himself 'against any dealings by any Irish government with any communist country',[39] accused Fianna Fáil of being communist when Ireland voted in favour of the admission of the People's Republic of China to the United Nations,[40] and voted against a Bill to make contraceptives legally available. In most political systems these two individuals would have belonged to opposing parties; the fact that in this case they belonged to the same one made it impossible to present an image of anything like unity.

Despite the depth of feeling manifested by ordinary delegates that the disputes should cease, it was not long before the familiar round of attempted expulsions began again. After a brief flurry involving Stephen Coughlan and Jimmy Kemmy, a prominent left-winger from Limerick who resigned from the party in January 1972,[41] the former stirred up a fresh hornet's nest by giving an interview to a Sunday newspaper.[42] Defining his political philosophy as 'Christian Republicanism', he criticised 'parlour socialists' who had forced the party too far to the left, and, when asked whether legislation should be subject to rulings by the Church, he counterposed the question of why anyone should try to 'deny' the 'rights' of the clergy. Most controversially, when asked to explain his 1970 remarks about the Jewish moneylenders, he claimed that he had been misrepresented; he had merely been comparing the present position with that of 1904, 'when the people were in dire straits, thanks largely to the Jews of Limerick'.[43] A week later Dr Noel Browne contributed an article to the same newspaper, in which he described the Catholic Church as 'arrogant, petulantly intolerant of criticism, authoritarian and unjust' and called for the secularisation of the educational system.[44]

The next meeting of the AC was, inevitably, faced with a motion from the Dublin Regional Council calling for the expulsion of Coughlan, and a counter-proposal from David Thornley that Browne should be expelled; for good measure, Thornley urged that Conor Cruise O'Brien be 'disciplined' for having questioned RTE's twice-daily broadcasting of the Angelus. Although the expulsion of Coughlan had at one stage seemed a foregone conclusion in view of the AC's 1970 ruling that anti-semitic comments would in future automatically incur this fate, he averted it by making a remarkable speech in Limerick in which he called for a 'new Ireland, which must be a secular, pluralist state'.[45] His 'deathbed conversion' to ideals to which he had previously been opposed was greeted first with 'incredulity and then with derision', and it was speculated that it had been 'inspired' by another TD,[46] but it served its purpose. The AC defeated the expulsion motion by twenty votes to seven, and Thornley's motion was not put.[47] In an attempt to dispel the impression of weakness thus given, both the PLP and the AC set up sub-committees to deal with disciplinary matters, and James Tully was named deputy leader of the party.[48] The AC declared solemnly that 'sectarian' utterances would not be tolerated in future, although the warning inevitably carried less credibility than the one issued after Coughlan's 1970 remarks.

6.3 The referendums of 1972

The referendum on a proposal to add a sub-section to Article 29.4 of the Constitution, so as to permit the State to join the European Community, brought about some temporary unity in the Labour ranks. Fianna Fáil and Fine Gael favoured entry, leaving the anti-EEC position to Labour, the ICTU, Official Sinn Féin and Provisional Sinn Féin. Labour maintained that joining the EEC would raise food prices, would jeopardise 35,000 jobs because Irish industries could no longer be protected from competition from other EEC countries, and would open Irish territorial waters to all other EEC fishermen.[49] It suggested that associate membership could be considered instead, and called the government's pro-EEC case 'unsustained and dishonest'.[50] However, although Labour distributed 1·5 million pieces of literature during the campaign,[51] the two major parties' support for entry made the result entirely predictable, and the party's campaign lacked conviction. Although some Labour TDs, particularly Justin

Keating, campaigned vigorously, others did not feel strongly on the issue or had reservations about the campaign,[52] and were absent from the fray. Moreover, Labour feared that the government might call a general election once the campaign was over, in the belief that the opposition parties would be unable to form a credible coalition, so it was reluctant to expend all its resources on the referendum campaign.

The referendum was held on 13 May, and the results showed a massive vote in favour of entry, with almost five votes being cast in favour for every one against.[53] The No vote in the referendum correlates strongly with Labour's strength in 1969 ($r = 0.82$) and in 1973 ($r = 0.81$), suggesting that most Labour supporters voted against EEC entry, and it has been concluded that the referendum confirmed the 'highly entrenched character of party loyalties' in the Republic.[54] Another study suggests that 60 per cent of Labour's 1969 supporters voted Yes,[55] but its authors acknowledge that there is no way of estimating the degree of confidence which may be reposed in their findings.

After a satisfactory by-election campaign in Mid Cork, which managed to produce a dispute in which two Labour TDs exchanged accusations of adolescence and irresponsibility,[56] Labour offered united and consistent opposition to the Offences against the State (Amendment) Bill debated by the Dáil in November and December 1972. The Bill was part of a government drive against the IRA, and the opposition parties claimed that it was cynically timed to benefit Fianna Fáil electorally, arguing that having been too tolerant of IRA activity in the past, it was now enacting unduly repressive legislation in the hope that the other parties would oppose it and enable the government to go to the country on a law-and-order platform. At first it seemed likely that the Bill would be defeated and precipitate a general election, for both opposition parties and the former Fianna Fáil 'dissidents' seemed likely to vote *en bloc* against it, but it then emerged that about seven Fine Gael TDs, including Liam Cosgrave, were determined to abstain. Preparations for a change of leadership had reached an advanced stage when two bombs exploded in Dublin, killing two people and wounding over a hundred.[57] As a result, all but a handful of Fine Gael TDs followed Cosgrave's lead and abstained, and the second stage of the Bill was passed by seventy votes to twenty-three.

Two further referendums were held towards the end of the year, neither causing any division between or within the parties. One was on the lowering of the voting age from twenty-one to eighteen, and the other involved the deletion of the two sub-sections of Article 44 which acknowledged the 'special position' of the Catholic Church and 'recognised' the other Churches. Although some politicians later suggested that this was a gesture to which northern Protestants should have responded favourably, it did not in fact denote any assertiveness on the part of the state *vis à vis* the Church, for three years earlier the Catholic Primate of Ireland had said that he 'would not shed a tear' if the change were made, and the Hierarchy endorsed his attitude.[58] On the occasions when the question was raised in the Dáil only one TD, Labour's Michael Pat Murphy, expressed any reservations, although he did not explicitly declare his opposition.[59] Labour favoured both proposals, but since the results were never in doubt it did not campaign vigorously; in the words of one constituency organisation report, 'the December referenda were the occasion of a "low profile" approach by the Party organization'.[60] Each proposal was carried by a majority of over six to one; turn-out was low, reflecting the lack of interest.[61] Curiously, the voting on these two entirely different proposals was almost identical, as if the No voters were undiscriminating conservatives. Even more curiously, the No vote correlates positively ($r=0.63$, significant at the 0.001 level) with Labour's 1969 support, and McCarthy and Ryan conclude that 20 per cent of Labour's 1969 supporters, as against much lower proportions of the other main parties' supporters, may have voted against both proposals. Such figures raise the interesting possibility, untestable on the evidence so far available, that Labour's most conservative supporters may be more conservative than the other parties' most conservative supporters.

The 1969–73 period was a difficult one for all three major parties. Fianna Fáil was in a state of almost permanent crisis from May 1970, but the threat to the leadership would have been greater had the three ex-Ministers adopted a common front. Instead, they went in entirely different directions. Neil Blaney and two other dissidents were expelled from the Oireachtas Party in November 1971 and from the national party the following year.[62] Kevin Boland's supporters engaged in unprecedented heckling and booing of the leadership at the Fianna Fáil Ard-Fheis in February 1971, but Boland resigned in May and formed a new party, Aontacht Eireann. It claimed to be the true heir of the traditional Fianna Fáil, whose attitude to the north had been 'betrayed' by Jack Lynch, and argued that while force was not necessarily the best way to solve the northern problem, the Republic's government should not hamper those nationalists in the north who used this method. It made no attempt to develop policies on social or economic issues, on which Boland was regarded as a right-winger. Although its first convention was attended by about 1,100 delegates,[63] its support dwindled rapidly, and only one Fianna Fáil TD, Sean Sherwin, joined it. The third ex-Minister, Charles Haughey, who was to become party leader and Taoiseach in December 1979, was among those put on trial as a result of the arms smuggling accusations. After all the defendants had been acquitted, Haughey described it as 'a political trial' for which those responsible had 'no alternative but to take the honourable course that is open to them', to which Lynch responded that, despite the verdicts, it was undeniable that 'there was this attempt to import arms illegally'.[64] With this exception, there were few public exchanges between leadership and dissidents, and Fianna Fáil remained remarkably united in appearance considering the issues at stake.

During the same period Fine Gael was beset by internal rivalry, the conservative leadership group feeling itself threatened by more liberal, pro-coalition elements. Two front-benchers made allegations of a left-wing plot in December 1969,[65] and after a reshuffle of the front bench in April 1972 had acknowledged the growing strength of the liberal wing by promoting leading coalitionists, tension remained high within the party for the rest of the year. In May an opinion poll found that only 19 per cent of those sampled supported Fine Gael, and only 40 per cent of these regarded Cosgrave as the best leader the party could have.[66] At his party's Ard-Fheis a fortnight later, Cosgrave launched a bitter attack on his enemies within the party, whom he described as 'mongrel foxes' whom he would flush out for 'the pack' to 'chop'.[67] His position remained uncertain almost up to the 1973 election.

The only other political party to enter the election was Sinn Féin, known familiarly as 'Official' or 'Gardiner Street' Sinn Féin. It was one of the products of a split in December 1969, when a majority of Sinn Féin's 'Army Convention' voted to end the policy of abstention from the Dáil. The minority withdrew to form Provisional Sinn Féin and the Provisional IRA.[68] Although an 'Official' IRA remained in existence, Sinn Féin began to play down its military connections and nationalist issues in general and to present an image of itself as a socialist party.

6.4 **The 1973 general election**

The nineteenth Dáil was dissolved early in February and the general election was held on the 28th of the month. The campaign was a dull one, fought between two centrist, pragmatic groups and revolving around promises on jobs, prices and other costs of living. Labour and Fine Gael hastily concluded a coalition agreement (see Chapter 8.7 below) and issued a fourteen-point programme which declared that the coalition's aim would be to 'transform Ireland into a modern progressive society based on social justice' and consisted largely of platitudes.[69] It contained a few specific promises: a coalition government would build 25,000 houses a year, end 'the policy of selective compulsion' on the Irish language and set up an independent body to deal with planning applications. The influence of Fine Gael could be seen in the first point, which asserted that the 'first responsibility' of the government would be to protect the safety of the individual and to uphold the institutions of the State. Labour's influence could be detected in the promise to evolve 'a programme of planned economic development' and to introduce worker participation in State enterprises. It contained no proposals which were not entirely acceptable to both parties. Fianna Fáil, as usual, issued no manifesto; it emphasised the need for a 'united' government rather than a coalition to deal with the important issues due to arise shortly.[70] It made little use of the red smear approach, about the only exception being the allegation of a Parliamentary Secretary that farmers in the west could be ruined if a coalition government implemented Labour's 'communist' policies.[71] Labour nominated only fifty-six candidates, forty-three fewer than in 1969, a strategy officially described as 'confining the Labour challenge to areas with proven organizational ability and concentrating the Party's central resources'.[72] Most of the candidates campaigned on the merits of the fourteen-point programme instead of expounding the 1969 policies.

The results contrasted with those of 1969, when Fianna Fáil had lost votes but gained seats, for it now gained votes – remarkably, in view of its troubles of the previous three years – but lost seats and office. Labour, on the other hand, lost votes but gained a seat, an outcome due mainly to the coalition's transfer agreement, and Fine Gael gained four seats. Neither Aontacht Eireann nor Sinn Féin won a seat, and only one candidate from each party saved his deposit. Overall, the two coalition parties won seventy-three of the 144 seats, while Fianna Fáil had sixty-nine and the other two were held by Independents.

Labour lost votes in all regions of the country (see Appendix 2), and outside Ulster, where it nominated only one candidate, its losses were heaviest in Dublin, where it fell back by 16,000 votes. In percentage terms, it fell back by an average of 8·7 per cent in the four Dublin constituencies in which there was a Sinn Féin candidate in 1973, and by only 6·9 per cent in the other three. Bearing in mind that Sinn Féin issued a fairly left-wing set of policies described as 'very much like a resumé of Labour's radical policies of their 1969 manifesto',[73] it may well be that Labour's losses in Dublin were caused partly by anti-coalition 1969 supporters switching to Sinn Féin. It fell back by three seats in Dublin, but only one outgoing TD was defeated here, Seán Dunne having died in 1969 and Noel Browne standing down in 1973. It gained four rural seats, all of them traditional Labour seats which had been lost in 1969. In Kildare and North Tipperary Joe Bermingham and John Ryan, both hard-working county councillors, were elected for the first time, while in Mid-Cork and Waterford TDs defeated in 1969 regained their old seats. Three of these gains were due to high transfers from Fine Gael as a result of the coalition agreement; the fourth, in Mid-Cork, was made at Fine Gael's expense with the aid of Fianna Fáil transfers. Overall, Labour was satisfied with the results, for although the steady growth in votes achieved at each of the previous three elections had been reversed, it had gained a seat, and moreover the result might have been worse in view of the party's internal problems. Most important, the Coalition's victory meant that Labour was in government for the first time since 1957.

7

Labour and Irish nationalism, 1957–73

7.1 **Irish nationalism since the Treaty**

Pre-1922 Irish nationalism fits fairly comfortably Minogue's definition of nationalism as 'a political movement depending on a feeling of collective grievance against foreigners'.[1] Viewed through the green haze of the Easter Rising and its aftermath, even the most insignificant and discrete incidents can be linked and said to constitute a 'tradition'. The mountain of literature on the subject contrasts with the limited analysis of the less romantic cause of Loyalism,[2] and of the unglamorous record of post-1922 Irish nationalism. Indeed, the very concept of Irish nationalism since the Treaty is a controversial one, of which at least three different interpretations – one sympathetic, one unsympathetic and one cynical – are possible.

The essence of the first, which might be called the traditional nationalist view, is that post-1922 Irish nationalism is the same phenomenon as pre-1922 Irish nationalism. It has the same goal, an independent thirty-two-county Irish Republic, and faces the same problem, British interference in Irish affairs. It made significant progress towards its aim in 1916–21, but the national task is not completed. The partition of Ireland, in this view, is the root cause of 'the problem'. Britain imposed partition on an outraged nation, and Britain could, and should, end it. What an Act of a British parliament had done, another Act could undo. Partition has greatly hindered the 'national advance'; in the words of a Fianna Fáil TD in 1937,[3]

the main cause of all that emigration, of all the poverty, and of anything else that is wrong politically, nationally and economically with the country is due to the partition of Ireland.

The existence of the northern Protestants does not justify partition, for the differences between them and the rest of the Irish people are no greater than the differences to be found within any nation. Their reluctance to join a united Ireland is caused mainly by British manipulation and British-fostered myths; if they threw in their lot with the rest of the Irish people, they would in fact receive more than fair treatment. In this view, which has been increasingly on the defensive since 1970, the problems of Northern Ireland spring from a conflict between British colonialism and Irish nationalism.

The second, which could be called the two communities interpretation, maintains that Irish nationalism emerged from the 1916–22 period looking surprisingly like colonialism. Before then it had rested on a belief that a community of people (the Irish) had the right to its independence from a larger nation (Britain) which claimed jurisdiction over it, but after 1922 it held that the northern Unionists had no such right *vis à vis* the Irish Republic. Indeed, it could be claimed that inherent in Irish nationalism had always been the contradiction of denying to others what it claimed for itself, but that this had remained latent while the Irish nation had itself been under the colonial yoke. The root of the problem in the north, in this view, lies not in a conflict between Britain and Ireland, but in the existence in Ireland of two communities with very different traditions and aspirations. Any political creed advocating that one community be compelled to be governed by a State dominated by the members of the other community, it is argued, is not nationalism at all but colonialism. Protagonists of this view see partition as a symptom of the problem rather than its cause, regard violence in Northern Ireland as springing from conflict between the two communities *within* the north rather than conflict between Britain and Ireland *about* the north, and advocate that the south should concentrate its efforts on improving relations between the two communities. As Whyte points out, internal conflict theories of the problem were surprisingly late in emerging, but are now widely accepted.[4]

The third interpretation regards post-1922 Irish nationalism as an ersatz version of what went before, espoused for purely functional reasons and not to be taken seriously. By 1922 the three major grievances which had fuelled Irish nationalism throughout the nineteenth century – alien rule, landlordism and religious discrimination against the bulk of the population – had been resolved to the general satisfaction of most Irish people. The continued use by politicians of nationalist rhetoric represented the vestigial traces of a habit ingrained in Irish political thought over several centuries, and did not betoken any genuine desire for a united Ireland. The people of the south, in this view, soon came to think in twenty-six-county terms, and from Fianna Fáil's entry into the Dáil in August 1927 there was a tacit consensus that parties should frame their policies with an eye only on the twenty-six-county electorate. The tendency of de Valera and others to equate Irishness with Catholicism[5] is often cited to illustrate the point that the northern Protestants, and by extension the counties in which they were in a majority, were not really regarded as an integral part of 'the nation' but as external to it. Nationalist rhetoric was employed not in the hope that it would bring a united Ireland any closer but because it seemed to be electorally popular. For Fianna Fáil in particular the goal of 'ending partition' became a nominal *raison d'être*, a goal especially useful for its purpose since it was never likely to be attained. According to this interpretation, partition served the same function for Fianna Fáil as 'the threat from the south' did for the Unionist Party, an external 'problem' which diverted attention from internal social and economic problems and reinforced conservatism on both sides of the border.

The traditional nationalist view, that the island of Ireland is, without qualification, one nation, was enshrined in the 1937 Constitution:

Article 2. The national territory consists of the whole island of Ireland, its islands and the territorial seas.

Article 3. Pending the re-integration of the national territory, and without prejudice to the right of the Parliament and Government established by this Constitution to exercise jurisdiction over the whole of that territory, the laws enacted by that Parliament shall have the like area and extent of application as the laws of Saorstat Eireann and the like extra-territorial effect.

Until the late 1960s it was almost unchallenged as the dominant southern perception of 'the problem'. The north was not an issue at elections in the Republic, because there was no division of opinion between the parties. That the political elite believed that Britain should 'end partition' went without saying; its members felt no more need to state their views on this subject than on sin. The consensus was so fundamental as not to need extensive reiteration. The few voices raised against it, such as those of the Independent TD Frank MacDermot in the 1930s and Donal Barrington in the late 1950s (see below), were left unanswered. Occasionally the southern elite gave vent to its feelings, most notably in the late 1940s, when all the major parties took part in the creation of the Mansion House Committee. This raised money in the south which was used to finance anti-partition candidates in the Northern Ireland general election of February 1949; its main achievement, not surprisingly, was 'to unite and solidify the Unionist camp', and the Unionist Party gained three new seats at the expense of Labour candidates.[6]

Overall, there can be little doubt that 'anti-partitionism', the active political expression of the traditional nationalist view, has been sterile and counter-productive in terms of its stated end. Its practitioners, like nineteenth-century colonialists, addressed themselves not to the inhabitants of the disputed region but, directly or indirectly, to London. Virtually the only people the anti-partitionists did not try to convince of the rightness of their cause were the northern Protestants, who have been the blind spot of post-1922 Irish nationalism.[7] Officially, they were misguided Irishmen, 'our fellow-countrymen in the Six Counties who are opposed to national reunion'.[8] Unofficially, they were not liked, and tended to be perceived as 'Orange bigots'. Mac Gréil's 1972–73 survey found that out of seventy stimulus categories, 'Unionists' came sixty-third, ahead in popularity only of the two wings of the IRA, drug addicts, drug pushers, communists, criminals and Pakistanis.[9] De Valera in 1949 characterised them as an insignificant minority whose inconvenient aspirations should no longer be permitted to poison relations between Britain and Ireland.[10]

The chances of persuading northern Protestants to come voluntarily into a thirty-two-county Republic were tacitly written off. Successive governments pressed ahead with the incorporation of specifically Catholic values into the laws and Constitution of the southern State. Anti-partitionism emphasised not the improvement of relations between the two traditions on the island but territorial unity, and it was often expressed romantically as the recovery of the currently occupied 'fourth green field'. Its hope of success lay not in persuading northern Protestants to join the southern State but in convincing Westminster and the world that the south had a quasi-legal right to the north. Articles 2 and 3 of Bunreacht na hÉireann, asserting a claim rather than expressing an aspiration to unity, are thus regarded as essential from the traditional nationalist viewpoint, for if the claim were dropped the case would be conceded.

7.2 **Labour and post-Treaty Irish nationalism**

Some writers have attributed Labour's third-party status to inept behaviour at key moments in the 1918–27 period. Most important, Farrell suggests that by not contesting the 1918 election, at which two-thirds of the electorate was on the register for the first time, Labour allowed the new voters to form voting habits which persisted subsequently and were passed on from generation to generation.[11] Since Sinn Féin won 65·5 per cent of the votes cast in the twenty-six counties at the election, it is argued, Labour's absence from the fray meant that it was thereafter attempting to wean voters away from attachments they had already formed.

While there is no doubt that Labour would have been better placed if it had stood and done well at the 1918 election, it is difficult to accept that Labour's subsequent position was significantly and adversely affected by its decision not to contest it. For one thing, this underestimates the influence of the many other factors, social structural and cultural, which militate against a strong Irish Labour Party. Secondly, it could be argued that Labour had no real option but to abstain from the election, and that any other course would have been even more damaging;[12] if this was so, then Labour's absence was a symptom rather than a cause of its weakness. Thirdly, the 1918 election may not in fact have been as important as sometimes imagined. Fifty-five per cent of the twenty-six-county electorate did not vote at all in 1918,[13] and only 29 per cent of the electorate voted for Sinn Féin. The fact that Sinn Féin did not secure for its descendants a monopolistic hold on the political affections of the electorate is further demonstrated by the fact that at the June 1927 election the three parties whose origins lay in Sinn Féin won only 57·2 per cent of the votes cast. Moreover, Labour does not seem to have been weakened by its lack of exposure in 1918, for its performance at the 1922 election, when it won more votes than de Valera's anti-Treaty Sinn Féin, was probably its best ever.[14]

Other writers argue that Labour's attitude to the Treaty and the civil war was mistaken. The party tried hard to remain neutral, and was inevitably criticised by each of the rival wings of Sinn Féin. It entered the Dáil and took the oath in 1922, which earned it the opprobrium of the anti-Treatyites. However, acceptance did not imply support, and when its TDs took the oath they stated that this was 'a formality implying no obligation of citizenship', and was being performed under duress, since the Treaty had been 'imposed upon Ireland by threat of superior force'. They added that if the electorate later changed its mind on the Treaty, they would not regard their having taken the oath as a barrier to their freedom of action.[15] Labour argued that social and economic issues, with which its 1922 manifesto was exclusively concerned, were more important than the Treaty. Similarly, during the civil war it urged the anti-Treatyites to end their struggle and condemned some of the harsher government measures like the Mountjoy executions, and was again attacked bitterly from both sides.

Most of Labour's critics believe that it should have taken the anti-Treaty side. According to Thornley, Labour's neutrality during the civil war 'may well have been yet another tactical blunder', and a wiser course might have been to join with the 'radical' wing of the anti-Treatyites, 'best personified in Liam Mellows'.[16] Mellows shared this view, claiming shortly before his execution that by failing to oppose the Treaty 'the official Labour Movement has deserted the people for the fleshpots of the empire'.[17]

However, there are many objections to the argument that Labour should have opposed the Treaty. First, if it had committed itself strongly to one side or the other, it would almost certainly have split. Secondly, once the electorate had delivered its pro-Treaty verdict in the 1922 election, to have supported the taking up of arms against the government would have been to renounce its long-standing support for democracy and opposition to militarism. Thirdly, it seems that Labour supporters themselves favoured working within the framework of the Treaty; an analysis of Labour transfers at the 1922 election shows that when faced with a choice between pro-Treaty and anti-Treaty Sinn Féin candidates, about one and a half times as many Labour voters (44·1 per cent as opposed to 27·9 per cent) gave their next preference to a pro-Treatyite.[18] Fourthly, there was a certain irony, of which he was no doubt unaware, in Mellows's accusing Labour of having 'deserted the people' less than six months after he had lost his Dáil seat in Galway to a Labour candidate. Fifthly, it would have been incongruous for Labour, which always maintained that bread-and-butter issues were of more importance than nationalist abstractions, to have joined in the anti-Treatyites' indignation over the oath to King George V. It would also have increased still further the polarisation of politics along the line of the Treaty, and reduced still further the likelihood of social and economic issues ever coming to the fore.

Finally, the anti-Treatyites' rejection of the Dáil led them into a cul-de-sac, and only the consummate political skill of their leaders allowed them to retrieve their position without humiliation.[19] When they finally entered the Dáil in 1927 they treated the oath as Labour had in 1922, even down to the description as a 'formality'.[20] If Labour had followed the anti-Treatyites into the cul-de-sac, it would have had either to follow them back out again or perish slowly in the electoral wilderness. In other words, later events seemed to bear out the wisdom of Labour's, rather than the anti-Treatyites', course of action in 1922.

The fact is that the Treaty split and the civil war would have posed huge problems for Labour no matter what it did, and its neutral line achieved what was probably the most obtainable under the circumstances, namely the preservation of party unity without the abandonment of its principles. The disruptive potential of nationalism, and the need to steer a careful path, were demonstrated by one Labour TD's defection in 1922 because he refused to take the oath, and the expulsion of two others in 1931 for supporting anti-IRA legislation not approved of by the party.[21]

The latter incident marked the beginning of a trend that saw Labour become the most republican of the three main parties by 1957. In the early 1930s it fully supported Fianna Fáil's nationalist actions, such as the removal of the oath, but in 1936 it took up a more nationalist position than Fianna Fáil, opposing a government Bill brought forward after the abdication of King Edward VIII. The Bill provided for the retention of the functions of his successor with regard to the State's external affairs, to which William Norton objected, maintaining that since the former British king had 'broken the link', it could be allowed to remain broken as far as Ireland was concerned.[22] All five votes cast against it were those of Labour TDs. In 1939 Labour opposed Fianna Fáil's own anti-IRA emergency legislation.[23] The party inserted into its constitution Article 2 of Bunreacht na hÉireann, almost verbatim.[24] In 1954 Labour supported a Bill introduced by two Independent TDs of strong republican views to allow elected representatives from 'the six occupied counties of Ireland' to speak in the Oireachtas, while the two major parties opposed it.[25] There were no signs of dissent from the traditional nationalist view; in 1947 Norton called on Britain to unify the island, stating that 'Mr Attlee's government has it in their [*sic*] power to end Partition in six months'.[26]

Although no internal disputes arose, the fact remained that Labour was always vulnerable to a split on such issues, precisely because, unlike Sinn Féin, it had not split in 1922. In consequence, whereas Sinn Féin's successor parties each tended to be more or less of one mind on nationalist issues, Labour members had a wide diversity of views. Indeed, the left as a whole has tended to hold an extremely wide range of opinions on the subject of the north, and on what approach socialists should take to it, manifested after 1970 in differing attitudes to the Provisional IRA. At one extreme, Eamonn McCann maintains that 'there is no such thing as an anti-imperialist who does not support the Provos and no such thing as a socialist who is not anti-imperialist'.[27] At the other, in the eyes of the British and Irish Communist Organisation (BICO), 'the IRA is a petit-bourgeois nationalist organisation whose fundamental objective is to incorporate, by physical force, the Protestant population of Northern Ireland into an all-Ireland nation dominated by Catholic nationalism ... The IRA, therefore, is the vanguard of the Catholic nationalist movement for the national subjugation of the Ulster Protestant community.'[28] While the differences of opinion within Labour generally remained latent, they were liable to come to the surface if nationalist issues again forced themselves into the centre of political debate, as was to be the case in the early 1970s.

7.3 The IRA campaign 1956–62 and the 1960s

In December 1956 the IRA began a campaign of violence which, it stated, would continue 'until the invader is driven from our soil'.[29] In fact it soon fizzled out, being finally called off in 1962, and was condemned by all the main parties. The condemnation of the Minister for Justice, James Everett, was couched in rather lukewarm terms; he described the 'occurrences in the Six Counties', which consisted mainly of attacks of RUC barracks, as 'a deplorable waste of life and of youthful endeavour', and later described the campaign as 'counter-productive', while stating that he 'detested partition'.[30] County councils all over the country discussed the topic, most of them passing votes of sympathy with the relatives of two IRA members killed in a raid, and some adding approval for their efforts. Labour's public representatives expressed differing views. On Waterford Corporation Tom Kyne TD condemned 'physical force', and said that attempts to achieve the freedom of any country should be on constitutional lines. James Hickey, a former TD, was slightly more militant, stating at a

Cork Corporation meeting that although he did not believe in force, the blame for 'the present situation' lay with Britain for maintaining an army in Ireland. A view of almost complete support for the IRA was expressed by a future TD, Seán Treacy, supporting a motion before South Tipperary County Council which urged the government to 'give the Republicans fighting the common enemy the full support of our army and police force'. He expressed pride that he had witnessed this upsurge of patriotism, and added that because of the IRA's actions this generation of Irishmen would not pass away in shame.[31]

None of these views was incompatible with traditional nationalism, and Labour's thinking remained firmly within that framework. At the 1957 annual conference William Norton stated that partition should be ended, 'full stop', irrespective of the standard of living in the north or the south. Labour's opposition to partition, he said, was based on the belief that Ireland had been one and indivisible before the British partitioned it. Labour denied 'the right of Britain or any power to occupy any part of our territory'.[32] Later in the year Dan Desmond seemed to hint that he would be willing to endorse the use of violence, suggesting that a 'more direct' approach to the problem of partition was needed, since young people 'are not content to live under foreign domination'. It was a shame, he added, to see so many young people 'suffering in internment camps because of this abomination of Partition'.[33] Nine Labour TDs (the other two did not vote) supported a motion calling for a thirty-two-county plebiscite on the ending of partition, a measure perhaps comparable to a 1938 plebiscite of all Germans and Austrians on the Anschluss. Brendan Corish declared that the government should attempt to convince the United Nations that partition was the responsibility of the British government, and did not represent a dispute between Irishmen from the north and south or between Protestants and Catholics.[34] The only sign of deeper thinking came from a Fianna Fáil TD, Frank Loughman, who argued that a thirty-two-county plebiscite would be a pointless exercise. Although an overall majority would obviously vote for reunification, he said, the Unionists of the north would vote against it, and any all-Ireland government would have to be as coercive towards them as they had hitherto been towards the northern nationalists.[35] Corish replied that he would 'be prepared to chance that'.[36]

The first sustained critique of the traditional nationalist approach came in 1957 from Donal Barrington, a lawyer and later a Fianna Fáil member. In a paper published by the research group Tuairim[37] he argued that anti-partitionism had in fact 'tended to strengthen and perpetuate' partition.[38] Past anti-partition campaigns had alienated the Unionists and had simply induced Westminster to give them firmer guarantees.[39] He took issue with the familiar argument that partition had been imposed on an unwilling Ireland by Britain, so that it was Britain's responsibility to end it. Instead, he said, partition had been 'forced on the British Government by the conflicting demands of the two parties of Irishmen'.[40] He described as absurd the widely held views that the British troops in the north constituted 'an army of occupation' and that the north was 'British-occupied territory'.[41] The anti-partitionist approach, he wrote, seemed to consist of a demand 'that England should force the people of the north to come into a United Ireland against their will'; such a demand, he continued, 'was utterly reprehensible and ought never to have been made in the name of Irish nationalism'.[42] The complete failure of anti-partitionism to bring reunification any nearer meant that an entirely new approach was needed. Instead of regarding the north as occupied territory and insisting that the British hand it back, the Republic should grant recognition to the Northern Ireland government and declare that it acknowledged that unification could not come about until Stormont gave its consent. The emphasis should be on appealing to and trying to win the trust of the Unionists rather than on attempting to persuade Britain to force them into a thirty-two-county Republic.[43]

The pamphlet, according to its foreword, was intended as 'a basis for rational discussion', but it provoked very little discussion, rational or otherwise, despite, or perhaps because of, its originality, and it took the bloodshed of the 1970s to stimulate new thinking, much of it on the same lines as Barrington's. The only politicians to whom fresh ideas seemed to occur in the late 1950s were William Norton and Declan Costello. Norton's speech to Labour's February 1958 consultative conference suggested that he may have read Barrington's pamphlet, for he too argued that there was a need for a completely new approach.[44] Labour, like the other parties, had 'adopted a rather ostrich-like policy, ignoring inconvenient or unpalatable facts'. It must do some fresh thinking, whatever the political risks involved, and 'not just remain stuck in the same old groove that has, in the past, served for policy not just in the Labour Party but indeed in all parties'. He suggested that in each party there were some members who did not really agree with the prevailing policy, but 'always a public front is presented that frequently conflicts with private conviction'.

Labour rejected force, he said, and aimed for 'not merely territorial unity, but a unity of hearts and minds with our fellow-countrymen in the Six Counties'. It had to face the fact that the northern majority supported the constitutional connection with Britain, and had to adjust its thinking accordingly. The Republic should aim to extend the forms of association between north and south, and should seek talks at government level between London, Belfast and Dublin, on economic as well as political and constitutional matters. In order to enable these talks to take place, he said, 'it may be necessary to recognize the political facts as they exist today', perhaps a veiled suggestion that Dublin recognise the legitimacy of the Stormont regime. This alone could break the deadlock. A similar point was made by Declan Costello in May 1959, when he stated that the south 'must accept and recognise the *de facto* existence of the Northern Government'.[45]

However, Norton's thoughts on this, as on the need for Labour to adopt a new approach on all issues (see Chapter 2.2 above), were not followed up, and as the IRA campaign faded away, so did perceptions of the need for fresh thinking. Few attitudes of any sort were expressed until the civil rights movement again raised the problem in the late 1960s, except for the occasional remark at a party conference. In 1958 James Tully, the party chairman, suggested that the British troops should be withdrawn, after which the future of the north would be discussed 'round a table', while in 1960 he stated that 'some type of federal association seems to be the best solution at present',[46] an idea which was ahead of its time but was not developed. In 1967, however, he returned to the traditional nationalist line, opposing the idea of Ireland's entry into the EEC partly because this would mean it was abandoning its 'right to demand freedom for the six north-eastern counties', which at present the British were 'holding . . . by force' with an 'army of occupation'.[47]

Under Seán Lemass there was something of a thaw in southern attitudes to the north. The government began to lay less verbal emphasis on the need to end partition and more on the need for economic growth. Lemass himself tried to gain currency for the term 'Northern Ireland' instead of 'the six counties', the term then most often used by anti-partitionists, since it implied that the area under discussion was not in any significant way different from the rest of the country except that it had been artificially separated by the Treaty boundary. In January 1965 he visited the northern Prime Minister, Terence O'Neill, triggering a series of meetings over the next five years between northern and southern Ministers. Labour was not entirely enthusiastic about this development, for whereas Corish welcomed it as a first step towards better north–south relations and ultimately towards unity, Michael O'Leary declared that 'partition is still a problem' and described the Lemass–O'Neill meeting as 'probably the complete metamorphosis of the Fianna Fáil party, the salvaging of Ulster Unionism instead of support for the non-Unionist forces'.[48]

Unlike the other parties, Labour had tenuous links with northern parties, and in the late 1960s an attempt was made to institutionalise them through an 'All-Ireland Council of Labour'. This council was, probably unknown to many of those involved in its creation, simply the latest in a seemingly interminable series of such bodies set up over the years to try to bring the northern and southern political labour movements closer together. The Northern Ireland Labour Party (NILP), like the ILP, had its roots in the decision of the 1912 ITUC Clonmel conference. After the establishment of the Irish Free State, the Labour leadership concentrated on events south of the border. Feeling neglected, some northern members in March 1924 established the 'Labour Party (Northern Ireland)', which in 1927 rejoined the party-congress.[49] The separation of the ILP from the ITUC in 1930 also cut it off from the LP(NI), but the party's constitution stated that Labour

deems it expedient to leave the work of political organization in Northern Ireland to be dealt with through machinery specially established for that area. The Labour Party, therefore, recognizes the Labour Party (Northern Ireland) as providing the appropriate machinery and will maintain close contact with that Party by means of a joint council.[50]

A joint council was duly established, and was supposed to meet twice a year and issue an annual report, but the AC's reports speak instead of very infrequent meetings involving 'general discussions' or 'an exchange of views'. Every few years a new joint committee was established to try to increase contact and co-operation between the parties, but since they were fighting in different political arenas, and were both very weak in any case, neither had much to offer the other.[51] Fraternal delegates to conferences were exchanged for a while, but this practice ceased in the late 1930s. The ILP leadership took offence when an anti-partition motion was defeated at an LP(NI) conference, while at the latter's 1936 annual conference there were allegations that the ILP was attempting to 'dictate' to it over the question of a possible united front with the Communist Party.[52] Labour's new constitution continued to 'recognise' the LP(NI) in almost exactly the same words as the first constitution had, except that now such recognition existed only 'pending the ultimate destruction of the alien influences which, by means of an unnatural division of the country, separated Ireland into two political entities'.[53]

A liaison between the LP(NI) and the British Labour Party led to the ILP declining an invitation to send a fraternal delegate to the LP(NI)'s 1938 conference, and when the northern party told Labour that the conference had passed a motion calling for closer trade links between Northern Ireland and the southern state the AC sent back a cold reply to the effect that it did not support a trade agreement while partition continued to exist, since in its view 'the territorial reintegration of Ireland must precede economic co-operation'.[54] However, at Labour's 1939 conference delegates criticised this attitude, asking why, if the AC could (as it did) co-operate with the Old IRA in the creation of a 'National Anti-Partition Council', it could not co-operate with the representatives of the northern workers. Against the wishes of William Norton and Senator Luke Duffy, the party's strongly nationalist general secretary, the conference passed by sixty-two votes to twenty-seven a motion calling for a resumption of contact with the LP(NI).[55] Arising out of the motion, a meeting took place in Waterford in August 1939 between representatives of the two parties, at which they appear to have agreed to disagree as to whether the LP(NI) should declare itself anti-partitionist. However, when the northern party pledged its full support to the Unionist government in its prosecution of the war effort the AC, in view of Labour's support for Irish neutrality, decided to cease communicating with it, and there were no further contacts until the war was over.[56] Late in 1945 representatives of the two parties met in Belfast, and agreed yet again to establish a joint committee, to facilitate an exchange of views, advice, information and speakers between the parties. The committee was duly set up in March 1946, but then lapsed.[57]

The LP(NI) had always avoided committing itself on the question of the border, but a number of factors, among them the increasing anti-partition activity in the south, the interest of an anti-partition group of British Labour MPs at Westminster, and the Unionist Party's reaction to these developments, made continued playing down of the issue impossible. Late in 1948 the national executive approached the British Labour Party to discuss reconstituting the LP(NI) as a regional council of that party. The ILP protested, and Luke Duffy sent a letter on behalf of the AC threatening that Labour might start organising in the north if the merger went ahead.[58] Even though in fact it never did, a number of anti-partition members of the LP(NI) now broke away, and, along with other anti-partition Labour groups, held a meeting in Belfast in January 1949, with Duffy and Roddy Connolly TD present, which decided to set up a provisional committee to extend the ILP's activities to the north.[59] Later that month, and again in April, the NILP (as it was now called) declared itself committed to preserving the constitutional link with Britain, and informed the ILP that in view of its threat to organise in the north and its co-operation with dissident and expelled members, fraternal relations between the two parties were over and the joint committee was dissolved.[60] The way was now clear for the ILP to become the first southern party to cross the border. After meetings in Dublin and Belfast, those who had attended the January meeting agreed in April 1949 to start setting up ILP branches in the north, initially under the uninspiring title of 'The Irish Labour Party in the Six County Area' until the recognition accorded to the NILP could be excised from the party constitution.[61]

The party in the north began with two Stormont MPs and one Westminster MP (the anti-partitionist Protestant Jack Beattie), but it rapidly fell apart. Few southern members took much interest in the northern wing, and those who did were bemused by its byzantine and highly personalised factionalism, which soon led to a proliferation of mini-parties. At the 1953 Stormont election one of its original MPs, Frank Hanna, now Independent Labour, defeated both an Irish Labour Party and an Independent Irish Labour Party candidate to win re-election, while the other, Harry Diamond, formed his own Republican Labour Party (RLP) and also defeated ILP and Independent ILP candidates.[62] Indeed, of all the factions the official Irish Labour Party fared worst, its candidates generally finishing bottom of the poll. It found it hard to win Protestant support – the local press always referred to it as 'Eire Labour' – while on the other side its ostensible non-sectarianism made it easy prey for explicitly Catholic Labour politicians like Hanna. During the 1950s it was quite strongly represented on Belfast Corporation, by Paddy Devlin among others, but it lost all seven of its seats to Hanna's group in May 1958.[63] The AC got as far as establishing a committee to examine the effectiveness of the Belfast organisation, but the committee did not find time actually to visit the north.[64]

The idea of Labour becoming involved in northern politics was not, then, quite as original as some of the advocates of the Council of Labour imagined it to be in the mid-1960s. It arose this time round when the NILP's June 1966 conference passed a resolution moved by the Queen's University Belfast branch, which called for 'a Council of Labour in Ireland', and was taken up by Labour's 1966 conference, which called on the leadership 'to take the initiative in calling together a Council of Labour, representative of all democratic political Labour movements in Ireland, which would help to co-ordinate the policies and actions of political Labour, North and South'.[65] Difficulties arose because the ILP wanted the inclusion of the Belfast-based RLP while the NILP feared the loss of Protestant working-class support if it seemed to be in any way linked to the RLP. Moreover, none of the parties gave the establishment of the Council very high priority, and discussions dragged on for some time, with the unions exerting some pressure to try to bring them to an agreement.[66]

The Council was finally set up in March 1968, with Brendan Corish as chairman, Gerry Fitt of the RLP as vice-chairman, and Sam Napier of the NILP as secretary.[67] It was declared to have 'the purpose of bringing to an end conservative rule in both parts of the island' and would aim to 'secure the return of socialist governments' north and south, and it would also provide the means for consultation between the various Labour parties. In general it proved as ineffectual as all previous joint councils and joint committees; only in its last capacity did it serve a useful purpose, especially when the northern crisis began to develop, but it faded from the scene as events gathered pace. When the NILP decided again to seek a merger with the British Labour Party in 1970, Michael O'Leary declared that the Council was 'dead'.[68] This merger, like that projected in 1948, never materialised, but the picture was further complicated by the virtual disappearance of the RLP as an electoral force and the emergence of the Social Democratic and Labour Party (SDLP). A brief attempt to revive the Council, with the SDLP and NILP as co-members, was made late in 1971.

The Belfast Corporation rout of May 1958 had brought Labour's own organisation in the north to an end, with the exception of what a delegate to the 1970 conference called 'a few lingering limbs' in Newry and Warrenpoint, near the border in County Down. In an attempt to apply artificial respiration, the conference empowered the AC to co-opt an additional member from the north, and the 1972 conference empowered it to co-opt two additional members.[69] Despite these measures, the disastrous performance of the party's candidates in the northern local elections of May 1973 led to the resignation of all the members of what seems to have been the only functioning branch in the north.[70] The northern organisation's obituary was noted in the party's next annual report, which commented laconically that 'the Administrative Council decided not to exercise its right to co-opt members from the North of Ireland in view of the fact that no Party organisation now exists in the North of Ireland'.[71]

During the 1960s, then, Labour's thinking on the north had remained within the framework of the traditional nationalist approach. There was no awareness of the limitations of this approach, and no realisation that Catholics in the north were coming to see that anti-partitionism, pursued doggedly by the Nationalist Party, was sterile. A more profound analysis of the problem was simply neglected by Labour and the other southern parties. There were, of course, excuses for this neglect. Northern politics were fairly quiescent until the late 1960s, and there were no stimuli to fresh thinking. Moreover, in failing to think deeply about the north, southern parties were doing no less than successive British governments, which were nominally responsible for the welfare of its people.[72]

7.4 Dispute and disunity, 1968–71

In the late 1960s there was a change in the political attitudes of the Catholic community in the north, which manifested itself politically in a sharp decline in support for the Nationalist Party and the emergence of the civil rights movement. The former had concentrated on the unattainable goal of abolishing partition and had made no attempt to highlight or rectify the problems of people within the State. It had been the sectarian obverse of the Unionist Party, in effect a Catholic party for a Catholic people, and had never tried to appeal to, for example, the Protestant working class, many of whose members did not fare very well under Unionist rule. Its strategy was guaranteed to be a losing one, since there was an in-built majority against removing the border, and so it had posed no threat to the fundamentally sectarian nature of the State. The civil rights movement, in contrast, concentrated on reform within the north, was overtly non-sectarian, and in practical terms achieved more in two months than the Nationalists had in forty-seven years.[73] Its strategy undermined the institutions of the State, by demonstrating, not least to Westminster, that although they were democratic in form, they were not infused with a democratic spirit. It triggered off violent resistance by militant Protestants, and after several nights of attacks by Protestants on Catholic areas the British army was introduced.

To some in the south, this deployment of the British army, traditionally regarded as an 'army of occupation', was a confusing development. Labour, however, sent two delegations to the north, which used the contacts existing with the northern Labour parties and concluded that the presence of the British troops was desired by, and was in the interests of, the people in the besieged Catholic areas.[74] It also sent a delegation to London, and its care to make an on-the-spot assessment before issuing statements drew praise from political commentators.[75]

At this stage Labour was able to display a united attitude, whereas divisions were apparent within Fianna Fáil. The Taoiseach's statements were generally mild, ruling out the use of force to try to achieve unity, but a minority of Cabinet members, spearheaded by Neil Blaney, favoured a much harder line. Late in 1968 Blaney launched a fiery attack on partition, Terence O'Neill, the 'bigoted junta' in the north and Gerry Fitt.[76] Clearly undisturbed by gentle remonstrations by the Taoiseach, he made a particularly controversial speech a year later:[77]

I believe, as do the vast majority, that the ideal way of ending partition is by peaceful means. But no one has the right to assert that force is irrevocably out ... The Fianna Fáil Party has never taken a decision to rule out the use of force if the circumstances in the Six Counties so demand.

Once again, Lynch stated that the government had no intention of using force, but since he recognised that Blaney's 'feelings on the partition issue are very deeply felt' he would not discipline him.[78]

Under the appearance of unity within Labour it was possible to discern embryonic outlines of the divisions which were to rend the party in the second half of 1971. In a Dáil debate in 1969 three TDs' sympathies seemed to tend towards the two communities view. Brendan Corish argued that the withdrawal of the British troops would not solve the problem. Continually pointing out that no Irishman had voted for partition served no useful purpose; they should recognise that partition existed because a majority in the north wanted it to stay. Conor Cruise O'Brien stated explicitly that 'partition is not the root cause of this matter', and Michael O'Leary suggested that the

Republic concentrate on removing sectarian features from its own life and Constitution.[79] In contrast, Justin Keating put forward the traditional argument that partition had been 'a manoeuvre by British imperialism', and added that 'the struggle against imperialism will have to go on because it is the source of the oppression'.[80] Similarly, whereas at the 1970 conference Corish suggested that the south adopt a policy of peaceful persuasion towards the north, party chairman Dan Browne spoke of London as the place 'where the power lay ultimately to smash Unionist fascism', and Jimmy Kemmy, referring to 'the capitalist partition of our country', said that Labour must become 'a militant socialist republican party'.[81] Later in the year David Thornley told the ITGWU annual conference that he hoped no one would derive the impression that any TDs were 'abdicating from our Republican traditions'.[82]

This variety of views did not create an image of Labour disunity, because they differed only implicitly. Labour members were not attacking each other direct, and there was no argument about whether any particular views were consistent with Labour's policy, because it did not have one – remarkably, the 150 page book of policy documents issued in 1969 did not contain a single word on the subject of the north. However, this indulgence was no longer possible once internment had been introduced in the north on 9 August 1971. The scale of violence there increased greatly, and feelings in the south became more passionately held.

Many of Labour's arguments centred on the position of Dr Conor Cruise O'Brien as party spokesman on the north. There was an element of chance in the fact that he held the position at this sensitive time. He had been appointed foreign affairs spokesman after the 1969 election because of his international experience, and it had not been foreseen that Northern Ireland would be by far the most important area covered by his portfolio. Nor was it fully realised that he had little sympathy with traditional nationalism, even though he had criticised it caustically in a newspaper article in 1966.[83]

Two rival camps began to develop within the PLP, their interpretations of the situation corresponding closely to the traditional nationalist and two communities views outlined earlier. Nominally the two groups clashed most frequently over whether O'Brien should be removed from the party's spokesmanship, but one of the main substantive points at issue was whether or not the IRA's campaign of violence should be unequivocally condemned. The arguments were at

their most heated between August 1971 and the prorogation of
Stormont in March 1972, seven months during which it seemed to
many people in Ireland and elsewhere that the Stormont regime, with
the backing of Westminster, had embarked on a policy of systematic
repression of the Catholic community with the aim of imposing a
military solution to the 'troubles'.

Many of the traditional nationalists opposed violence, but the more
militant were inclined to regard the IRA's campaign as a justifiable
means of defence against the institutionalised violence of the Northern
Ireland State, and the idea of helping the northern government to
quell it was in their eyes akin to 'felon-setting'. Moreover, its campaign
might make the northern State 'unworkable' and precipitate a British
withdrawal, after which partition would disappear, so that although
many of its actions were distasteful, they were 'objectively' bringing
nearer the only real solution to the problem. Its campaign was the
quickest, and perhaps the only, way of bringing down the inherently
undemocratic system of government in the north. Their opponents, in
their eyes, were abandoning the northern Catholics to their fate and
conceding the Unionist claim that the north was part of another
country. In essence, they were pro-British rather than pro-Irish, and
most traditional nationalists would have endorsed George Colley's
description of O'Brien as 'the Tories' favourite Irishman'.[84]

Those inclining towards the two communities view, on the other
hand, believed that the IRA had no redeeming features at all. It was
worsening relations between the communities in the north, and might
precipitate a civil war there – in which, incidentally, the Catholics
would suffer most. It was providing the Unionist government with an
excuse for its own intransigence and letting it off the hook on which
the civil rights movement had impaled it, for while Westminster had
refused to tolerate its continued reluctance to grant basic democratic
rights to a third of the citizens under its jurisdiction, the British were
bound to support it if the threat to it became a violent one directed
against its very existence. To this group the traditional nationalists
were, often unintentionally, since many of them opposed violence,
providing an ideological umbrella for the IRA.[85] They themselves, in
their own eyes, were not 'anti-Irish' or betrayers of the patriot dead,
but were confronting the officially sanctioned and propagated myths
which had left the two communities in Ireland as far apart in 1971 as
they had been in 1921.

The first sign that Labour was heading into stormy waters emerged

from the June 1971 annual conference of the ITGWU, in a debate on a
motion calling for 'the immediate release of Irish political prisoners
being held in England and Northern Ireland'.[86] A query from Conor
Cruise O'Brien as to whether the term 'political prisoners' included
people who had been found guilty of murder or planting bombs drew
hostile comment from several delegates. One, who said that he 'was a
dynamiter and I am proud of it', declared that he would not condemn
'the men who take their stand now to drive the last vestige of British
imperialism from this country', and another said that they need make
no apology for demanding 'the release of Irish republican prisoners'.
Despite reservations expressed by Brendan Corish and Fintan
Kennedy, a Labour Senator and general president of the union, the
motion was carried by a large majority.

Three months later David Thornley criticised O'Brien and Noel
Browne for having condemned the IRA, since, he said, the use of force
could not be ruled out in all circumstances. Taking up a recent speech
by Browne, he described the view that James Connolly should not have
participated in the Easter Rising as 'incompatible with membership of
the party which Connolly founded'.[87] The Dublin Regional Council
declared that O'Brien's views on the north were not those of rank-and-
file members, mentioned 'the republican principles and traditions' of
the party, and called for a phased withdrawal of the 'colonial force'
from the north.[88]

The divisions within the PLP were made obvious in a Dáil debate in
October 1971. Five TDs opposed the traditional nationalist view,
while three endorsed it. Brendan Corish maintained that 'territorial
unity alone is not real unity'; for genuine unity 'there must be unity of
peoples', which in turn 'must be based on consent'. Perhaps alluding to
some Labour TDs, he referred to 'those who by their silence or tacit
approval, or by their nods and winks to those who use force in the
North, are merely inviting their own destruction as democratic
representatives'.[89] Barry Desmond criticised 'the reactionary brand of
sectarian nationalism which has cursed this country', and stated that
since 'violence and its by-products will not bring about a solution',
Labour condemned all violence, including that of the IRA.[90] Noel
Browne also condemned violence and its glorification, and said that
the Republic had to recognise the genuine fear of the northern
Protestant worker that he would suffer discrimination in a united
Ireland.[91] Michael O'Leary took issue with the suggestion that the
departure of the British army would be conducive to peace.[92] Conor

Cruise O'Brien described Articles 2 and 3 of Bunreacht na hÉireann as an 'irredentist annexationist claim', and said that the Irish government should work 'towards adjustment in Northern Ireland, towards structural reform there, not by emphasising our claim to unity though without concealing our aspirations towards that'.[93]

The traditional nationalist viewpoint was expressed eloquently by Seán Treacy, who stated that he deplored 'physical violence', but continued:[94]

Equally, I deplore the insidious violence and repression which emanate from a one-party system of government, a totalitarian system of government, a system which relegates one section of the community to the role of second-class citizens bereft of fundamental rights, civil or political, a system which discriminates and differentiates on a class and religious basis, a system of government which in its origin is unnatural because it seeks to opt out of the historic Irish nation and to perpetuate the myth of two nations in this our island home, ignoring the obvious fact and the great truth that God fixed the boundary for the Irish nation when he fixed as its frontier the encircling sea.

North-east Ulster, he said, was 'the last bastion of British imperialism in all its abominable features', and the violence there was 'the natural reaction of an outraged people, victimized, persecuted and brutalized'. He added, 'We must come to the defence of our too-long oppressed people quickly and effectively by all the means at our disposal . . . If we will not help them in their hour of need let us not hinder them.' When he had finished, two other Labour TDs indicated their agreement, David Thornley saying pointedly, 'This is the authentic voice of the Labour Party,' and Stephen Coughlan adding, 'Definitely.'[95]

Thornley soon hammered his point home by describing O'Brien as 'the so-called spokesman on Northern Ireland', and argued that O'Brien's criticism of Article 2 of Bunreacht na hÉireann, coupled with the fact that that Article appeared also in Labour's own constitution, meant that 'the abandonment of party policy automatically disqualifies Dr O'Brien from membership of the party let alone being a spokesman for it', drawing a public rebuke from the party whip, Frank Cluskey.[96] The Minister for Finance, George Colley, alleged that O'Brien's policy amounted to 'nothing less than acquiescence in the right of the national minority [i.e. the northern Protestants] to dictate the destiny of our people', adding that 'all our troubles began when 50 years ago a British government made a similar mistake'.[97] O'Brien's 'abandonment of the national position' went beyond any concession the IPP leader John Redmond would have made. This attack disturbed some Labour members, who feared that Fianna Fáil might win over some of its supporters if Labour seemed 'soft on the national question'. Voters might not take the trouble to think about the complexities of the two communities view; they might simply see the issue as one of how strongly parties were prepared to stand up for Ireland against Britain. The private arguments within Labour became more bitter, and in December 1971 an attempt within the PLP to have O'Brien removed from the northern spokesmanship was defeated, apparently by just one vote.[98]

Labour's disunity emerged even more starkly after the killing in County Tyrone of the Northern Ireland Senator John Barnhill by a unit of the Official IRA, which explained that Barnhill had attacked it when it came to blow up his house.[99] Michael O'Leary, deputising as party spokesman for Dr O'Brien, who was abroad, stated that the onus rested on the Taoiseach to bring the officers and members of the IRA executive before the courts as accessories to the crime.[100] At a PLP meeting David Thornley suggested wryly that O'Brien should be asked to return at once, since his surrogate was even worse than he was. In the Dáil he said that Barnhill's death had been 'excessively deplored' by some people, and went on:[101]

If the implication of that statement [i.e. O'Leary's] is that Irish soldiers or Irish police are ever to be put into a position where they act as felon-setters for Mr Brian Faulkner, I want to dissociate myself totally from that statement ... I think that those who go across the border into Northern Ireland to carry out armed attacks upon Unionist installations should not be placed in the same category as ordinary criminals in this part of Ireland. I do not propose that it should be the function of the gardai to collect them and to hand them over for extradition.

When a Fianna Fáil TD asked whether his view was Labour policy, he replied, 'It is the policy of the grassroots of the Labour Party.' He also accused some of his 'colleagues' of 'repeating the historical mistakes made in the past and apparently turning the path of Labour away from the Republican tradition'.

Stephen Coughlan, who had sat next to Thornley and shown his approval throughout his speech, stated that he was 'not a party' to the Treaty 'and never will be'.[102] Seán Treacy, who was away from Leinster House through illness, sent Corish a telegram saying, 'Dump O'Brien and O'Leary fast. Only hope of saving party from national disgrace and political annihilation. What price internment and repression now?' and he too said that he would not act as a 'felon-setter' for the northern government.[103] Thornley's speech drew criticism from outside the party ranks. The Fine Gael deputy leader, Tom O'Higgins, alluding to Thornley's attitude to the use of violence, commented sharply that 'we can afford no fifth column in this Parliament',[104] and the parliamentary correspondent of the *Irish Times* suggested that Thornley had come close to describing Barnhill as a legitimate target for the IRA, and called his speech the most 'chilling' of all the 'shabby notes' sounded in the Dáil in the previous two years.[105]

Thornley's claim that his views were those of the 'grass roots' of the party is impossible to verify, but contemporary opinion poll evidence, from a survey carried out by Irish Marketing Surveys in May 1970, suggests that Labour supporters were more republican than supporters of the other two main parties, while only a minority favoured the most militant options offered in the questionnaire. If the events of August 1969 happened again, 24·6 per cent of Labour supporters thought the Irish army should move into the north, as opposed to 18·1 per cent of Fianna Fáil supporters and 12·0 per cent of Fine Gael supporters, and 16·7 per cent approved of arms being supplied from the Republic to 'people in the North'.[106] Thirty per cent of Labour supporters wanted the British troops to leave the north at once, and 18·3 per cent said that they would prefer to see the border go than stay even if this could be achieved only by the use of force; lower proportions of the other parties' supporters agreed with these views.

The 1972 conference was to suggest that, whatever their views on the north, most Labour members did not want to see the party torn apart over the issue, and an IMS survey conducted during the 1973 election campaign found that only 5 per cent of Labour supporters regarded it as the most urgent problem, and only 23·5 per cent ranked it among the three most urgent problems facing the Republic, as against higher proportions of Fianna Fáil and Fine Gael supporters.[107] Consequently, something of a backlash developed towards the end of 1971, with a growing feeling among party members that the PLP's bickering was getting out of hand. The mood was given expression by John O'Connell, who warned that Labour was heading for self-destruction if it continued in its present manner, called for firm leadership, and referred to 'prima donnas' within the party who seemed to consider themselves above criticism.[108] The last point struck a responsive chord among many party supporters, in whose eyes the behaviour of Dr O'Brien and Dr Thornley, both of whom had entered the party only three years earlier, was better suited to a university debating society than to a political party. Some, indeed, were beginning to wonder whether the inflow of the 'intellectuals' had been such a good thing after all. Thornley seemed impetuous and unconcerned by the need for party discipline, while a journalist wrote of Labour TDs' irritation at O'Brien's frequent 'abrupt departures to foreign capitals' to attend showings of his play *Murderous Angels*.[109]

7.5 Defusion and resolution 1972

The focus for party unity was to be a policy statement on the north issued in January 1972. By September 1971, as the next annual report euphemistically observed, 'it was evident that disagreement existed as to the nature of party policy regarding the North',[110] so that the AC and the PLP set up a thirteen-member Northern Committee to prepare a policy statement to be submitted to the next party conference. The committee was on paper a high-powered one, containing three TDs associated with the two communities approach – Barry Desmond, Conor Cruise O'Brien and Michael O'Leary – and the two most prominent traditional nationalists, David Thornley and Seán Treacy, as well as the party leader and the party chairman.[111] Its statement was accepted by a joint meeting of the AC and PLP by twenty-seven votes to three – those opposing it appear to have been two hard-line nationalist TDs and an AC member – and was later accepted also by the 1972 annual conference.[112]

The document was very obviously shaped by more than one hand, and Corish was to admit at the 1972 conference that it had been 'a hurried effort in order to get a sense of unity in the party'. Labour's 'fundamental objective' was 'the establishment of an all-Ireland Socialist Republic', and its main principle was 'the voluntary reunion of all Irish people and territory'. It unequivocally repudiated the use of force to achieve a united Ireland. However, it stated, this was not to be interpreted as 'acquiescence in . . . the political division of the island'; on the contrary, Labour was 'unconditionally opposed to the built-in official violence practised by the Unionist Government'. The party demanded 'that the sectarian Unionist regime in the North must be brought to an end', aimed at 'the withdrawal of the British Troops as soon as a political solution permits', called for the ending of internment, and supported the idea of 'talks between the elected public representatives of all the parties concerned'. Finally, it 'recognised' that the present troubles were caused partly by 'the deliberate worsening of relations between Catholics and Protestants by landowners and capitalists' and by 'the economic situation in the whole island'.

Overall, the statement was such that no one person could agree with it in its entirety, but on certain crucial points it marked a defeat for the most militant members of the traditional nationalist wing. Violence was repudiated, the stipulation that those involved in talks should be elected public representatives ruled out the IRA, and it implied that the achievement or imminence of a political solution had to precede the withdrawal of the British troops. The desire for 'the voluntary union of all Irish people and territory' was highly ambiguous, for, like the phrase 'unity by consent', it did not make clear what was needed before union could be considered 'voluntary'. It did not state whether a majority vote in an all-Ireland plebiscite would suffice, or whether there must be a majority within the north, or whether unanimity throughout the island was necessary.

After the document was published Labour's rows subsided briefly, with a tacit agreement that the matter would be resolved by the party conference. The nationalist mood in the country was strengthened after 'Bloody Sunday', 30 January 1972, when thirteen unarmed demonstrators were shot and killed in Derry by British paratroopers, and when, in O'Brien's words, England 'seemed to be acting in the way we often accused her of acting but of which we had not, for decades, really believed modern England capable'.[113] In an understandably emotional Dáil debate held a few days later, those Labour TDs who spoke called for a withdrawal of the British troops, at once or at some future date to be specified, although some, for whom these views were uncharacteristic, soon reverted to their former positions. Conor Cruise O'Brien, Frank Cluskey and Michael O'Leary advocated withdrawal of the troops.[114] James Tully said that Britain should now give freedom to the north, as it had to other areas which it had previously held 'in thrall'. He added, 'This is the old battle of Ireland *v.* England . . . This is an island, thirty-two counties of Irish soil, and we are entitled to every square inch of it.'[115] Stephen Coughlan came close to expressing outright support for the IRA, which, he said, 'speak for more than 80 per cent of the people of Ireland'. When the Minister for Finance appealed to the IRA to leave the task of ending partition to the politicians and 'get out of the way', Coughlan interjected, 'The Minister should get out of their way.'[116]

A fortnight later David Thornley returned to the fray, arguing that Labour should not condemn unreservedly the violence being employed in the north.[117] Instead, it should

identify, as Connolly did, those aspects of the Republican struggle which are essentially reactionary and those which are essentially social, and . . . disown the former and make ourselves the spokesmen of the latter. This we are signally failing to do.

He did not suggest how the party might identify the two aspects. A number of members resigned from the West Galway constituency council out of dissatisfaction with Labour's 'drift to the right', citing O'Brien's attacks on the IRA as an example.[118] The council's secretary stated that he could understand their feelings, since 'we have repeatedly protested about the Quisling attitude to British imperialism'.

The annual conference, held at the end of February, spent a lot of time on the north, debating both the policy statement and a motion to remove O'Brien from the spokemanship.[119] In the end both issues were decided against the more extreme members of the traditional nationalist wing, but the divisions within the party were made very clear by the range of views expressed. The opening speech of the conference, the address of the party chairman, Roddy Connolly, the son of James Connolly, was strongly nationalist in tone. Using terms like 'the British army of occupation', 'the terrorists of the British army' and 'the six-county statelet in the north-east of our country', he too drew a parallel between Brian Faulkner and Vidkun Quisling. Tragedies such as Bloody Sunday sprang from 'the violent occupation of part of our country by troops of a foreign power' and from the continued denial by the 'non-nationalists' of the nationalists' 'right to merge into a new Ireland'. He contrasted the civil rights movement of 'the working people of Derry, of the Falls Road and Ardoyne areas in Belfast' (all Catholic areas) with 'the destructive violence of the lumpen proletariat of the Shankill ghettoes' (a Protestant area). He added, in what did not sound like an unequivocal repudiation of force, that 'non-violent means . . . are the much to be preferred methods in the present circumstances in trying to achieve a solution of the north-east problem'.

Brendan Corish, in his leader's address, took a more nationalist line than he usually did, although the general emphasis was on reconciliation. He put forward four proposals, including the withdrawal of British troops from Catholic areas, the ending of internment, and the replacement of Stormont by a representative commission. The fourth was more controversial; the British government 'should announce a date by which it will withdraw its army and end its control of the area'. This, he maintained, would bring the Unionists to the realisation that they had to live in peace with the rest of the Irish people. In saying this, four weeks after Bloody Sunday, he was expressing a widely held view that Britain was not playing a constructive role in the north, and that it should withdraw before it exacerbated the harm it had already done. This view was by no means confined to Ireland. The fraternal delegate from the British Labour Party, Tony Benn, also said that he felt there was no justification for continued British involvement in Ireland; Britain's role in the north must now be only temporary, and hindered the working out by the Irish people of their own future.

The northern policy statement was generally approved, although without much enthusiasm, since, as several delegates pointed out, it contained many platitudes. Most of the criticism, however, concerned a point on which it was not platitudinous, namely its firm rejection of violence. David Thornley reminded the conference that James Connolly had employed 'physical force', and argued that both wings of the IRA were facts of life and should be brought into any talks held. A Dublin delegate accused the party spokesmen on the north of failing to stress that the northern Protestants 'are a minority of the Irish people, and that they have no right to tell the majority of the Irish people what they want'. A South Tipperary delegate advocated the policy statement's complete rejection and its replacement by a call for the ending of internment, the withdrawal of the British forces, and 'support for the freedom fighters in Northern Ireland in their struggle against British imperialism'. Violence, he said, had 'worked before', most notably between 1916 and 1921.

However, the mood of the conference was clearly against violence. The IRA was no more popular than the British army, for the wave of support it could have expected after Bloody Sunday had been largely dissipated during February 1972 by the burning of the British embassy in Dublin, the killing by the Official IRA of a number of women cleaners in Aldershot, and an assassination attempt on a Northern Ireland Cabinet member. Gerry Fitt, the leader of the SDLP and its fraternal delegate, stated that no Labour member should give any support to either wing of the IRA. The conference accepted the policy statement, and rejected all those amendments which the leadership had declared unacceptable.

The composite motion calling for the removal of O'Brien from the northern spokesmanship was moved by Seán Treacy. He referred to O'Brien's 'conservative, right-wing expressions' and accused him of having denigrated James Connolly, betrayed Labour's constitution and, along with Noel Browne, given comfort and solace to the Stormont regime. He could no longer subscribe to 'a brand of spineless, supine, unprincipled shoneenism' which was 'anti-Irish and anti-Labour'. He had been amazed, he said, that 'the extreme socialists in this party were the first to renege when the war of liberation was on in this country'. Among those opposing the motion were two Dublin TDs, Barry Desmond and Frank Cluskey, the latter saying that he supported O'Brien's position because he believed it had 'a tremendous amount of socialist content'. O'Brien himself denied that he had denigrated the dead or that he was, as some of his critics alleged, 'peddling any so-called two nations theory'.[120] The censure motion had arisen mainly because of his repudiation of violence, he said, and if it were passed it would consequently cast doubt on the earlier acceptance of the policy statement.

Treacy's speech was greeted with as much booing as applause, and the motion would undoubtedly have been defeated, but in the event it was withdrawn, after Paddy Devlin of the SDLP had urged this in the cause of party unity. Treacy stated that he had been heartened by O'Brien's speech; many of the uncertainties had been cleared up, and Labour now had a policy document with which they could all agree. The debate ended with O'Brien and Treacy shaking hands, to general applause.

The conference debates unquestionably cleared the air, and led to a sharp reduction in the amount of public argument between Labour TDs on the north. The conference had come out in favour of the unequivocal repudiation of violence, and O'Brien had been in effect confirmed in his spokesmanship. However, it would be wrong to conclude that the conference had endorsed all of O'Brien's views and rejected the traditional nationalist interpretation which he opposed so strongly. For one thing, the policy statement which it approved was a rather incongruous mixture of views from the two wings of the party. For another, many centrist delegates, while uneasy about O'Brien's soft-line approach, were even less attracted by the apparent readiness of some of his opponents, including Treacy, to tolerate violence, and if the anti-O'Brien motion had been passed Treacy would have had a strong claim to the spokesmanship.

Thirdly, many delegates seem to have regarded the real issue at stake as being not the party's attitude to the north but the wider one of whether it should revert to its pre-1967 non-socialist image. Tension between right and left was high, partly because of the contraceptives Bill vote only three weeks earlier. Many rural delegates of traditional nationalist views seem to have regarded O'Brien's northern policy as merely another aspect of an attempt by the new members of the late 1960s to swing the party away from its 'tried and true' approach to politics. In his speech Treacy stated, with allusions that were not lost on either left-wing or right-wing delegates, that he was 'asking this conference therefore, the rank and file, the poltroons and the backwoodsmen, to win back the soul of this party, to take over once again and control its destiny'. Similarly, some left-wing delegates whose views on the north differed from O'Brien's spoke against the motion to remove him from the spokesmanship. One, Brendan Scott, acknowledging that many 'sincere socialists' did not like O'Brien's policy, warned, referring to the contraception vote, that 'their sincere desire for a change of policy might be used by some of the unholy relics of Sadleir and Keogh's Brass Band, the pre-Vatican I crozier-shying rump who have proved their contempt for any form of civil rights only recently in the Dáil'.[121]

The conference itself, then, did not unequivocally mark the defeat of the traditional nationalist wing, but events in the north now began to undermine completely the position of its most militant members. Stormont was prorogued on 24 March 1972, and the British government appointed a Secretary of State for the north. He appeared to operate the policy of direct rule even-handedly, which inevitably brought him into conflict with Unionist politicians more often than with Catholics, further blurring the traditional southern perception of the British as the instigators of Unionist obduracy. A British Green Paper issued in October drew favourable responses from the southern parties.[122] Support for the IRA was also much harder to justify, since once Stormont had gone it had no credible defence to the accusation that it was attempting to 'bomb a million Protestants into the Republic'.

No more serious disputes arose within Labour until October 1972, although hints of division surfaced twice. In March Dr John O'Connell arranged talks between the Provisional IRA and the British opposition leader Harold Wilson, and described proposals by the former, which included a demand that the British declare an intention to leave the north, as 'responsible and realistic', while stating that 'I will not ever condone violence or brutality, no matter for what justification'.[123] There were suggestions of an attempt to expel him from the PLP, some TDs feeling that to involve members of paramilitary bodies in talks confers legitimacy on them and encourages them to believe that they can 'bomb their way to the conference table',[124] but in the end a new 'code of party conduct' was adopted. No action was taken when O'Connell arranged further Wilson–IRA talks in July.[125] Some disagreement also arose at the ITGWU annual conference, when some delegates sought to have the union disaffiliate from Labour mainly because of the 'anti-national views' of some Labour TDs, but it was withdrawn at the request of the general secretary, although the conference went on to call for the immediate withdrawal of British troops from the north, and one delegate urged Labour to 'get rid of the people who advocate the policy of felon-setting' if it wanted to regain its 'image as an Irish socialist party'.[126]

The basic division within the PLP still existed, even though it was no longer being exposed to the public gaze, and it erupted for the last time in the autumn of 1972 after the SDLP published a policy document, *Towards a New Ireland*. The document advocated joint British–Irish sovereignty over the north, and called on the British government to state that it believed that it would be in the best interests of all if Ireland were eventually united. Fianna Fáil reacted enthusiastically to the proposals, but Labour's response was cooler.[127] There were no formal links between Labour and the SDLP, although in November 1971 Brendan Corish had mooted the curious idea of a complete merger, to form a thirty-two-county socialist party to work for a thirty-two-county socialist republic.[128] Attempts to revive the Council of Labour, with the SDLP and NILP as co-members, had failed, owing mainly to differences between the northern parties, and it did not meet again.[129]

Nevertheless, the SDLP had expected better from Labour, and its chief whip, Paddy Devlin, stated that relations between the two parties had been permanently damaged. Its deputy leader, John Hume, clashed with Conor Cruise O'Brien in a radio debate, since O'Brien's view was that the substance of the document was such as to weaken moderate Protestant opinion, and that to insist on progress towards unity in present circumstances was 'unwittingly and unintentionally a formula for civil war'.[130] In mid-October John O'Connell tabled a motion at a PLP meeting declaring that the PLP supported the document, which was opposed by O'Brien. A victory for the motion, which would probably have ended O'Brien's shaky reign as spokesman, was forestalled only by an amendment by Corish which suggested that the party meet the SDLP for discussions. The amendment was passed, but only on Corish's own casting vote, and it seems that several TDs supported it only out of loyalty to the leader, and on the following day the AC accepted the motion O'Connell had put before the PLP.[131] More SDLP criticism followed, Austin Currie alleging that the PLP's refusal to support the SDLP document was a 'face-saving charade' for O'Brien's benefit.[132] However, the ILP–SDLP discussion meeting itself was not quite as explosive as had been feared, and although some of the SDLP participants were very critical of O'Brien the ILP members present explained that their criticisms of the document sprang not from hostility to the SDLP but from a feeling that they should be honest with their friends, and the two party leaders managed to prevent an open breach developing.[133]

This proved to be the last serious challenge to O'Brien's position. His own constituency council, with which he had had his differences, declared its support for the January policy statement, and the West Galway constituency council, which earlier in the year had been critical of him, now stated that it would oppose any attempt to replace him as northern spokesman.[134] Noel Browne denounced both the SDLP, which he described as a new version of the Nationalist Party, and its 'silly, pretentious, irresponsible and pompous' policy document.[135] Gerry Fitt indicated some agreement with O'Brien's views, and accused Fianna Fáil, which he described as the 'political Siamese twin' of Unionism, of having 'done nothing' for the north over the years.[136] A PLP meeting at which yet another attempt to displace O'Brien had been expected passed off peacefully, with an agreement to consign a discussion of the Northern Ireland question to the safe limbo of the non-existent Council of Labour.[137]

A visit paid by David Thornley to the Provisional IRA leader Seán MacStiofain in the Mater Hospital in Dublin served only to emphasise his isolation within the PLP. MacStiofain had been sentenced to six months' imprisonment for being an IRA member, and had been taken to the hospital because he was on hunger strike. After an unsuccessful armed attempt to free him, an estimated 7,000 demonstrators marched to the hospital to demand his release.[138] They included Thornley, who said he could not stand by and see an Irishman die of a hunger strike and urged that MacStiofain be released while the Dáil 'debated the issue'. Several public bodies around the country, mirroring the behaviour of county councils in 1957, called for his release on 'humanitarian grounds'. Thornley was reprimanded in the Dáil by Noel Browne, who also criticised the visits paid to MacStiofain by John Charles McQuaid and his successor as Archbishop of Dublin,[139] and drew no public support from any Labour member. Indeed, Labour was able to put on a rare show of public unity in the Dáil vote on the controversial Offences against the State Bill in late 1972, since it was unanimously opposed to such measures while in opposition, some members being concerned that they were illiberal and others that they were anti-republican.

The question of the north played little part in the 1973 election campaign, even though it seemed to have dominated Irish politics since 1971. Apart from suggestions that 'subversives' would have an easy time under a divided, indecisive coalition government, the only serious Fianna Fáil attack on Labour's approach came from George Colley, who argued that O'Brien was in effect suggesting that the Republic wash its hands of the fate of the northern Catholics, who would have been 'at the mercy of the Unionists' for the previous three years had not the Irish government been looking after their interests.[140] At the election Conor Cruise O'Brien's vote rose numerically but fell slightly in percentage terms, David Thornley's fell sharply, while Seán Treacy's rose considerably. The low importance accorded by voters to the northern question, however, means that these fluctuations in individuals' votes can by no means be attributed entirely to their perceived attitudes to Northern Ireland.

7.6 Conclusion

Many of Labour's problems on this issue were caused by the fact that the views of its TDs alone covered virtually the whole spectrum of opinion within the Republic, and were exacerbated by the circumstance that its spokesman was near to one end of the spectrum rather than in the centre, and was setting out deliberately to challenge the interpretation which had hitherto been taken for granted in the south. It was the sort of subject on which feelings were inevitably strong and passionate, and there was often a genuine fear that the PLP might split or at least suffer defections.

Very often the public wrangling of Labour TDs was not edifying, and their remarks were sometimes couched in unnecessarily personal terms, but underneath the mud-slinging serious issues were being aired. In a way, Labour's reaction was a more honest one than the other parties', in that it reflected the confusion felt by many in the Republic. Open debate is all too rare within Irish parties, and the arguments within Labour on this issue meant that the electorate was given much more food for thought than it would have received if the party's internal dissent had been stifled. Similarly, Irish parties have been justifiably accused of not displaying leadership and of moving at the pace of the most conservative sections of the electorate, but in this instance Labour could not be said to have adopted a safe and traditional line. Whatever the merits of the rival views of the combatants, they were not expressed with one eye on the opinion polls.

The apparently widespread belief that socialism and republicanism are related creeds is not borne out by Labour's experience in the early 1970s. Although each of the conflicting groups accused its rivals of holding the more right-wing views, of those TDs most closely associated with the traditional nationalist viewpoint – Stephen Coughlan, John O'Donovan, Dan Spring, David Thornley and Seán Treacy – only Thornley was on the left of the PLP when it came to social and economic matters, and Coughlan and Spring were among the most right-wing TDs. Of their most prominent opponents – Noel Browne, Frank Cluskey, Barry Desmond, Conor Cruise O'Brien and Michael O'Leary – all were on the left of the PLP, of which Browne was certainly the most left-wing member.

In fact the division largely, though not entirely, followed the lines of the urban–rural divide noticeable within the PLP after the 1969 election. A more republican attitude among TDs from rural constituencies – especially those in the south-west, such as Kerry, Limerick and Tipperary, represented by Spring, Coughlan and Treacy respectively – could be attributed either to a direct relationship between ignorance and distance from the border[141] or to the traditionally republican nature of these constituencies, which were the strongholds of the IRA in the 1918–21 period and of the anti-Treatyites during the civil war. However, this does not wholly explain the relationship between republicanism and general conservatism. The most likely explanation is that many traditional nationalists saw the emergence of the two communities approach as yet another step on the road away from the pre-1967 party to which they wanted to return, a point which emerged during the 1972 conference debates. It is reasonable to assume that those who clung to traditional views despite the fresh developments of the 1970s were those who were least receptive to new ideas in general, and such people could be expected to be on the right of the party.

8

The coalition question, 1957–73

8.1 The background, 1922–57

During the first thirty-five years of the State, Labour had experience of all three options open to a minor party. It spent twenty-five years in opposition, six in government as part of a coalition with other parties, and four giving external support to a single-party government.

None of these experiences was very satisfactory. In theory, a party might benefit from being in opposition, by developing a coherent overall policy and a long-term strategy. It might, indeed, consciously choose to remain in opposition; it might feel, for example, that if it joined a coalition it would be breathing life into a dying party, or would be preventing the emergence of a new political alignment in which its prospects would be much more favourable. Labour, however, evolved no striking set of policies while out of office, and the twenty-five years it spent there were due not to a careful balancing of long-term considerations against short-term opportunities but to the simple fact that no alternatives were on offer.

Between 1932 and 1936 Labour gave external support to Fianna Fáil administrations. After the 1932 election the seven Labour TDs voted for de Valera when the Dáil met to elect a new President of the Executive Council, a crucial decision, since Fianna Fáil held only seventy-two of the 153 seats. For a while Labour was consulted on projected legislation in return for supporting the government in the Dáil, but the relationship, whose exact nature is still unclear, broke down around 1936 for reasons which are also unknown.[1] Although in theory a minor party giving external support to a government might enjoy power without responsibility, and might be able to take credit for the government's popular policies while avoiding both the odium of its unpopular ones and the risk of losing its identity, in practice things did not work out like that for Labour. Voters who approved of the nature of Fianna Fáil's policies do not seem to have attributed them to any extent to Labour's efforts, while Fine Gael and its allies accused Labour of being partly responsible for them. The alliance nearly cost Labour not only its identity but its very existence; at the 1933 election it won only eight seats and 80,000 votes out of the 1·4 million cast. In 1932 it had hoped that enabling Fianna Fáil to enter office might be to its own electoral advantage, since it might now attract the working-class protest vote which had previously gone to Fianna Fáil.[2] It soon came to realise, however, that helping Fianna Fáil into power was a lot easier than getting it out again, and during the 1930s Fianna Fáil increased its working-class support, especially in Dublin.

During the 1930s relationships between the two parties cooled. The passage of transfers between them declined greatly,[3] and Labour abstained on the vote on de Valera's renomination after the 1938 election. Labour grew steadily more disenchanted with what it saw as Fianna Fáil's increasing conservatism, and was inclined to blame Fianna Fáil for engineering the 1944–45 split in the ITUC and the party itself. After the 1944 election, consequently, Labour joined Fine Gael for the first time in voting against Fianna Fáil. Seven of its eight TDs opposed de Valera's renomination, the eighth abstaining, whereas three of the four National Labour TDs supported it, the fourth being 'detained at a meeting of Kerry County Council'.[4]

After this vote, it was only a matter of time before the opposition parties realised the logic of their position and accepted that a coalition was necessary if Fianna Fáil was ever to be prised out of office. Up to this point Labour in particular was trapped in a vicious circle (see Fig. 8.1). If it did well at an election, the ensuing single-party government was not stable and consequently called another election as soon as possible. In this, Labour suffered, partly because its resources had been drained by the previous election, and partly because voters gravitated towards the larger parties in the hope that a stable government would emerge. Thus Labour fared worse in 1923 than in 1922, in September 1927 than in June 1927, in 1933 than in 1932, in 1938 than in 1937, and in 1944 than in 1943. The party did well if it had had a chance to build up its resources after several years of stable government, but this simply set the cycle off again. The vicious circle could be broken only by ensuring that an election at which Labour did well produced a stable government, which in practice meant a coalition involving Labour.

Figure 8.1 Labour strength and government stability, 1922–44

The idea of an anti-Fianna Fáil united front was given impetus by the success in the 1945 presidential election of the Independent Patrick McCartan, whose candidacy was supported by Labour,[5] and by Clann na Poblachta's success in the October 1947 by-elections.[6] In Labour's official newspaper there was a lot of discussion of the possibility of a coalition – though Fine Gael was not envisaged as a participant – and at the 1948 election the paper advised its readers to give a preference to all candidates when voting, and to put the Fianna Fáil candidates last.[7] During the same campaign a Cork Labour candidate, who later became a TD, declared that coalitions were stable, progressive and democratic, and that the workers must ensure that they were represented by a 'strong and virile force of Labour TDs in a coalition government'.[8]

Fianna Fáil's failure to come close to a majority of seats at the election led to discussions among the other parties and the eventual emergence of the first Inter-Party government.[9] Labour's decision to participate did not require a special conference, and does not seem to have attracted much criticism from the rank and file.[10] The National Labour Party posed the biggest problems, since its five TDs were urged by the CIU to support de Valera's renomination, but the TDs flatly refused to do so and were accused of 'betrayal of the Trade unions' at the next CIU conference,[11] an episode which shows that the traditional perception of National Labour as simply a CIU Party is inaccurate. Labour received two of the thirteen Ministries; discounting the Independent Minister and the Independent TDs who supported the government, this amounted to 16·7 per cent of the Ministries, which meant that it was slighly under-represented, since its seats amounted to 20·9 per cent of the coalition's total.

On the whole, both the party itself and its supporters seem to have been reasonably satisfied with this first experience of government; at the 1951 election Labour won 11·4 per cent of the votes, as against the 11·3 per cent won by Labour and National Labour combined in 1948. At the 1954 election Labour campaigned on its own policies while advocating the reinstatement of the coalition, and again its votes rose. Again, it did not need to do much heart-searching before deciding to join the second Inter-Party government; a special conference unanimously decided that it should do so, whereas Clann na Talmhan decided to join the government only after twelve hours of meetings.[12] On this occasion Labour was slightly over-represented in the government, supplying 25·7 per cent of the coalition's Dáil strength but receiving 30·8 per cent of the Ministries.

The second Inter-Party government was a much less satisfactory experience for Labour. Between 1948 and 1951 it had been reasonably effective in the areas under its control, especially social welfare and housing, and had kept its own supporters contented. Between 1954 and 1957, however, it suffered the fate always feared by a minor party entering a coalition government: it was unable to prevent the government adopting policies to which it objected, but it was criticised by its supporters for apparently backing them, since the constraints of collective Cabinet responsibility meant that it could not make its opposition to them public. The last year of the second Inter-Party government, as has been seen (see Chapter 2.1 above), was a very unhappy one for Labour.

Although the question of whether a party should join a coalition is one which actually arises only at an indecisive general election, all parties, especially those with some sort of distinct ideology, are likely to have contingency plans to deal with such a situation, particularly if such factors as the electoral system and recent political history suggest that it is highly likely to arise. Such an important issue cannot be divorced from the party's overall long-term strategy, and in Labour's case the question of whether or not it should be prepared to enter a coalition government as a junior partner was the most important item of strategy facing it at all times between 1957 and 1973.

Irish political scientists frequently take pleasure in arguing that the theories, models and categorisation schemes which seem to be appropriate for most countries do not fit the realities of political life in Ireland, and certainly the large and growing amount of literature[13] whose aim is to formulate a theory of coalitions, or to predict the combination of parties most likely to form a coalition after an indecisive election, does not help much in the Irish context. The nature of the party system ensures that there is never any suspense about which parties might be involved in a possible coalition. Because Fianna Fáil invariably either wins, or comes close to winning, a majority of the seats at each election, it has come to the conclusion that its 'winning strategy' is to have nothing to do with any proposed coalitions, and to make a virtue of its position by attacking the very concept of coalition government whenever it raises its head.

Fianna Fáil's enviable strategic position in the Irish party system can never be overlooked, for it enables the party to make capital out of whatever relationship exists between the opposition parties. If the possibility of coalition is in the air, it can and does raise the issue of the supposed advantages of single-party governments over coalitions, which must inevitably, it maintains, be weak, indecisive, vacillating and rent by internal conflicts. Thus in 1973 Jack Lynch declared, 'Coalitions are formed on platitudes. They fall apart on fundamentals.'[14] In addition, it can take advantage of its image, accurate or not, as the centre party to attract some Labour supporters by arguing that their party is selling them out to a right-wing party, while at the same time winning votes from Fine Gael supporters disturbed by the prospect of a government with a Labour component.

On the other hand, if one of the opposition parties rules out the idea of a coalition, then Fianna Fáil can point out that there is no alternative government and argue that political instability will ensue unless it wins a majority. Its ability to use this 'Heads we win, tails you lose' argument against the opposition makes it extremely unlikely that Fianna Fáil will ever take part in a coalition unless it suffers a sustained and significant drop in support. With Fianna Fáil thus out of the market, the important question is not which parties will combine, but whether the other parties are prepared to combine with each other. Labour, unlike most social democratic parties, has to decide only whether it should be prepared to take part in a coalition; it is spared the dilemma of whether a centre–left alliance is to be preferred to a united-left alliance.

8.2 The coalition and the 1957 general election

Labour entered the 1957 election campaign with little enthusiasm for the coalition idea and emerged from it with less. Indeed, none of the parties in the outgoing government was very keen to prolong its suffering, and so none of them offered more than vague and half-hearted defences of the coalition's record. None of the parties informed the electorate, and in the pre-press conference era none was asked, whether it would take part in another Inter-Party government after the election if the possibility arose. A suggestion from John Costello that Fine Gael supporters vote 'all the way through',[15] imprecise as it was, seems to have been the only call from any party for an exchange of transfers with its coalition partners.

Labour's already lukewarm feelings about the alliance with Fine Gael were cooled further by two factors. The first was that Gerard Sweetman, the Fine Gael Finance Minister and in Labour's eyes the architect of the government's austerity policies, made it clear that he had no sympathy with suggestions that government policy move to the left. Fine Gael, he said, stood for unbridled free enterprise and a minimum of State intervention; 'we reject socialism with its planned direction of capital and labour as something foreign and detestable to our way of life'.[16] Even though Labour eschewed the word 'socialism', Sweetman's message was unambiguous. The policy of another coalition government, it seemed to Labour, was likely to be as conservative as that of the last one.

Secondly, Labour was alienated by Fine Gael's apparent readiness to ditch it in favour of an alliance with Fianna Fáil. This possibility, or that of an all-party 'national government', remains a shadowy episode, and it is not clear how much fire there was beneath the smoke. The idea of an all-party government was first floated by William Norton in July 1956, and he repeated the suggestion six months later,[17] but for a while it seemed likely to rebound on Labour. A 'grand coalition', or even a merger, between Fianna Fáil and Fine Gael was promoted by two national and several provincial newspapers, and by Deputy Anthony Barry and Senator James Crosbie of Fine Gael. It was alleged that these two had had discussions with Seán Lemass and Seán MacEntee, and perhaps with de Valera. According to some accounts, they had proposed that de Valera and Mulcahy would retire from politics and the two parties would merge under the leadership of Lemass.[18] Norton claimed that Lemass and MacEntee had reacted favourably but de Valera had vetoed the proposal; from the Fianna Fáil side there were denials that the idea had ever got off the ground.[19] Attempts to maintain that the President favoured the plan, on the ground that in 1952 he had called for the restoration of the pre-1922 unity in 'the Republican ranks', were of no avail,[20] for de Valera killed the idea by issuing his familiar condemnation of coalitions.[21] Norton repeated his allegations of secret talks and called for a full disclosure of the facts 'even if it causes embarrassment to all connected with the negotiations'.[22] Less ardent coalitionists than he were even more annoyed, and for many Labour members the affair reminded them that, in the last analysis, Fianna Fáil and Fine Gael both 'came out of the same pod'.[23]

Although the flow of transfers between parties may not provide entirely reliable evidence about the feelings of party supporters,[24] there seems little doubt that in 1957 Labour voters were not keen on the idea of another coalition. After all the Labour candidates had been eliminated, little more than a third of Labour transfers went to Fine Gael candidates in situations where the latter were available to receive them (see Table 8.1). Since this figure is based on counts in fourteen constituencies, more than half those in which Labour candidates stood, it can be taken as a reliable indication of Labour supporters' feelings. Over 70 per cent of Fine Gael transfers went to Labour in corresponding circumstances, but this situation arose in only two constituencies. With a higher rate of transfers from Labour, Fine Gael would have gained an extra seat in both Dún Laoghaire and South Tipperary.

Table 8.1 *Cross-transferring between Fine Gael and Labour, 1957–81*

	1957	1961	1965	1969	1973	1977	1981
From Labour to:							
Fianna Fáil	20.8	30.6	23.9	14.2	7.6	12.5	19.2
Fine Gael	37.3	34.1	52.7	34.5	71.9	58.8	56.6
Others	27.0	24.1	10.8	4.6	5.8	13.5	7.7
Non-transferable	14.9	11.1	12.7	46.6	14.7	15.2	16.5
N (constituencies)	28,110(14)	18,537(14)	17,374(12)	49,843(21)	31,470(16)	30,497(14)	43,513(19)
From Fine Gael to:							
Fianna Fáil	11.3	17.5	14.6	16.0	7.5	10.3	13.2
Labour	70.0	21.5	55.0	33.4	70.9	72.3	86.8
Others	2.6	14.5	—	1.8	0.8	—	—
Non-transferable	16.1	46.5	30.4	48.7	20.7	17.4	0
N (constituencies)	4,548(2)	10,548(4)	15,951(8)	19,131(9)	12,270(7)	13,221(9)	1,915(2)

Note. The figures, in percentages, show the destination of transfers from each party when no candidate of that party, but a candidate of the other party, was available to receive transfers. The N refers to the total number of votes involved in such transfers, and the figures in brackets to the number of constituencies in which such situations arose.

In 1957 2·0 per cent of the Labour transfers, here recorded as having passed to 'Others', went to Clann na Talmhan, which was another of the coalition parties.

The comprehensive defeat suffered by the government, which won only fifty-five seats against Fianna Fáil's seventy-eight, made completely hypothetical the question of whether Labour would have joined another coalition if the possibility had arisen. The only answer which can be given is that the factors which were responsible for Labour's dissatisfaction, such as high unemployment, were also responsible for the government's defeat. Only if they had not existed could the government have won the election, and in such circumstances Labour would have had no reason to be reluctant to take part in a third Inter-Party government.

8.3 The success of an independent strategy, 1957–65

The 1957 election result, terminating as it did a very unhappy period in government, reinforced a growing belief within Labour that participation in coalitions was not in the party's interests. The 1957 annual conference, held mainly in private sessions, overwhelmingly passed a resolution calling for 'the drafting of a comprehensive statement of policy on the basis that Labour will not again take part in an Inter-Party government'. It would remain in opposition until it achieved a parliamentary majority. Party chairman James Tully maintained that Labour had gained a little and lost a lot by taking part in previous coalitions; in future, it should stick to its own programme, put up enough candidates to form a government, and 'not deviate one inch' until it reached its goal.[25]

This decision, an ambitious one to be taken by a demoralised party with only twelve TDs, was the starting point of the policy which was to culminate in the 1969 election campaign. It was not only an emotional reaction to the disappointment of the last coalition; it was a conscious decision, the first ever taken, to pursue an independent line. The party's strategists believed that Fianna Fáil would be seriously weakened when de Valera stepped down, and that Fine Gael was probably moribund, since it did not appear to stand for anything in particular. Consequently, they believed, the existing party system was in its death throes, and Labour should remain aloof until it had collapsed and the dust had settled, after which a new left–right party system would emerge.

Although there was not much sense in Labour's attempting to grow to majority status without distinctive policies, these took another ten years to arrive. A Dublin Regional Council motion passed by the 1959 annual conference, calling on the AC to publish a comprehensive policy document within a year on the basis of the assumption that Labour would not be taking part in any further coalitions,[26] produced no result. Nevertheless the anti-coalition policy was confirmed by the 1960 conference, and by Brendan Corish in two interviews,[27] in which he reaffirmed that Labour would not join a coalition, although it might support a minority government, and suggested that 'the conservative elements' in the two major parties should merge. The very fact that Corish was now party leader was of significance, for he had always seemed less impressed by the coalition idea than Norton, and had on occasions been very critical of the previous government's record.[28] Labour voters too seemed anti-coalition, for only 29·1 per cent of Labour transfers went to Fine Gael at by-elections between 1957 and 1961.

Nevertheless, as the 1961 election approached, not all political commentators, and presumably not all of the electorate either, were certain that another Fine Gael–Labour coalition was not on the cards. Not many Labour TDs had actually endorsed the go-it-alone approach, while one, Michael Pat Murphy, who in 1969 was to acknowledge that he had never been an anti-coalitionist, had spoken approvingly of Labour's particpation in the second Inter-Party government.[29] Moreover, in 1960 Dan Desmond, the party's deputy leader, had admitted that not all PLP members felt bound by the anti-coalition decision of the 1957 conference, which they believed could easily be overturned by calling a special conference after the next election.[30] Fine Gael certainly seemed willing. James Dillon declared that his party had 'no objection in principle to working with other parties' and 'would be quite prepared to do so',[31] although in fact he was not as attractive a prospective Taoiseach in Labour's eyes as Costello had been, being more of a committed right-winger and less of a pragmatist.

During the campaign itself, though, no Labour candidate deviated from the line that the party would not participate in a coalition after the election whatever the result. Fianna Fáil and Fine Gael were branded 'the twin reactionary parties' or the 'anti-Labour' parties. A Laois-Offaly candidate declared that Labour would not repeat the mistake of joining a coalition, because it had learned that 'when you lie down with the dogs, you get up with fleas'.[32] Fine Gael became cautious, not willing to seem enthusiastic if Labour intended to reject any advances, and aware that the tide was flowing in its favour. Dillon stated that the party would enter government only on the basis of its own policies.[33] The results showed very little transferring between the two parties; barely a third of Labour's terminal transfers went to Fine Gael candidates when these were available, and only a fifth of Fine Gael transfers went to Labour in corresponding circumstances (see Table 8.1). In Wexford, for example, only 39·9 per cent of Brendan Corish's surplus went to the Fine Gael candidate, while in Kildare William Norton's surplus divided practically three to two in favour of Fianna Fáil. With a higher rate of cross-transferring Labour would have won seats in Dublin South Central and Laois-Offaly, and Fine Gael would have gained an extra seat in Longford-Westmeath.

Fianna Fáil's loss of its overall majority at the election seemed to raise the possibility of another coalition, but Corish at once stated that Labour would not join one.[34] In fact the electoral arithmetic virtually ruled one out anyway, for Fianna Fáil had seventy of the 144 seats and Fine Gael and Labour only sixty-three between them. Since the two NPD TDs would not have joined any alliances, the would-be coalition would have needed the support of the Clann na Poblachta TD, both Clann na Talmhan TDs and five of the six Independents to overtake Fianna Fáil. An attempt to construct such an alliance would have been unlikely to succeed, and even if it had the resulting government would have been very shaky, so that if Labour had participated in such an attempt it would have been throwing away its independent image and its credibility for a very meagre price. In other words, expediency alone would have been sufficient cause for Labour to adhere to its independent position, and the sincerity of its anti-coalition statements was not really put to the test.

There was no internal pressure to change the anti-coalition policy in the wake of the reasonably satisfactory election results, and it was reaffirmed by the 1963 annual conference, which also empowered the PLP to try to form a minority government after the next election if the opportunity arose.[35] It was elaborated in the same year by Labour TD Seán Treacy, who looked forward to a merger between the two major parties; there was 'a fundamental difference in outlook' between Labour and Fine Gael, and his party would 'never again permit ourselves to be associated with a party that has so little in common with us from the social and economic point of view'.[36] Corish's reply on the only occasion when he was asked whether Labour might join a coalition was an equivocal one,[37] but this can probably be explained by the imminence of two by-elections at which Labour was hoping to attract Fine Gael supporters' lower preferences.

In fact the evidence of the by-elections held between the 1961 and 1965 general elections suggested that Labour supporters were beginning to look more favourably on Fine Gael, because over half their transfers went to that party in each of the three by-elections in which the Labour candidate was eliminated, while over 70 per cent of Fine Gael transfers passed to Labour in Mid-Cork. Allowance must be made for the fact that in three of the four cases the recipient of the strong transfer was a close relative of the TD whose death had caused the vacancy, and as such would naturally attract transfers from all other candidates on personal rather than party grounds. Moreover, all sorts of local tactical ploys are likely to come into operation at by-elections. Nevertheless, there seems little doubt that as the memory of the second Inter-Party government faded so did Labour voters' aversion to the idea of another coalition.

Despite this, Labour remained adamantly anti-coalitionist during the 1965 election campaign. The party leader, in what became known as 'the Tullamore speech', reiterated that Labour would not enter a coalition after the election, although he did not say what it would do if it held the balance of power, or rule out the possibility of its supporting or trying to form a minority government.[38] James Tully, asked whether a coalition might follow the election, replied that the onus was not on Labour to decide that; it was 'open to Fianna Fáil and Fine Gael to amalgamate and thereby form a Tory administration',[39] and this was the line taken by most Labour candidates. Few Fianna Fáil candidates suggested that a Fine Gael–Labour coalition was likely, and it seems that whereas in 1961 not everyone believed Labour's protestations that it would not participate in another coalition, in 1965 it was accepted that the party would not be joining one.

Once again, the election results ruled out a coalition regardless of the inclinations of the opposition parties, but they also confirmed the evidence of the 1961–65 by-elections by showing a high degree of transferring between Labour and Fine Gael (see Table 8.1). Over half Labour's last transfer went to Fine Gael where possible, a figure higher than that for any previous election, including those of 1951 and 1954, and the figure for transfers from Fine Gael to Labour was the second highest ever. This increase in inter-transferring was probably partly due to the 1963 Electoral Amendment Act, which allowed party labels to appear on the ballot paper for the first time; hitherto, supporters of one party may simply not have known who the other parties' candidates were. In addition, the fall in the number of Independent and minor-party candidates – in 1961 there had been sixty-three, with at least one in thirty-four of the thirty-eight constituencies, but in 1965 there were only twenty, standing in just seventeen constituencies – meant that Labour voters who wanted to maximise the damage done to Fianna Fáil usually had little option but to give their next preference to Fine Gael, and, as Table 8.1 shows, the increase in Labour transfers going to Fine Gael was accounted for by the decrease in the proportion going to other candidates. As before, though, much of the increase must be attributed to the blurring with the passage of time of Fine Gael's image as the villain of the second Inter-Party government, and the development of greater hostility towards the government than towards the other opposition party.

Over the whole country Fine Gael and Labour won 20,000 more votes than Fianna Fáil but won three fewer seats. If transfers had pased between them at the 1973 rate, Labour would have won two extra seats, in Dublin South East and Kerry South, and Fine Gael three, in Dublin South West, Longford-Westmeath and Louth. This would have given Fine Gael fifty seats and Labour twenty-four, so that the two parties could have prevented Fianna Fáil retaining power after the election had they called explicitly for an exchange of lower preferences on tactical grounds.

The go-it-alone strategy had clearly worked very well for Labour between 1957 and 1965. The party had almost doubled its number of seats, had won back its self-respect, and was probably stronger and more cohesive than ever before. On the other hand, it had not managed to win the balance of power, and the reshaping of the party system for which it had hoped had not materialised. De Valera's departure had produced not the collapse of Fianna Fáil but an economic boom and widespread expressions of regret that Lemass had not succeeded him earlier. Fine Gael's *raison d'être* was as hazy as ever, but it had gained more votes between 1957 and 1965 than Labour had. Labour's argument that the two major parties were essentially the same and should merge was falling on deaf ears. Within Labour there remained a minority which was unhappy about the no-coalition strategy and the move to socialism, but the party's course had been set, and there were no attempts to bring about a rethink until after the 1969 general election.

8.4 'The opposition of the Opposition', 1967–69

The coalition question was not debated again until the 1967 annual conference, which discussed a motion stating that since Labour's aim was to present an alternative to 'the two civil war parties', it would not take part in another coalition except as the majority partner.[40] Almost all speakers supported it. Michael O'Leary declared that Labour would be cutting its own throat if it participated in another coalition; its role 'must be to polarize Irish politics, to drive the other parties into one great camp so that we will be left to represent the real interests of the people'. Brendan Corish stated, 'I am against coalition,' but added, 'I am one who abides by the decision of the party whether it is the annual conference, the Administrative Council or the parliamentary party.' After this apparent hint that he would allow his personal anti-coalition feelings to be overruled by the parliamentary party, if the situation arose, he continued in the same curiously ambivalent vein:

What do we do in the event of no party having an overall majority at the next election? We have to decide what our stand is to be. I cannot tell you what we may do. It is a decision that will have to be made by the parliamentary party and the Administrative Council. But having made that decision we should not in any way appear to be giving the kiss of life to the dying parties of Fine Gael and Fianna Fáil.

A few individuals mustered the courage to put the opposing viewpoint, but to most delegates their arguments seemed to betray defeatism and the lingering presence of Nortonism. A delegate from Kiltegan maintained that if Labour wanted political power it would ultimately have to join some sort of coalition, and another said that Fianna Fáil had made 'coalition' seem 'a dirty word', and argued that Labour should take the opportunity of 'getting men into government' when it was offered. Predictably, the motion was passed overwhelmingly.

The statement that Labour hoped to force the two major parties into 'one great camp' is worth considering further. A surprisingly large number of Labour members have always hoped that Fianna Fáil and Fine Gael would 'recognise' that they are at bottom identical and would merge, to form an explicitly conservative party. The workers and small farmers who had hitherto supported one or other of these parties would realise that the new party did not represent their real interests and would switch to Labour. The other parties would be forced to acknowledged that they represented the wealthier sections of society, politics would become realigned along left–right lines, and eventually a Labour government would be elected.

Such a hope has always been completely unrealistic. The absence of basic policy differences between the two parties is only one factor affecting their relationship. Each is steeped in its own traditions, and, for many members, opposing the other party at every turn is the essence of political activity; a merger would take all the fun out of politics. Moreover, Fianna Fáil's record of success is such that the party could not hope to gain by a merger, and indeed there is little to attract either party in the idea. The hope that the major parties would be prepared to form an ugly Goliath is the product of wishful thinking on Labour's part. A Fianna Fáil TD's comment that Labour 'wants the role of the good guy and wants everyone else to play the baddies'[41] seems apposite.

In addition, there is no certainty that a merger really would be in Labour's interests. Labour may be fortunate that the class enemy is politically divided, since this gives it the opportunity to play off one party against the other. If they merged, Labour would have no leverage at all, and if they simply formed an alliance, Irish elections might come to resemble 1945–66 Austrian elections, with two large parties fighting only to increase their representation in the 'grand coalition' they would inevitably form after the election, with the other parties being almost irrelevant.[42] Labour's dream of seeing the two major parties united on one side of an important issue, with itself on the other, finally materialised in the 1972 EEC referendum campaign. The outcome on that occasion – 83·1 per cent of the votes in favour of the course advocated by the major parties – does not support an optimistic assessment of Labour's prospects were the situation to become a regular one.

To force a merger was Labour's long-term aim, but in the short term it hoped to gain mainly at the expense of Fine Gael. With that party disposed of, the way would be clear for a left–right showdown with Fianna Fáil. In 1967 Michael O'Leary described Fine Gael as 'an alliance between the most reactionary elements of the countryside and a certain section of the professional classes of the towns'; it was dominated by the Irish Bar, whose 'antediluvian social views' were well known.[43] Nevertheless, it was hard for Labour to keep maintaining that it had no more in common with Fine Gael than with Fianna Fáil. Fianna Fáil's attempt to change the electoral system gave the two opposition parties a common cause. At a special Labour pro-

PR conference James Tully said that the party should concentrate its fire on the real enemy in the campaign, not on 'those going the same road'. This produced a minute-long standing ovation,[44] possibly an indication of a lurking pro-coalition sentiment that dared not speak its name, but in fact there was little co-operation between Labour and Fine Gael; each ran its own campaign, and there was no sharing of platforms.

During 1967 and 1968 Fine Gael made a number of overtures to Labour. In private discussions some Oireachtas members on the liberal wing of Fine Gael tried to persuade Labour TDs to change their minds on the question of a coalition, and expressed their willingness to give Labour half the seats in a coalition government. They also pointed out that their own position within Fine Gael was weakened, and that of the old guard was strengthened, by Labour's attitude; one of the arguments they used to move their party to the left, that this would facilitate a coalition with Labour, was completely undermined. It is probable, for example, that Declan Costello's decision in January 1969 to retire from politics was caused partly by the weakening of his position as a result of Labour's refusal to consider a coalition. However, their arguments had no impact on Labour, whose leadership's private attitude matched its public one. In fact it is doubtful whether the liberal–conservative balance within Fine Gael would have been significantly altered even if Labour's attitude had been different. Moreover, none of the Fine Gael members making the attractive proposal of half the Cabinet seats in a 'progressive' coalition government was a wholehearted supporter of, or was regarded with much favour by, the leadership of his own party, and it is unlikely that the party as a whole would have ratified the terms of their offer. For its part, Labour made some attempts to entice Costello into the party, but without success.

Overtures were also made in public. Garret FitzGerald maintained that both Fine Gael and Labour were 'parties of the left', and that the future development of Irish politics lay in a closer alliance between them.[45] The Fine Gael backbencher Surgeon Patrick Hogan called for a 'united Party' on the opposition benches, and Senator Benignus O'Quigley advocated a 'united front'.[46] At by-elections Fine Gael TDs urged an exchange of preferences with Labour,[47] and in East Limerick about two-thirds of over 10,000 Fine Gael second preferences went to Labour. At the four by-elections between the 1965 and 1969 elections at which a Labour candidate was eliminated, 51·0 per cent of the

Labour transfers went to Fine Gael and only 23·8 per cent to Fianna Fáil.

These long-range appeals reached a climax in May 1968, when Michael O'Higgins, a senior Fine Gael TD enjoying the confidence of the party leader, made a speech which had previously been approved by the front bench.[48] He called for a 'united front' between Fine Gael and Labour to defeat the government and replace it by a coalition with policies based on Fine Gael's *Just Society* programme. He pointed out that, because of the disunity of the opposition parties, Fianna Fáil had won six of the seven by-elections held since the 1965 general election, even though Fine Gael and Labour combined had won a majority of first preferences in five of them. Labour needed to gain fifty-four seats for a Dáil majority, which would take decades and would mean that 'those now in the party will lose the opportunity to use their talents in government'.

In a statement issued the following day[49] Corish rejected O'Higgins's proposal and reaffirmed Labour's desire to force a realignment in Irish politics:

Fine Gael are a private enterprise party. We are Socialists. It is not sufficient, as Deputy O'Higgins pointed out himself, merely to get rid of Fianna Fáil. The alternative government must have positive policies to implement immediately it comes into office . . . Our aim is, and always has been, to form a Labour government. I do not intend to sacrifice that goal for what may appear as a short-term advantage.

We are at the end of an era in Irish politics and I believe the beginning of a new attitude by the electorate to parties, and particularly policies. Of the three parties one is superfluous. I don't believe that either Fianna Fáil or Fine Gael would suggest it is Labour. We are moving towards a two-party system of the left and the right. The logical and desirable development in Irish politics would be for those who believe in the socialist philosophy and the just society in either of the other two parties to join Labour and work for a Labour government.

He declared that Labour and Fine Gael differed on many issues, including the role of the State, the Anglo-Irish Free Trade Agreement, the promotion and management of industry, legislation against trade unions, the EEC, taxation, and public control of financial institutions. Within a fortnight this drew a cold rejoinder from Liam Cosgrave, who declared that only Fine Gael had the capacity to provide an alternative to Fianna Fáil. He continued, obviously alluding to Labour: 'Political theorists may get emotional satisfaction by talking about Utopian conditions in the future, which they will never have responsibility for bringing into effect'.[50]

Public pressure from Fine Gael now came to an end, but the question was raised again from a surprising quarter when Dr Noel Browne, the most prominent anti-coalitionist of the post-1969 period, argued the pro-coalition case in a long newspaper article.[51] The party, he said, was unnecessarily frightened by the word 'coalition'. The one-party versus inter-party debate was 'completely irrelevant'; the reason Labour had lost support after the second Inter-Party government was that none of its Ministers had achieved anything worthwhile in office. Here he was repeating an argument put forward in 1957 by James Larkin, that the important question was not whether Labour joined a coalition but what it did once inside a coalition government.[52] Labour's reluctance to consider a coalition, continued Browne, suggested that it did not trust itself to 'outwit' Fine Gael within the Cabinet. Many Continental socialist parties had gone into coalition with conservative ones; did Ireland's workers' republic have to have 'a purely Labour gestation'? For a party in Labour's position to insist that it did was 'an absurdly doctrinaire and bigoted and above all unrealistic decision'. Later in the year Browne pointed out that he, like most Labour TDs, had been elected in the past on Fine Gael transfers, and argued that it was inconsistent for Labour to support PR while ruling out coalition.[53]

The last point was given added relevance by Fianna Fáil's heavy defeat in the PR referendum. Corish insisted that the result did not alter the position at all, but in fact the electoral system which the country had voted to retain could almost have been designed to facilitate a coalition between Labour and Fine Gael. In 1965 these parties had won 49·5 per cent of the votes, against Fianna Fáil's 47·5 per cent. A 'first past the post' system would have given Fianna Fáil a comfortable majority, while a pure PR system might have left Independents holding the balance of power. Under the Irish electoral system, however, they could be virtually certain of winning a Dáil majority provided they exchanged transfers. Shortly after the result David Thornley commented that it was 'ludicrous' for Labour, with its small number of seats, to pursue a Dáil majority; ten years in the wilderness might be acceptable to Labour politicians, but it was not acceptable to those with immediate problems such as unemployment or bad housing.[54]

As the general election approached, Labour's position hardened. Not only would it not take part in a coalition; the idea of supporting a minority government which had undertaken to implement some of Labour's 'short-term proposals', an option which in 1967 Michael O'Leary had suggested could be workable,[55] was now also ruled out. Conor Cruise O'Brien declared that Labour should oppose any government proposed in the next Dáil in an attempt to force Fianna Fáil and Fine Gael to merge.[56]

The position was set out explicitly at the January 1969 conference. Brendan Corish stated that after the next election Labour would propose its own nominee for Taoiseach and would vote against all others; it would not support 'a minority government of either conservative party'.[57] It was fortunate that, when deciding its attitude to coalition, Labour had the benefit of its experience in two previous coalition governments:

On both occasions, in subsequent elections, the electorate showed us what they thought of us for submerging our identity. Does anyone believe that it will be any different the next time? . . . I cannot see how, after a coalition government, the Labour Party could fight an election as a party with a separate identity.

Fine Gael was no better than Fianna Fáil; it wanted 'power for power's sake'. Its members 'have no interest, I believe, in changing the system. Their only claim is that they might make a better job with the system.' The most warmly applauded part of the speech was the section in which Corish set out his personal position. The last conference's decision against coalition, he said, was one

which at the time I supported and will continue to uphold so long as I am leader of the party. If conference should in the future decide by its democratic choice to change its mind, I will, as I have consistently done since I became a member of the Parliamentary Party 24 years ago, accept that decision. But the party must appreciate that to me this is a matter of conscience and that in such an eventuality, my continued support for socialism will be from the back benches.

It need hardly be said that this passage proved something of an embarrassment when, at the Cork special conference the following year, Corish proposed the motion changing the party's policy.

The conference spent little time discussing coalition, since Labour's attitude to the idea was by now as clear-cut as its attitude towards sin. An anti-coalition motion was discussed briefly and passed overwhelmingly. Its mover stated that Labour would be postponing the progress of history and giving the kiss of life to a conservative party if it joined a coalition. Its seconder, who went on to win 900 votes and lose his deposit in a Dublin constituency at the 1969 election, declared that there were only two sides in Ireland: Labour's side, the side of the workers and the people, and the other side, the side of the exploiters and oppressors of the people. If Labour agreed to a coalition, he said, 'we cease to be the people, we cease to represent the people'. During another session of the conference Denis Larkin TD warned that if he was re-elected at the next election – in fact he did not contest it – and if the PLP decided to take part in a coalition, he would resign his seat.

The conference seems to have finally convinced Fine Gael that Labour was not open to persuasion to join a coalition. A few days after it ended, Fine Gael issued a statement describing Labour's no-coalition decision as 'the result of a takeover by an extreme and irresponsible element'.[58] Michael O'Higgins declared that Fine Gael had no further interest in a coalition with Labour; in present circumstances consideration of the idea was neither necessary nor desirable.[59]

Labour's 1969 election manifesto restated the position. 'All eyes are on the next Dáil,' it said, 'and most are on Labour.'[60] What would Labour do?

The answer is clear. Policy in the Labour Party is determined by its Annual Conference. The last two Conferences have declared against coalition. And there Labour stands. In Dáil Éireann, after the next election, Labour will propose its own nominee for Taoiseach. It will not support the nomination of either of the other two parties. Should a majority of conservative deputies be returned to the Dáil, then the responsibility is on the two civil war parties to give the nation a government. The responsibility is on those who believe in the same conservative attitudes to bury their personal differences and stop play-acting. The difference between the two Civil War Parties is in name only. The past is past and best forgotten. The responsibility of the future is for them to come together and to give the country a Government – if they have the majority in the Dáil. Labour cannot be asked to bury its real and legitimate policy differences with other parties solely for the purpose of displacing any Government by a coalition. That would be the path of political dishonesty. For Labour to renege on its coalition policy would be to betray those who voted for it.

During the campaign Brendan Corish stated categorically that 'the Labour Party will not in any circumstances whatever enter a coalition'.[61] Labour would support only a Labour nomination for Taoiseach, and would adhere to this course even it meant that there had to be one or two further elections.

Despite all this, some Fianna Fáil Ministers, perhaps from force of habit, maintained that Fine Gael and Labour would form a coalition if they got the opportunity. The Tánaiste-to-be, Erskine Childers, said that the 'dirty trick' of coalition might well be played, and the outgoing Tánaiste, Frank Aiken, believed that a coalition was possible despite 'the old bluff'.[62]

Fianna Fáil's achievement of an overall majority, against most expectations, meant that yet again Labour was not actually put to the test, although there can be no doubt that the PLP would not have done a coalition deal, despite the reservations of some TDs, if it had held the balance of power. Transfers between Labour and Fine Gael were low (see Table 8.1); only about a third of the last transfer from each went to the other opposition party, and about half became non-transferable, indicating the mutual antipathy between the two parties. As a result the opposition parties forfeited eight seats to Fianna Fáil. In Dublin South West, for example, a low transfer from Labour to Fine Gael meant that these two parties won only two of the four seats with 58·6 per cent of the votes, while Fianna Fáil, with 33·8 per cent, won the other two. In seven other constituencies Fine Gael and Labour together won more first preferences than Fianna Fáil but fewer seats. If transfers had passed between the parties at the 1973 rate, Labour would have won seats in Kildare and Waterford, and Fine Gael would have picked up an extra seat in Laois-Offaly, Longford-Westmeath, Louth, Roscommon-Leitrim and Sligo-Leitrim, as well as Dublin South West.

If Labour supporters had given their lower preferences to Fine Gael – purely as a tactical measure, and not in any way as part of a coalition arrangement – Fine Gael would have won six extra seats at the expense of Fianna Fáil. Fianna Fáil would then have had only sixty-nine of the 144 seats, with Fine Gael having fifty-six and Labour eighteen, and Labour would have held the balance of power, its expressed aim throughout the campaign. There was, of course, the risk that if it had advised its supporters to give their lower preferences to Fine Gael, suspicions would have been raised that it was planning a coalition after all, but experience shows that voters are usually willing to follow their party's advice, and provided Labour had explained carefully the reasons why it was in the party's interests for lower preferences to be given to Fine Gael, there is every likelihood that Labour supporters would have made full use of their votes in this way. Labour's failure to issue this advice must be regarded as a major tactical mistake which nullified its chances of achieving its strategic objective, and resulted partly from its obsession with long-term strategic questions and the consequent neglect of tactics.

Whether the balance of power was really worth pursuing is, of course, another matter. Labour had already declared that it would neither join a coalition nor support a minority government, and certainly neither major party would have supported a Labour minority government. That Fianna Fáil and Fine Gael might form a coalition or even merge, as it hoped, was never a remote possibility. If Labour actually had gained the balance of power after the 1969 election there would almost certainly have been another general election practically at once, and Labour would have been most likely to suffer, as it had from 'snap' elections in the 1922–44 period.[63]

Labour's whole approach during this period is, obviously, open to the charge of being unrealistic. Just as there was no chance of a merger between the major parties, so there was no evidence to suppose that either would disappear. There was some incongruity in Corish's May 1968 assertion that one of the major parties was 'superfluous', for in the post-1932 period Fine Gael at its weakest was stronger than Labour at its strongest, and Fianna Fáil was almost three times as strong. Similarly, Labour might be accused of having let Fianna Fáil off the hook in the late 1960s, for the governing party was disturbing many even of its own supporters by the air of complacency and indifference – which in the case of certain Ministers reached arrogance – it exuded. Its main electoral asset was the fact that unless it won an overall majority there would be no stable government after the election, and for this reason Labour may be said to have failed to capitalise on its unpopularity at this time.

However, Labour was looking ahead to more than just one election. It could probably have ousted Fianna Fáil at the election had it joined a coalition with Fine Gael, but the latter party was still dominated by conservatives, and a Fine Gael–Labour government would have been a far cry from the prospect of the 'progressive', social democratic alliance which Fine Gael liberals held out to Labour. Labour's go-it-alone strategy was one part of a package, the other component being the socialist policies; had it not adopted the former there would have been no point in developing the latter. The strategy also enabled it to attract members in the late 1960s who later proved an asset but who would probably not have joined had its sights been set on nothing higher than a third coalition.

The 1969 election demonstrated that some of the assumptions on which Labour built its hopes in the late 1960s were unrealistic, but it does not follow that the party should not have nurtured those hopes. It is probably good for a party, especially a minor party, to entertain an optimistic view of its prospects, and in some circumstances, as Irish history shows, an unrealistically favourable assessment may become a self-fulfilling 'myth'. Labour's assessment during the 1960s of the likely development of Irish politics made it inevitable that it would pursue an independent, socialist line, but the 1969 election made a reassessment equally inevitable.

8.5 The reassessment, 1969–June 1970

Like a decapitated chicken, the anti-coalition policy showed vigorous signs of life for a while after the 1969 election. At first, indeed, the two opposition parties drifted even further apart. When the nineteenth Dáil met for the first time, the Fine Gael liberal Tom O'Higgins described Corish and 'the horny-handed sons of toil who sit behind him' – a sarcastic reference to Labour's new 'intellectual' TDs – as Fianna Fáil's greatest friends in the Dáil, because they had helped it back into power.[64] The more conservative Mark Clinton described Labour as the 'surplus party' in the Dáil,[65] and the coalitionist Garret FitzGerald, while differing from most of his colleagues by accepting that Labour had been the victim of a smear campaign, accused it of 'opting out of parliamentary politics' by demanding control of any government in which it took part; this, more than the smears or any fear of socialism, was responsible for Labour's disappointing performance at the election.[66] Conor Cruise O'Brien reciprocated the hostility, commenting that O'Higgins's remarks made it clearer than ever that Fine Gael 'is, as it has been for almost forty years, not an alternative to Fianna Fáil but an auxiliary to it'.[67]

The following month Liam Cosgrave delivered a fierce attack on Labour and its 'theoretical policies incapable of being put into practice'; his party would not be deflected from its task by 'any crazy ideas suggested by political neophytes, or others, remote from reality and divorced from responsibility'.[68] Fine Gael's spokesperson on health and social welfare, Richie Ryan, criticised coalitionists in both opposition parties, and accused both Declan Costello and Brendan Corish of having 'done nothing for some years past to assist in the replacement of Fianna Fáil with a progressive government'.[69] Garret FitzGerald, in contrast, argued that the failure of the two opposition parties to offer even the prospect of an alternative government had created in the country a sense of frustration which could be dangerous if allowed to persist.[70]

Labour's next annual conference, in January 1970, was presented with three composite motions calling respectively for the existing strategy to be reasserted, reviewed and altered.[71] For the first time since 1957 the question became an item of disagreement within the party, and all points of view were put at length; the arguments advanced at the conference, and throughout the whole of the year following the 1969 election, are discussed below. Corish took the opportunity to prepare the ground for a retreat from his apparent promise to retire to the back benches if Labour changed its mind on coalition. Even before the 1969 election he had said that 'there is no man quicker to take the lesson from the Irish electorate than myself', and that the party would have to review its policy if the electorate rejected its approach.[72] He now stated that while he was still opposed to coalition, he was 'open to conviction', and would accept whatever decision any conference might make. This conference in fact made no decision, as all three composites were referred to the incoming AC without any votes being taken on their substance.

It was clear to most political observers that the failure to uphold the no-coalition strategy would almost inevitably lead before long to its complete abandonment, and another straw in the wind appeared in April 1970, when two by-elections were held. Each opposition party asked its supporters to give their second preferences to the other; Labour's campaign director in Longford-Westmeath, David Thornley, said it was ludicrous to keep PR and then not use the opportunity to halt Fianna Fáil's 'march to dictatorship'.[73] Over 64 per cent of Labour's transfers in each constituency, the highest proportion at any by-election since March 1954, went to Fine Gael, which won both seats. In the Dublin South West by-election held in March, the Labour candidate, a strong anti-coalitionist, attracted only 31·1 per cent of Fine Gael's transfers, the lowest proportion in a by-election since the Inter-Party era began in 1948. Although there were a number of special factors operating, this defeat in a strongly working-class area, plus the fact that Labour would have won the seat had it received 37·1 per cent of Fine Gael's transfers, just a few hundred more, did nothing to convince wavering Labour members that there was much future in an independent strategy. Finally, in April, even Liam Cosgrave said he felt there was an obligation on Fine Gael and Labour to provide an alternative to Fianna Fáil.[74]

A *détente* approaching the warmth of an official friendship between Fine Gael and Labour was, then, growing even before May 1970, and in all probability a coalition arrangement would have been reached at the next election even if the Arms Crisis had never arisen. In any case, the affair forced the two opposition parties much closer together, and a full debate sprang up within Labour on the coalition question.

The coalitionists' case rested on two arguments: first, that all the evidence showed that if Labour adhered to the no-coalition strategy it would remain in sterile opposition for the foreseeable future, and second, that the two major parties were no longer, as they had been during the 1960s, equally objectionable.

They argued that Labour's previous belief that the Irish political system was on the verge of a fundamental realignment had been shown to be false. It had, on the contrary, unnatural, illogical and hideous mutant of a normal party system though it might be, withstood everything Labour could throw at it. Labour had believed that Fine Gael, which was unable to offer any convincing justification for its own existence, would wither and die if kept away from the wells of power for long enough, but in fact it had picked up over 120,000 votes between 1957 and 1969, while Labour had gained 113,000. In a world of political Darwinism both Fine Gael and Fianna Fáil, bizarre anachronisms which would soon go the way of the dinosaur if transplanted to another environment, seemed only too well adapted not just to survive but actually to flourish in the Irish Republic. Moreover, pleasant as it might be if the two major parties announced that they were going to merge and form an 'Irish Conservative Party' whose aim was to ease the lot of large farmers and businessmen, such a development did not seem imminent.

The coalitionists were not, they said, turncoats but simply realists. While Labour's day might eventually come, it would be self-delusion to believe that a major breakthrough was around the corner. Elaborating Lord Butler's definition of politics as 'the art of the possible', David Thornley argued that 'those of us who practise the vocation of politics must accept the realities of the context in which we work, with all its attendant frustrations, not invent a more agreeable fantasy'. Sometimes, he wrote, 'it is a nobler role to embrace reality and seek to change it even marginally than to stand apart from it in glorious and impotent righteousness'.[75] A delegate at an ITGWU conference said that they would all like Labour to be a majority party, free from the need to make compromises, but 'when you are not the majority party you have got to make whatever strength you have pay as effectively as possible'.[76] In their eyes the anti-coalitionists' attitude was an all-or-nothing one; they themselves believed that half a loaf was better than no bread. Labour now had nothing to gain from remaining in opposition any longer than necessary; as one coalitionist was later to put it, 'opposition is hell, it's sterile, and has no validity for a political party unless it's a time of preparation'.[77]

The second argument used by the coalitionists was that the two major parties were no longer Tweedledee and Tweedledum; as a result of recent changes it would now be worth while allying with Fine Gael to eject Fianna Fáil from power. The government party had earned the hostility of all Labour members by its conduct during the 1969 election campaign; one prominent party member, a strong anti-coalitionist until 1969, has stated that after that campaign he determined to dedicate himself henceforth to opposing Fianna Fáil.[78] This distaste was reinforced by its behaviour during the Arms Crisis, and Fianna Fáil's general reaction to events in the north, and the nature of the views expressed by Neil Blaney and others, convinced some erstwhile anti-coalitionists that the party must be removed from office as soon as possible.

At the same time Fine Gael had become slightly more attractive to Labour. Three powerful conservative TDs disappeared at the 1969 election: James Dillon stood down, and Michael O'Higgins and Patrick Lindsay lost their seats. Most importantly, Gerard Sweetman, probably the second most powerful individual within Fine Gael, was killed in a car crash in January 1970. Sweetman was a highly articulate right-winger, once described as having 'one of the keenest minds in the nineteenth century',[79] and those who remembered the second Inter-Party government would have had serious reservations about an alliance with Fine Gael had it seemed likely that he would play a significant role in a future coalition government. The conservative wing of Fine Gael, then, had been weakened considerably, while on the liberal wing Declan Costello's departure had been balanced by the emergence of Garret FitzGerald, whose views seemed similar to Costello's but who was much more active politically.[80]

These two lines of thought explained why many who had previously supported the go-it-alone strategy now changed their minds, but it must not be forgotten that a sizeable section of the party had never been anti-coalitionist at heart. In many rural constituencies Labour and Fine Gael are in a sort of unofficial coalition, and co-operate on matters like transporting voters to the polls and the deployment of personation agents, which means that they need only ensure that every booth is covered by one or other of them instead of being compelled each to station an agent at every one. On many county councils it is usual for the Fine Gael and Labour members to vote together on such matters as the election of council and committee chairmen. Even in Dublin in 1968 the Labour TD Frank Cluskey was elected Lord Mayor as part of an agreement with Fine Gael under which the two parties would share the mayoralty for four years.[81]

Between 1965 and 1969, at most five Labour TDs spoke publicly in favour of the anti-coalition line. After 1969 several were prepared to admit that they had never really agreed with it. The first to do so openly was Michael Pat Murphy, who stated his dislike for what he termed 'the opposition of the Opposition' and continued:[82]

I believe Opposition parties should be more co-operative and that there should be some common ground for agreement and certain policies which could be put forward in this House on which the people could pass judgment. I agree the people did not accept independence of attitude by Labour or Fine Gael. Let me say, whoever likes it, that I have never been opposed, while I have been here, to the concept of groups of parties joining together if necessary to oust a Government that should be ousted when there is no alternative. That is a personal viewpoint.

In a later recantation he stated that during the 1960s Fine Gael and Labour had 'adopted the foolish idea that they could get into government on their own'.[83]

The anti-coalitionists' case was essentially a reaffirmation of pre-1969 orthodoxy. The plethora of arguments advanced to prove that Labour should never again enter a coalition as a minority partner were, they maintained, as valid as ever. They believed that the coalitionists were over-reacting to the 1969 election results, from which too much had been expected. It had never been realistic to expect a massive Labour breakthrough only six months after the party had finally adopted socialist policies. Given the conservative outlook of many Irish people, converting the electorate would be a long process requiring commitment and hard work. Labour had to forego the temptations of office and instead assume the long-term role of 'an educator–leader–élite'.[84] The reluctance of most Labour TDs to seek this role suggested to the anti-coalitionists that they had never had a sincere attachment to them; they had adopted them out of expediency when they thought they might be swept into office on the crest of a socialist wave, but were now rushing to abandon them since they had not, after all, proved the means to the desired end. To some extent, some coalitionists, especially rural ones, might have accepted this argument, although they would have recast it somewhat. They would have acknowledged that they had always harboured doubts as to whether the 1969 policy was going to be acceptable to the electorate, but had been willing to 'give it a try'.[85] Once their suspicions had been confirmed they saw no point in persisting with the policies.

The anti-coalitionists argued that if Labour changed its strategy, all the time and energy spent during the late 1960s in formulating new policies would be rendered worthless, for it was obvious that these policies could not be implemented from within a Fine Gael-dominated coalition. Those coalitionists who actually felt some attachment to the 1969 policies maintained, rather unconvincingly, that Labour would not be abandoning them if it entered a coalition; they were only to be put 'on the shelf' or 'into cold storage' to await their time, and the party would some day return to them. The anti-coalitionists maintained that Labour would be humiliating itself if it went back to Fine Gael and asked for fresh coalition terms. One likened Brendan Corish's December 1970 advocacy of coalition at Cork to Moses telling the Israelites that there was no Promised Land after all, but that they need not worry, since Pharaoh had agreed to take them back.[86] The coalitionists, of course, believed that to adhere to the anti-coalition line would be to stay in the wilderness.

Nor were the anti-coalitionists much impressed by changes in the other parties. Despite the Arms Crisis, they said, Labour should not become part of an alliance whose aims went no further than to 'get Fianna Fáil out'. Moreover they believed that, despite the turnover of a few individuals, Fine Gael was still a very conservative party, as Labour had maintained up to the 1969 election. Another point which should not be overlooked is that some Labour members not on the left of the party were consistently opposed to coalition, disliking Fine Gael not on socio-economic grounds but because of its image as the pro-Treaty party or the Blueshirt party. This feeling, indeed, was shared by some Labour TDs, although in the final analysis none allowed it to determine his attitude.

The differences within the party on this question, then, were fundamental ones, and concerned ends more than means. Most anti-coalitionists believed that Labour should aim to transform Ireland into a socialist society in which the workers would own and control the means of production and distribution, and had little interest in the limited social democratic reforms which were all that would be possible in a Fine Gael-dominated coalition. Most coalitionists believed that Labour should concentrate on the nearer future, and should attempt to make incremental improvements to Irish society and to the position of the working class, even though this would involve compromise, on the ground that it was better to implement some of Labour's policies than none of them. Some maintained that the argument actually concerned means rather than ends; they claimed that their desire to achieve a majority Labour government and a socialist society was no less deep than that of the anti-coalitionists, and that participation in coalition governments was at least as likely to produce these outcomes as remaining permanently in opposition. Most, however, were openly or privately sceptical about these goals being attained, at least during their lifetimes.

8.6 'Operation Houdini': towards a new coalition

By mid-1970 the party establishment, including probably every TD except Noel Browne, favoured a change of strategy, as did probably a majority of members. It remained only to escape from the straitjacket of the no-coalition policy with as little loss of face as possible. This task was named 'Operation Houdini' by Conor Cruise O'Brien,[87] perhaps an allusion to a Cumann na nGaedheal advertisement of 1932 entitled 'Devvy's Circus', which purported to advertise the Fianna Fáil Party as a circus.[88] Among the acts to be seen, it proclaimed, was 'Señor de Valera, World-Famous Illusionist, Oath Swallower and Escapologist. See his renowned Act: "Escaping from the Straight Jacket of the Republic"'.

There were certainly parallels between the position of Labour's leadership in 1970 and of de Valera in 1923–26. Both had staked out a clear position and had portrayed compromise as the equivalent of betrayal. Both had become convinced by events – Labour by the 1969 election result, and de Valera by the decline of the Sinn Féin organisation – that their present course was sterile, and that to win political power they would have to make compromises of the sort they had previously condemned. Both, pragmatists at heart, knew that they would face bitter internal resistance to any change of policy from those they regarded as fundamentalists but who regarded themselves as idealists.

After the Arms Crisis calls for a coalition were heard openly. Barry Desmond, Conor Cruise O'Brien and John O'Connell argued that the opposition had a duty to offer an alternative administration.[89] Michael O'Leary argued that Labour would become irrelevant unless it changed its strategy; the idea that Labour would win enough seats to become a majority partner in a coalition was 'a false expectation', and in any case Fine Gael had been 'profoundly affected' by the *Just Society* policies.[90] Responding to pressure from Fine Gael liberals, Declan Costello announced that he had accepted an invitation to stand in Dublin South West at the next election, and called for a coalition between the opposition parties, which, he said, had a lot in common with regard to policies.[91] These moves were criticised by Noel Browne, Matt Merrigan and Labour's Dublin Regional Council.[92]

The decisive phase of the argument was reached late in 1970. As a result of an incorrect belief that a general election was imminent, Labour's AC, which had been given responsibility by the 1970 conference to deal with electoral strategy, decided that the party should be freed quickly from the anti-coalition line, and a special conference was called, to be held in Cork on 13 December.[93] It prepared a motion, preceded by a long statement, which was published two weeks before the conference was held.[94]

The statement affirmed that Labour was 'a Socialist Party' whose aim was to win a majority of seats in the Dáil. However, since, it said, no party was likely to win an overall majority at elections in the 1970s, there was an obligation on Labour to 're-examine' its 1960s electoral strategy. Labour's enhanced strength and 'new sense of purpose' justified a 'more flexible' approach to strategy; its interests might sometimes demand, and sometimes prevent, participation in government, and the question of coalition was basically 'a matter of political judgment'. Moreover, Labour had a 'responsibility to the nation' because there were policies and viewpoints which it alone could contribute to government. By taking part in a coalition, it continued, 'Labour is aware that it cannot expect to secure all of its aims but believes that even their partial achievement will transform society for the better ... Labour's policies were not designed for permanent opposition but for implementation. To be a socialist is not to be condemned to perpetual opposition, but rather is to be committed to achievement, whenever the opportunity arises to do so, with honour'. After this lengthy preamble, the actual motion to be put before the conference was one giving the PLP and the party leader power to negotiate participation in a government.

The motion, which few doubted would be passed, was at once criticised by Noel Browne, who argued that if Labour had anything to do with 'a right-wing conservative party' like Fine Gael, it could not call itself 'the party of Connolly'.[95] In response, Liam Cosgrave assured members of his party that Fine Gael would not barter its principles to attain office, or allow the State's foundations to be 'undermined by any crazy verbal extremist theoreticians',[96] a comment probably directed against Browne rather than Labour as a whole. However, the coalitionist mood was strengthened just before the conference by a very high transfer (67·9 per cent) from Labour to Fine Gael in a by-election in Dublin, where most party members were anti-coalition.

The Cork conference was attended by 858 delegates and was held in an atmosphere of virtual civil war.[97] The anti-coalitionists by this time constituted almost a party within a party, and many of them alleged that the conference had been 'rigged' or 'stage-managed', allegations which were the product of their frustration at the fact that everyone knew in advance what the result would be rather than serious suggestions of malpractice. It began with a protracted attempt to reject the standing orders report outlining the conference agenda; during its course one delegate raised, as a point of order, the claim that a pro-coalition TD was 'openly sneering' at anti-coalition speakers; many speeches were interrupted by loud and angry heckling from the floor. The conference also brought out clearly the rift between Dublin and rural members; about 90 per cent of Dublin speakers were opposed to coalition (see Table 8.2), while speakers from outside Dublin were split evenly in their attitudes. The contrast is even more marked when it is borne in mind that two of the three pro-coalition speakers from Dublin were TDs.

The AC's motion was proposed by Brendan Corish, who reiterated the arguments for a change of strategy. After the 1969 result it had to be accepted that the two major parties could not be forced together in the foreseeable future. Labour should not stand by and permit Fianna Fáil to govern indefinitely. An anti-coalitionist pointed out that it was generally accepted that Labour had suffered by joining previous coalitions, and asked what was the 'miraculous new ingredient' which would enable it to succeed next time. Anticipating this, Corish acknowledged that past coalitions had been unhappy experiences for

Labour, but claimed that the situation was different now because the party had clear policies and TDs of a high calibre. He dismissed the idea of supporting a minority government; this, he said, would be 'responsibility without power', a claim he backed up by referring to the 1932 experience. A Dublin TD accused some anti-coalitionists of being 'addicted to protest' and of wanting to see party policies rot in impotence while they expressed sterile opposition to everything. A rural delegate said he had never been opposed to coalition, and accused some anti-coalitionists of wanting to introduce a brand of socialism which was 'diabolically repugnant to the Irish way of life'.

Table 8.2 *Location of branch belonged to, and attitude to coalition, of speakers at Cork Special Conference, December 1970*

Location of branch belonged to	Anti-coalition	Pro-coalition	Total
Dublin	20	3	23
Rest of Ireland	8	8	16
Total	28	11	39

Note. The table excludes one anti-coalition speaker whose branch could not be ascertained.
Source. Labour Party record of conference.

Most speakers, however, opposed the motion, arguing that it would transport Labour back to the 1950s. The party had been given a new lease of life by the approach of the 1960s, which was now being reversed. It should adhere uncompromisingly to its aim of winning a Dáil majority. Labour, said one delegate, 'if it's a genuine socialist party, must be in permanent opposition until this rotten capitalist system comes down', an attitude reminiscent of that used by de Valera's opponents within Sinn Féin in 1926, who argued that the party should have nothing to do with the northern or southern legislatures but should wait for them to collapse.

An amendment to the AC's motion, to forbid the PLP to join a coalition but allow it to support a minority government, was defeated by 522 votes to 288; another amendment, forbidding a coalition with either Fianna Fáil or Fine Gael, was defeated by 526 to 250. A third amendment, submitted by the ITGWU, attracted rather more support. It argued that Labour should not play its cards too early; it should not make any decision on a coalition until after the next election, which it should fight on its own policies to see whether support for socialism was still increasing. A special conference should be held two days after the election results were known to decide what Labour should do in the light of the situation thrown up. The AC, its movers suggested, had rushed into the present conference because they wrongly imagined that a general election was about to be called, and postponement of a decision would also allow tempers to cool. However, this too was defeated, by 470 votes to 307.

While the final series of amendments was being voted on a number of delegates left the hall, some in dissatisfaction with the whole conference, but most simply to catch trains. By the time the AC motion was finally put, fewer than three-quarters of the original delegates were still present. The motion was passed by 396 votes to 204; a comparison with the voting on the first amendment suggests that most of those who had left were supporters of coalition. Of the forty-three amendments submitted between the first publication of the motion and the conference, five had been accepted by the AC. These reduced the PLP's freedom of action slightly, by requiring the AC's approval for any step taken, and by specifying that Labour could remain within a coalition government only while its policies were being implemented. The motion, as approved by the conference, now read:[98]

That this special meeting of National Conference affirms that circumstances exist in which participation by the Labour Party in Government is in both the national interest and the interest of the Party, and pending the return of a majority Labour Party representation in Dáil Eireann, which is our aim, Conference empowers the Leader and members of the Parliamentary Labour Party, subject to consultation with the Administrative Council on the terms thereof, to negotiate participation by the Labour Party in a Government that would guarantee the implementation of Labour policies and to participate in such a Government for such time as it is in the nation's interests to do so and for so long as Labour Party policies are being implemented.

The motion, then, did not state that Labour actually would join a coalition. It declared, like de Valera's motion at the 1926 Sinn Féin Ard-Fheis, that the question should cease to be a matter of principle and should become one of policy. As with the 1926 motion, however, it was clear that those who had fought for its passage would not have gone to the trouble of unlocking the door if they had not intended to go through it. Corish, like de Valera after he entered the Dáil, was left to explain how he reconciled his position with his earlier undertaking to retire to the back benches if Labour changed its mind on coalition. He informed a post-conference press meeting that he regarded the pro-coalition vote as one of confidence in himself.[99] He had told the conference, he said, that

with regard to my 1969 attitude, as long as my informed assessment of the political situation suggested to me in the context of 1969 that coalition was wrong, then, in conscience, I was bound to retire to the backbenches. In drastically changed circumstances, when in my judgment it is right for the party to negotiate for participation in government and to adopt this policy, I found no reason to retire to the back benches.

Although Noel Browne described his turn-about as the biggest *volte-face* since de Valera entered the Dáil, there was no significant pressure on Corish to resign the leadership, since all his potential successors had undergone the same change of mind as he had.

The prospect of a general election disappeared as suddenly as it had arisen, giving some validity to the ITGWU's argument that the conference had been ill timed, although in fact it may well have been in the party's interests to have the question resolved. There was not much discussion of the question until 1972, the main exception being a speech by Corish in May 1971 which briefly recalled an earlier era. He declared that Labour would fight the next election, if it came soon, 'as an independent party standing on socialist policies'.[100] A coalition might be agreed after an election, but Labour would be tough in any negotiations, and

If the party with whom we negotiate proves to be conservative in its approach, then it will be up to Labour not to give way to conservatism. If conservatism is the price of coalition, then we don't go in . . . We didn't bargain hard enough in 1948, and again in 1954. There are many lessons to be drawn from these two experiences.

After an attack on his internal critics, whom he accused of being self-proclaimed 'paragons of socialism' who were weakening Labour's negotiating position by alleging that the party would be prepared to enter a coalition on any terms, he stated that 'Fianna Fáil and Fine Gael should know their real enemy, the democratic socialism of the Labour Party'.

This, however, was the last time such rhetoric was heard from the party establishment. In May 1972 the Dublin South West TD, John O'Connell, began to nudge the party towards a pre-election agreement with Fine Gael. He pointed out that the motion passed by the Cork conference did not in any way rule this out, and also argued that the party's apparent intention of fighting the next election independently and deciding its attitude to a coalition only when the results were known was dishonest.[101] It would enable Fianna Fáil to claim that the electorate did not know what alternative was on offer, and that those voting for Fine Gael or Labour would be 'buying a pig in a poke'. Instead, said O'Connell, the opposition parties should make their decision known before the election, and should spell out to the electorate the economic and social policies they would hope to implement. His thoughts were endorsed by the coalitionist Fine Gael TD Paddy Harte, and, thus encouraged, he developed them further, even outlining a coalition Cabinet, in which Tom O'Higgins was Taoiseach and neither Corish nor Cosgrave had a place.[102]

O'Connell encountered criticism from within the party for openly advocating a coalition, but he was known to keep his finger firmly on the pulse of Labour supporters, a process aided by opinion polls regularly conducted for him in his constituency and testified to by his high first preference vote at successive elections. Partly at his urging, Corish now made a major speech to a meeting of the Dublin South West Constituency Council.[103] Whereas the Cork statement had discussed the coalition option in a somewhat hypothetical, quasi-academic manner, albeit favourably, Corish now openly argued the case for a coalition. It would be 'an act of irresponsibility' not to give the electorate the opportunity to elect an alternative government at the next election; Labour must 'clearly indicate to the electorate' that it would be willing to take part in the formation of such a government. On this occasion he neither attacked Fine Gael nor ruled out the possibility of a pre-election agreement. The PLP endorsed the speech, and on 28 June authorised Corish to engage in discussions with Cosgrave 'on the feasibility of a Coalition Government'.[104]

O'Connell's omission of the Fine Gael leader from his proposed government had in fact touched on a sensitive spot, for Cosgrave's name did not spring readily to the minds of those casting around for the leader of a 'reforming' or 'progressive' coalition. Labour regarded him as excessively conservative, while Cosgrave himself was known to be wary of an alliance with Labour and to cherish lingering hopes of a Fine Gael government. Some Fine Gael liberals, dissatisfied with his leadership in any case, hoped to replace him by a more centrist figure who would be more likely to attract Labour into partnership. As a result, Fine Gael was in a state of tension throughout 1972, and at its May Ard-Fheis Cosgrave attacked not only the 'mongrel foxes' but also Labour, perhaps in the hope of weakening those within his own party who favoured a coalition with it. He suggested, in an obvious reference to Labour, that those who had campaigned in the EEC referendum alongside 'subversive' groups had become tainted by the latter, and it would 'take them a long time to wash those stains away'.[105] However, he reacted warmly to Corish's Dublin South West speech, issuing a statement an hour before it was even made, having received an advance copy. The speech, he said, 'changes the political climate dramatically and must be so recognised by all responsible elements in the community', and he added that 'the possible seems more probable now'.[106]

Anti-coalitionists in both parties reacted unfavourably to these developments. Noel Browne wrote another anti-coalition article, David Thornley expressed reservations, and the West Galway Constituency Council declared itself against coalition.[107] Dermot Boucher, a Dublin member, suggested that Labour 'must withdraw from the mainstream of Irish politics and abandon for ever the illusion that "power" may be obtained through the parliamentary process'. It should try 'to achieve a final organizational and ideological rapprochement with the Republican movement', and 'the use of force as a means of combating the institutionalized violence of the capitalist state must be investigated in a sober and unromantic fashion'.[108] These rather enigmatic arguments were probably not intelligible, let alone attractive, to coalitionists within the party. On the other side, a newspaper published an anonymous letter, seemingly written by a member of the Fine Gael Oireachtas Party, expressing hostility both to the idea of a coalition and to the liberal wing of the party.[109]

However, the coalitionist tide in both parties was by now unstemmable. Early in October Fine Gael's parliamentary party held a series of meetings, lasting eighteen hours in all, at which each TD and Senator gave his or her views on the idea of a coalition.[110] Only about ten per cent of those present opposed the idea, some because of concern about the position of some Labour TDs on law-and-order questions, and others because of a fear that traditional Fine Gael supporters might desert the party if it was part of an alliance that included Noel Browne, something of a bogey-man to those to the right of centre. Overall, the meeting favoured not only joining a coalition but also negotiating a pre-election pact, if Labour agreed; it gave the negotiators a free hand, subject only to the condition that they report back to the parliamentary party. It was followed by an invitation from

Cosgrave to Corish to participate in exploratory talks on the formation of an alternative government, in which the respective deputy leaders would also participate. Corish accepted the invitation, an action endorsed by the PLP and the AC and condemned by the Liaison Committee of the Labour Left, a loose organisation of left-wing Labour members.[111]

Although it seemed that the stage was now set for a rapid move towards a coalition arrangement, there were no public developments, and scarcely any private ones, until late January 1973. Indeed, prospects of a coalition seemed to recede when the two parties adopted different attitudes to the Offences against the State Bill in November and December 1972, and particularly after Liam Cosgrave's speech. The Fine Gael leader, who throughout his political career displayed a tendency to speak rather wildly when not adhering to a prepared script, declared that 'Communists and their fellow-travellers and soft-headed liberals are always talking about repression';[112] it was, of course, Labour's contention that the legislation under discussion was repressive. He went on to attack 'movements which started out legitimately, like the anti-apartheid protest marches, which degenerated into a rabble and were a disgrace to all associated with them';[113] among those prominently 'associated with' anti-*apartheid* marches in the early 1970s had been many Labour politicians, as well as some from Fine Gael, such as Garret FitzGerald.

8.7 The formation of the 1973 coalition government

When the general election was announced, on 5 February, the coalition negotiations had made virtually no progress.[114] One meeting had been held in October, shortly after Labour had accepted the Fine Gael invitation to talks, but only one other had taken place. This, which was held just before the dissolution, left the prospect of a coalition as distant as before, since both sides were still cautious. However, the announcement of the election, and the near certainty of a further term of Fianna Fáil government unless they could form an alliance, spurred the parties into action. The leaders and deputy leaders at once met and agreed that they would fight as a coalition, and they also agreed, without ado, that if they won the election Cosgrave would become Taoiseach and Corish Tánaiste. An eight-man team was established to draw up a manifesto.

Working from a Labour draft, the committee took only about three hours to produce the final version (see Chapter 6.4 above). Three matters were agreed privately and not included in the manifesto. First, it was agreed that a wealth tax would be introduced – this was strongly hinted at in the manifesto but not made explicit. Second, farmers were to be brought into the income tax net. Third, the Fine Gael leader secured Labour's agreement that a coalition government would not repeal the December 1972 Offences against the State legislation, despite the strong doubts expressed about it by members of both opposition parties at the time.

After the election some Labour anti-coalitionists made much of the publication in a periodical of an anonymous article which quoted from what it claimed was a document summarising an address made by Garret FitzGerald to a meeting of 'stockbrokers, bankers and industrialists'.[115] FitzGerald had allegedly assured his listeners that there would be no major changes in economic policy, that Labour's 1969 policies would not be put into effect, and that Labour's 'doctrinaire views' on nationalisation 'will have no part of the National Coalition's policy'. The authenticity of the document was never either denied or reliably confirmed, and in fact is immaterial, since it was obvious to everyone by the time of the election that Labour was not expecting to implement its 1969 policies while in coalition. The real argument, as during the previous three years, was whether this was a necessary compromise or a betrayal.

The name 'National Coalition' implied that the projected government was not in any way a successor to the 'Inter-Party' governments of the 1950s, and it also suggested that the participants would be sinking their differences and operating much more as a unified team than those rather loosely co-ordinated governments had. The two parties ran separate campaigns; there was no joint advertising and no co-ordination when it came to nominating candidates, but it was agreed that each party's director of elections in each constituency would maintain 'maximum co-operation' with his counterpart in the other party throughout the campaign, and that each party would urge its supporters to give their lower preferences to the other.[116] The election manifesto was approved by Labour's AC, with just one dissentient, and by the PLP, with the exception of Noel Browne, who did not stand in the election; David Thornley at first refused to sign it, but later changed his mind.[117] All Labour candidates had to sign a 'party pledge' promising, among other things, to campaign 'in support of the Statement of Intent on the formation of a National Coalition

Government' and, if elected, to 'vote in support of the National Coalition Government in the Oireachtas'.[118] Every Fine Gael TD endorsed the manifesto.

At the local level, most of Labour's campaign literature contained a brief summary of the fourteen-point programme, with some emphasis on those parts thought likely to appeal especially to Labour voters, and contained a reminder that the party was in alliance with Fine Gael. The exceptions were constituencies where there was strong electoral competition between the two parties, such as South Tipperary, or where the candidates were not enthusiastic about coalition, such as Galway West and Dublin North West. In the latter, David Thornley's constituency, the pamphlet issued made no mention of the coalition arrangement, and printed some 'excerpts from Labour's policies', including the nationalisation of banks, mines and building societies.

The coalition was attacked not only by Fianna Fáil but also by Labour's anti-coalitionists. Noel Browne said that the fourteen-point manifesto represented an unconditional surrender by Labour to Fine Gael, and accused other Labour TDs of reneging on the socialist policies on the basis of which they had been elected,[119] yet another echo of Sinn Féin in the 1920s. Matt Merrigan accused Labour's leadership, hungry for 'a place in capitalism's squalor', of having betrayed the Irish working class by pushing its political organisation into a 'class-collaborationist' role, and warned that the wedding of 'irreconcilable class and social forces' in the name of 'the national interest' could lead to a corporate fascist State.[120] The leadership was trying 'to create a delusion that a section of [the] property-owning class, represented by Fine Gael, is in some way anti-capitalist or progressive and is prepared to act against its own class interests'. The 'middle-class leaders of the Labour Party' were being used by Fine Gael 'as a decoy for working-class support for their tatty rag-bag of democratic aims, which will not in any way affect the bosses . . . who hold the lives of Irish workers in thrall'. In order to create the revolutionary socialist party envisaged by Connolly, he said, 'the wretched middle-class careerists and carpet-baggers, together with their working-class sycophants, must be driven out of the leadership of the Labour Party', and he urged workers not to be 'deluded by this temporary pawning of the Labour Party to the Fine Gael pawnbrokers'. This speech, in comparison with which most of Fianna Fáil's attacks on the Coalition seemed insipid, was followed by condemnation from the Liaison Committee of the Labour Left, who called on Labour supporters to vote only for the Labour candidates and not to give lower preferences to any other party; two left-wingers were later disciplined for their connection with the statement.[121]

The victory of the National Coalition was seen by the coalitionists as a vindication of Labour's change of strategy, especially as the party gained three seats, in Mid-Cork, Kildare and North Tipperary, as a result of Fine Gael transfers, and might have lost three others, in Carlow-Kilkenny, Meath and Wicklow, had it not been for the high transfer rate from Fine Gael. Fine Gael also picked up three seats, in Laois-Offaly, Longford-Westmeath and Sligo-Leitrim, as a result of Labour transfers. Overall, as Table 8.1 shows, supporters of each coalition party obeyed the advice to give lower preferences to the other, and altogether 82·5 per cent of coalition transfers went to other coalition candidates when these were available to receive them, a figure almost as high as that of 84·5 per cent for Fianna Fáil's internal solidarity. In three three-seat constituencies, Kildare, Sligo-Leitrim and North Tipperary, Fianna Fáil won more than 50 per cent of the first preference votes but won only one seat, because the transferring between its candidates was less solid than that between the coalition candidates. The LCLL's call to Labour voters not to give lower preferences to Fine Gael does not seem to have had much impact. In Dublin, where the LCLL was strongest, an average of 68·6 per cent of the final Labour transfers went to Fine Gael candidates when these were available to receive them, a figure very close to the national average of 71·9 per cent. The situation in fact arose in only two Dublin constituencies; there was an above-average transfer (80·8 per cent) in Dublin Central, and a below-average transfer (56·3 per cent) in Dublin North West.

The distribution of government posts between the two parties had not been decided before the election, but it had been agreed that they would receive 'pay-offs' in proportion to their respective strengths. Labour won 26·0 per cent of the Coalition's seats and 28·1 per cent of its votes, which on a *pro rata* basis would have entitled it to four (26·7 per cent) of the fifteen government positions.[122] However, when the party leaders met to apportion Ministries, Cosgrave at once offered Corish five, an offer which was accepted. It has been noted that, in all European countries, when deviations from strict proportionality occur in the composition of coalition governments, small parties are the most likely beneficiaries.[123] This is partly because one Ministry more or less means more to a party with few Ministries than to one with many, and partly because, in a 'minimum winning' coalition,[124] all the parties contributing to the government's strength are essential, so small parties can claim that they are as important as large ones in real if not in numerical terms. Ten non-government posts were also distributed, and Labour received three. It obtained two of the seven parliamentary secretaryships, and a Labour TD, Seán Treacy, became Ceann Comhairle; five Fine Gael TDs were made Parliamentary Secretaries, one became Attorney General, and another became Leas-Cheann Comhairle (Deputy Speaker) of the Dáil. The question of which party would supply the EEC Commissioner to be appointed in January 1977 was not decided until much later.

The question of which Ministries each party should get, potentially a divisive one, was settled easily and amicably. Hardly any bargaining was involved. The Labour leader, who seems to have consulted only the party chairman and secretary in advance, specified the five he wanted, and this was agreed. Labour received Health and Social Welfare (which, although two separate Ministries, counted as one), Industry and Commerce, Posts and Telegraphs, Labour, and Local Government. It is, of course, impossible to tell whether the party could have got more had it demanded it. Finance is the most important Ministry in any government, but whether Fine Gael – which had it in both of the Inter-Party governments – would have been prepared to forego it, even if Labour had agreed to take some minor Ministries instead of its more powerful ones, remains an open question. Labour did not seek Finance, partly because no Labour TD had any expertise in economic and financial affairs, and partly because Labour, like everyone else, assumed that if Fine Gael got the Ministry it would be given to Garret FitzGerald, who would have been quite acceptable to the Labour Party. In the event, it was given to a Fine Gael TD in the centre of his party, and although he had no training in economics he did not appear out of his depth in the job.

Health, Social Welfare and Local Government (which had responsibility for housing) were obvious choices, as they dealt with areas of particular concern to Labour. So did Industry and Commerce, which covered the exploitation of natural resources and also had the first responsibility for dealing with price rises, and Labour, which was responsible for industrial relations. The selection of these two Ministries was criticised by the Labour left, which argued that by possessing them Labour would be seen by the public to be responsible for price rises, strikes and relations with the trade unions, and would thus be acting as Fine Gael's 'mudguard'.[125] Labour's other Ministry, Posts and Telegraphs, covered the sensitive area of government control over broadcasting, but was otherwise one of the least important in the government. Its selection, and its allocation to Conor Cruise O'Brien, was probably a case of picking a Ministry for a man rather than a man for a Ministry. O'Brien was also made responsible for the government's public relations. Overall, both the quantity and quality of Labour's posts compared favourably with its size. As a result of the distribution, eight of the nineteen Labour TDs (42·1 per cent) were given something, as against seventeen of the fifty-four Fine Gael TDs (31·5 per cent).

The selection of TDs to fill Labour's Ministries was entirely in the hands of Corish. The Labour Ministers in the Inter-Party governments had been elected by the PLP, but it changed its rules in 1972, partly as an expression of confidence in Corish, and partly at the instigation of TDs who felt they were more likely to be selected than elected. The change was also seen as bringing the party's procedures into line with general practice, since Ministers of the other Irish parties, and of the British parties, had always been appointed by the leader, although some parties, such as the Australian Labor Party, elect their Ministers. Moreover it was generally recognised, not least by the TDs concerned, that the 1965 and 1969 intake would stand a better chance of entering the Cabinet if the rules were changed. The election of Labour Ministers in 1948 and 1954 had produced some surprising results. One of the Ministers elected in 1954 was suffering at the time from a protracted bout of hiccoughs, which had lasted several months, and seems to have received a sympathy vote in consequence. On the other hand, one of the party's most able TDs, James Larkin, was not elected on either occasion; admittedly, he would probably not have been selected by William Norton either.

Corish selected TDs to fill Labour's Ministries on the basis of his assessment of which would be best for the jobs, with due regard for other factors like seniority; there was no attempt to distribute them evenly between, say, urban and rural TDs. Corish became Minister for Health and for Social Welfare; the only other rural TD given a portfolio was Jimmy Tully, who received Local Government. The other three Ministers were graduates representing Dublin constituencies. Michael O'Leary became Minister for Labour, Conor Cruise O'Brien was given Posts and Telegraphs, and Justin Keating got Industry and Commerce. One of Labour's Parliamentary

Secretaries, Frank Cluskey, was from Dublin, and the other, Michael Pat Murphy, represented rural South West Cork.

The four Ministers were asked, individually, by Corish whether they would be prepared to serve in the government. They were offered specific Ministries, but were given no assurance that if they declined what they were offered they would be invited to choose another one. Tully and Keating were both pleased with what they were given; O'Leary was known to be unhappy with the choice of Labour, but took it anyway. Within Fine Gael, Cosgrave sought the advice of some of his front-benchers and closest confidants, but made the final decision himself. Some of the Fine Gael TDs appointed were given little notice that Cosgrave intended to offer them a post in the administration, and some were told only at the last moment exactly what he had in mind for them. Each party leader chose his own appointees; his selections were not subject to the approval of the other. The Dáil met on 14 March 1973, and endorsed the composition of the government by seventy-two votes to sixty-nine.

9
Labour in government, 1973–77

The National Coalition government held office for four and a quarter years, before being defeated at a general election held in June 1977. It began very brightly, and had a 'honeymoon period', lasting for about a year, during which a large number of popular decisions were made. Some of the early press comment, indeed, was almost embarrassingly sycophantic. Before the Cabinet was picked, one political correspondent wrote of the likelihood that a 'Government of all the talents' would be forthcoming and of the Coalition's 'problem of too much Ministerial talent'. Even after the government's composition had been revealed, he insisted that it was 'showered with talent', and the Coalition's first budget was hailed as 'the greatest social welfare budget of all time' and the 'most progressive budget yet'.[1]

After such lavish initial praise the Coalition was almost bound to disappoint. The greatest problems arose in the area of economic policy. The fivefold increase in oil prices after the 1973 Yom Kippur war reduced economic growth and led to massive inflation and unemployment throughout the Western world, and had a particularly strong impact on the Irish Republic, which was almost entirely dependent on imported energy sources. Consequently the government's performance fell far short of its promises. The 1973 manifesto had included the sentence: 'The immediate economic aim of the new government will be to stabilize prices, halt redundancies and reduce unemployment under a programme of planned economic development'.

In the event, prices rose by about 90 per cent during the first four years of the Coalition's term, and almost doubled over the whole period, an average rate almost twice that experienced during the previous four years of Fianna Fáil government. In 1974 inflation exceeded 20 per cent, although it was beginning to fall by 1977. The suggestion that prices could be stabilised was in fact an unrealistic one, which would have been quite unfulfillable in any event. The government removed Value Added Tax from food, as it had promised, and in July 1975 introduced subsidies on some basic items such as milk, bread, butter and gas. Attempts to 'introduce strict price control' proved unavailing, despite a number of measures taken, mainly because no amount of controls could remove the causes of inflation. The government argued during the 1977 election campaign that it had kept inflation as low as possible under the circumstances, claiming that the rise in consumer prices had been a third lower than the import price rise whereas under Fianna Fáil it had been nearly 50 per cent higher. However, the electorate was unmoved by such arguments, and what the Labour Senator Fintan Kennedy was to call 'the rising tide of public opinion' over inflation,[2] which inevitably bore most heavily on the least well-off, played an important part in sweeping the Coalition out of office in 1977.

The aim of halting redundancies and reducing unemployment was another which looked rather tattered by 1977. The recession caused many firms to cease production or cut down their work force, and redundancies increased rapidly, exceeding 19,000 in 1975. The number of unemployed rose from 71,435 when the Coalition entered office in March 1973 to 115,942 (the highest March figure since 1936) four years later, representing an increase from 7·9 per cent to 12·5 per cent of the insured labour force.[3] Once again the government could claim only that this was the result of factors outside its control, and that other countries were suffering just as badly. Once again, though, traditional Labour supporters were worst affected, and Fianna Fáil, recalling the position in 1957, attempted to capitalise during the 1977 election campaign on what it suggested was an inevitable link between a Coalition government and high unemployment. One of its advertisements tried to drive a wedge between the Coalition parties. It featured a picture of unemployed people queueing at a labour exchange, and read, '160,000 workless – that's the *real* cost of Fine Gael. And they expect Labour to vote them back to power!'[4]

The 1973 manifesto suggested that the 'programme of planned economic development' would be a central feature of the government's policy, just as the idea of an economic plan had been a central feature of Labour's 1969 policies. Here, too, the performance did not match the promise. No economic plan of any sort was drawn up. The government was generally responsive to, rather than an initiator of, economic events, trying to cope with problems as they arose. It had to face a long succession of crises, and felt it had no time to take a long, contemplative look at the future direction of the economy; in any case, the uncertainty of world economic conditions made long-term planning in an open economy seem to many a pointless exercise. The nearest it came to setting out any long-term economic objectives was in a long-awaited Green Paper (a discussion document) published in September 1976.[5] Far from outlining a new programme of economic development, as had been anticipated, it seemed to be little more than an extended argument in favour of pay restraint. It said that 'consideration' would be given to the idea of establishing an Industrial Development Corporation, which might allow State investment in industry, and a National Development Fund, but since the government had already had three and a half years to consider the ideas, such undertakings did nothing to prevent the paper looking very bland and disappointing.

The sharp rise in inflation and unemployment, and the absence of any kind of economic plan, was inevitably displeasing to the Labour Party. In 1975 the AC called twice for a change in the direction of government economic policy. In February it circulated to the Cabinet and the PLP a document drawn up by the general secretary, Brendan Halligan, one of the few trained economists in the upper echelons of the party. The document called for an increase in State investment to boost output and employment, the establishment of a State Holding Company and a State Building Company, the imposition of import controls in certain areas, and the ending of the link between the Irish pound and sterling. Echoing a grievance felt by the non-government members of every left-wing party in office, it also suggested that 'The Parliamentary Party and the AC should be more closely involved in policy formation and should be given precedence over officials and the Central Bank'.[6]

In June the AC drew up another document and circulated it to the Cabinet and affiliated trade unions. This repeated some of the points in the earlier statement, and also urged that 'proper economic planning be introduced without delay so as to provide the true foundation for economic growth'.[7] In 1976 Halligan called for economic planning, a National Development Corporation, a partial take-over of the commercial banks, and in general increased particpation by the State in economic life, on the ground that private enterprise had failed to provide the number of jobs needed, and he repeated his appeal later in the year following his election to the Dáil.[8] It does not seem, however, that much attention was paid by the Labour Ministers to these efforts, or that they had any impact at all on government policy. Another disappointment for Labour in this area was the failure of the government to increase the power of the Central Bank *vis à vis* the commercial banks, or its own power *vis à vis* the Central Bank, steps the party had long advocated in order to increase State control over the economy.

With the admittedly large exception of the impact of the recession, Labour could feel reasonably satisfied with the government's record. One of the most specific pledges made in the 1973 manifesto was that housing output, which came under the Ministry of Local Government, would be increased to 25,000 a year. Although most commentators had doubted whether this could be achieved, over 100,000 houses were built during the first four years of the government's term, an increase of about 50 per cent, in both the public and the private sector, over the previous rate. Moreover, the quality of new local authority housing was improved considerably.

The government's record in the field of social welfare was another positive consequence of Labour's presence. The Exchequer allocation rose from £91·6 million in 1972–73 to £274·5 million four years later, and gross expenditure on social welfare rose from about 6·5 per cent of gross national product to 10·5 per cent.[9] Most benefits rose by about 125 per cent, considerably more than both wages and prices. Rates were increased twice a year, instead of annually as previously. The qualifying age for old age pensions was reduced by three years, and various minority groups with little electoral muscle – unmarried mothers, single women over fifty-eight, and prisoners' wives – received allowances for the first time. Many other improvements were made in this field. However, the government came nowhere near achieving 'the elimination of poverty and the ending of social injustice', adumbrated in the 1973 manifesto.

The Ministry of Labour was also used to good effect. Legislation was passed to protect workers against unfair dismissal and to protect young workers against exploitation. Employment Premium Acts provided for State payments to employers increasing their work force, as a result of which over 6,000 workers entered or returned to full-time employment. Voluntary mergers between trade unions were encouraged, and steps were taken to improve the wages and conditions of farm workers. Under the 1977 Worker Participation Act a third of the directors of seven semi-State companies were elected by and from the companies' workers, an advance which fell a long way short of the 'worker democracy' advocated in the 1969 policies. Legislation was also passed, following an EEC directive, to try to ensure that men and women be paid equally for doing the same work, but the government lost much of the credit it had earned for promoting the Bill when it tried unsuccessfully late in 1975 to avoid having to be bound by it when it came to public service pay.[10]

The Minister for Industry and Commerce was unable to prevent prices rising, but in other respects his record was better. The terms on which private firms could exploit the country's natural resources were tightened considerably. In 1974 legislation was passed ending the twenty-year exemption from taxes which the previous government had granted to companies on their profits from certain mining operations. In 1976 agreements were signed with the major oil companies licensing them to prospect off the coast; the agreements ensured that through State participation, plus the payment of royalties and taxation, the State would receive about 80 per cent of the value of any oil discovered. The role of the Industrial Development Authority in promoting new industry and attracting foreign investment was expanded, and the rate of grant-aided industrial jobs approved increased by about 50 per cent, although this came nowhere near balancing jobs lost because of the recession.

Posts and Telegraphs was essentially a 'technical' Ministry, and there was no Labour policy on the subject by which the Minister could be guided or judged. Some improvements were made in the communications system – about 140,000 new subscribers were connected to the telephone system, annual capital expenditure on which expanded threefold – but it remained very poor by EEC standards. The only contentious area under the Minister's control was broadcasting. Here the relationship between the government and RTE was altered so as to give the latter's controlling body rather more autonomy and to limit the Minister's power to issue directions. However, Dr O'Brien's frequent criticisms of the media for allegedly portraying the IRA too favourably, and his use of his statutory powers to prohibit RTE from broadcasting interviews with members of the Provisional IRA, Provisional Sinn Féin or the Official IRA, made him unpopular with many journalists.

Of the Ministries under Labour's control, possibly least was achieved in Health. Corish's two Ministries had the largest and second largest Exchequer allocations, and the burden of running them both, as well as continuing to lead the party, was a very heavy one. Free medical care was extended to an extra 10 per cent of the population, new hospitals were opened, and expenditure on the health services increased almost threefold. However, no dramatic changes were made. In August 1973 the Minister announced that everyone would be entitled to free hospital services as from the following April, but the medical profession refused to work the scheme. The Minister was forced, humiliatingly, to announce that it had been postponed, and in fact it was abandoned.[11] Perhaps disheartened by this experience, he did not embark on any further ambitious projects.

The most spectacular failure in this area came in the field of contraception. A 1935 Act made both the sale and the importation of contraceptives illegal, but in 1973 the Supreme Court found that the ban on importation was unconstitutional. Consequently, all sides saw a need for reform; conservatives wanted restrictions on the right to import contraceptives, and liberals wanted legalisation of their sale. Responsibility for reform was given, following tradition, not to the Ministry for Health but to Justice. In June 1974 the government introduced its 'Control of Importation, Sale and Manufacture of Contraception Bill', which would have permitted contraceptives to be imported and sold, under licence, by chemists to married people only. The government permitted its TDs a free vote on the Bill, since some claimed conscientious objections to the idea of legalising 'artificial' contraception, regarding it as contrary to Catholic teaching. Some time earlier, the Hierarchy had declared that it was up to the legislators to decide whether the law should be changed; although the Catholic Church taught that the use of contraceptives was wrong, it said, it did not follow that the State was bound to prohibit their sale and importation.[12] Fianna Fáil consistently opposed the Bill, which it maintained would be inoperable.

The vote on the second stage was taken on 16 July, and it was defeated by seventy-five votes to sixty-one. To the astonishment of observers, those voting against it included the Taoiseach, Mr Cosgrave, and the Minister for Education, Richard Burke, as well as five other Fine Gael TDs. One Labour TD, Dan Spring, who was still annoyed that he had not been 'reappointed' to the Parliamentary Secretaryship he had held in 1956–57, did not travel to Dublin for the vote. This perhaps unprecedented example of a Prime Minister voting against one of his own government's Bills was a surprise also to the Cabinet, for Cosgrave had given no prior indication that he opposed the Bill. When the subject had come up at Cabinet meetings he had confined himself to keeping the business moving, and it had never occurred to any Minister, as far as can be told, that he might vote against it.

Immediately after the vote the opposition leader asked, 'Were the Government really serious in putting this Bill forward when the Head of the Government voted against it?'[13] and his question found private echoes on the government side. What was at issue was not Cosgrave's right to avail himself of the free vote, and to vote in accordance with his conscience, but the question of whether he should have let the Cabinet know that he opposed the Bill. Several Ministers were extremely annoyed – more than one seems to have considered resignation – since the work involved in drafting the Bill and steering it through the Dáil had been rendered almost pointless, and the government as a whole had been made to look foolish. Cosgrave explained to government critics that he had kept silent so as not to influence others against the Bill, but since he must have known in advance that it would be defeated without full support from the government benches, this explanation was not regarded as very satisfactory. Despite this, it does not seem that the matter was even raised at a Cabinet meeting. The incident did nothing for the mutual trust, depending partly on predictability of behaviour, which Cabinet members should have in each other, and also put an end to hopes that the government would be a liberal one or that it would, in the words of the 1973 manifesto, 'transform Ireland into a modern progressive society'.

This first attempt at reform having foundered, the subject was left to rest by the established parties, but was kept alive by a group of Independent Senators, two of whom tabled a Family Planning Bill in the Seanad and then joined the PLP. The matter was discussed in December 1976 by the PLP, which, because of the reservations of some members, refrained from adopting the Bill itself. However, it was decided that Corish would ask the three parliamentary groups to participate in an all-party committee to try to produce 'agreed legislation'. The PLP naturally accepted the invitation, but Fianna Fáil declined, and the Fine Gael parliamentary party informed Corish that it had 'deferred a decision'.[14] The Senators' Bill was then adopted by the Labour Party and was defeated in the Seanad in May 1977 by twenty-three votes to twenty, most of those opposing it being Fine Gael Senators.[15]

Of the Ministries under Fine Gael's control, four – Transport and Power, Defence, Lands and the Gaeltacht – covered fairly non-contentious areas on which Labour had no strong feelings. Foreign Affairs and Agriculture were rather more 'political' Ministries, but Labour was generally satisfied with the way each was handled.

The other three Fine Gael Ministries were more sensitive. With respect to Finance, Labour was unhappy with the government's record on prices, planning and unemployment, but the Minister's taxation measures were more to its liking. A White Paper published in February 1974 announced the government's intention to introduce a capital gains tax of 35 per cent, an annual wealth tax on estates of over £40,000, and a tax on capital acquisitions. In return, death duties were to be abolished. Following strong representations from those who would be affected, the package was diluted somewhat.[16] Labour's AC, having initially congratulated its Ministers for securing the party's objectives, expressed its concern when the modifications were made.[17] The Labour Ministers, however, made little attempt to prevent the changes being made, feeling that the finally agreed version was as much as Fine Gael would stand for, and content that the principles behind the taxes had been accepted. Fianna Fáil opposed the wealth and capital gains taxes vigorously in the Dáil in 1975, and abolished the wealth tax (without restoring death duties) after it returned to office in 1977, and it could well be argued that during this period it moved to the right of Fine Gael. The government also brought farmers into the income tax net, ending the anomaly whereby a farm labourer paid tax while his much wealthier employer did not.

Labour was less satisfied with progress in the other two Ministries under Fine Gael's control. The Minister for Education, Richard Burke, proved a very conservative figure, who alienated teachers' and students' organisations by his failure to consult them fully. He took no steps to reduce the clerical domination of the educational system, and was unsympathetic to attempts by some parents to establish interdenominational or non-denominational schools. On one occasion he replied to his critics by quoting from an encyclical of Pope Pius XI, and spoke of 'those who would wish us to cast aside our traditional loyalties in favour of new-fangled materialistic philosophies which have proved to be pitiable failures'. They should, he said, 'come out boldly and state where they stand in relation to the Christian ethic in education and in our national life'; the Christian ethic 'must be accepted in its totality'.[18] Not surprisingly, his conservative and high-handed approach made him extremely unpopular with the Labour Party, to the extent that its 1974 conference took the unusual step of passing, by overwhelming margins, votes criticising his record, including one demanding that he be withdrawn from office. No Labour Minister spoke in his defence, and the TD who replied to the debate commented that many of the criticisms were 'richly deserved'.[19]

The Minister for Justice, Patrick Cooney, was forced by circumstances to devote most of his attention to security problems rather than to social reform. The violence in the north spread increasingly to the Republic. There were three escapes by IRA prisoners, one of which involved the use of explosives in the centre of Dublin. In March 1974 a Fine Gael Senator, Billy Fox, was murdered by the IRA, who were also responsible for assassinating the British ambassador in July 1976. In May 1974 no-warning car bombs planted by northern Loyalists exploded in Dublin and Monaghan, killing twenty-eight people and wounding over 100. Twice, Provisional IRA prisoners in Portlaoise jail staged hunger strikes in support of a demand that their conditions be improved. On the first occasion, in February 1975, threats were relayed to the government that two Ministers would be killed if a hunger striker died; on the second, in April 1977, two Labour TDs were attacked at their homes by Provisional IRA supporters. In each case the hunger strikes were called off without any concessions having been extracted.

Since the IRA did not recognise the legitimacy of the political institutions of either the northern State or the southern State, regarding both as having been imposed upon Ireland by the British, the government took the view that the violence it used in the south was directed ultimately at the very existence of the State, and reacted accordingly. In April 1975 it introduced the Criminal Law Jurisdiction Bill, which had originally been part of the Sunningdale package (see below) and was intended to ensure that those committing serious offences in the north could not use the Republic as a safe haven. The Bill ran into protracted opposition from Fianna Fáil, and took eleven months to pass through the Houses of the Oireachtas. There were also reservations within the Labour Party, including the PLP. One of Labour's Senators, ITGWU general secretary Michael Mullen, voted against the Bill's first reading, after which the PLP changed its rules, so that henceforth any Labour TD or Senator voting against a government measure would automatically forfeit the whip, unless the measure was one the PLP had decided not to support or on which it allowed a free vote.[20] Consequently, when Mullen went on to vote against the final stage of the Bill he was expelled from the PLP. He had earlier declared that he would resign from the Seanad as soon as possible, but in fact he never did so, and he was readmitted to the PLP on 16 February 1977.[21] In January 1976 Dr John O'Connell put down a critical amendment to the Bill, but when it was pressed to the vote he abstained so as not to suffer Mullen's fate.[22]

Two further pieces of security legislation, introduced in the autumn of 1976 following the killing of the British ambassador, also caused some disquiet. The Bills gave increased powers to the police and the army, increased penalties for offences against the State, and created new offences in respect of recruiting for or inciting to join an illegal organisation. Both Houses of the Oireachtas were brought back from their summer recess to discuss the Bills for two heated weeks. Fianna Fáil opposed them skilfully; its front bench's performance was probably the most effective since the 1973 election, and played a part in reviving the confidence of the party as a whole.

The debates found the Labour Party in some disarray. A specially called PLP meeting on 11 August gave the Labour Ministers its support, in advance, for whatever measures the government decided to introduce, but some members regretted giving this blank cheque when they actually saw the proposed legislation. There was in any case a feeling throughout the party, extending from ordinary members up to some Ministers, that the government's reaction savoured of panic behaviour, and of what has been termed 'the politics of the last atrocity'. Outside parliament, the Dublin Regional Council and some branches were vocal in their criticism.

When the Bills came before the Oireachtas, Labour's parliamentarians reacted in five different ways. Most said nothing, and voted for them. Four Labour members who were not in the PLP – Noel Browne, Michael Mullen, Mary Robinson and David Thornley – spoke and voted against them.[23] Three who were in the PLP – John O'Connell, Michael D. Higgins and John Horgan – also spoke against them, but abstained on the votes. Three others – Barry Desmond, Brendan Halligan and Ruairi Quinn – expressed reservations but voted for the Bills. Only one Labour member spoke in support of the measures. This was Conor Cruise O'Brien, who said he hoped they would lead to a reduction in the amount of 'pro-IRA propaganda' published by newspapers, citing particularly letters appearing in the correspondence columns of the *Irish Press*,[24] which produced allegations that he favoured press censorship. The impression that O'Brien was rather out on a limb within both his party and the government as a whole was reinforced when the Minister for Justice accepted a Fianna Fáil amendment which diluted precisely the section to which he had attached so much importance.[25]

Overall, Labour's obvious unhappiness with the package, and the apparently embarrassed silence of most of its Ministers and TDs, prompted Charles Haughey to comment sarcastically that 'the Labour Party always wrestle with their consciences but I am afraid the Labour Party always win'.[26] Another consequence was that abstention, described during the debate by chief whip Barry Desmond as 'a soft option', ceased to be so, for the PLP tightened its rules still further so that even abstention on a government measure would in future incur the automatic removal of the whip.[27] The measures had still further ramifications, for a sequence of events arising out of their passage led to the Minister for Defence calling the President a 'thundering disgrace', and to the subsequent resignation of the latter.[28] While there were those who felt the President had over-reacted by resigning, there was no denying that the Minister's remarks were beyond justification, and tarnished the whole government. There was some feeling within the PLP that the Minister should have been dismissed, as the opposition claimed, but on the whole Labour kept out of the argument, its leader declaring that 'to the Labour Party, quite frankly, it is not that important'.[29]

Labour's concern was that while there might well be a need for tough security legislation, there was also a need to guard against the erosion of civil liberties. Some leading Fine Gael members seemed to feel that there were no valid libertarian objections to their security measures, and that all those expressing such objections must be tacit supporters of the IRA. Labour's unease was heightened by a speech made by the Taoiseach in May 1977 to his party's Ard-Fheis.[30] He dismissed complaints that some suspects' civil rights had been violated by asking what civil rights had been possessed by Senator Fox or by two policemen murdered in the course of their duty, and declared that a carefully researched newspaper inquiry into police interrogation methods had been 'a malicious campaign of vilification' against the police, a claim backed up by the Finance Minister. He also claimed that over the previous four years Fine Gael had 'not for the first time

... stood between the people of this country and anarchy'. The fervent
enthusiasm with which his remarks were greeted by delegates enabled
the opposition to speak of triumphalism, right-wing militancy and a
Nuremberg rally atmosphere.

This reluctance to concede that the institutions of state could be
secure in hands other than Fine Gael's manifested itself again during
the 1977 election campaign; for example, Fine Gael's leader in the
Seanad, Michael O'Higgins, stated that 'It is because of the calm,
courageous and cool hand of Liam Cosgrave at the helm that every one
of us is able to go home tonight and sleep soundly in our beds'.[31]
Similar rhetoric undoubtedly contributed to Cumann na nGaedheal's
defeat in the 1932 election, and did not help the Coalition in 1977.
However, unpleasant as it was to Labour, the party did nothing
whatever to dissociate itself from it.

Progress in the non-security aspects of the Justice Ministry was
rather disappointing for Labour. The 1973 promise to introduce
legislation 'to end all forms of existing discrimination against women'
was not fulfilled; for example, the archaic laws of 'criminal
conversation', treating a wife as her husband's property, were not
repealed. No attempt was made to remove the constitutional ban on
divorce, and the government did not really try to promote public
discussion on the issue. It was raised in March and April 1976 by
Conor Cruise O'Brien and Garret FitzGerald, but after the latter had
declared that there was a need for a fresh approach with regard to
divorce, contraception and interdenominational education, the
Taoiseach stated that his speech had not reflected government policy,
and the prospects of reform were killed.[32] Later in the year the
Attorney General, Declan Costello, published a discussion paper
advocating an extension of the granting of decrees of nullity, which
some saw as divorce under another name.[33]

The 1973 manifesto had also committed the government to
attempting 'to promote a peaceful solution in the North', and its policy
here differed from that of the previous administration. Whereas
Fianna Fáil repeatedly called on Britain to declare an intention to
withdraw from the north, the Coalition put the emphasis on the
establishment there of a power-sharing government, based on both
communities, an aim the British were also striving for from 1973
onwards. The British Prime Minister visited a Dublin military airport
for nine hours of discussions with the Taoiseach in September 1973,
and in October the main northern parties (except the Loyalist groups)

agreed to set up a power-sharing executive. In December a four-day conference was held at Sunningdale, in England, between the British and Irish governments and the parties in the executive. According to a declaration issued afterwards, the executive agreed to the establishment of a two-tier Council of Ireland, with representatives from north and south, and in return the Republic's government stated that it 'fully accepted and solemnly declared that there could be no change in the status of Northern Ireland until a majority of the people of Northern Ireland desired a change in that status'.[34] In addition, an Anglo-Irish Law Commission was to be set up to examine ways of dealing with 'fugitive offenders'; out of its work came the Criminal Law Jurisdiction Bill, which became law about two years after all the other parts of the Sunningdale agreement had collapsed.

The government at once ran into trouble when the Aontacht Eireann leader Kevin Boland challenged the constitutionality of the package in the High Court. The government won the case and Boland's subsequent appeal to the Supreme Court, but the victory was a pyrrhic one, for in its defence it was compelled to deny that it had stated that a part of 'the national territory', as defined by Article 2 of the Constitution, belonged to the United Kingdom, or that it had reached an agreement which prejudiced the right of the Oireachtas to exercise jurisdiction over the whole of the national territory. Moreover, it emerged that the Sunningdale declarations were not in fact an agreement but merely an agreement to sign an agreement (which in the event never was signed).[35] The point that a united Ireland could be achieved only with the consent of a majority of the people in the north remained, and a few days after the Supreme Court judgement the Dáil passed by seventy-three votes to sixty-eight a motion reaffirming this and ruling out the use of violence.[36] However, the damage had been done; the power-sharing Unionists' claim that they had secured *de jure* recognition for Northern Ireland from the southern government was seen to be false, and this certainly contributed to some extent to Protestant opposition to the executive, which was finally brought down by a Protestant workers' strike in May 1974.

The idea of removing or amending Articles 2 and 3 was not given serious consideration by the government as a whole, although it was occasionally raised. Late in 1974 Patrick Cooney suggested removing the Articles as a gesture of reconciliation, but hastily withdrew the idea after it had attracted vehement criticism from Fianna Fáil and from

John Hume and Seamus Mallon of the SDLP.[37] Conor Cruise O'Brien made the same suggestion some time later, drawing criticism from the same quarters and a deep silence from his Cabinet colleagues.[38] Although the Cabinet did have some discussions on the possibility of drafting and submitting to the people a new Constitution, its attitude was that attempts at significant constitutional reform would be divisive unless there was all-party agreement. Since Fianna Fáil has argued against such reform until the northern Protestants 'get around a table' to discuss the future of the whole island,[39] the effect of the Coalition's approach was to give Fianna Fáil, and thus ultimately northern Protestants, a veto over the possibility of change. Both O'Brien and Garret FitzGerald spoke on a number of occasions in favour of the idea of making the Republic a pluralistic society, but no specific proposals emerged from the government.

O'Brien remained Labour's spokesman on the north during this period, although parties in government do not usually have spokesmanships, and he was the only 'spokesman' Labour had on any subject. Within the government, responsibility for the north was shared between the Taoiseach and the Minister for Foreign Affairs, but O'Brien spoke more frequently on the subject than either. In June 1974 he stated that he was not personally working actively for Irish unity, since it was not a practicable goal,[40] the first such declaration ever made by an Irish Minister. Three months later a storm broke round his head when a document presented by him to Labour's AC was leaked to the press.[41] It argued that to prevent the risk of a 'doomsday situation', in which there would be civil war in the north and a flood of refugees into the south, with the Republic's army unable to intervene decisively, the government should present 'a relatively low profile'. This, he suggested, might allow the emergence of 'a non-Loyalist Protestant vote' in the forthcoming Convention elections, whereas 'a noisy and threatening posture by Dublin would play into the hands of Loyalists and help to make a Loyalist victory certain'. The leak of the document in effect caused the idea to backfire, since the Loyalists claimed that it demonstrated that even an ostensibly non-interventionist policy by the Dublin government was in fact part of an overall plot to manipulate internal events in the north. It was also condemned by Fianna Fáil and the SDLP, and drew support only from the centrist Alliance Party.

O'Brien's vigorous articulation of his views on the north made him even more unpopular than previously with Fianna Fáil. The party's

Health spokesman, Desmond O'Malley, once referred to the 'anti-national semantics' of O'Brien and FitzGerald,[42] and O'Brien's support for almost any idea became enough to turn Fianna Fáil against it. More important, the point was eventually reached where members of the Coalition parties began to feel that politically he was more of a liability than an asset to the government. He did not deviate from the Coalition's policy – which remained to work for a settlement within the context of the northern State, and to keep Britain committed to the establishment of a power-sharing government there – but he expounded it much more often than most Ministers thought necessary. Even those who agreed with almost everything he said felt that what had once been a courageous challenging of sterile orthodoxy had now become an obsession. The frequency and predictability of his comments – 'like Radio Tirana', in the words of one member of the administration – and the generous coverage guaranteed by their stylish formulation led to a feeling that by identifying a certain viewpoint too closely with himself he might actually be reducing the support which that viewpoint would otherwise have had. Since he had no formal Ministerial responsibility for the north, it is almost certain that, had the government been a single-party one, the Taoiseach would have asked him either to adopt a lower profile himself or to give his views from the back benches. It may be that Cosgrave was prevented from taking such action by O'Brien's anomalous position as Labour's northern spokesman, and by Corish's support for O'Brien.

The rows on the north which had wracked Labour before 1973 ceased. To some extent this was a consequence of developments in the north. The collapse of Sunningdale, on which so much hope had been pinned, brought home to people in the Republic and in Britain both the intractability of the problem and the depth of Protestant aversion to a united Ireland. The continuing violence led increasing numbers of people in the Republic to wonder whether 'unity or close association with a people so closely imbued with violence and its effects' was really what they wanted, in the Taoiseach's words; President Childers once expressed a similar view.[43] Indeed, the findings of opinion polls carried out in the north and the south in 1978 suggested that only about 50 per cent of the people of all Ireland actually wanted a united Ireland.[44]

Partly for this reason, Labour's traditional nationalist wing gradually subsided into silence. In addition, two of its most vocal exponents before 1973 were no longer vocal; Seán Treacy had been neutralised by becoming Ceann Comhairle, while David Thornley spent much of his time out of the country as a result of being appointed a member of the European Parliament. However, Thornley retained his capacity to embarrass the party, for at Easter 1976 he attended an illegal march staged by Provisional Sinn Féin and sat on the platform while speeches were being made. He said afterwards that he had taken part not because he supported the Provisionals but to protest against government curtailment of freedom of expression, although he was also reported to have declared that if he was sent for trial before the Special Criminal Court, he would refuse to recognise it.[45] On 28 April the PLP voted by twenty-two votes to three to withdraw the whip from him, but it was restored the following February.

O'Brien's line came in for some internal criticism, especially from anti-coalitionists. His leaked 'doomsday' document had been part of a party discussion on the north, and the opposite point of view was put by Matt Merrigan, who argued that the government should urge the British to disengage politically, militarily and economically from the north. Its existing policy, he said, was 'appeasement of British and Orange/Loyalist intransigence and arrogance' and involved abandoning the Catholic community.[46] Labour critics of the government's line linked it with its security policy, and with the ever-tightening rules of the PLP after No votes and abstentions on security legislation, and argued that, as in the Communist Party of the Soviet Union in the early 1930s, external repression was necessitating internal repression. However, O'Brien's position was never seriously challenged after 1973, and there was little open expression of any Labour dissatisfaction with government policy on the north.

Another aspect of government behaviour worthy of examination was patronage, and here the Coalition's record was poor. One of its first acts upon entering office was to install two of its own TDs as Ceann Comhairle and Leas-Cheann Comhairle, breaking a long-standing tradition that one of the two posts should be held by an opposition TD. In a similar spirit the government revised the constituency boundaries in a way obviously designed to favour itself, even though several Ministers had urged, while in opposition, that an independent commission be asked to perform the task.[47]

Members and supporters of the government parties, particularly Fine Gael, were appointed to the boards of semi-State bodies and the judiciary at a staggering rate.[48] Patronage continued even after the 1977 election defeat; in the fortnight before the government handed over office, one defeated Fine Gael TD was appointed to an £11,000 a year Land Commissionership, and another became a judge.[49] In most of this, admittedly, the government was continuing the practice of the previous administration, but it disillusioned those who had hoped that Fianna Fáil patronage would be replaced not by Fine Gael and Labour patronage but by an end to patronage. Indeed, in 1968 the then Senator Garret FitzGerald had stated that Oliver J. Flanagan should resign from the Fine Gael party and that he was not fit to hold office in a Fine Gael government after he had spoken in favour of jobbery;[50] in 1976 Flanagan was made Minister for Defence.

The government did leave two positive achievements in this field, however. It established the office of Director of Public Prosecutions, one of whose functions was to distribute briefs among barristers on an impartial basis rather than to government supporters as hitherto. In addition, it set up an independent Planning Board, to take over from the Minister for Local Government the job of deciding appeals against the decisions of planning authorities.

There were very few public disagreements between the Coalition parties. The calls from Labour, particularly Brendan Halligan, for a State development corporation drew a response from John Kelly, one of Fine Gael's Parliamentary Secretaries; he attacked the suggestion, without mentioning who had floated it, and argued against 'a massive extension of State ownership'.[51] Shortly before the 1977 election the Taoiseach declared that he had 'no ideological bias one way or the other' on the idea, while expressing a number of non-ideological reservations.[52] Late in 1976 the Minister for Finance suggested it was 'worth studying' the possibility of reducing or eliminating subsidies in areas like free school transport, children's allowances and disability benefits, but the Labour leader at once stated that he was 'firmly opposed' to any such changes, and the ideas were not mentioned again.[53]

During this period Labour rank-and-file opposition to coalition continued at much the same level as before. The Liaison Committee of the Labour Left emerged as a distinct faction within the party; in March 1975 the AC declared membership of it incompatible with membership of Labour.[54] During 1976 the LCLL, together with the Communist Party of Ireland and Official Sinn Féin, established a 'Broad Left' or 'Left Alternative' grouping, which in September published a 14,000 word plan to tackle the unemployment crisis, including proposals to nationalise the banks and to create a National Development Corporation.[55] By the end of the year, however, the alliance had collapsed.

Labour's October 1974 annual conference heavily defeated a motion calling on the party to withdraw from the coalition, but it passed, by a margin of about three to two, a resolution to the effect that a special conference be held to discuss the coalition question unless the PLP got 'an assurance from the Cabinet of a statement of intent to implement Labour policies'. Nothing was done in response until July 1975, when the party leader formally informed the PLP of the 'elements of Labour policy' so far implemented by the government and assured them that more would be implemented in the future. The PLP declared itself satisfied, and the AC too held that this met the terms of the resolution, so that no special conference needed to be held.[56] The whole incident demonstrated how weak was the phrase in the 1970 special conference resolution to the effect that Labour could remain in government 'for so long as Labour Party policies are being implemented', since almost any government at any given time is bound to be doing something which is 'Labour policy'. In any case, while the party was in government the question of what was Labour policy was not to be solved by line-by-line analysis of the 1969 documents or conference resolutions; when doubt or ambiguity existed, party policy was simply what the PLP, and in particular the Ministers, said it was.

The coalition question was fully aired at the 1976 annual conference, which discussed an AC motion calling on the conference to authorise the party leader, in consultation with the PLP and the AC, to negotiate a new election programme.[57] The resolution noted a number of areas where the conference might approve the government's record, but also recorded disappointment with the lack of progress in certain fields, such as economic and social planning, the control of the banking system, the reform of the educational system, and the introduction of comprehensive health, social and legal services.

The debate was conducted at a much higher, less personalised and rancorous level than the 1970 debate, but most of the arguments were fairly predictable.[58] The anti-coalitionists pointed to the government's poor record on jobs, prices and planning, claimed that Labour had got nowhere near enough in return for its participation in the government, and argued that by tarnishing its record it was damaging both its short-term and its long-term electoral prospects. The coalitionists pointed out that defeat for the motion would simply hand the country back to Fianna Fáil, emphasised the features of the government's record which could be attributed to Labour's presence, maintained that support for coalition was not a sacred principle for all time but merely a tactical expedient which they favoured in present circumstances, and argued that, even if the party's image was being tarnished, Labour should be prepared to get its hands dirty in the interests of working people.

Some coalitionists suggested that if the Coalition won the next general election, the 'myth of Fianna Fáil's invincibility' would be shattered. Once this happened, they argued, its internal contradictions, springing from its position as a right-wing party with extensive working-class support, would come to the fore, and it might start to disintegrate. At its most optimistic, then, the coalitionist strategy has Fianna Fáil as its intended victim, whereas during the 1960s the most optimistic anti-coalitionists had hoped that Labour would gain at the expense of Fine Gael and emerge as the main opposition to Fianna Fáil.

As in 1970, most of the opposition to coalition came from Dublin delegates, while rural delegates were overwhelmingly in favour of a further coalition. The PLP, too, was almost unanimously in favour, the only serious reservations about the motion coming from Dr John O'Connell, who in October 1973 had been the first to end the government's honeymoon period by criticising Labour's performance.[59] The motion was carried by about six to one.

Five of the seven by-elections between the 1973 and 1977 general elections arose in areas with very little Labour support. The only two where the party's 1973 strength was enough to constitute a valid base for comparison were in Galway West in March 1975, where the Labour vote rose by 5·4 per cent, and in Dublin South West in June 1976, where it dropped by 8·2 per cent. The Dublin result should have given the party a warning of the fate it would suffer in the city at the general election, but the fact that its support was slipping was not noticed because Labour won the seat, its first by-election success since 1965. Its candidate, Brendan Halligan, went on leave of absence from his job as party secretary. Transfers between the Coalition parties remained high; there was a 70 per cent transfer from Labour to Fine Gael in Galway West, and a 75 per cent transfer in the other direction in Dublin South West. Party membership remained fairly stationary, at around 5,000, throughout the government's term (see Appendix 3); most of the fall between December 1976 and December 1977 took place after Labour had left office.

The general election was called for 16 June 1977, about nine months earlier than was legally necessary.[60] The government had decided about three weeks earlier to go to the country when it did. Four of the Labour Ministers, the exception being the party leader, wanted the election held later, on the ground that the economy was recovering and that this would have reached the public consciousness by the end of the year. However, the government allowed election fervour to build up among backbenchers and ordinary members, and finally trapped itself in a position where it felt it had to call an election or seem to be afraid to face the country. Although the Constitution gives the Taoiseach the power to seek a dissolution, the decision in this case was a Cabinet one, reached after a vote.

The 'renegotiation' approved of by the 1976 conference produced a twenty-six-page manifesto drawn up by a committee composed of members of the two government parties. In essence, it offered more of the same, although it did contain a few new Labour-inspired proposals. It spoke unconvincingly of a 'plan', to be updated annually, which would provide an unprecedented rate of growth and would allow investment decisions to be 'taken with greater certainty and knowledge'. It also promised a National Development Corporation, which would 'make proposals for new economic enterprises which will not compete unfairly with the private sector' and would co-ordinate the activities of semi-State bodies. The manifesto looked hastily put together, as indeed it was, and was later described by Labour's National Director of Elections, acting general secretary Seamus Scally, in a report adopted by the AC, as 'dull and unimaginative'.[61] Fianna Fáil's well marketed manifesto, full of attractive promises, together with the unemployment rate, meant that the Coalition was on the defensive throughout the campaign.

Labour also ran into problems from its anti-coalition wing. In the Dublin Artane constituency Noel Browne was selected by local branches as a Labour candidate, but the AC refused to ratify his selection, having passed, a month earlier, a clearly *ad hominem* resolution to the effect that no party member who was also an Oireachtas member but did not belong to the PLP could be ratified.[62] Another prominent anti-coalitionist, Matt Merrigan, withdrew his candidacy shortly before the selection conference in Dublin Finglas, alleging that supporters of Brendan Halligan were attempting to rig it. Browne and Merrigan then stood as 'Independent Labour' candidates, on a socialist, anti-coalition platform, and were helped by anti-coalition Labour members and supporters from other Dublin constituencies, some of which also witnessed Labour rows. A different case arose in East Limerick, where the local party organisation, controlled by the constituency TD Steve Coughlan, decided that Coughlan should be the only Labour candidate, a decision which led to his long-standing party rival Mick Lipper standing as a 'Democratic Labour' candidate.

The results were disastrous for both Coalition parties. Fine Gael fell from fifty-three seats at the dissolution to forty-three, and Labour from twenty to seventeen. The Labour vote dropped by about two per cent, back to the 1961 level. Labour lost votes in every part of the country (see Appendix 2), especially in the Dublin region, where the recession was felt most strongly and where hostility among members to the coalition idea was greatest. Four Labour TDs, Brendan Halligan, Justin Keating, Conor Cruise O'Brien and David Thornley, lost their seats here, although two new ones were elected. Thornley actually lost his deposit, the first Labour TD to suffer this fate since 1923. Outside Dublin the party held its own in terms of seats. It lost its Waterford seat – its veteran TD there, Tom Kyne, stood down – but an outgoing Senator, Patrick Kerrigan, was elected in Cork City. In Limerick Coughlan lost his seat to Lipper, but since the latter was admitted to the PLP four months later, this amounted only to a turnover in personnel.

Since Labour had expected to lose seats, it was not too disappointed with the result, especially since Fine Gael, which had been expecting to gain significantly, fell back heavily. Moreover, in five constituencies – Dublin Cabra, Clontarf, Finglas and Rathmines West, plus Kerry South – the leading Labour candidate came within 1,000 votes of election. Given the internal problems in Dublin, the party was able to convince itself that it had almost managed to increase its Dáil strength, completely against the odds. The impression that it had fared better than Fine Gael was in fact inaccurate; Fine Gael had lost more heavily mainly because it had had more to lose, and Labour's losses in proportion to its strength were actually greater. Labour's share of the total Coalition vote fell from 28·1 per cent in 1973 to 27·6 per cent, with Fine Gael's rising accordingly.

The Coalition transfers held up fairly well. Fine Gael's transfers to Labour rose slightly, but the transfer in the other direction fell from 71·9 per cent in 1973 to 58·8 per cent, and in Dublin to 50·4 per cent. Of the two Independent Labour candidates, Browne was elected –

neither of the Coalition parties won a seat in his constituency – but Merrigan only just saved his deposit. It seems fair to conclude that most Labour voters favoured a continuation of the Coalition, although they were less enthusiastic than in 1973.

The defeat of Halligan, Keating, O'Brien and Thornley did not mark a reversal of the transition of the 1960s even at the level of personalities, for both the new Dublin TDs were recognisably post-transition figures. One, John Horgan, a former journalist, had been an Independent Senator, representing the National University constituency, for six years before joining the Labour Party and the PLP in September 1975. The other, Ruairi Quinn, was an architect in his early thirties. One of the narrowly defeated Dublin candidates, Mary Robinson, had been an Independent Senator for Trinity College since 1969; she joined the party in August 1976 and the PLP two months later. A lawyer, she had a long record of involvement in civil liberties issues and, like Horgan, had made innumerable attempts to liberalise the contraception laws. After the Dáil election she was re-elected to her Trinity Seanad seat.

Overall, Labour's period in government was one which contained many lessons for the party, lessons frequently overlooked. Many anti-coalitionists were reinforced in their belief that all the party's ills sprang from its willingness to take part in coalitions, a simplistic conclusion which opts out of trying to face up to the problem of how a minor party, operating in an unsympathetic social and political environment, can make the best use of the strength it has. Far too many coalitionists, on the other hand, were content to maintain that the coalition strategy had been vindicated by the fact that Labour did at least manage to get some of its policies implemented. The fact is, however, that although Labour conferences had been assured during the early 1970s that a future coalition would not be like the previous ones, because the party now had clearer policies, TDs of a higher calibre and a greater sense of purpose, Labour did lose its sense of identity to almost as great an extent as in the Inter-Party governments.

The important lessons for the party were tactical rather than strategic, and bore on the effectiveness of its Ministers in the government. Labour had nearly 200,000 voters, it had 5,000 members, and hundreds of people spent many hours formulating its policies, but in the last analysis everything rested on the shoulders of just five individuals. There can be little doubt that these individuals, whatever their personal merits and achievements, did not operate well collectively.

To many observers, one of the most remarkable things about the Coalition government was its unity. It faced economic and security problems far greater than those which beset the Inter-Party governments, but it held together much better than they had, and indeed better than the preceding and succeeding single-party governments. Some felt that the government's greatest achievement had been simply this, that it had remained united, and, by showing that a coalition could work, had disproved the Fianna Fáil argument that coalitions are inherently unstable and disintegrate when serious problems arise.[63] Moreover, there is no doubt that this appearance of unity was not deceptive. Although there were occasions when the Cabinet divided along party lines, they were few and far between, were not on fundamental issues,[64] and never provoked any sort of 'crisis'. Much of the credit for this must go to the Taoiseach, who, although on the right of his party, operated, in the opinion of the Labour Ministers, as an extremely fair chairman.

While all this was good for the government as a whole, however, it may not have been good for the Labour Party specifically. The Labour Ministers did not act as a bloc within the government. At Cabinet meetings they did not sit together: the decision not to do so was taken at the start, as a token of the two parties' willingness to operate amicably. They sometimes held their own meetings beforehand – incurring some disapproving noises from the Fine Gael Ministers – but rarely acted in unison around the Cabinet table. Even some of those occasions when the Cabinet did split along party lines seem almost to have happened by chance. Some of the Labour Ministers made powerful contributions to the government's record, to the extent that fifty-seven of the 156 Bills passed during the Coalition's terms of office, 36.5 per cent of the total, emanated from Ministries controlled by Labour,[65] but they did so as individuals. Moreover, even some of their most commendable achievements, such as the construction of over 100,000 houses, resulted from the drive and hard work of the Minister concerned rather than from an attempt to implement Labour policy specifically. One Minister at least decided at the outset that he would devote all his energies to his own Ministry rather than dissipate them by taking an interest in the activities of other departments.

There were several reasons why the Labour Ministers did not act as a bloc. The first was the general dilemma faced by any party in a coalition government, that of being pulled in two directions. On the one hand, it wishes to steer government policy as far as possible in its own direction, and will be under internal pressure to do so. On the other, a spirit of unity within the government is not something to be destroyed lightly. The latter consideration was felt with particular acuteness because of the sixteen years of Fianna Fáil rule which had just passed, and a feeling among both Coalition parties that they had an obligation to provide a stable alternative government, even though this involved compromise on both sides. In addition, Fine Gael, certainly in the early days, bent over backwards to be fair to Labour, in matters like the apportionment of Ministries, and for Labour to have behaved in too prickly a fashion might have seemed ungracious and churlish.

Another, curiously, was the impact of the economic recession and the problems it produced. Although in some circumstances adversity might shatter a government, as it did in 1957, in this case it led to a greater degree of unity and mutual loyalty between Ministers, to the extent that they each reportedly took an oath that even if one of them was kidnapped and threatened with death the government would make no concessions to the kidnappers.[66] Crisis circumstances do not encourage boat-rocking, and militated against the muscle-flexing and testing of ideas which might have been indulged in a period of tranquillity.

A third was that Labour possessed no policies designed for implementation within a coalition. It still had its 1969 policies, but these were clearly intended for a situation in which Labour was in government on its own. The party had no intermediate policies behind which its Ministers could throw their weight, and had given little thought to the question of what exactly they should try do do.

The structure of the government also played a part. The key role of the Minister for Finance, in all governments based on the British model, was appreciated by many Ministers only after they took office. The Finance Minister must approve of every Ministerial project which has a financial aspect, which gives him a power almost of veto over other Ministers' activities. While it is true that ultimately a Finance Minister must implement government decisions, it is nevertheless the case that he can delay a project about which he is unenthusiastic, by questioning costings, asking for clarifications, and so on. Consequently, his goodwill, and the revenue in his possession, are much sought after, and unless some Ministers are acting as a bloc, each one, especially those in charge of large spending departments, is in competition with the rest of the Cabinet for a greater share of the available money.[67] A related factor was that the civil servants in the Department of Finance have always been regarded as extremely conservative[68] – this was certainly the impression of the Labour Ministers who came into contact with them – so that Labour's chances of achieving a radical departure from economic orthodoxy were reduced still further.

In addition, the Coalition government seems to have made more use of Cabinet committees than did earlier governments. One reason, no doubt, was to facilitate 'horizontal looks' across departmental boundaries.[69] Another was that Ireland's recently acquired membership of the EEC greatly increased the government's work-load. Ministers were frequently away on EEC business, and attendance at the twice-weekly Cabinet meetings averaged only about ten. The difficulty of getting all fifteen Ministers together was one factor leading some Ministers to feel that the pace of decision-making in the Cabinet was too slow, and that smaller, specialist bodies might resolve problems more quickly. The capital taxation package was drawn up by a Cabinet committee, for example. The most powerful proved to be the security committee, whose recommendations, when they were unanimous, were often passed virtually without discussion by the full Cabinet. Labour's representatives on it were Conor Cruise O'Brien and Jimmy Tully, who of all the Labour Ministers were probably closest to the traditional Fine Gael viewpoint on law-and-order questions. In general, the likelihood of two Labour Ministers acting as a 'bloc' in a small informal body of only five or six Ministers was even less than that of five acting as a bloc in a body of fifteen, and the Cabinet's use of committees reduced the likelihood of decisions running along party lines.

The other reasons related to the individuals involved. Although there were only five of them, the Labour Ministers had widely differing views on a number of subjects, from the economy to the north. These political differences were sometimes accompanied by personal differences; there was deep antagonism between two of them in particular. Such disunity could not be concealed from the Fine Gael members of the government. Personal – and even political – closeness was to be found as often across party lines as within them; Jimmy Tully and Fine Gael's Mark Clinton had played football together as boys, for example, while Justin Keating and Garret FitzGerald took holidays together. In some cases there was a complete lack of trust. One Labour Minister suspected another of being in secret contact with Fine Gael, so that even if the Labour Ministers had decided on a policy of brinkmanship, Fine Gael would always have known exactly how little they needed to concede.

The other relevant personality factor was the character of the Labour leader. In a parliamentary party often marked by backbiting and intrigue, Corish enjoyed widespread respect and even affection for his decency, integrity and lack of cynicism. However, he was by no stretch of the imagination a tough leader, and now, approaching sixty, clearly running out of steam, and trying to cope with two large Ministries, he lacked the inclination to try to whip his Labour colleagues, three at least of whom were more forceful personalities than he was, into a cohesive unit, as a different type of leader might have been able to despite all the other difficulties. Corish had been relatively young and inexperienced during his previous period as a Minister, and his best years were spent on the opposition benches. Although it had been decided in advance that he had the power to 'hire and fire' the Labour Ministers, in other respects he did not act as a mini-Taoiseach for them. Cosgrave and the other Labour Ministers contacted each other direct when the need arose, without feeling any obligation to channel communications through Corish.

Almost certainly, if the Labour Ministers had acted as a bloc, they would have been able to extract more from the government, by demanding the right to control policy in certain areas in return for giving Fine Gael control over others. Of course, such an approach would have had its drawbacks. It would have forfeited Fine Gael's goodwill, and might have produced a government of two parts, each pulling in different directions, a situation on which Fianna Fáil would have been quick to capitalise. It would have led to a great increase in the number of Cabinet votes going along party lines, and while Labour could have countered this by threatening to withdraw unless it received fair treatment, an implementation of this threat would also have given Fianna Fáil much straw from which to make anti-coalition bricks.

However, Labour could have been more assertive than it was without pushing matters to breaking point. As things were, the party never flexed its muscles; it never attempted to find out exactly where breaking point was, or just how much ground Fine Gael would have been prepared to yield. Perhaps cowed by Fianna Fáil's attempts to make the viability of coalitions a key issue in Irish politics, and unduly fearful of the *Schadenfreude* with which that party might greet the collapse of a coalition government, Labour never behaved in the obdurate, even recalcitrant manner which a minor party must be prepared to adopt if it is not to lose its identity.

Altogether, the party's experience in government was an unimpressive sequel to the period of transition. The transition, it was true, had attracted individuals who performed more effectively within the government than most of its pre-transition Ministers had, but apart from this, the previous sixteen years, during which the party had supposedly been steeling itself in the fires of opposition, honing its policies to a fine edge, might never have happened.

The main lesson for Labour to draw from its participation in the National Coalition government was that it had devoted too much time in the past to grand strategy and not enough time to tactics. The whole coalition question is of course an important one, but all too often Labour has seemed unhealthily obsessed by it. In complete contrast, it gave no thought before 1973 – and has given not much more since – to the basic tactical question of what approach it should take once inside a coalition government. On this crucial question the Ministers received no guidance from the PLP, and the PLP received no guidance from the annual conference. Other things being equal, carefully formulated policies are worth having, but they remain in limbo, at one level removed from reality, unless thought is given to the question of how they can be implemented. This question, contrary to what Labour has generally seemed to imagine, involves much more than simply deciding whether or not to join a coalition.

10

Marking time, 1977–81

10.1 Labour in the interregnum

The four-year period after the 1977 election was not one of advance for Labour, as the aftermath of the 1957 election had been. Indeed, the result of the 1981 election was to suggest that things actually got worse after the humbling 1977 result. While there was some new thought on matters of party policy, and a fresh approach to party strategy, there was no organisational overhaul, and no radical departure from the methods of the past.

The party spent this period under a new leader, Frank Cluskey. Ten days after the 1977 election Brendan Corish announced that he would not seek re-election as leader when the Dáil reconvened, and would not have done so whatever the outcome of the election. In his resignation statement he said that during the period of his leadership Labour had 'emerged as a National Party with clearly defined Socialist policies and a national organization'.[1] The statement ended, perhaps characteristically:

The people of County Wexford have honoured me as one of their Deputies in the Dáil for thirty-two years. I trust I have served them well in the past and hope that I will continue to do so throughout this incoming Dáil. Their continued support has been at all times a source of great consolation throughout the trials of public life and particularly over the last four difficult years.

When the PLP met to elect a new leader on 1 July the only nominees were Frank Cluskey and Michael O'Leary. Only sixteen TDs were eligible to vote,[2] and the first ballot produced an eight–eight tie. In the vote, it appears, the PLP split partly on union lines and partly on an urban–rural basis.[3] Cluskey belonged to the WUI, all three members of which supported him, while six of the eight ITGWU members supported O'Leary, a long-time member of that union. It was also noticeable that, of the five longest-serving rural TDs, only one (Corish) supported Cluskey, while only two of the six Dublin TDs supported O'Leary. A second ballot was held at once on the proposal of one of Cluskey's supporters, and this time Cluskey won by nine votes to seven; it is believed that the Wicklow TD Liam Kavanagh was the only one to change his vote. Kavanagh then proposed that O'Leary be elected deputy leader, which was unanimously agreed.

Cluskey had been in the Dáil since 1965, and had been a Parliamentary Secretary in the coalition government. Aged forty-seven when he became leader, he was a Dubliner who had been a trade union official before entering full-time politics. Cluskey's style of leadership, and his electoral fate, resembled in many ways those of Tom Johnson, the party's first leader. He too was an excellent parliamentarian; one reviewer of the 1977–81 Dáil described his 'tactical skill, political judgement and performance within the Dáil' as 'quite outstanding'.[4] He was a particularly sharp critic of Charles Haughey after the latter became Taoiseach in 1979, and was much more effective than the Fine Gael leader in piercing his defences. Cluskey was widely respected for his sincerity, his tenacity and his capacity for hard work. Like Johnson, however, he lacked popular appeal, and appeared dogged, unimaginative and colourless to television audiences, in whose eyes he was overshadowed by the other two party leaders. He lacked charisma and did not appear to enjoy meeting people *en masse* during election campaigns. His own Dáil seat was never secure – his first preference vote slid steadily from its 1965 level – and it was no great surprise when he lost his seat in 1981. His defeat, like that of Johnson fifty-four years earlier, was due partly to the intervention in his constituency of an Independent Labour candidate (see below).

The party faced few electoral tests during these four years. It contested only one of the three by-elections to arise; this was in Cork City, where the vacancy was occasioned by the death of the Labour TD Pat Kerrigan. A strong Labour candidate, Toddy O'Sullivan, actually doubled Labour's percentage vote (from 10·2 to 22·6 per cent), but finished only third; the Fine Gael candidate took the seat as a result of receiving 58·5 per cent of O'Sullivan's transfers, with only 18·6 per cent passing to Fianna Fáil.

The five-yearly local government elections were held in June 1979, on the same day as the first direct elections to the European

Parliament. Labour fared slightly worse than it had at the 1974 local elections; its percentage vote on both the twenty-seven county councils and the four main city councils fell by one per cent, and it won seventy-seven of the 806 seats on these thirty-one authorities, having won seventy-seven out of 795 in 1974. This lacklustre performance contrasted with that of Fine Gael, which gained twenty-nine seats and used the elections as a springboard for its advance at the general election. For this reason it was in the long run the more important of the two elections held at that time, but it took second place in the public eye to the European elections, at which Labour seemed at first sight to have done remarkably well, winning four of the fifteen Irish seats, the same number as Fine Gael and just one fewer than Fianna Fáil.[5]

The superficial impression of a leap forward to a position of near equality with the two major parties was, however, entirely misleading. Only in Dublin, where each of the three parties won about 30 per cent of the votes, did this happen. In the country as a whole Labour's share of the votes rose only slightly, from 11·6 per cent at the 1977 general election to 14·5 per cent. Labour did so well in terms of seats mainly because the potential for disproportionality inherent in the STV system when small constituencies are employed for once manifested itself, and whereas at general elections the disproportionalities generally even themselves out across the country, on this occasion they were cumulative. In consequence, Fine Gael won no more seats than Labour despite receiving well over twice as many first preferences, and minor parties and Independents, with 40,000 more votes, won two fewer seats. Given that Labour, unlike the other parties, nominated its strongest possible candidates in each constituency, and that the government's popularity was then at its nadir partly owing to a postal strike which had already lasted four months, Labour should have done very much better if it was really on the road to recovery.

In addition, the outcome of the election weakened the party by taking four of its small Dáil group to Europe.[6] As a result Michael O'Leary, the party spokesman on Finance, John O'Connell (Health and Social Welfare), Eileen Desmond (Justice) and Liam Kavanagh (Foreign Affairs until a reshuffle in May 1980) became infrequent Dáil attenders, and the party's voice in these areas was muted, at least until the TDs, disillusioned after a year or so by the powerlessness of the European Parliament, switched their attention back to Dáil Eireann.

In comparison with the previous eight years, the party was fairly united during this period. This was partly a consequence of the departure, in some cases enforced, of those who had constituted an anti-coalition thorn in Labour's flesh since 1970. At its meeting on 29 September 1977 Labour's AC passed a motion, proposed by its new leader, to the effect that Noel Browne and Matt Merrigan had '*de facto* formed another political Party' by standing on their own manifesto during the election, and that they had consequently ceased to be party members by violating the party's constitution. Another anti-coalitionist, Dermot Boucher, had been expelled six months earlier.[7] Those expelled, with their supporters and others, proceeded to form the Socialist Labour Party (SLP), which adopted the anti-coalition approach taken by Labour in 1969.[8] Shortly before it was formed, Boucher suggested that it sprang from the fact that Labour's internal contradictions, resulting from the changes of the previous fifteen years, could no longer be resolved:[9]

Perhaps the time has come for a parting of the ways; for terminating the endless, futile, fratricidal civil wars which benefit no one except Fianna Fáil; for abandoning the ludicrous pretence that the Socialism of Noel Browne and Matt Merrigan has anything in common with the mild reformism of Brendan Corish and Frank Cluskey, not to mention the true blue conservatism of Jimmy Tully and the rural TDs.

Labour's view of the cause of the parting of the ways was simply that the 'dissidents', unlike the silent coalitionists in the late 1960s, were not prepared to accept conference decisions on policy and strategy when these were not to their liking.

The only internal dispute of any note culminated in the resignation of Dr John O'Connell in February 1981. The revision of constituency boundaries meant that O'Connell's base was split between two of the new constituencies, and while O'Connell wanted to opt for Dublin South Central, where party leader Frank Cluskey would also have been standing, the AC insisted that he stand in Dublin West. The AC was breaking the unwritten law that TDs are allowed to decide for themselves where they stand and how they run their bailiwicks. It did so partly to protect Cluskey, who was thought more likely to lose his seat than O'Connell should only one of the two be elected in Dublin South Central. In addition, O'Connell was still regarded as something of a maverick in the party; he had been critical of Corish's record as Minister for Health, but praised his Fianna Fáil successor Charles Haughey, and in July 1978 had described as 'progressive' a health scheme about which Labour expressed 'very considerable reservations'.[10]

Rather than move to Dublin West, O'Connell resigned from the party to contest Dublin South Central as an Independent Labour candidate, although in his resignation letter he said that 'my heart will always be with the Labour Party and all it stands for'.[11] The outcome of the election – O'Connell swept to re-election at the head of the poll, while Labour did not win a seat in either constituency – did not endear him to Labour members, some of whom held him personally responsible for Cluskey's defeat. However, it added substance to O'Connell's claim that both he and Cluskey could have been elected in South Central had they been standing on a united ticket, and suggested that the AC had been over-protective towards Cluskey. It also reaffirmed the lesson that the national executive of a party of Labour's size is ill advised to attempt to dictate to a sitting TD in the matter of where he should stand.

Several other figures who had been prominent in the party during the early 1970s now faded away. David Thornley drifted out of the party, joined the SLP, and died in June 1978, nine years to the day after the 1969 election. Conor Cruise O'Brien was elected to the Seanad from the Trinity College constituency, but resigned the Labour whip in October 1977 so as to enable him to speak more freely on Northern Ireland. He subsequently became editor of a British weekly newspaper, resigned his Seanad seat in June 1979, and played no part in party activities except to address annual conferences. Justin Keating was also elected to the Seanad, where he became Labour leader, but although he remained close to the decision-making core of the party for a while, he did not stand for either the Dáil or the Seanad in 1981. The fourth defeated Dublin TD, Brendan Halligan, returned to his former position as party general secretary, from which he resigned for personal reasons on 28 October 1980; he was succeeded by Seamus Scally, formerly the assistant general secretary.

There was a certain amount of policy development, although inevitably most of the party's policy statements were reactions to the government's actions and were predictable responses for an opposition party to make. Thus Labour opposed Fianna Fáil's abolition of the wealth tax in 1978, and its phasing out of food subsidies, which were partially restored early in 1981. It opposed a Family Planning Bill brought forward by the government to legalise the sale of contraceptives to married people on presentation of a doctor's prescription, a Bill which the sponsoring Minister, Charles Haughey, said sought 'to provide an Irish solution to an Irish problem'.[12] Although most members of the PLP thought it ludicrously conservative, there remained a section which was opposed to legalising contraception at all, and the impossibility of devising amendments with which all TDs would agree caused the party not to table any amendments on the pretext that the Bill was so bad as to be beyond improvement by amendment.[13] Fine Gael took the same approach, for the same reason, so that line-by-line opposition to the Bill (which came into operation late in 1980) was offered only by the SLP deputy Dr Noel Browne.

A clear-cut stand on divorce took a long time to emerge, and when, in June 1980, Browne introduced a Bill to permit the holding of a referendum on the Article (41.3.2) forbidding the enactment of any law legalising it, no other TD supported his attempt to have the Bill formally introduced, Labour explaining that it was still formulating its policy. Two weeks later it announced that it wanted the establishment of an all-party committee to seek agreement on the need to amend Article 41.3.2. Its annual conference in October 1980 passed a motion calling on the PLP to introduce a private member's Bill to permit a referendum, one of the few opposing voices coming from Michael Pat Murphy, who said that if the motion was passed Labour would lose seats at the next election.[14]

In fact the PLP had already decided to bring in a less ambitious Bill, which was introduced three days later. Its motion called on the Oireachtas to set up an all-party committee to report 'on the appropriate form of amendment to Article 41 of the Bunreacht na hEireann',[15] a form of words designed to make it clear that the committee was to decide how, rather than whether, the constitution was to be amended. The government declared itself firmly against the introduction of divorce, but Fine Gael, which was deeply divided on the question, sought to avoid the issue by tabling an anodyne amendment seeking a committee 'to consider problems of supporting marriage and the family under modern conditions'.[16] When the vote was taken the Labour motion was defeated by sixty-two votes to fifteen, with Fianna Fáil voting against and Fine Gael abstaining; two Labour TDs, Michael Pat Murphy and Dan Spring, also abstained.[17]

Shortly before the 1981 election an anti-abortion group, the 'Pro-Life Amendment Campaign', approached each of the three main parties asking them to undertake to amend the Constitution by inserting an article forbidding the legislature to legalise abortion. Although such a move seemed unnecessary, since no party had ever suggested introducing such legislation, both Fianna Fáil and Fine Gael enthusiastically promised to introduce an amendment to this effect if returned to power. Cluskey also met the group, but promised only that Labour would 'consider the need' for a constitutional amendment, adding that the anti-abortion group should also be putting forward proposals to improve facilities for poor and single-parent families. The party did, however, make clear its opposition to the idea of legalising abortion.[18] Labour also urged that Irish neutrality be made a constitutional stipulation rather than merely a matter of government policy, but drew no support from the other parties.

Responsibility for Northern Ireland policy during this period lay with the party leader, who had always been an adherent of the two communities view. In the aftermath of the 1977 election Fine Gael appeared to become slightly more republican than heretofore, leaving Labour as the least republican of the main parties. Cluskey continually spoke in favour of power-sharing within the north, while Charles Haughey, after becoming Taoiseach, repeatedly expressed the opinion that Northern Ireland had failed as a political entity, so that no purely internal northern settlement could achieve peace. A profile of Cluskey spoke of him as being 'determined that Labour will continue, alone if necessary, to insist that the achievement of unity must not come before the achievement of reconciliation, and that there will be no succour for men of violence'.[19] After losing his seat in the 1981 election, he said that he did not regret the line he had taken even if the party had suffered electorally in consequence.[20] In 1980 Justin Keating suggested that the party should adopt a more nationalist approach, and was criticised by Conor Cruise O'Brien for doing so, but since neither man was any longer a TD the disagreement was of little consequence.[21] The party's 1979 conference passed a motion, proposed by O'Brien, that the Council of Labour, including representatives of the SDLP, the NILP and the ICTU, be reconvened, but since only the NILP responded favourably no action was taken.[22]

On one issue on which many Labour supporters felt strongly, the party resisted, for obscure reasons, the temptation to float with the tide of public opinion. This was the question of taxation, a major source of irritation to many PAYE (pay as you earn) taxpayers who felt that their share of the tax burden was unjustly high while that of farmers, the self-employed and professional people was unjustly low. On 20

March 1979 there were nation-wide strikes and massive marches – in Dublin alone at least 150,000 people took part – by workers protesting about the government's taxation policies. These were organised by local trades councils and not by the ICTU, which was clearly unhappy with the whole affair. Labour, remarkably, made no attempt to capitalise on the protestors' displeasure. The reason was that the party leadership, like that of the ICTU, while favouring increasing taxes on the groups singled out by the marchers, did not favour reducing employees' taxation, since it would be inconsistent with their desire for increased government expenditure. In consequence, the party maintained an embarrassed silence on the question, breached only by one of its TDs actually expressing disapproval of the strikes,[23] a self-effacing attitude, possibly the result of Cluskey's closeness to some senior figures in the ICTU, which suggested a lack of political astuteness.

In 1980 the party brought forward a new programme of policies, the successor to the 1969 policy documents. The 1980 programme was shorter and less detailed than they had been, but did not mark any move towards the centre. Once again, Labour was defined as a socialist party, working to create a classless society in which the people as a whole owned and controlled the means of production, distribution and exchange. The mixed economy was dismissed as merely a modified form of capitalism.[24] The section on the economy again made mention of a fifteen to twenty-year national plan, and this time explicitly called for the nationalisation of the banks.[25] The programme advocated a free and comprehensive national health service, including the nation-wide provision of family planning clinics, and proposed the election, on a one-person-one-vote basis, of local education authorities, which would presumably reduce or even eliminate clerical control of education.[26] It also called for a new non-sectarian Constitution and, in the interim, for the removal from Bunreacht na hEireann of the Article forbidding divorce.[27] The programme contained sections on women's rights, the travelling people, the reform of parliament, and energy, where an 'unequivocal' opposition to nuclear power was expressed.[28] Unlike the 1969 programme, this one included a section on the north, which was largely the same as the 1972 policy. One difference was that it stated explicitly that the party believed that the immediate requirement was an internal settlement within the north, and that 'longterm solutions can only be considered when the political vacuum within Northern Ireland is filled',[29] an approach which reflected Cluskey's attitude to the question and distinguished Labour's policy from those of the two major parties.

As always, the question of coalition loomed over many of the party's deliberations. The alliance with Fine Gael ended with the 1977 election defeat, and for the next four years each of the two parties went its own way. Three annual conferences were held between the 1977 and 1981 general elections; only at the second of these, held in Killarney in April 1979, was party strategy discussed. The conference considered an AC motion, supported by most members of the PLP, to the effect that Labour should contest the next election on its own independent manifesto, and that if no party won an overall majority of seats the party leader would be authorised to enter into negotiations with other parties to see if a coalition was possible. A special conference would then be convened to hear his report of the negotiations, and would decide what course the party should take.

Most of the discussion of the motion revolved not around the niceties of these tactics but around the inevitable question of whether the party should or should not rule out coalition.[30] Opponents (who included both the party chairman, Michael D. Higgins, and the vice-chairman, Pat Carroll) argued that as long as there remained a prospect of coalition the process of creative thinking within the party would be stunted; a 'cautious self-censorship' would creep into the formulation of policies, which would be framed with one eye on the question of whether they would be compatible with Fine Gael policies. Supporters maintained that the motion simply advocated keeping all options (except that of a pre-election pact) open, and that the anti-coalitionists wanted Labour to be an ideologically pure sect rather than a broad national party. Barry Desmond declared that he believed in government 'in the here and now, not in some kind of militant hereafter'. The motion was carried by a majority of about two to one, a demonstration that most of the pre-1977 Labour anti-coalitionists had remained within the party rather than join the SLP.

The effect of this decision was to postpone a firm commitment on the coalition question until after the 1981 election, and although some were later to blame the strategy for Labour's losses in 1981, it at least had the merit of removing this always contentious subject from the arena of internal debate. Other discussion of the issue dealt only with whether Labour should lay down certain 'non-negotiable' conditions before agreeing to coalition talks, and in particular whether it should insist on any future coalition government introducing a wealth tax, which Fine Gael had made it clear it opposed. Early in 1980 Cluskey gave an apparently binding commitment on the subject, declaring that 'If Fianna Fáil do not legislate for an effective wealth tax, as seems likely, we will contest the next general election with a programme which will include a commitment to its reintroduction. That commitment will not be negotiable in any conceivable circumstance.'[31] However, this declaration was not incorporated into the motion passed at Killarney, and in the event the Coalition programme did not include a wealth tax.

The Fianna Fáil government had no more success than the National Coalition in dealing with unemployment and inflation, although as late as January 1979 it was still speaking optimistically of actually eliminating unemployment by 1983.[32] Whatever chance its ambitious plans had of success were swept away by the economic recession of the late 1970s which followed the overthrow of the Pahlavi regime in Iran. By the time it left office in 1981 unemployment, inflation and foreign borrowing were all higher than they had been in 1977, and were much higher than the 1977 manifesto had predicted.[33] Unemployment, for example, which had been 109,439 in June 1977, was 123,472 in June 1981.

Fianna Fáil, after its poor showing in the European Parliament elections, entered a state of internal tension. Backbenchers criticised Lynch, usually for not being sufficiently republican, in terms which no previous party leader had had to endure. He resigned from the leadership in December 1979, maintaining that the backbench criticism had not affected his decision, as he had always planned to step down then. The two contenders for the vacant position, as in 1966, were Charles Haughey and George Colley. The latter was supported by nearly all the members of the Cabinet, including Lynch, while the former drew heavy support from backbenchers who wanted the party to adopt a more republican line, or resented having being passed over for promotion by Lynch, or simply thought that Haughey would be more popular than Colley with the electorate. Haughey's narrow victory, by forty-four votes to thirty-eight, caused bitter resentment among the defeated group, which was headed by Colley and the Industry and Commerce Minister, Des O'Malley. Soon after Haughey's election Colley, who remained Tánaiste, declared that in his opinion the behaviour of Lynch's backbench critics had 'legitimized the withholding of loyalty to, and support for, the elected leader', and he denied that, in a conversation with Haughey after the latter's selection as leader of the parliamentary party, he had used either of the words 'loyalty' and 'support' which Haughey later attributed to him.[34] For the next eighteen months commentators painted a picture of a party in a state of civil war.

Fine Gael was undergoing its own period of transition during these years, and it too suffered from internal tensions. Liam Cosgrave resigned the party leadership a few days after the 1977 election, and at the first meeting of the Fine Gael parliamentary party Dr Garret FitzGerald was unanimously elected leader. FitzGerald was firmly on the liberal wing of Fine Gael, and had a background as an economist, boundless energy and a personal popularity second only to that of Jack Lynch. He supervised the overhaul of the party organisation, which involved bringing in new head office staff, moving the head office to larger and more modern premises, introducing a new party constitution which made the party more democratic and ended the virtual control over their constituency organisations previously enjoyed by some TDs, and developing a youth wing of the party, Young Fine Gael.

The party did not do particularly well in either the local government or the European Parliament elections of June 1979, but its new organisation was gaining valuable experience. Membership rose rapidly, and Young Fine Gael in particular flourished. Some of Liam Cosgrave's closest confidants faded from public visibility, and people who could without incongruity have been members of Labour moved into senior front-bench positions. A clear division arose between the 'Old Guard' and those identified with, or to the left of, the new leader, leading to FitzGerald appealing openly on one occasion for unity between the two.[35] Once the renovation of the party got under way, its new organisers declared that their aim was to bring Fine Gael up to the strength of Fianna Fáil, and to form a single-party government at the next election, and it is very doubtful whether the party would have agreed to a pre-election coalition agreement with Labour even if Labour had been willing.

On the left of Labour, 'Official' Sinn Féin changed its name to Sinn Féin the Workers' Party at its January 1977 Ard-Fheis, and concentrated on questions like job creation, housing and economic growth. On the north, it and its northern wing (the Workers' Party Republican Clubs) maintained that while their ultimate objective was a united socialist Ireland, this could come about only with the consent of the people in the north and the development of class politics there, and in the interim the party recommended a return to majority rule in the north with a Bill of Rights to protect the minority. Despite this abandonment of the traditional nationalist line, and the strenuous efforts of the leadership, the party's previous militaristic associations could not be entirely erased from the elecorate's memory, and other left-wing groups accused it of being uncritically pro-Soviet in its opinions on international affairs. It won nine of the city and county council seats in the 1979 local elections, including one in Dublin, and appeared to be building up a respectable if limited degree of working-class support. It attacked the two major 'capitalist' parties, but was generally not hostile to Labour, and at its 1980 Ard-Fheis its leader, Tomás Mac Giolla, said he looked forward to 'fruitful co-operation' with it.[36]

The SLP began from a stronger position than most previous small left-wing parties in that it possessed, in Noel Browne, a Dáil voice, but it showed no signs of taking off as an electoral force. Organisationally it was almost confined to Dublin, with a scattering of members in other parts of the country. In the June 1979 local elections it was able to nominate only eighteen candidates for the major council seats; none was elected. The party was riven by a number of factions, and was beset by differences on the northern question. The militantly nationalist line taken by the party's January 1979 conference caused Noel Browne to resign the following month from his position as its parliamentary spokesperson, although he later resumed it. Browne took no other position in the party, stressing on several occasions that he was simply a rank-and-file member, and was not identified very closely with it in the public eye.

10.2 The 1981 general election

The general election was held on 11 June 1981. Fianna Fáil issued a 'Programme for the 80s', but fought mainly on its record, claiming that it was 'steering Ireland safely through the recession' and that unemployment would have been much higher were it not for its achievements in the field of job creation. Fine Gael's manifesto offered large cuts in income tax, as well as many other benefits for particular groups, which the party maintained would be paid for by an increase in indirect taxation, an employment levy on large salaries, and increased health contributions. Sinn Féin the Workers' Party proposed a central planning authority to produce 500,000 jobs by 1990, a price freeze on basic foods, plus subsidies on a number of items, while the SLP manifesto called for nationalisation of the banks, a secular education system, and divorce legislation.

The election was also contested by nine 'H Block/Armagh' candidates, eight of whom were republican paramilitary prisoners in the H Blocks in the Long Kesh prison near Belfast, the ninth being in Armagh women's prison. When the campaign started, four of them were on hunger strike in support of demands relating to their treatment in the jail; four hunger strikers had died within the previous month as part of the same protest, and inter-communal tension in the north was high. Republican feeling was running strong in the border constituencies, and in Louth it was reported that the chairman of Labour's Dundalk branch, along with another member, had left the party to campaign for the local H Block candidate.[37]

Labour's manifesto, its first for twelve years, stated that the economy was in a state of crisis, and proposed a three-year economic and social plan, under a National Planning Board, to overcome it. There would be a National Development Corporation to create wealth and employment, and a youth employment scheme, guaranteeing three years of work or job training for young unemployed people, to be funded by a one per cent levy on employed people's incomes. The manifesto spoke of a wealth tax and a comprehensive capital taxation system, but fought shy, like the 1969 manifesto, of mentioning the party's policy of nationalising the banks. It favoured a comprehensive, free health service for all, increased food subsidies, and amendments to the Constitution to affirm Irish neutrality and to remove the prohibition of the legalisation of divorce, though the party's view on legalisation itself was not stated. The section on the north said that while Labour aspired to the unity of the island, that unity could come about only through reconciliation between the two communities in the north and the creation of institutions there built on power-sharing. The programme was not costed.

Although the Labour manifesto was longer than those of the two major parties, it received very little attention. Since Labour was nominating only sixty candidates, and was expecting to win fewer than twenty-five seats, there was no possibility of its policies being implemented in full, whereas both Fianna Fáil and Fine Gael cherished hopes of winning an overall majority. In consequence, and much to Labour's irritation, most of the questions at press conferences were about the prospects of the party agreeing to a coalition with Fine

Gael rather than about Labour's own policies.

It was at this point that the wisdom of Labour's electoral strategy was put to the test. The Killarney decision, which was similar to that advocated by the ITGWU delegates at the 1970 Cork special conference, had certain advantages for the party. It bought two years of internal peace, it made it worth while to think about fresh policies, and it did not tie the party's hands. Its disadvantage was that Labour appeared to be attempting to achieve two mutually irreconcilable feats during the campaign: it wanted to establish that its policies were distinct from, and yet compatible with, those of Fine Gael. If they were genuinely and fundamentally different from Fine Gael's policies, then how could a workable coalition agreement be reached on the basis of the two sets of policies? If they were not fundamentally different, then was there any point in voting for Labour rather than Fine Gael?

Each opposition party advised its supporters to give their lower preferences to the other, since otherwise Fianna Fáil was likely to remain in office. Labour explained that this did not mean it was committed to forming a coalition government; it was simply keeping its options open, and the question of a coalition would be settled by the post-election conference. Fianna Fáil, not unreasonably, adopted its familiar argument that the opposition parties 'are so deeply divided on fundamental issues as to make Coalition completely unworkable', so that voting for either would be 'like buying a pig in a poke', and that if Fianna Fáil did not win an overall majority, 'prolonged government instability is the prospect'.[38] Fianna Fáil advertisements drew voters' attention to a tactless remark made early in the campaign by a Fine Gael front-bench spokesman, John Kelly, who said that he hoped his party would be able to form a single-party 'uncontaminated' government; Charles Haughey declared that his party would not feel contaminated if it received votes from Labour supporters insulted by Kelly's remark.[39]

Much of the argument focused on the question of a wealth tax. At the press conference where the Labour manifesto was launched Cluskey appeared at first to suggest that such a tax was a non-negotiable demand on Labour's part, but then hinted that Labour would insist only on increased capital taxation rather than a wealth tax specifically.[40] As the campaign progressed, Fine Gael's position hardened. Its leader stated that he expected Fine Gael to win an overall majority on its own, but that if this did not happen, and Fine Gael required 'support' to form a government, it would be 'prepared' to discuss with Labour the formation of a government 'on the basis of our programme'. He gave 'an unqualified assurance that the programme which we implement in government will be the Fine Gael programme'. There would be 'no compromise on fundamental issues or on ... the fundamental elements of the programme which we have put forward'; in particular, there would be 'no resurrection of the wealth tax'.[41]

As well as attacking the prospect of a coalition, some Fianna Fáil speakers attacked Labour in terms reminiscent of those employed during the 1969 campaign. In Kerry a Minister of State, Tom McEllistrim, was reported to have said:[42]

> If you don't vote Fianna Fáil, Garret FitzGerald will become Taoiseach and Frank Cluskey will be the next Minister for Agriculture. And farmers of Abbeydorney you know what that means. The Labour Party is committed to a policy of nationalizing all farming land. Vote for a Coalition and they will move in and take your land.

Although Labour's Eileen Desmond stated half-way through the campaign that Labour was 'totally and unequivocally opposed' to legalising abortion,[43] it was alleged that the true position was otherwise. Albert Reynolds, Minister for Communications, said that 'the Labour Party seek to bring in divorce and abortion which is totally against the wishes and values of the Irish people. Abortion is murder – and the people want no part of it.'[44]

Another Minister of State, Seán Doherty, said that the ambivalence on, and in some cases the support for, divorce and abortion on the part of the opposition parties meant that they were not fit to participate in government; he also maintained that Labour's call for a referendum on the constitutional ban on divorce was 'an attempt, typical of some members of the Labour Party, to impose by stealth a view of society not shared by the majority of our people'.[45] A Fianna Fáil county councillor said that a vote for Labour would not be 'a vote for marriage at all, but for living in sin'.[46] Some Labour candidates took steps to protect themselves against such attacks. The party candidate in Sligo-Leitrim declared that he was a 'Christian Socialist', and had his nomination papers signed by the local bishop. In Limerick the party's outgoing TD, Mick Lipper, said, 'I will not be telling people that they have minds of their own to challenge the word of the Almighty God.'[47]

The election results showed an upsurge of support for Fine Gael, with both Fianna Fáil and Labour slipping back. Fine Gael won more seats, and a higher share of the votes, than ever before; it was also closer to Fianna Fáil than ever before. Sinn Féin the Workers' Party won its first-ever seat, in East Cork, and two other left-wing TDs, former Labour members Jim Kemmy (in East Limerick) and Dr Noel Browne were also elected. Kemmy was a member of the small but vociferous Socialists against Nationalism group, vehement critics of the traditional nationalist approach, which, they argued, was a barrier to the development of working-class unity in the north; they advocated a recognition by the southern State that the northern majority had a right to self-determination, and the removal from Bunreacht na hEireann of Articles 2 and 3. Two of the H Block candidates were elected, but neither was in a position to take his seat; both were, in any case, abstentionists. One died a month later after a ten-week hunger strike.

Fianna Fáil's losses were expected, given that its vote in 1977 had been abnormally high and that the economic situation had worsened since then. Labour's dismal performance, however, had not been predicted, for it seemed that since it had done so badly in 1977 it was bound to pick up strength, especially since it was in opposition at a time of very high unemployment and inflation. In contrast, the party's share of the votes dropped below 10 per cent (see Appendix 1), and it fell to fifteen seats in a much larger Dáil. Four Labour TDs lost their seats: Cluskey, John Horgan and Ruairi Quinn in Dublin, and Mick Lipper in East Limerick. In addition, two of the 1977 TDs were no longer in the PLP (Pat Kerrigan having died and John O'Connell having left the party), and two of Labour's longest-serving rural TDs, Michael Pat Murphy and Dan Spring, did not contest the election. Five new TDs were elected: Mervyn Taylor in Dublin South West, Michael D. Higgins in Galway West, Toddy O'Sullivan in Cork North Central, Michael Moynihan in South Kerry and Dick Spring in North Kerry.

In terms of votes, Labour was at its weakest since the traumatic result of 1957. It fell back heavily in Dublin, suffered slight losses in rural Leinster and Connacht-Ulster, and gained very slightly in Munster. In Dublin, where it won only three of the forty-eight seats, it was scarcely any stronger than in the rest of Leinster or in Munster, a reversion to the 1965 position (see Appendix 2). Some of its limited successes outside Dublin, moreover, seemed to owe little to a more favourable perception of the party. Moynihan was establishing a record by finally winning a seat on his seventh attempt, his first having been in 1954; an archetypal rural Labour TD, his eventual success was due primarily to his assiduous constituency work over the years. Spring won his seat only narrowly, and would almost certainly not have been elected had he not been the son of the outgoing Labour TD. The other three new TDs had all stood before for the Dáil and were strong candidates in their own right. Higgins's election in Galway gave Labour its first Connacht seat since T. J. O'Connell lost his in 1932. An eloquent university lecturer, he stood well on the left of the party and did not trim his sails for fear of alienating floating voters. While in this sense his election marked a gain for Labour rather than a purely personal achievement, there is no doubt that his own energy and commitment, as well as his work as a county councillor, contributed greatly to his success. His support, it was generally believed, came almost wholly from urban voters in Galway City rather than from the many small farmers in the constituency.

Even though a third of the TDs were newly elected, the post-1969 trend of an aging Dáil party continued (see Appendix 5). The average age of Labour's 1981 TDs was fifty-one, about four years above that of the Dáil as a whole. Four Labour TDs were in their sixties, and only one, Dick Spring, was younger than forty. Eight of the fifteen had first entered the Dáil in 1969 or earlier.

Transfers from Labour to Fine Gael, in situations where there were no Labour candidates remaining, passed at much the same rate (56·6 per cent) as in 1977, reflecting the fact that while the party had urged its supporters to carry on their preferences against the government, there was no explicit coalition agreement. The high figure for transfers from Fine Gael to Labour (86·8 per cent) is based on the distribution of small surpluses in only two constituencies, and thus is not very reliable as a guide to the feelings of Fine Gael supporters in general.[48] The transfer pact played a crucial role in determining the outcome of the election, for Fianna Fáil had won an overall majority of seats in 1969 with a slightly smaller share of the votes. In 1981 Labour won two seats thanks to Fine Gael transfers, in Carlow-Kilkenny and Wexford, while Fine Gael won three (in Cork North West, Cork South West and Dublin North), which would otherwise have gone to Fianna Fáil, owing to Labour transfers. Without the transfer arrangement Fianna Fáil would thus have won five extra seats, which, given the absence of the two H Block TDs, would have given it a clear overall majority. Only one seat was lost to the opposition parties by poor transferring; this was in Dublin North East, where a terminal Labour to Fine Gael transfer of only 35 per cent led to an Independent rather than a Fine Gael candidate winning the last seat.

The question of why Labour had done so badly, losing votes for the third election in a row despite the high level of unemployment, was one which produced many different answers from within the party. Michael O'Leary, who from the start had criticised the strategy of aiming for the balance of power, argued that because Labour did not declare its position on coalition in advance, potential Labour supporters who wanted to be certain that their vote would count against the government had voted Fine Gael; he, like John O'Connell from outside the party, maintained that there should have been a pre-election pact between the opposition parties.[49] Anti-coalitionists drew quite the opposite conclusion. The left-wing Militant group, among others, claimed that Labour had done badly because it had not ruled out coalition; at a time when conservative policies had clearly failed the country, it would have done better by fighting on a go-it-alone socialist platform than it did by leaving open the door to another coalition.[50]

Almost certainly neither of these arguments is entirely valid. It is not at all certain that a newly aggressive Fine Gael, intent on overtaking Fianna Fáil, would have been prepared to conclude a pre-election agreement with Labour, or that Labour would have fared any better if it had appeared before the electorate as Fine Gael's junior partner. On the other hand, the anti-coalitionists' argument seems invalidated by the poor performance of the parties that took the course they prescribed for Labour. Apart from Noel Browne, who had already demonstrated his ability to win a seat on almost any party label, the SLP fared disastrously; none of its other six candidates, who included Matt Merrigan, won even 600 votes, and all lost their deposits. One of the six, former Labour member Dermot Boucher, admitted that his party had 'failed to provide a credible alternative'.[51] Sinn Féin the Workers' Party's vote scarcely rose, and ten of its fifteen candidates, including six out of eight in Dublin, lost their deposits. The inability of either party to make a real impact was in fact the only consoling feature of the results for Labour; it had lost votes on its right flank but not, as it had feared, on its left as well.

Others suggested, probably rightly, that factors other than strategy were mainly responsible for the party's disappointing performance. Its vice-chairman, Michael Ferris, argued that Labour's undeniably poor organisation in Dublin bore a greater responsibility for its losses there than did any decision on strategy.[52] It was noticeable that none of the three Labour TDs defeated in Dublin was on a local authority, unlike all bar one of Labour's successful candidates. Indeed, all three had seemed more interested in their political and parliamentary role than their brokerage role (Horgan had even founded a journal, *Left Perspectives*), reinforcing the view that TDs neglect immersion in local work at their peril.

Mary Robinson, who had polled poorly in West Dublin, said that she had discovered a lack of political consciousness among working-class people: they 'did not respond with any degree of political awareness of their critical position and seemed to have no perception of the degree of social change necessary to alter their predicament'.[53] This reflected a view held by some Labour politicians, generally expressed only privately, that the people had allowed themselves to be bought again by the highest bidder; many potential Labour voters had been lured by Fianna Fáil's promises in 1977, and in 1981 had switched to a party offering tax cuts rather than one advocating fundamental societal change. One defeated candidate reportedly went so far as to state on television that the Dublin working class should be 'examining its conscience' for having rejected Cluskey.

10.3 The formation of the 1981 coalition government

Labour had now to select a new leader and decide what attitude to take to the formation of the next government. The first question was easily resolved; on 17 June Michael O'Leary was chosen unanimously as leader by the Labour TDs, with Jimmy Tully, Labour's oldest TD, being elected to his former position of deputy leader by defeating Michael D. Higgins by ten votes to five. The second, which was to be settled by the special conference laid down by the Killarney motion, was more complicated, because even though Fine Gael and Labour combined had more seats than Fianna Fáil, they were still short of an overall majority. The possible options of supporting a minority Fianna Fáil government, or even joining a coalition with that party, were ruled out by a progressively cooler series of public statements by the two party leaders; Labour believed that Fianna Fáil wanted its support but was not prepared to offer anything in return. There were no discussions between the parties. The idea of a national all-party government was agreed by all parties to be out of the question.

This left just three possibilities, each of which had its supporters among Labour members: a coalition with Fine Gael, support for a Fine

Gael minority government, or opposition to both major parties. The third course was advocated by anti-coalitionists, who suggested that if Labour went into 'Socialist opposition', trade union activists and young voters would flock into the party, which would be 'transformed in a matter of weeks' and would double its vote in one Dáil term, while the two major parties would be forced together.[54] They pointed out that in view of the high budget deficit and the high level of foreign debt, the next government would have to pursue unpopular policies, so that Labour would be best advised to remain in opposition. Their critics believed that, once again, their assessment of the likely reaction of the electorate and the two major parties to a go-it-alone decision by Labour was wildly over-optimistic. Moreover, although the idea of going into safe but vociferous opposition was attractive, the respective parties' Dáil strengths meant that it was not an option, because if Labour were to vote against both major parties' nominees for Taoiseach, both would almost certainly be defeated. There would then be another general election, at which Labour, directionless and short of funds, would probably do even worse than before.

The idea of supporting a minority Fine Gael government gradually faded out of contention. Its advocates argued[55] that Labour, backed up by the left-wing Independents, could have as much influence on government policy as if it was in coalition, but would be in less danger of losing its identity.[56] However, they found little support. Coalitionists argued that the arrangement would amount to responsibility without power; Labour would be held responsible for government policy to just the same extent as if it were in formal coalition, but would be left 'outside the door', unable to ensure that its 'demands' were being implemented in the manner agreed, and overshadowed by publicity-conscious Ministers. Many anti-coalitionists also dismissed the idea, the Militant group describing it as simply 'coalition by another name'.[57]

That left only a coalition, favoured by many only reluctantly as the least undesirable option on offer. After his election as party leader, O'Leary entered into the negotiations with Fine Gael envisaged by the Killarney resolution, to produce a coalition manifesto which would be endorsed by Labour's special conference.[58] The negotiators (mainly the party leaders, with the deputy leaders and one or two advisors also playing important roles) found enough in common between the two parties' manifestoes to produce a joint programme, although some areas proved troublesome. The most difficult was perhaps that of industrial relations, where the Fine Gael manifesto had called for the licensing of trade unions, the withdrawal of legal protection from pickets of unlicensed unions and from all secondary pickets, and cooling-off periods before strikes could take place in essential public services. Labour, fearful of union reaction and convinced that the ideas were unworkable, succeeded in keeping the undertakings out of the coalition programme, which, like Labour's own manifesto, said little on the subject. On taxation, Labour, like the ICTU, had strong reservations about shifting the tax burden from direct to indirect taxation. Labour suspected that Fine Gael's hope that, as a result of the income tax cuts, the unions would not seek compensation for the price rises caused by the indirect taxation increases betrayed a complete lack of understanding of the unions on the part of the middle-class Fine Gael leadership group. However, Fine Gael would not yield on the point, which it believed had been central to its success in the election, and so the coalition taxation policy was the Fine Gael policy along with some protection for those on low incomes. Labour was also unable to persuade Fine Gael to hold a referendum on divorce, which the Fine Gael negotiators thought might lead some of their party's TDs to oppose the whole agreement, and the joint programme spoke only of establishing an all-party committee to report on the subject. The topic of a constitutional amendment to rule out the legalisation of abortion was not discussed.

Labour's successes in the negotiations included the incorporation, in considerably diluted form, of its youth employment scheme, and agreement to establish a National Development Corporation to engage in economic activity; Fine Gael, while not opposed to the latter, was initially reluctant to commit to it the full sum (£200 million) eventually agreed. In addition, government policy was to be guided by a series of 'rolling' (i.e. annually updated) four-year plans, which would be reviewed by a National Planning Board. Capital taxation was to be increased, and bank profits would be subjected to a special levy, though there would be no wealth tax. The Fine Gael commitment to eliminate the current budget deficit over four years was watered down slightly (it was now to be only an 'aim'), and there would be higher subsidies on basic foodstuffs. It was also agreed, though not made public, that a scheme of State financing for political parties would be introduced, which Labour hoped would solve its recurrent financial problems.

The negotiations were completed only on the day before Labour's special conference, held in Dublin on 28 June. While they had been in progress, branches had been discussing the question and selecting conference delegates. A number of branches, mainly in Dublin, decided to mandate their delegates to vote against coalition no matter what terms were agreed. The two largest affiliated unions also came out against coalition, the ITGWU favouring opposition to all governments and the FWUI preferring support for a Fine Gael minority government, in response to which several PLP members argued that to make a decision before the results of the negotiations were known defeated the purpose of the Killarney resolution, which the ITGWU had supported.[59] An opinion poll conducted five days before the conference found that 50 per cent of Labour supporters wanted a Fine Gael–Labour coalition and another 19 per cent wanted a national all-party government, with only 8 per cent favouring a Fine Gael minority government and one per cent a Fianna Fáil–Fine Gael coalition; the rest either wanted a Fianna Fáil–Labour coalition or a Fianna Fáil minority government or, quite understandably, did not know what they wanted. When they were asked to choose between a Fine Gael–Labour coalition or a Fianna Fáil minority government, 74 per cent chose the former, 12 per cent the latter, and 14 per cent did not know.[60] The poll's findings were by no means conclusive, but they did suggest, as had generally been assumed, that Labour voters were on the whole pro-coalition.

The conference itself was held in private session. The new leader recommended the deal he had struck, and Frank Cluskey seconded the pro-coalition motion. As usual, most speakers were anti-coalition, and most of the pro-coalition speakers were TDs. Three of the newly elected TDs (Higgins, O'Sullivan and Taylor) spoke against coalition, but the rest of the Dáil party clearly favoured it. Some anti-coalitionists acknowledged that O'Leary had extracted more from Fine Gael than they had expected, but maintained that it was still not enough. In general the discussion was reasoned and temperate; whereas in 1970 there had been heckling and threats of resignation, on this occasion the rousing anti-coalition speech of Michael D. Higgins received a standing ovation, although another anti-coalitionist, ITGWU president John Carroll, was booed. The coalition motion was passed by 737 votes (60·7 per cent) to 477 (39·3 per cent); it was generally believed that most of the 320 Dublin delegates and of the 150 trade union delegates had voted against coalition, with rural delegates heavily in favour.

The distribution of Ministries between the two parties had been raised right at the start of the negotiations. Labour, which had won half as many votes as Fine Gael in 1969, now had barely a quarter as many, and with only 21·3 per cent of the total Coalition vote, and 18·7 per cent of the Coalition's Dáil seats, it was entitled to only three of the fifteen government posts, and three of the fifteen Ministries of State, on a pro rata basis. FitzGerald suggested that Labour receive this bare entitlement, but O'Leary asked for five Ministries, as in 1973, and five of the junior Ministries. The negotiators then decided to leave resolution of this question until the end. When they eventually returned to the subject, Fine Gael agreed to give Labour one extra Ministry, though no extra junior Ministry; it was also agreed that the question of who would be appointed the next Irish EEC Commissioner was to be decided amicably between the parties when it arose late in 1984 (assuming the government was still in office) rather than by majority vote in the Cabinet.

O'Leary became Tánaiste and Minister for Energy; in addition, some of the functions of the Department of Industry and Commerce, such as those relating to industrial development, were transferred to his department, which would also be responsible for the National Development Corporation.[61] In addition, he was given a responsibility, along with FitzGerald and the Foreign Minister, in shaping the government's Northern Ireland policy. Two of the other Labour Ministers occupied positions also taken by Labour in the 1973–77 government. Eileen Desmond was given Health and Social Welfare, and became only the second woman Minister since the establishment of the State, while Liam Kavanagh became Minister for Labour and the Public Service. These three Ministries had all been sought by Labour; it also wanted that of Environment (as Local Government had been renamed) for James Tully, but the Fine Gael deputy leader had already earmarked this, and Tully had to be content with the relatively minor department of Defence.

Labour's three junior Ministries included that of Economic Planning (given to Barry Desmond), potentially a more important post than several of the full Ministries. Dick Spring was given responsibility for Law Reform and Justice; he was a trained barrister (the Minister at the department had no legal training), and his appointment also ensured that Labour's only youthful Dáil face would be in the public eye. The third, the Office of Public Works, was given to PLP chairman Joe Bermingham. As in 1973, the TDs involved were simply offered a specific position; they were not invited to choose a Ministry. The Ministers were notified the day before the government took office, and the junior Ministers only after the Dáil had elected FitzGerald Taoiseach. The party leaders discussed with each other their possible nominees to the government, although neither had a veto over the other's selections. Three of the Labour Ministers, O'Leary, Kavanagh and Eileen Desmond, held seats in the European Parliament which they now had to vacate; O'Leary's seat went to Cluskey, and the other two were given to Labour TDs Seamus Pattison and Seán Treacy.[62] In consequence, no fewer than nine of the fifteen Labour TDs received some 'pay-off' from the coalition agreement.

The only remaining hurdle was to ensure that the Dáil selected FitzGerald as Taoiseach when it reconvened on 30 June. With only eighty of the 164 attending TDs, the Coalition needed support or benign abstention from the six Independent and minor-party TDs if it was to enter government. These TDs were subjected to blandishments from all sides; four of them (John O'Connell, Jim Kemmy, Noel Browne and Sinn Féin the Workers' Party's Joe Sherlock) were told that if they wished to join (or rejoin) the Labour Party the door was open. None accepted, though one seemed likely to do so before long, but in the event the Coalition won the vote quite comfortably. O'Connell agreed to become Ceann Comhairle, and Kemmy voted with the Coalition when the Dáil considered the nominations of Haughey and FitzGerald as Taoiseach. Browne and Sherlock both voted against Haughey and then abstained when FitzGerald's name was put to the vote. His nomination was approved by eighty-one votes to seventy-eight, and the composition of the government was endorsed by eighty-two votes to seventy-eight. At the early Cabinet meetings of the new government the Tánaiste sat at one end of the table next to the Taoiseach, but the other three Labour Ministers sat together, as they had not done in the 1973–77 government, in a small bloc at the other end. Whether this had any long-term significance, as a pointer to the *modus operandi* of the new government, remained to be seen.

10.4 The fourth coalition government, 1981–82

The fourth coalition government lasted only eight months before losing office in the February 1982 general election, precipitated by a budget defeat. Its term in power had been too short for any far-reaching policy decisions to be made. Of the Labour policies incorporated in the coalition manifesto, a Youth Employment Agency, designed to implement its scheme for youth employment, was set up but had not yet become operational, while a National Development Corporation was unveiled a week before the election. Legislation to abolish the death penalty was to have been introduced a week after the government fell, and corporal punishment in schools was abolished. No four-year plans were produced.

Most of the government's time was occupied by the economy, which, it claimed immediately upon entering office and looking at the books, was in a far worse state than Fianna Fáil had admitted, with the current budget deficit for 1981 likely to reach ten per cent of Gross National Product and foreign debts amounting to £1,500 per head of the population. In July 1981 it brought in a hard budget, which was narrowly passed by the Dáil, and throughout its period in power it attempted to convince the public that its predecessor's high level of foreign borrowing had left the country at the mercy of foreign bankers. Should they recall their loans, Ireland would have to seek assistance from the International Monetary Fund, which would be forthcoming only if the government of the day agreed to draconian policies that would bear hardest on the weakest sections of society. To obviate this danger, the government argued, it was necessary to put the economy in order, by phasing out the current budget deficit and reducing reliance on foreign borrowing.

This approach, which involved both spending cuts and tax increases, was broadly supported by most independent economists but, not surprisingly, did not find an enthusiastic response among Labour members. At the end of October the AC declared that the Labour Ministers had exceeded their mandate from the June special conference when they agreed to the provisions of the July budget, and there were constant calls from individual members, and from the party's youth wing, for a withdrawal from the government. The Labour Ministers argued that to take such a step would be to abandon their national responsibilities, but within the government they behaved somewhat more assertively than their counterparts in 1973–77. Late in September Michael O'Leary suggested that the proposed income tax cuts be applied only to those whose incomes were below £9,000 a year, and in January two other Labour TDs, Barry Desmond and John Ryan, called for the entire package to be postponed or even abandoned. One striking success for Labour came when in

December, largely at Desmond's instigation, the government announced that it would not be providing any further funds for a proposed airport at Knock in the west of Ireland, which according to independent assessments would be an expensive white elephant, even though Fine Gael had undertaken before the election to build it.

The government fell on 27 January when its budget was defeated in the Dáil by one vote. It had been even tougher than the July 1981 budget, raising indirect taxes, imposing new taxes on clothing and footwear and reducing food subsidies, although social welfare benefits would have risen by twenty-five per cent. The promised income tax cuts, against which Labour had spoken out, were not implemented. At the Taoiseach's request, President Hillery dissolved the Dáil and a general election was called for 18 February.

Most, though not all, Labour TDs favoured fighting the election on a coalition platform, as in 1977, but the AC decided that the party should fight on its own policies, as in 1981, and that after the election it would decide, after consultations with the leader, whether there was a need for another special conference to decide what Labour should do. During the campaign Michael O'Leary and other coalitionists stated repeatedly that if Fine Gael and Labour together won a majority of seats the government would remain in office, without the need to seek approval from a Labour special conference, but anti-coalitionists insisted that any fresh coalition would need a fresh mandate from party members, and some candidates refused to ask their supporters to give their second preferences to Fine Gael as Labour advertisements urged.

The government announced that if it was returned to office it would reintroduce the budget on which it had been defeated, except that it would exempt children's clothing and footwear from tax. At the start of the campaign most commentators thought that the unprecedented severity of the budget would mean an easy victory for Fianna Fáil, but opinion polls suggested that most people believed that the budget had been necessary. The polls also showed that subjects like the current budget deficit and the extent of foreign borrowing, hitherto concepts of interest only to economists, had become matters of widespread concern, and were regarded as more important than any other issues apart from unemployment and inflation.

Labour nominated only forty-one candidates, its lowest number since 1961, with only one candidate in thirty-one of the thirty-six constituencies it contested. This strategy was adopted in the belief that, since its vote was likely to fall in view of the nature of the proposed budget, it could best preserve its existing Dáil strength by allowing its strongest candidates to run personalised campaigns in their constituencies, without the risk of antagonising and losing transfers from running-mates. Two veteran Labour TDs, former leader Brendan Corish and deputy leader Jimmy Tully, stood down at the election, and another notable retirement was that of Dr Noel Browne, who in November had severed his connection with the SLP.

The results of the election were very similar to those of June 1981, with most of the fourteen seat changes being attributable to the retirement of individual TDs and the main parties' absorption of the H Block vote. Fianna Fáil's vote went up to 47·3 per cent, and it won eighty-one seats; Fine Gael's vote also went up, to a record 37·3 per cent, but it fell back to sixty-three seats. Labour's vote went down from 9·9 to 9·1 per cent, but it won the same number of seats as in 1981; all of its thirteen outgoing TDs were re-elected, and although it failed to hold the seats vacated by Corish and Tully, two former TDs, Frank Cluskey and Ruairi Quinn, regained their old seats in Dublin, which now provided five of the fifteen Labour TDs. At the first post-election meeting of the PLP, Michael O'Leary was unanimously re-elected leader and Barry Desmond was unanimously elected deputy leader. Labour's vote fell back slightly in Dublin (to 11·2 per cent), in the rest of Leinster (to 10·0 per cent) and in Munster (to 11·3 per cent), and rose marginally in Connacht–Ulster (to 2·4 per cent).

A significant advance was made by Sinn Féin the Workers' Party, which, having won its first seat eight months earlier, retained this and added two more, in Waterford and Dublin North West. Neither gain was at Labour's expense – one came from Fianna Fáil and the other from Fine Gael – and the pattern seemed to be that SFWP was attracting working-class votes in areas where there was no strong Labour presence, rather than winning votes from Labour where Labour was strong. Three Independents were elected, along with Ceann Comhairle John O'Connell, and two of these stood on the left of the political spectrum. One, Tony Gregory, was elected ahead of the Labour leader Michael O'Leary in an inner-city Dublin constituency. The other, Jim Kemmy, who had been a consistent Dáil supporter of the coalition government before voting against its budget, announced that he would soon set up a 'post-nationalist' Democratic Socialist Party.

The pattern of transfers between Labour and Fine Gael seemed to show general approval among both parties' supporters for the continuation of the coalition, despite prior speculation that Labour voters would have been alienated by the austere nature of the government's economic policies. In seventeen constituencies the final Labour transfer took place when both Fine Gael and Fianna Fáil candidates were available to receive transfers, and 59·4 per cent of the transfers passed to Fine Gael, a figure slightly up on 1977 and 1981 (cf. Table 8.1). Fianna Fáil received 18·3 per cent, 8·6 per cent went to other candidates, and 13·6 per cent became non-transferable. Of terminal Fine Gael transfers, 69·1 per cent went to Labour, 13·9 per cent to Fianna Fáil, and 17·0 per cent became non-transferable; this situation arose in six constituencies. A high rate of Fine Gael transfers secured a Labour seat in Carlow–Kilkenny; high rates of Labour transfers were responsible for Fine Gael retaining seats in Cork North West, Dublin North and Dublin West, and contributed to Fine Gael TDs being elected in Dublin North East and Waterford. Only in one constituency, Louth, was a coalition seat lost because of poor inter-party transferring.

With no overall majority in the 166-member Dáil, there followed, as in the previous June, two and a half weeks of intense negotiations between the various parties and the Independents. Believing, probably mistakenly, that the Coalition's continuation in office was possible, Labour's AC and the PLP held meetings early in March, which produced a 'list of priorities' to be circulated to the other parties, as a basis for negotiations rather than as a *sine qua non* for Labour support in the Dáil. The 'priorities' included modifying the harshest features of the budget, increased capital taxation, much more money for the National Development Corporation, measures to prevent land speculation, and a programme of urban renewal. This belated stiffening of Labour's position was criticised by Jim Kemmy, who argued that what the party was now advocating was virtually the same as what he had called for before the budget; if the Labour Ministers had stood up for themselves then, they could have ensured that the budget was acceptable to him and there would have been no election. There was, indeed, a widespread feeling that the budget defeat could have been avoided had the government been more adroit politically and more sensitive to the feelings of Independent TDs.

On the day before the Dáil met, Labour's AC held a six-hour meeting to decide the party's position. O'Leary was able to report that Fine Gael had agreed to some of its proposals, including the removal of tax on clothing and shoes and the restoration of food subsidies, and it was also apparent that a large majority of PLP members favoured a continuation of coalition. Nonetheless, the AC decided, by eighteen votes to sixteen, that Labour would not participate in government in the new Dáil; instead, its TDs could support a minority Fine Gael government.

In the event the decision had no bearing on the outcome. Fianna Fáil won the support of the three TDs of Sinn Féin the Workers' Party (which in April changed its name to simply 'The Workers' Party'), Neil Blaney and Tony Gregory, who secured a remarkable list of commitments in return for his Dáil vote, so on 9 March Charles Haughey was elected Taoiseach by 86 votes to 79. In fact, Haughey ran into more trouble from within his own parliamentary party than from the Dáil, having to quell an abortive coup led by Desmond O'Malley before being confirmed as the Fianna Fail nominee for Taoiseach. Even so, the AC's decision caused deep resentment among most TDs, much of it directed against party chairman Michael D. Higgins, who was accused by Barry Desmond of 'an incredible piece of dilettantism' and of having played 'a negative and destructive role' by his influential advocacy of an end to the coalition. Desmond accused 'the closed minds and the ideologues' on the AC of having made a decision which conflicted with the wishes of most Labour voters, and the incident certainly raised the question of whether TDs were answerable in the first instance to those who had voted for them or to party members, a question which had never previously arisen in Irish politics because of the generally deferential nature of party members. PLP members' anger at being overruled by the AC was not assuaged by a statement from the party's youth wing containing the blithe assurance that a majority Labour government would be in power 'within a few years' as a result of the anti-coalition decision. Whatever transitions had taken place in the party since 1957, there remained room for a lot more thinking on the question of how to make the transition from a party of protest to a party of power.

11
Conclusion

During the period 1957–82 the nature of the Irish Labour Party changed fundamentally, but its electoral strength remained fairly constant. In 1957 it had been almost incongruously conservative by European standards; it shunned the word 'socialist' and seemed to regard even 'liberalism' as a dangerous creed. Its goals were much the same as those of all parties – higher employment, better social services, and so on – but it proposed no particularly distinctive or controversial methods to achieve them. Throughout the 1960s, however, it moved steadily to the left. It began, cautiously at first, to assert that it was 'socialist', and in 1969 it adopted new policies, the fullest and most left-wing ever evolved by any Irish party. It could no longer be argued that it had generally reacted timidly and defensively to change; by 1982 its position on both social and economic questions placed it in advance of the two main parties and indeed of the electorate.

Organisationally, too, there was significant change. Up to the mid-1960s Labour was a loosely linked collection of individuals, and although some had built up efficient constituency parties, there was little central co-ordination of these local organisations. Annual conferences were attended by hardly more than 100 delegates, most of whom were supporters of individual TDs, and were not forums for the formulation of policies. During the 1960s Head Office, which had previously had a purely administrative role, became much more political, and tightened up the party machinery considerably. Annual conferences became much larger affairs, with up to 1,000 delegates attending, and became the arena for decisions on party policy and strategy. They became much less sycophantic towards the parliamentary party, which came to expect vituperative criticism from some delegates, but were still unable to exercise effective control over the PLP, which for the most part was able to go its own way virtually unchecked.

The nature of Labour's parliamentarians also changed considerably. Before 1965 most Labour TDs had been primarily constituency representatives, with a limited interest in national politics, but something of a transformation took place during the 1960s. Partly as a result of its move to the left, it attracted members of the intelligentsia, an important component of most socialist parties, and its proportion of university-educated TDs, the lowest of the three main parties in 1961, was the highest in 1969.[1] There was a marked rise in the number of professional people among its Dáil candidates, and very few of the workers among its candidates ever reached the Dáil party. Of eight major European social democratic parties surveyed in the late 1970s, the post-war average proportion of manual workers in the parliamentary groups of all but one was higher than the figure for Labour TDs between 1957 and 1982.[2]

As a result, the party became a much more effective parliamentary force, and was able to make much better use of television and radio than the pre-1960s party could have. At times, indeed, the PLP seemed over-endowed with people interested in ideas, which partly accounted for the endless arguments of the early 1970s. At the same time, though, the proportion of trade union officials among its Dáil candidates and TDs remained high, and the proportion of women remained very low.

There was also a shift in the nature of the party's support, which before the 1960s had come mainly from rural Ireland, especially farm labourers. Its traditional weakness in Dublin was dramatically overturned during the 1960s; it rose from just one seat in the Greater Dublin area in 1957 and 1961 to ten in 1969, reflecting gains among both working-class and middle-class groups in the capital. Despite the subsequent erosion of its position, even in 1981 it was still stronger there, albeit only marginally, than in any other region of the country (see Appendix 2). Its already low appeal to farmers diminished further; there were no farmers among its Dáil candidates at either the 1973 or 1977 elections, and only one in 1981 and 1982.

In one important respect, though, there was little change. Labour was the third strongest party in the State in 1957, and it still occupied this position in 1982. It had had its electoral successes in the intervening years – the equalling of its previous highest number of seats in 1965, a record number of votes in 1969 – but it never broke out of the pattern of its pre-1957 experience. In 1982 it was weaker in terms of its percentage vote than it had been at fourteen of the previous twenty general elections, and it was further adrift of Fine Gael than it had been since 1932. No 'Labour breakthrough' had materialised, and Labour had come nowhere near overturning the established political order.

The considerable change within the party, viewed in conjunction with the lack of change in its relationship with the wider political system, led certain members, particularly those on the right, to argue that the internal transformation had been unnecessary and indeed unhelpful. Labour had done just as well when Head Office was run on a shoestring, when its conferences had not been dominated by 'theoretical' socialists, and when it had not bothered to elaborate lengthy policy documents which hardly anyone was going to read anyway but which unscrupulous opponents could easily use against the party to damage it in rural Ireland. Echoing Downs,[3] they argued that since almost all those who did not support Labour voted instead for parties to the right of it, it made no sense for Labour to move to the left.

However, although it is true that many of those instrumental in effecting the transition were disappointed that it had not had more impact on Labour's electoral position, it cannot be seriously maintained that the changes were unnecessary. The modernisation of the Labour Party was necessary to keep pace with the modernisation of Irish society. The pre-1960s party of like-minded independents with a trade union base would have been an anachronism in the 1980s. Without the new policies, the new image and the overhaul of the organisation, Labour would neither have made the major advances it did in Dublin nor have attracted the new members who enabled it to perform as well in the Oireachtas and the mass media as the two larger parties. To some extent, then, Labour had to run simply to stand still.

The reason why the transition had less impact than anticipated was that the forces making for change were weaker than they appeared, while the *status quo* was more firmly entrenched than it appeared. In 1967 Labour's general secretary had outlined a number of reasons for believing that the party's immediate future would be brighter than its past.[4] First, he suggested, the two major parties had failed to move with the times; they lacked distinctive identities, and had suffered because of the disappearance of their 'old guard'. In fact the passage of the veterans helped the parties to adapt to changing circumstances. Moreover the fact that it remained difficult to pin either party down to a firm spot on the left–right spectrum did not seem to disturb their supporters. Secondly, it was suggested that young voters had no formed allegiances and would decide which party to support on the basis of the issues of the 1960s and 1970s rather than what happened in the 1920s. However, the results of subsequent elections have suggested that in Ireland, as elsewhere, voting habits are passed on strongly from generation to generation; the only alternative explanation is that young voters without inherited affiliations prefer the major parties' policies to Labour's.

A third sign of change, it was said, was the upsurge in trade union affiliations. These, however, proved to have very little significance. The affiliation fees, it is true, were helpful financially, although in 1980 they amounted to only £6,748, just over an eighth of the party's reported income of £52,079.[5] The unions' main financial contribution, though, took the form of subventions to individual members standing as Labour candidates, which had been made before they affiliated. If the financial impact of the affiliations was limited, the electoral impact was negligible; it might even be doubted whether all the affiliations together caused even one extra vote to be cast for the party. Moreover, it was only at the institutional level that the relationship became closer. There were no signs at any stage that a majority of union members thought of Labour as 'their' party, and in 1972 it was estimated that only about 41 per cent of trade unionists in the Republic were contributing to Labour's funds through union affiliations, about half the British figure.[6] Neither do Irish unions have a bloc vote at Labour conferences, as British unions do. The number of delegates each union can send depends on the number of members for which it is affiliated, and is approximately one for each thousand members.[7] Each trade union delegate has just one vote, like all other delegates, and the number of union delegates is usually about ten per cent of the total number.

Too much, then, was expected of these changes by the New Wave of the late 1960s, and the unrealistically high expectations were partly responsible for the great sense of disappointment felt after the 1969 election results, and the subsequent abandonment of the anti-coalition approach. The propensity of people to vote on the basis of the respective parties' policies rather than on the basis of inherited allegiance was greatly overestimated. However, this is merely to say that some of the innovators were in some respects naive and starry-eyed. Some of the problems of the transition arose simply because it took place so quickly; in the space of only about ten years Labour changed from being little more than a collection of well-meaning, hard-working individuals to a party fitting into the Western European social democratic tradition. The transition did not bring the electoral success some had hoped, but it was none the less necessary.

Finally, it is worth considering the party's future prospects in the light of the situation existing after the 1982 election. Before the 1981 election, Labour feared being squeezed between parties to its left on one side and a centre-left Fine Gael on the other. The former threat did not materialise, although it remains possible that in the future Sinn Féin the Workers' Party, uninhibited by the need not to alienate a conservative rural wing and unencumbered by a rather disappointing record of participation in coalition governments, could eat into its working-class support. The latter threat did, and Labour lost some of its liberal middle-class support. Indeed, it might be argued that if Labour could not do better than it did against the pre-1977, poorly organised, patrician Fine Gael party, it will have difficulty even surviving against the post-1981, professional and populist Fine Gael party and the equally professional and populist Fianna Fáil party. As against this gloomy analysis, it must be observed that there is still no credible left-wing alternative to Labour, and that Fine Gael remains an alliance of differing viewpoints. Indeed, that party's 1981 success, especially in Dublin, may bring to the fore its own internal divisions, between rural traditional conservatives and urban liberals.

The coalition question is likely to continue to loom large in Labour's eyes. Despite the SLP split, there remains a sizeable section of Labour members which is opposed to coalition under any circumstances, and which believes that the party should concentrate on working for a majority Labour government. While an anti-coalition strategy may well become the right one to pursue for a while, the aspiration of a Labour government remains as remote as it was in the early 1970s. Even if the party were to gain five seats at every election, an unrealistically optimistic assumption, it would take about fourteen elections, perhaps fifty years, before it won an overall majority. To adopt and adhere rigidly to such a strategy would make it difficult to attract candidates, who would have no chance of attaining political power within their lifetimes, and would not appeal to voters who wanted to see radical change come rather more quickly.

At the same time, there are those on the right of the party who

favour the idea of a coalition virtually regardless of the terms offered
or of the policies a coalition government might follow. Many, indeed,
would prefer the policies of coalition governments to undiluted Labour
policies. For Labour to adopt this strategy would in effect be to pass a
vote of no confidence in its own future. With such an attitude, there
would be little point in developing its own policies, or indeed in
maintaining an existence separate from Fine Gael, and the danger of
being outflanked from the left would become a real one.

Tension within the party on this issue is unlikely to decrease in the
near future. The increase in the number of professional people and
university graduates – government-oriented rather than brokerage-
oriented individuals – and the high proportion of full-time career
politicians among Labour TDs is a powerful internal factor disposing
the PLP to favour participation in government except in a context of
exceptional external factors. This inevitably leads to rank-and-file
accusations of careerism, and, given that the proportion of conference
delegates willing to be 'guided' by their local TD seems to be declining
steadily, conflict between the PLP and the annual conference on this
issue during the 1980s is quite conceivable. In addition, the success of
British Labour Party members in increasing their power in the party
vis à vis the parliamentary party in the late 1970s and early 1980s did
not go unnoticed by Irish Labour Party members, and 'contagion from
the east' may also contribute to a more assertive annual conference.

In fact, despite the heat which the coalition question has often
generated within the party, there is much to be said for Noel Browne's
1968 suggestion that it is 'completely irrelevant' and for James
Larkin's 1957 argument that the question of whether Labour should
or should not join a coalition is less important than the question of how
it behaves once inside a coalition government.[8] There is no harm in
Labour's being permanently in a coalition government, provided that
it makes sure it preserves its own identity, and provided that it can
demonstrate to its own supporters that it is having a significant impact
on government policy. In contrast, there is little point in its spending
any time at all in coalition unless it can show that the end result has
been substantially better than would have been the case under a
government without a Labour component.

So far, Labour has not made the most of its opportunities. In the two
Inter-Party governments the party lacked clear policies and so was not
quite sure what it wanted from government. By the time of the
National Coalition government its long-term policies were clearer, but

partly because of the world recession, and partly because of weak tactics and its lack of medium-range policies, it was not as assertive as it might have been. A minor party in government must use every weapon at its disposal, including if necessary the threat to withdraw, if it is not to risk losing its identity. A militant party conference can strengthen a parliamentary party's position, by convincing the coalition partner that its continued participation in government cannot be taken for granted and may end unless it receives more from the government. However, the Labour Party establishment, though admittedly not to quite the same extent as the other parties' establishments, has never given the impression that it welcomes being put under pressure by a 'fire-breathing' Conference. In any case, the importance of party strategy as a determinant of Labour's strength tends to be much overrated; the dismal record of class-based parties in Northern Ireland emphasises the point that no amount of strategy can steer a party to a position of strength if it operates in a fundamentally unsympathetic social and political environment.

In the long run Labour's prospects depend on much more fundamental questions than which individuals happen to be leading the main political parties, or what attitude it takes towards coalition. In 1982 there were still five counties in the Republic which had never been represented by a Labour TD, and several others which had only rarely, or only in the distant past, returned one. There had been only one Labour TD in Connacht and Ulster since 1932. After the 1982 election Labour had TDs in only nine of the twenty-six counties, and was so weak in many parts of the country that it could hardly be called a national party.

This very weakness in many areas sets up a vicious circle. Because Labour has no TDs there, and often no county councillors either, it has no links with the areas; it cannot respond to their problems, and is perceived not to do so, which makes it much harder for it to gain a foothold. In addition, although the electoral system ensures that it does not suffer from the 'wasted vote' argument, it is the victim of a 'wasted candidacy' factor. Aspiring TDs from such areas, even if their political views are close to Labour's, are more likely to seek a political career through one of the major parties than to embark on the hopeless task of creating a Labour seat out of nothing.

Labour still has very little support from farmers, partly because of its abiding image as the political arm of the trade union movement. It has never worked out a coherent attitude to farmers. Many of its members have a sometimes slightly sentimental sympathy for small farmers, and dream of a party which would link them, agricultural workers, industrial workers and the liberal bourgeoisie, like the Norwegian Labour Party. However, their feeling that workers and small farmers are 'natural allies', and that there is a fundamental incompatibility between the interests of large and small farmers, does not appear to be shared by the small farmers themselves. In the circumstances Labour might do better not to attempt to become a third catch-all party, by trying to appeal to virtually all sections of society except for obvious 'villains' like land speculators and large farmers, but instead to exploit some of the existing cleavages in Irish society. During the 1970s a strong cleavage developed between the urban and rural communities, based on the resentment felt by many urban dwellers at the EEC-based wealth of the agricultural sector and the relatively low taxes paid by farmers. If Labour tried harder to capitalise on this resentment it might well win urban votes at the expense of both major parties, especially Fianna Fáil, and although it might be branded an 'anti-farmer' party its support among farmers has always been so low that this would cost it very few votes and might win it many more. It would also be accused of fomenting sectional conflict in society, and its attractiveness in Fine Gael's eyes as a coalition partner might be reduced, although probably not significantly.

Labour is the victim of a vicious circle in another way. Because it is weak, the onus lies on it, rather than on the other parties, actually to convert voters, obviously a much more difficult task than simply retaining their allegiance. A strong left-wing party does not have to convince its supporters afresh of the merits of socialism at every election; it can rely on an automatic, almost inherited, loyalty, perhaps because its supporters think of it instinctively as 'the party of the working class'. The force of habit, an asset to a strong party, is a liability for a weak one. A weak left-wing party can progress only by winning converts, a difficult task to achieve on a large scale, in the absence of a collapse on the part of one of the major parties, in a settled political system sixty years after the establishment of a full adult franchise, particularly when so many 'natural' Labour voters are linked to the major parties by brokerage ties to individual politicians.

Neither major party seems at all likely to forfeit its position of strength by electorally 'irrational' behaviour. Both, at all levels, are oriented towards maximising votes rather than preserving ideological purity. Their members tend to be more deferential towards their respective leadership than Labour members,[9] willing to go out and canvass votes on the basis of whatever set of policies their leaders hand down to them; Fianna Fáil's 1977 manifesto and that of Fine Gael in 1981 were unveiled by the leaderships only at the start of the election campaigns, and had never been seen, let alone debated, by party members, even though they contained several new proposals. Labour members, at least in Dublin, bear more resemblance to Duverger's 'militants', more concerned with the nature of policies than their electoral appeal, insistent on their right to decide what the policies should be, and suspicious of the motives of the parliamentarians. The major parties' members also seem more keen than Labour's to involve themselves in local organisations, such as residents' associations, community associations, sports clubs and indeed any other body which can be joined, thus increasing their party's local profile and the support it can expect to receive on non-political grounds. In purely electoral terms, the differing nature of the parties' memberships may thus be another retarding factor on the growth of the Labour vote.

In the short term, at least, the odds are heavily against any radical transformation of Labour's position. It is true that, in some respects, the pattern of change seems favourable to the party. Industrialisation and urbanisation have both been, and will continue to be, features of Ireland, north and south, during the present century. Growth in the industrial working class should in theory be reflected in a concomitant growth in support for Labour. Some rural Labour TDs believe that during the 1970s their support came increasingly from workers in the towns in their constituencies, rather than mainly from agricultural workers as hitherto. Irish political culture is becoming more secular, and the strength of the Church is much less of a barrier to the growth of the left than it once was, for on questions like the desirability of State involvement in the economy or the provision of social services it cannot be said to be more conservative than society as a whole. Social attitudes too are becoming more liberal; indeed, political attitudes in general are becoming less conservative. Words like 'socialism' and 'communism' are losing the ominous overtones they possessed for previous generations, and the development of a liberal middle class means that a party repeating Fianna Fáil's 1969 'red smear' campaign might alienate more votes than it attracted. The decline, temporarily at least, of emigration, together with a young population, rising expectations and high unemployment, might cause a build-up of pressure for radical change.

On the other side of the coin, individualism seems to be growing stronger, reducing the likelihood of a socialist programme attracting voters.[10] The reservations about ideology and 'isms' remain, and a left–right dialogue is still conspicuous by its absence. In the broadest terms, elections may now be about social and economic subjects rather than constitutional ones, but the main 'issue' at elections tends to be competence rather than a difference in goals or even policies. The liberalisation of social attitudes, on which Labour is the most progressive of the main parties, may not help it very much, given that the two major parties have always practised the 'chameleon conformism' of which Noel Browne once accused the Church. If the considerable social structural and cultural changes in Irish society since 1960 have not produced any appreciable difference in Labour's strength, a continuation of such changes in the future may not do so either.[11]

Labour's main problem – though potentially its greatest opportunity – lies in Fianna Fáil's continued capture of a large proportion of the working-class vote. Fianna Fáil built up this support base during the 1930s, partly by the programme of industrial expansion linked to protectionism, and partly by being markedly the more left-wing of the two major parties. Since the late 1950s its position in both these respects has been reversed. The first economic programme, with its emphasis on exports, the attempts to attract foreign capital during the 1960s and 1970s, and entry into the EEC in 1973, have all led to a much greater integration of the Irish economy into the world-wide capitalist economy. The party's attitude from the mid-1970s onwards to capital taxation and social issues placed it at least on a par with, and probably to the right of, Fine Gael. Despite this, opinion polls showed it to have at least twice Labour's working-class support.

The main reasons, of course, are the durability of inherited allegiances, which in all countries have a tendency to persist despite changes in the voter's views or the party's policies, and the continued existence of a 'national question'. For as long as Ireland is politically divided Fianna Fáil will have something to 'stand for', a cause far more inspiring than anything either of the other main parties can offer, and will continue to win votes which in other circumstances would go to Labour. Because Fianna Fáil's appeal in this regard is based more on image than on actual policies, let alone performance, it would not necessarily avail Labour much to espouse traditional Fianna Fáil policy on the north in the hope of winning over its working-class supporters. Such a move would in any case alienate some of its own members. The third main reason for Fianna Fáil's possession of so many 'natural' Labour voters is the nature of the party system, which makes it impossible for Labour to wield any effective power except as the junior partner in a coalition with a party perceived by many working-class voters to be a party of the middle class and the large farmers. Fianna Fáil may some day crack up under the weight of its internal contradictions, but so far it has been remarkably successful in defying predictions that it is about to do so.

Labour's main potential for growth certainly seems to lie in the working class rather than among farmers or middle-class liberals, in that the disparity between its expected and its actual vote is widest here, but it is not so easy to offer a formula which would greatly increase its working-class support. The party's constant advocacy of more State involvement in the economy can hardly be said to be a vote-winner, since existing State-run industries seem to be associated in the public mind, rightly or wrongly, with inefficiency, high costs and poor industrial relations. Issues of concern to workers, like prices, jobs, health services, housing and urban transport, are ones where the record of the political and economic systems is open to a lot of criticism, but it is difficult for a minor party to make credible promises of fundamental change, or to explain where it would raise the money to finance them, and so its statements on such subjects look like aspirations rather than policies. Ironically, the party may be hampered in its attempts to gain greater working-class support by its persisting image of closeness to the trade union establishment; in the late 1970s, for example, it did not commit itself fully to wage-earners' demands for tax reform partly at least because the ICTU had reservations about them.

Labour's relatively liberal stance on social and moral matters – divorce, contraception, the role of the Church in education – might in theory cost it support from workers, in view of Mac Gréil's conclusion that those in manual employment and with least education were most conservative,[12] but in fact in electoral terms the gains almost certainly outweigh the losses. It is unlikely that many workers actually withhold support from the party on these grounds, while among the liberal bourgeoisie and the young and, perhaps, minority religious groups it probably gains by appearing to be the most willing of the main parties to resist clerical pressure. For the first time in the State's history there is a small but not negligible anti-clerical vote which Labour is best placed to receive. Liberalism on subjects on which the Church is conservative alienates some rural TDs and their supporters, but even if such votes are lost this can be regarded as an inevitable shedding of pre-transition elements whose support for the party was a historical aberration, due to local circumstances or attachment to a personality rather than sympathy with left-wing policies.

For many years Labour was trapped in a dilemma, feeling compelled to steer a very careful course between Scylla and Charybdis. If it moved to the left the Church or its lay allies would accuse it of being communist; if it did not it would be barely distinguishable from Fianna Fáil. While there is no longer a danger of being eaten by a six-headed monster if it espouses socialism, the party still finds itself in positions from which all possible escape routes seem blocked. If it moves closer to the trade union movement, it is liable to alienate those non-union members who do or might support it; if it does not, it must find another way of attracting that majority of union members who do not support it. If it adopts a left-wing, anti-coalition approach it may win more votes and even more seats, but not enough to have any impact at all on government policy; if it appears ready to join a coalition it reduces its chances of winning working-class support from Fianna Fáil.

The Irish Labour Party has a solid base, loyal supporters, distinctive policies, some backing from the trade union movement, and a long record of survival in circumstances more difficult than those it can expect to face in the future. For these reasons it will not disappear, but there are no signs either that it will grow dramatically, or throw off its third-party status, which has seen it oscillate between seven and twenty-two seats over its sixty-year electoral history. The impact of its period of transition will be permanent; it will not cease to be, in most respects, a modern West European social democratic party, though it is likely to remain an uneasy coalition of outlooks for some time yet. But even at the end of the period, there seemed no likelihood of a significant Labour breakthrough, let alone a majority Labour government, in the foreseeable future.

Notes

Chapter 1

1 Basil Chubb, 'Ireland 1957', in D. E. Butler (ed.), *Elections Abroad* (London: Macmillan, 1959), p. 190.

2 Seymour M. Lipset and Stein Rokkan (eds.), *Party Systems and Voter Alignments* (New York: Free Press, 1967), pp. 14–23. See also the discussion in J. H. Whyte, 'Ireland: Politics without Social Bases', in Richard Rose (ed.), *Electoral Behavior: A Comparative Handbook* (New York: Free Press, 1974), pp. 647–8.

3 Tom Garvin, 'Nationalist Elites, Irish Voters and Irish Political Development: A Comparative Perspective', *Economic and Social Review* 8:3 (1976–77), p. 161.

4 The name of the State was changed by law to 'The Republic of Ireland' in 1949.

5 For a concise history of modern Ireland see John A. Murphy, *Ireland in the Twentieth Century* (Dublin: Gill and Macmillan, 1975).

6 Maurice Duverger, *Political Parties*, 2nd edition (London: Methuen, 1959), pp. xxiii, xxxv.

7 For these developments see Arthur Mitchell, *Labour in Irish Politics 1890–1930* (Dublin: Irish University Press, 1974), pp. 35–6, 40, 278–80.

8 *IT* 7 June 1950, p. 1.

9 Emmet Larkin, 'Socialism and Catholicism in Ireland', *Church History* 33:4 (1964), p. 481; Brian Inglis, *The Story of Ireland*, 2nd edition (London: Faber and Faber, 1965), p. 214.

10 Motion passed unanimously by the Tralee Divisional Council, reported in the *Kerryman* 1 May 1943, p. 2.

11 Mitchell, *Labour in Irish Politics*, p. 279.

12 Maurice Manning, *Irish Political Parties* (Dublin: Gill and Macmillan, 1972), p. 83; Nicholas Mansergh, *The Irish Question 1840–1921* (London: George Allen and Unwin, 1965), p. 243; Morley Ayearst, *The Republic of Ireland* (London: University of London Press, 1971), p. 158.

13 Arthur Mitchell, 'The Irish Labour Party', Part 1, *IT* 27 February

1967, p. 10.

14 Mitchell, *Labour in Irish Politics*, pp. 37–8, 217–18. The British Labour Party too did not allow direct individual membership before 1918. See Ross McKibbin, *The Evolution of the Labour Party 1910–1924* (London: Oxford University Press, 1974), pp. 2, 94–5.

15 J. Dunsmore Clarkson, *Labour and Nationalism in Ireland* (New York: Columbia University Press, 1926), p. 296.

16 Jerome Joseph Joshua Judge, *The Labour Movement in the Republic of Ireland* (National University of Ireland: unpublished PhD thesis in the library of University College Dublin, 1955), p. 137.

17 Murphy, *Ireland in the Twentieth Century*, p. 112.

18 J. L. McCracken, *Representative Government in Ireland: A Study of Dáil Eireann 1919–1948* (London: Oxford University Press, 1958), p. 115; Mitchell, *Labour in Irish Politics*, pp. 242, 289.

19 Conor Cruise O'Brien, 'The Embers of Easter 1916–1966', in Owen Dudley Edwards and Fergus Pyle (eds.), *1916: The Easter Rising* (London: MacGibbon and Kee, 1968), p. 235.

20 Mitchell, *Labour in Irish Politics*, p. 285.

21 Whyte, 'Politics without Social Bases', p. 632.

22 For the circumstances surrounding the split see Donal Nevin, 'Industry and Labour', in Kevin B. Nowlan and T. Desmond Williams (eds.), *Ireland in the War Years and after, 1939–1951* (Dublin: Gill and Macmillan, 1969), pp. 94–108, and Charles McCarthy, *Trade Unions in Ireland 1894–1960* (Dublin: Institute of Public Administration, 1977), pp. 229–91, especially 251–4.

23 For the seriousness of their conflict, and the vitriolic nature of the Larkinites' attacks on the party, see J. Anthony Gaughan, *Thomas Johnson* (Dublin: Kingdom Books, 1980), pp. 265–77; Mitchell, *Labour in Irish Politics*, pp. 183–7, 274–6; Emmet Larkin, *James Larkin* (London: Routledge and Kegan Paul, 1965), pp. 261–74, 288–9.

24 As in Britain, all union members contribute automatically to their union's political fund unless they 'contract out'.

25 Introduction to Owen Dudley Edwards and Bernard Ransom (eds.), *James Connolly: Selected Political Writings* (London: Jonathan Cape, 1973), p. 15.

26 For his fullest biography, see C. Desmond Greaves, *The Life and Times of James Connolly* (London: Lawrence and Wishart, 1961).

27 Larkin's life is covered by Larkin, *Larkin*.

28 Cf. pp. 124–6 below.

29 David Thornley, 'The Development of the Irish Labour Movement', *Christus Rex* 18:1 (1964), pp. 7–8, 19, 16.

30 Larkin, 'Socialism and Catholicism in Ireland', p. 481.

31 Thornley, 'Development of the Irish Labour Movement', pp. 16–17.

32 Mitchell, *Labour in Irish Politics*, pp. 155–6.

33 Cf. ibid., and *Freeman's Journal*, 23 May 1922, p. 2.

34 McCarthy, *Trade Unions in Ireland*, p. 255.

35 Dennis Kavanagh, *Political Culture* (London: Macmillan, 1972), pp.

10–11.

36   Mansergh, *The Irish Question*, p. 244; Judge, *The Labour Movement*, p. 156.

37   *Bunreacht na hEireann* (Constitution of Ireland), Articles 43.1, 45.3.1.

38   Mícheál Mac Gréil, *Prejudice and Tolerance in Ireland* (Dublin: College of Industrial Relations, 1977), pp. 230–3.

39   Ibid., pp. 411, 241 and 298–9.

40   Communist Party of Ireland, *Outline History* (Dublin: New Books, nd [1973?]), p. 8.

41   Ronald Inglehart and Hans D. Klingemann, 'Party Identification, Ideological Preference and the Left–Right Dimension among Western Mass Publics', in Ian Budge, Ivor Crewe and Dennis Farlie (eds.), *Party Identification and Beyond* (London: John Wiley, 1976), pp. 247–51. There were 1,199 respondents to the survey in Ireland, of whom about 80 per cent were able to give some placement of their views.

42   Ibid., pp. 252–4. It was noted that the proportion of respondents identifying with a party was lower in Ireland (56 per cent) than in any of the other countries.

43   Ibid., pp. 254, 270.

44   Giovanni Sartori, *Parties and Party Systems* (Cambridge: Cambridge University Press, 1976), pp. 334–5.

45   *S Ind* 3 July 1977, p. 15.

46   Vivion de Valera, *DD* 278:1553, 5 March 1975.

47   Tom Garvin, 'Belief Systems, Ideological Perspectives and Political Activism: Some Dublin Evidence', *Social Studies* 6:1 (1977), p. 51.

48   *Census of Population Ireland 1971*, Vol. 9 (Dublin: CSO, 1977), Table 1A, p. 1.

49   James Lennon, Máire Nic Ghiolla Phádraigh and Thomas F. Inglis, 'Religious Practice in Ireland', *Intercom* (Bulletin of the Catholic Communications Institute of Ireland) 6:9 (1975), pp. 3, 5.

50   *Bunreacht na hEireann*, Article 44.1.2 and 44.1.3.

51   See e.g. Jean Blanchard, *The Church in Contemporary Ireland* (Dublin: Clonmore and Reynolds, 1963), p. 17.

52   Cf. Chubb, *Government and Politics of Ireland*, p. 55; J. H. Whyte, *Church and State in Modern Ireland 1923–1979* (Dublin: Gill and Macmillan, 1980), pp. 159–60, 265.

53   David W. Miller, *Church, State and Nation in Ireland 1898–1921* (Dublin: Gill and Macmillan, 1973), p. 270.

54   See the summary in Whyte, *Church and State*, p. 63.

55   Samuel Levenson, *James Connolly* (London: Martin Brian and O'Keeffe, 1973), p. 149. See also Greaves, *James Connolly*, pp. 319–20; Owen Dudley Edwards, *The Mind of an Activist* (Dublin: Gill and Macmillan, 1971), pp. 28–64; Edwards and Ransom (eds.), *Connolly: Selected Writings*, pp. 61–150.

56   Section 2, paras. 2 and 3; Section 3(b). The constitution is given in full in the Appendix to the *5th Annual Report 1936*.

57   *8th Annual Report 1939*, p. 166.

58   Ibid., pp. 162–4, 173, 174. For other accounts of this incident see
     Whyte, *Church and State*, pp. 81–6, and Donal Nevin, 'Labour and the
     Political Revolution', in Francis MacManus (ed.), *The Years of the
     Great Test* (Cork: Mercier, 1967), pp. 64–5.
59   See the Appendix to *10th Annual Report 1941*. The AC is Labour's
     national executive.
60   *5th Annual Report 1936*, p. 101. The delegate, Gilbert Lynch, was a
     former TD for Galway.
61   Warner Moss, *Political Parties in the Irish Free State* (New York:
     Columbia University Press, 1933), p. 170, n. 35.
62   *Limerick Leader* 21 November 1936, p. 6.
63   *4th Annual Report 1935*, pp. 113–18.
64   *7th Annual Report 1938*, p. 193. The displeasure caused by O'Brien's
     remark can be understood only if it is realised that in Ireland the
     Spanish Civil War was widely seen as one in which there was 'a Godless
     combination of Anarchists and Communists waging war with a satanic
     fury against the upholders of Christianity and civilization in that land',
     in the words of an editorial in the *I Ind* 18 February 1937, p. 8.
65   See Whyte, *Church and State*, pp. 85–6, and Nevin, 'Industry and
     Labour', pp. 101–2.
66   *Kerryman* 27 May 1944, p. 4.
67   From his election advertisement in *Wicklow People* 27 May 1944, p. 5.
68   For a full analysis of the episode see Whyte, *Church and State*, pp.
     196–272.
69   For the speech see *DD* 125:948–954, 17 April 1951.
70   Ibid., col. 952.
71   D. R. O'Connor Lysaght, 'Religion and Irish Labour', *International
     Socialist Journal* 2:10 (1965), p. 502.
72   *I Ind* 2 May 1957, p. 8.
73   *Dungarvan Leader* 30 September 1961, p. 1. For a similar editorial see
     Meath Chronicle 2 March 1957, p. 3.
74   See Whyte, *Church and State*, Chapter 10.
75   Ibid., pp. 355–6, and Cornelius O'Leary, 'The Catholic and Politics',
     Christus Rex 17:4 (1963), p. 295.
76   Gordon Smith, *Politics in Western Europe*, 2nd edition (London:
     Heinemann, 1976), p. 20.
77   See Frances Morrell, *From the Electors of Bristol* (Nottingham:
     Spokesman Pamplet No. 57, 1977), p. 6. Brokerage is by now a well-
     worn theme in studies of Irish politics; for two articles embodying
     active research see John Whyte, *Dáil Deputies* (Dublin: Tuairim
     Pamphlet No. 15, 1966), and Joseph F. Zimmermann, 'Role
     Perceptions of Dual Office Holders in Ireland', *Administration* 26:1
     (1978), pp. 25–48.
78   Chubb, *Government and Politics of Ireland*, p. 154.
79   See Jeremy Boissevain, 'When the Saints go marching out: Reflections
     on the decline of patronage in Malta', in Ernest Gellner and John
     Waterbury (eds.), *Patrons and Clients* (London: Duckworth, 1977), p.
     81. Cf. Mart Bax, *Harpstrings and Confessions* (Assen: Van Gorcum,

1976), p. 46.
80   Chubb, *Government and Politics of Ireland*, p. 217; Whyte, *Dáil Deputies*, pp. 15–16. Cf. Patrick Buckland, *Irish Unionism 1: The Anglo-Irish and the New Ireland 1885–1922* (Dublin: Gill and Macmillan, 1972), p. xx.
81   Bax, *Harpstrings and Confessions*, especially pp. 48–50, 64–5, 74–9, 113; Paul Sacks, *The Donegal Mafia* (New Haven: Yale University Press, 1976), pp. 7–8, 50–1, 211. See also John B. Keane, *Letters of a Successful TD* (Cork: Mercier Press, 1967).
82   Donogh O'Malley, *DD* 226:1892, 23 February 1967.
83   *DD* 255:415, 1 July 1971.
84   Oliver J. Flanagan, quoted in *IT* 8 November 1965, p. 11. In the 1951 election campaign he declared that 'he had placed his friends in good jobs in Clonsast and Portarlington, and as warders in prisons, and everywhere he could get in his foot', and made 'a promise that he would secure jobs for his friends . . . when the proposed new Ferbane Power Station was opened'. See *Offaly Chronicle* 30 May 1951, p. 3.
85   *DD* 123:2064, 13 December 1950.
86   Ian Hart, 'Public Opinion on Civil Servants and the Role and Power of the Individual in the Local Community', *Administration* 18:4 (1970) p. 383; John Raven *et al.*, *Political Culture in Ireland* (Dublin: Institute of Public Administration, 1976), pp. 32–3.
87   See Damian Hannan, 'Kinship, Neighbourhood and Social Change in Irish Rural Communities', *Economic and Social Review* 3:2 (1971–72), p. 167.
88   Hugh Brody, *Inishkillane* (Harmondsworth: Penguin, 1973), p. 36.
89   Chubb, *Government and Politics of Ireland*, p. 52.
90   Brody, *Inishkillane*, pp. 146–8. Cf. Hannan, 'Kinship and Social Change', p. 186.
91   Father James McDyer of Glencolumbkille, quoted in *IP* 7 April 1976, p. 9.
92   Donal Nevin (ed.), *Trade Unions and Change in Irish Society* (Dublin: Mercier, 1980), p. 171. For a survey of interest groups see Maria Maguire, 'Pressure Groups in Ireland', *Administration* 25:3 (1977), pp. 349–64.
93   Eric Jacobs, *European Trade Unionism* (London: Croom Helm, 1973), p. 31; Nevin, *Trade Unions*, pp. 170–1.
94   The atmosphere is perhaps most vividly evoked in Brinsley MacNamara, *The Valley of the Squinting Windows* (Tralee: Anvil Books, 1964).
95   Conrad M. Arensberg and Solon T. Kimball, *Family and Community in Ireland* (Cambridge, Mass.: Harvard University Press, 1968), p. 184; John C. Messenger, *Inis Beag* (New York: Holt, Rinehart and Winston, 1969), p. 64. See also Peter Gibbon and M. D. Higgins, 'Patronage, Tradition and Modernization: The Case of the Irish "Gombeenman" ', *Economic and Social Review* 6:1 (1974–75), p. 36.
96   See the *Kerryman* 21 June 1969, p. 1.
97   *Census of Population Ireland 1971*, Vol. 4 (Dublin: CSO, 1975), Table

2, p. x.

98   Ibid, Table 3, p. xi; Appendix B, pp. 188–9. The figures refer to both
      gainfully employed and not gainfully employed persons. For a general
      discussion of social stratification in Ireland see John Jackson, 'Ireland',
      in M. S. Archer and S. Giner (eds.), *Contemporary Europe: Class,
      Status and Power* (London: Weidenfeld and Nicolson, 1971).

99   Whyte, 'Politics without Social Bases', p. 631.

100   P. R. Kaim-Caudle, *Social Policy in the Irish Republic* (London:
      Routledge and Kegan Paul, 1967), p. 113.

101   *Census of Population Ireland 1971*, Vol. 4 (Dublin: CSO, 1975), Table
      3, p. 8.

102   *Census of Population Ireland 1971*, Vol. 1 (Dublin: CSO, 1972), Table
      5B, p. xvii.

103   Whyte, 'Politics without Social Bases', p. 634. Five per cent of the
      respondents appear to be missing from the table as presented.

104   1963 figure from D. E. Butler and Donald Stokes, *Political Change in
      Britain* (Harmondsworth: Penguin, 1971), p. 92; 1970 figure
      calculated from ibid., 2nd edition (London: Macmillan, 1974), p. 72.

105   Whyte, 'Politics without Social Bases', p. 645.

106   Ibid., p. 631; Richard Sinnott, 'The Electorate', in Howard R.
      Penniman (ed.), *Ireland at the Polls: the Dáil Elections of 1977*
      (Washington: American Enterprise Institute for Public Policy
      Research, 1978), especially p. 53.

107   Michael Gallagher, *Electoral Support for Irish Political Parties
      1927–1973* (London: Sage Professional Papers, Contemporary
      Political Sociology Series, Vol. 2, No. 06-017, 1976), pp. 42–4.

108   Richard Rose and Derek Urwin, 'Social Cohesion, Political Parties and
      Strains in Regimes', *Comparative Political Studies* 2:1 (1969–70), pp.
      10–11 and 13.

109   Robert Alford, *Party and Society* (London: John Murray, 1964), pp.
      79–80.

110   Whyte, 'Politics without Social Bases', p. 631.

111   Arend Lijphart, *Class Voting and Religious Voting in the European
      Democracies* (Glasgow: University of Strathclyde Occasional Paper
      No. 8, 1971), p. 8. It should be noted that most of the data from which
      his figures are drawn relate to the 1950s.

112   *Census of Population Ireland 1971*, Vol. 1 (Dublin: CSO, 1972), Table
      10, p. xxi.

113   Cf. Arensberg and Kimball, *Family and Community*, p. 143; Brody,
      Inishkillane, p. 68.

114   Cf. William Petersen, 'A General Typology of Migration', *American
      Sociological Review* 23:3 (1958), p. 263; Brody, *Inishkillane*, p. 7.

115   John Archer Jackson, *The Irish in Britain* (London: Routledge and
      Kegan Paul, 1963), p. 38.

116   See e.g. Whyte, 'Politics without Social Bases', p. 623.

117   John O'Donovan, *DD* 148:489, 16 February 1955. The speaker later
      became a Labour TD.

118   See John A. O'Brien (ed.), *The Vanishing Irish* (London: W. H. Allen,

1954), pp. 7, 41, 47. Cf. John V. Kelleher, 'Ireland . . . and where does she stand?', *Foreign Affairs* 35:3 (1957), p. 495.

119 See Tim Pat Coogan, *Ireland since the Rising* (London: Pall Mall Press, 1966), p. 107 and Garret FitzGerald, *Planning in Ireland* (Dublin: Institute of Public Administration, 1968), p. 17.

120 Thornley, 'Development of the Irish Labour Movement', p. 20.

121 Jean Blondel, *An Introduction to Comparative Government* (London: Weidenfeld and Nicolson, 1969), p. 162.

122 Stanley Henig and John Pinder (eds.), *European Political Parties* (London: George Allen and Unwin, 1969), p. 516. Henig does not attempt classification in the second (1979) edition of the book.

123 Smith, *Politics in Western Europe*, pp. 96–7, 313–14.

124 Blondel, *Introduction to Comparative Government*, p. 162.

125 Leon D. Epstein, *Political Parties in Western Democracies* (London: Pall Mall Press, 1967), pp. 4, 138.

126 Whyte, 'Politics without Social Bases', p. 648.

127 Epstein, *Political Parties*, p. 138.

128 This was de Valera's description of the 'dilemma'. See the Earl of Longford and Thomas P. O'Neill, *Eamon de Valera* (London: Arrow Books, 1974), p. 186.

129 Gallagher, *Electoral Support for Irish Political Parties*, pp. 19–20.

130 In an interview with Michael McInerney, *IT* 17 March 1967, p. 10. For similar comments see Chubb, *Government and Politics of Ireland*, p. 76; F. S. L. Lyons, *Ireland Since the Famine* (London: Weidenfeld and Nicolson, 1971), p. 520; Ayearst, *The Republic of Ireland*, p. 156.

131 See pp. 8–9 above.

132 Ayearst, *The Republic of Ireland*, p. 155.

133 *Tuam Herald* 28 June 1969, p. 7.

134 Murphy, *Ireland in the Twentieth Century*, p. 112; MacGréil, *Prejudice and Tolerance*, p. 205.

135 Brian Farrell, 'Labour and the Irish Political Party System: a suggested approach to analysis', *Economic and Social Review* 1:4 (1969–70), p. 486.

136 Henry Valen and Stein Rokkan, 'Norway', in Rose, *Electoral Behavior*, p. 334.

137 Walter Galenson, *Labor in Norway* (Cambridge, Mass.: Harvard University Press, 1949), p. 58.

138 Samuel P. Huntington, *Political Order in Changing Societies* (New Haven: Yale University Press, 1968), p. 375, quoted in Andrew Orridge, 'The Irish Labour Party', in William C. Paterson and Alistair H. Thomas (eds.), *Social Democratic Parties in Western Europe* (London: Croom Helm, 1977), p. 170. Cf. the comments of Moss, *Political Parties in the Irish Free State*, p. 34.

139 Cf. Orridge, 'The Irish Labour Party', p. 154.

140 Mitchell, *Labour in Irish Politics*, p. 215. For the background to the issue cf. pp. 213–16.

141 *Census of Population Ireland 1971*, Vol. 2 (Dublin: CSO, 1973), Table 2, p. ix.

Chapter 2

1   Clann na Talmhan (1938–65) was essentially a western-based small farmers' party. Clann na Poblachta (1947–65) was republican and in some ways relatively radical. For brief histories of these parties see Maurice Manning, *Irish Political Parties* (Dublin: Gill and Macmillan, 1972), pp. 99–106.

2   See *IT* 26 July 1956, p. 1, for details.

3   Garret FitzGerald, *Planning in Ireland* (Dublin: Institute of Public Administration, 1968), pp. 8, 16.

4   *Statistical Abstract of Ireland 1957* (Dublin: CSO, 1957), p. 189.

5   *IT* 19 September 1956, p. 1; *IP* 20 October 1956, p. 9.

6   *Liberty* January 1957, p. 20.

7   For details see *IT* 6 October 1956, p. 1. See also John V. Kelleher, 'Ireland . . . and where does she stand?', *Foreign Affairs* 35:3 (1957), pp. 485–95.

8   *IT* 6 October 1956, p. 1.

9   *Annual Report 1956–57*, pp. 13–14. The AC is charged under Labour's constitution with carrying out 'the control of the organization and the administrative affairs of the Party'. Seventeen members are elected by the annual conference, and three party officers elected at the conference – the party chairman, vice-chairman and financial secretary – are *ex officio* members, as are the leader and deputy leader of the party in the Dail. The party leader appoints another six PLP members (two before 1960) to the AC. In addition, the constitution is occasionally amended by an annual conference to allow other members – from western constituencies, for example – to be co-opted.

10 John O'Leary, in the *People* (Wexford), 2 February 1957, p. 8.

11 *DD* 160:2398–403, 13 December 1956.

12 Ibid, cols. 2403–4.

13 See e.g. the speeches of Sean MacBride, reported in *IT* 3 October 1956, p. 1 and *DD* 160:2435, 13 December 1956, and his letter to the Dublin Trades Council in *IT* 16 January 1957, p. 1.

14 *IT* 5 January 1957, p. 5; *Tipperary Star* 12 January 1957, p. 3.

15 *IT* 29 January 1957, pp. 1, 3.

16 This figure includes a Clann na Talmhan TD who went on to stand as an Independent in the 1957 election, but does not include an Independent who went on to stand for Fine Gael.

17 The recollection of a member of the government in interview, 1978.

18 There had been rumours that deputies of Clann na Talmhan, as well as Labour, had become increasingly unhappy about the policies pursued by the government. See *IP* 16 November 1956, p. 1.

19 For a study of the campaign see Basil Chubb, 'Ireland 1957', in D. E. Butler (ed.), *Elections Abroad* (London: Macmillan, 1959), pp. 183–226.

20 The manifesto is reprinted in the *Annual Report 1956–57*, pp. 26–8.

21 See e.g. his speech reported in *IT* 23 February 1957, p. 1.

22 *I Ind* 27 February 1957, p. 8.

23 *S Ind* 3 March 1957, p. 6.
24 *Leinster Leader* 2 March 1957, p. 5.
25 *IT* 2 March 1957, p. 1.
26 *Annual Report 1956–57* pp. 18, 1–2.
27 *Hibernia* December 1956, pp. 8, 13.
28 *S Ind* 16 June 1957, p. 11.
29 The section of his speech covering policy matters was published as a twelve-page pamphlet: William Norton, *Labour's Way* (Dublin: Irish Labour Party, nd [1958]). See pp. 4–7, 11–12. A brief report was carried in *IT* 10 February 1958, p. 4.
30 *IT* 24 January 1957, p. 7.
31 E.g. the speeches of James Larkin, *IT* 27 July 1957, p. 4; James Tully, *IT* 25 April 1958, p. 5, and 11 October 1958, p. 9; Brendan Corish, *IT* 21 May 1957, p. 6. See also *Annual Report 1957–58*, p. 2.
32 Ruaidhri Roberts, 'Trade Union Organization in Ireland', *Journal of the Statistical and Social Inquiry Society of Ireland* 20:2 (1958–59), p. 96.
33 For details see *IT* 22 February 1958, p. 9.
34 *IT* 14 March 1958, p. 5.
35 For details see *IT* 17 May 1958, p. 1.
36 Michael Kennedy, in *IT* 24 May 1958, p. 5.
37 *DD* 167:1462, 7 May 1958.
38 *IT* 28 November 1958, p. 6.
39 *IT* 5 July 1958, p. 1.
40 E.g. *Evening Mail* 12 June 1958, p. 9, and *I Ind* 27 June 1958, p. 11.
41 *IT* 21 October 1958, p. 7.
42 For a detailed account of the referendum campaign see Cornelius O'Leary, *The Irish Republic* (Notre Dame: University of Notre Dame Press, 1961) pp. 58–83, and Garret FitzGerald, 'PR – The Great Debate', *Studies* 48:1 (1959), pp. 1–20.
43 *IT* 13 October 1958, p. 1.
44 *Annual Report 1958–59*, p. 8.
45 *DD* 171:1047, 26 November 1958. Cf. his speech in *IT* 8 June 1959, p. 4.
46 Cf. Douglas Rae, *The Political Consequences of Electoral Laws*, revised edition (New Haven: Yale University Press, 1971), pp. 92–6; Maurice Duverger, *Political Parties*, 2nd edition (London: Methuen, 1959), pp. 223–6.
47 See Michael Gallagher, 'Disproportionality in a Proportional Representation System: the Irish Experience', *Political Studies* 23:4 (1975), p. 502.
48 John A. Murphy, 'The Irish Party System, 1938–1951', in Kevin B. Nowlan and T. Desmond Williams (eds.), *Ireland in the War Years and After, 1939–51* (Dublin: Gill and Macmillan, 1969), p. 154; O'Leary, *The Irish Republic*, p. 18.
49 *IT* 28 November 1958, p. 9.
50 Dominick Murphy, in *SD* 50:372, 5 February 1959.
51 *DD* 174:1971–75, 13 May 1959.
52 The precise figures were: for, 453,322 (48·2 per cent); against, 486,989

(51·8 per cent). Turnout was 56·1 per cent. The source of these figures and the results of other referendums and presidential elections is the official gazette *Iris Oifigiúil*.

53 *I Ind* 10 October 1959, p. 14.
54 *Annual Report 1958–59*, p. 13; cf. *Annual Report 1959–60*, p. 9.
55 *Annual Report 1958–59*, pp. 7–8; *IT* 21 November 1958, p. 10.
56 *IT* 21 December 1959, p. 1.
57 See e.g. the speech of de Valera in *IT* 4 March 1957, p. 1, and of Gerry Boland in *IT* 19 February 1957, p. 1.
58 E.g. *DD* 166:230, 13 March 1958.
59 E.g. Stephen D. Barrett in *DD* 162:683, 12 June 1957.
60 George Coburn, *I Ind* 16 August 1957, p. 8.
61 *IT* 3 October 1959, p. 4.
62 The speech was printed in full in *National Observer* 2:1, July 1959, pp. 5 and 8, and extensively in *I Ind* 2 May 1959, p. 14.
63 *National Observer* 2:1, July 1959, p. 4.
64 *IT* 22 October 1959, p. 9.
65 *National Observer* 2:5, November 1959, p. 1.
66 See e.g. *IT* 29 April 1957, p. 1.
67 *IP* 11 November 1959, p. 1, and *IT* 11 November 1959, p. 3.
68 For newspaper reports see *IT* 11 February 1960, p. 1, 18 February 1960, p. 9, and 25 February 1960, p. 1; *I Ind* 11 February 1960, p. 9; *IP*·10 February 1960, p. 7. Labour's *Annual Report 1959–60*, p. 5 states that Norton resigned on 3 February. Much of the remainder of this section is based on information derived from interviews, 1976–78.
69 *IT* 8 October 1960, p. 7.
70 See report in *I Ind* 6 June 1944, p. 3.
71 *DD* 138:840, 29 April 1953, quoted in Basil Chubb, *The Government and Politics of Ireland* (Stanford: Stanford University Press, 1970), p. 103.
72 *DD* 163:731, 4 July 1957. For a fuller account of the affair see J. H. Whyte, *Church and State in Modern Ireland 1923–1979* (Dublin: Gill and Macmillan, 1980), pp. 322–5.
73 Evelyn Bolster, *The Knights of St. Columbanus* (Dublin: Gill and Macmillan, 1979), p. 96. Norton was definitely a member; see ibid., p. 98.
74 *IT* 12 May 1960, p. 10.
75 See *IT* 21 September 1960, p. 6. The full text of the document is given in *Liberty* October 1960, pp. 8, 25.
76 *IT* 6 June 1960, p. 7.
77 *Hibernia* 22 July 1960, pp. 1, 9.
78 Although only 140 votes were cast, the chairman stated that attendance at the conference was the largest for many years, an indication of the poor state of the party. Reports of the conference were given in *IT* 8 October 1960, pp. 1, 5, 10 October 1960, p. 7, and 11 October 1960, p. 5; *I Ind* 10 October 1960, p. 2; *IP* 8 October 1960, p. 1.
79 See *IT* 12 December 1960, p. 1, and 18 March 1961, p. 8.
80 *IT* 12 March 1962, p. 9.

81 *Hibernia* December 1960, pp. 11–12.

82 *IT* 18 March 1961, p. 8.

83 *ICTU Annual Report 1960–61*, pp. 86–7. Cf. *IT* 18 March 1961, p. 8.

84 See *ICTU Annual Report 1961–62*, p. 93; *ICTU Annual Report 1962–63*, p. 166; *ICTU Annual Report 1964–65*, p. 98; *ICTU Annual Report 1965–66*, p. 108; *ICTU Annual Report 1966–67*, p. 109.

85 *ICTU Annual Report 1966–67*, p. 310.

86 *IT* 18 March 1961, p. 12, 17 June 1961, p. 15 and 28 July 1961, p. 9; *WUI Bulletin* June–July 1961, pp. 2, 6; *ICTU Annual Report 1960–61*, pp. 252–4.

87 E.g. *IT* 30 November 1959, pp. 1, 9 and 24 February 1960, pp. 1 and 9.

88 *IT* 2 May 1961, p. 7.

89 *IP* 5 May 1961, pp. 1, 9.

90 *IT* 9 August 1961, p. 7.

91 See *IP* 28 July 1958, p. 1, and *IT* 28 July 1958, p. 1, and 2 June 1959, p. 1.

92 See *IT* 12 December 1960, p. 1, and 25 May 1961, p. 6; *Westmeath Independent* 14 January 1961, p. 7.

93 E.g. the *Irish Times* (27 September 1961, p. 7) commented that 'there has never been an election campaign that made so little impact on the people at large', and similar reports can be found in some provincial newspapers.

94 See *IT* 13 September 1961, p. 1.

95 See *ICTU Annual Report 1961–62*, p. 113; *ICTU Annual Report 1956–57*, p. 68; *ICTU Annual Report 1964–65*, p. 113.

96 Michael Hilliard, in *IT* 26 September 1961, p. 9.

97 *Donegal Democrat* 22 September 1961, p. 6.

98 *IT* 14 September 1961, p. 1.

99 *Times* 7 October 1961, p. 9.

Chapter 3

1 *DD* 192:23–34, 11 October 1961.

2 Ibid., cols. 45–7.

3 Ibid., cols. 47–8.

4 Ibid., cols. 52–3.

5 Garret FitzGerald, *Planning in Ireland* (Dublin: Institute of Public Administration, 1968), p. 41.

6 J. H. Whyte, *Church and State in Modern Ireland 1923–1979* (Dublin: Gill and Macmillan, 1980), pp. 356–7.

7 See the speeches of James Tully (*IT* 5 May 1962, p. 11), and William Norton and Brendan Corish (*IT* 7 May 1962, p. 6).

8 *IT* 22 September 1962, p. 1, and 3 October 1962, p. 5.

9 *IT* 27 February 1963, p. 8, 13 March 1963, p. 8, and 27 March 1963, p. 8.

10 *IP* 21 November 1962, p. 5.

11 E.g. *DD* 197:18, 30 October 1962.

12 *DD* 202:305, 24 April 1963.

13 *IP* 19 October 1963, p. 3.
14 *IT* 20 November 1963, p. 5.
15 E.g. *IT* 25 April 1963, p. 9.
16 Cf. p. 11 above.
17 *Annual Report 1962–63*, p. 8.
18 Interviews, 1977 and 1978.
19 *IT* 14 November 1963, p. 1.
20 See e.g. Browne's favourable comments on Labour's 1961 manifesto (*IT* 20 November 1961, p. 9), and reports in *Sunday Review* 18 February 1962, p. 2 and 11 March 1962, p. 2.
21 *IT* 28 November 1963, p. 9; *Roscommon Champion* 30 November 1963, p. 8.
22 Interviews, 1976 and 1977.
23 *IT* 12 October 1967, p. 10; Michael McInerney, 'Noel Browne: Church and State', *University Review* 5:2 (1968), p. 205.
24 Gerald Bartley, in *DD* 174:1729, 6 May 1959.
25 Maurice Manning, *Irish Political Parties* (Dublin: Gill and Macmillan, 1972), p. 107.
26 A quorum in the Dáil is twenty TDs. The usual attendance during debates is five or fewer.
27 *DD* 171:571–2, 12 November 1958.
28 *S Ind* 8 December 1963, pp. 1, 4; *IT* 9 December 1963, p. 11.
29 *S Ind* 8 December 1963, pp. 1, 4.
30 See *Leinster Leader* 15 February 1964, p. 7; *IT* 21 January 1964, p. 9, and 23 January 1964, p. 1.
31 *IT* 21 January 1964, p. 9; *Leinster Leader* 25 January 1964, p. 11.
32 *Evening Echo* (Cork) 18 February 1964, p. 8. Hurley, like Norton, was the son of a former Labour TD.
33 *IT* 28 February 1962, p. 9.
34 See *DD* 205:1101–26, 7 November 1963.
35 See *IT* 16 May 1964, p. 10.
36 See *IT* 27 May 1964, p. 1.
37 *IT* 23 May 1964, p. 13. Some years later, he was to acknowledge that the programme had contained 'an element of socialism'; *DD* 257:2529, 16 December 1971.
38 *IT* 8 June 1964, p. 5.
39 *IP* 4 July 1964, p. 4.
40 A newspaper cartoon showed two elderly retired colonel characters, one saying, 'Soon, I fear, there'll be no party one can vote for, now that even Labour is moving to the Left.' *IT* 26 May 1964, p. 1.
41 *IT* 9 June 1964, p. 8.
42 *IT* 25 May 1964, p. 1. Cf. *WUI Bulletin* May–June 1964, p. 1, and, for some of the discussion at an earlier conference, ibid., June–July 1962, p. 2.
43 *IT* 30 June 1964, p. 7.
44 Ibid., and *IT* 2 July 1964, p. 8.
45 *Times* 6 April 1965, p. 5.
46 *IT* 5 April 1965, p. 1.

47 It was given in full in *IT* 24 March 1965, p. 6.
48 *IT* 13 March 1965, p. 15.
49 *IT* 5 April 1965, p. 6. Cf. *Fine Gael Policy 1965* (Dublin: Fine Gael, 1965), para. 9 pp. 9–10, para. 6 p. 13, and para. 12 pp. 14–15.
50 *IT* 26 March 1965, p. 6.
51 *S Ind* 28 March 1965, p. 9. Fine Gael advertisements offered the manifesto for sale at 1s 3d to those who 'applied' to party headquarters.
52 *IT* 20 March 1965, p. 11.
53 *IT* 25 March 1965, p. 11 and 27 March 1965, p. 13.
54 *IT* 29 March 1965, p. 6.
55 *IT* 19 October 1964, p. 1, and 31 March 1965, p. 6; *Western People* 27 March 1965, p. 13.
56 Michael Gallagher, *Electoral Support for Irish Political Parties 1927–1973* (London: Sage Professional Papers, Contemporary Political Sociology Series, Vol. 2, No. 06–017, 1976), pp. 38–40.
57 *Annual Report 1963–64*, p. 7.
58 *Annual Report 1964–65*, p. 14.
59 *IP* 18 October 1965, p. 4.
60 Ibid.
61 *IT* 6 October 1965, p. 10.
62 *Annual Report 1965–66*, pp. 6–7; *IT* 27 January 1966, p. 1, and 17 February 1966, p. 1.
63 *IT* 26 May 1966, p. 11.
64 *IT* 11 May 1966, p. 4.
65 The precise figures were: de Valera 558,861 (50·5 per cent); O'Higgins 548,144 (49·5 per cent).
66 The correlation coefficient (r) between Fianna Fáil's 1965 support and de Valera's 1966 support was $0·36$ ($n = 38$); for Fine Gael's 1965 support and de Valera's 1966 support, $r = 0·16$. These figures can be compared with a correlation of $0·78$ between Fianna Fáil's support at the 1961 and 1965 general elections.
67 *IP* 18 October 1965, p. 4.
68 *IT* 28 September 1966, p. 4.
69 *IT* 14 October 1966, p. 7, and 15 October 1966, p. 14.
70 *IT* 14 October 1966, p. 7, and 17 October 1966, p. 1.
71 *IT* 18 October 1966, p. 7.
72 *IT* 22 April 1965, p. 1.
73 *IT* 20 May 1964, p. 6.
74 *IT* 10 November 1966, pp. 1, 11.
75 *IT* 14 November 1966, p. 1.
76 The party's *Annual Report 1966–67*, p. 7 described the Kerry result as 'disappointing' and the Waterford result as 'not heartening'.
77 *IT* 12 December 1966, p. 11. The *Annual Report 1966–67*, p. 7 also concluded that there was a need for the organisation to be 'stepped up considerably'.
78 *S Ind* 18 December 1966, p. 4.
79 *ITGWU Annual Report 1959*, pp. 118–19.
80 *ITGWU Annual Report 1961*, pp. 113–15.

81   *ITGWU Annual Report 1962*, pp. 112–13.
82   *ITGWU Annual Report 1964*, pp. 100, 158.
83   *ITGWU Annual Report 1965*, pp. 151–2; *Liberty* July 1966, pp. 39–40.
84   See *Liberty* November 1966, p. 23.
85   *ITGWU Annual Report 1966*, p. 145. For a report of the conference see ibid., pp. 195–208. See also *Liberty* June 1967, p. 21.
86   *IT* 27 September 1967, p. 1.
87   *Liberty* June 1967, p. 21.
88   *Labour* May–June 1967, p. 8.
89   *IT* 16 May 1968, p. 15; *ITGWU Annual Report 1969*, p. 218.
90   *ITGWU Annual Report 1966*, p. 197.
91   *ITGWU Annual Report 1970*, pp. 159–60.
92   *ICTU Annual Report 1966–67*, p. 308.
93   Ibid., p. 311.
94   See *IT* 26 May 1967, p. 1.
95   *ICTU Annual Report 1967–68*, p. 140; *ICTU Annual Report 1968–69*, p. 154.
96   *IT* 4 February 1967, p. 6. Cf. *Annual Report 1966–67*, pp. 12–13.
97   *IT* 14 January 1967, pp. 1, 4.
98   *Hibernia* February 1967, p. 3.
99   *Catholic Standard* 20 January 1967, p. 6.
100 Proinsias Mac Aonghusa (ed.), *Corish Speaks* (Dublin: New Century Publications, 1966), p. 5.
101 *IT* 1 March 1967, p. 15.
102 *IT* 2 February 1967, p. 4.
103 *IT* 16 October 1967, p. 1.
104 *Business and Finance* 10 March 1967, pp. 10–11.
105 *IT* 16 October 1967, p. 9.

Chapter 4

1   See *Annual Report 1966–67*, pp. 5–6.
2   *United Irishman* October 1966, p. 4.
3   *IT* 29 March 1967, p. 9.
4   *Hibernia* August 1967, p. 4.
5   It is given in *Annual Report 1966–67*, pp. 28–39.
6   Ibid., pp. 8–10; *IT* 8 June 1967, p. 14.
7   *Annual Report 1966–67*, pp. 9–10; *IT* 1 July 1967, p. 1, and 4 July 1967, p. 11.
8   *Annual Report 1966–67*, pp. 10–11.
9   *IT* 19 July 1967, p. 1.
10   *IT* 10 February 1967, p. 11 and 23 January 1967, p. 9.
11   *IT* 19 September 1967, p. 8, and 26 September 1967, p. 8.
12   The speech was subsequently printed as a twenty-page pamphlet: Brendan Corish, *The New Republic* (Dublin: Irish Labour Party, 1968).
13   Michael McInerney, in *IT* 16 October 1967, p. 11.
14   *IT* 7 November 1967, p. 7.

15   *DD* 223:2550–1, 8 July 1966.

16   *IT* 23 November 1966, p. 6.

17   The first report of the new organisation was in *Business and Finance* 24 February 1967, p. 66.

18   See p. 18 above.

19   *IP* 30 October 1967, p. 4; *IT* 30 October 1967, p. 14.

20   See *IT* 15 December 1967, p. 1.

21   *IP* 16 December 1967, p. 8.

22   *Evening Press* 25 March 1966, p. 1.

23   *IT* 15 January 1968, p. 13.

24   *ICTU Annual Report 1966–67*, p. 109.

25   *ICTU Annual Report 1968–69*, p. 50; *ICTU Annual Report 1969–70*, p. 51.

26   *IT* 31 March 1966, p. 1.

27   *Evening Press* 25 March 1966, p. 1.

28   *IT* 23 March 1967, p. 9.

29   *IT* 8 February 1968, p. 13.

30   *IT* 24 April 1968, p. 8.

31   *IT* 10 May 1968, p. 11. The motion was referred to the executive committee.

32   *Roscommon Champion* 5 July 1968, p. 1. The paper drew the same conclusions from the affair as McQuillan did; see ibid., 28 June 1968, p. 1.

33   McQuillan moved to Spain soon after the affair, and refused to take any further interest in Irish politics until the 1977 general election campaign, when he worked for the Independent Labour candidates Noel Browne and Matt Merrigan.

34   *Annual Report 1967–68*, p. 9.

35   Ibid., p. 3, and *IT* 22 July 1968, pp. 1, 8.

36   *IT* 24 May 1968, p. 1.

37   E.g. Liam Cosgrave (*IT* 23 April 1965, p. 1, and 1 February 1968, p. 1); Gerard Sweetman (*IT* 10 June 1966, p. 1); Garret FitzGerald (*IT* 11 May 1959, p. 5); Oliver J. Flanagan (*IT* 5 February 1968, p. 11). For general accounts of the campaign see Enid Lakeman, 'The Irish Voter – 1968 Pattern', *Parliamentary Affairs* 22:2 (1968–69), pp. 170–4 and Cornelius O'Leary, *Irish Elections 1918–1977* (Dublin: Gill and Macmillan, 1979), pp. 66–70.

38   *Annual Report 1967–68*, p. 4; *S Ind* 3 March 1968, p. 1.

39   *IT* 4 March 1968, p. 11.

40   E.g. *IT* 14 October 1968, p. 5.

41   E.g. *IT* 25 September 1968, p. 12, and 1 October 1968, p. 7.

42   See *IT* 15 January 1968, p. 12.

43   The figures were: for, 423,496 (39·2 per cent); against, 657,898 (60·8 per cent). Turnout was 62·9 per cent.

44   *IT* 18 October 1968, p. 8.

45   *IT* 24 January 1969, p. 13.

46   *IT* 10 September 1968, p. 1.

47   *IT* 8 October 1968, p. 1.

48   *IT* 23 May 1969, p. 9.
49   *IT* Annual Review, 1 January 1969, p. 2.
50   *IT* 20 July 1968, p. 9.
51   See Steven B. Wolinetz, 'The Dutch Labour Party', in William E. Paterson and Alistair H. Thomas (eds.), *Social Democratic Parties in Western Europe* (London: Croom Helm, 1977), pp. 354–6.
52   Tom Kyne, in *DD* 233:930, 21 March 1968.
53   *IP* 16 September 1968, p. 4.
54   *IT* 14 October 1968, p. 6.
55   See *IT* 20 December 1968, p. 4.
56   Cf. his 1966 comments on Labour's domination by 'dismal poltroons', quoted on p. 4 above. The remark had not been forgotten, either within or outside the Labour Party.
57   Calculated from party records of the 1971 and 1972 conferences; *Annual Report 1974–75*, p. 24; *Annual Report 1975–76*, p. 9.
58   See Maurice Duverger, *Political Parties*, 2nd edition (London: Methuen, 1959), pp. 190–2; John D. May, 'Opinion Structure of Political Parties: the Special Law of Curvilinear Disparity', *Political Studies* 21:2 (1973), pp. 135–51.
59   *Labour Party Outline Policy* (Dublin: Irish Labour Party, 1969).
60   Ibid., Section 4, pp. 10–13.
61   Ibid., para. 6.1.3, p. 16; paras. 6.2.2 to 6.2.4, p. 17; paras. 6.3.2 and 6.3.3, p. 19.
62   Senator Jack Fitzgerald, in *IT* 25 July 1968, p. 14.
63   *Labour Party Outline Policy* paras. 1.2 and 1.5, p. 31.
64   Ibid., paras. 1.7, p. 32, and 8.1, p. 41.
65   Ibid., paras. 1.3.1 and 1.3.2, pp. 66–7.
66   Ibid., Section 3, pp. 79–80.
67   Ibid., paras. 4.7 and 4.2, p. 87.
68   Ibid., para. 1.3, p. 92; para. 5.7, p. 99; para. 4.1, p. 96.
69   Ibid., para. 4.2, p. 96; para. 5.5, p. 98.
70   Ibid., Section 2, pp. 101–2; para. 5.6, p. 108.
71   Ibid., para. 7.1, p. 110.
72   Ibid., Section 2, pp. 113–14; para. 3.1.4, p. 115.
73   Ibid., Section 4, pp. 138–40.
74   *IT* 28 January 1969, p. 13.
75   *IT* 1 February 1969, p. 13.
76   *IT* 22 February 1969, pp. 1, 4.
77   *IT* 11 February 1969, p. 7.
78   *IT* 24 February 1969, p. 13.
79   *IT* 1 February 1969, p. 15. Flanagan has been known to state that there was no sex in Ireland before television was introduced, and has described sex as 'foreign to Ireland'. See e.g. *DD* 252:657, 9 March 1971.
80   *IT* 10 December 1965, p. 11.
81   J. H. Whyte, *Church and State in Modern Ireland 1923–1979* (Dublin: Gill and Macmillan, 1980), Chapter 11.
82   *IT* 17 February 1969, p. 9. Cf. his comments in *IT* 29 March 1967, p. 9.
83   *IT* 27 February 1969, p. 15.

84   *IT* 11 December 1968, p. 1. See also the debate at the 1969 Ard-Fheis, reported in *I Ind* 29 January 1969, p. 15.
85   *IT* 9 February 1967, p. 1, 6 January 1969, p. 11, and 9 January 1969, pp. 1, 3.
86   *IT* 15 May 1968, p. 7, and 19 May 1969, p. 1.
87   *IT* 17 September 1965, p. 1.

Chapter 5

1   *IT* 6 January 1969, p. 15.
2   *Meath Chronicle* 14 June 1969, p. 9.
3   *IT* 4 June 1969, p. 9.
4   *IT* 19 June 1969, p. 1.
5   *IT* 18 June 1969, p. 8. See also some assessments cited in Brian Farrell, 'Dáil Deputies: "The 1969 Generation" ', *Economic and Social Review* 2:3 (1970–71) pp. 309–11.
6   *Annual Report 1969* p. 26.
7   Michael Gallagher, 'Candidate Selection in Ireland: The Impact of Localism and the Electoral System', *British Journal of Political Science* 10:4 (1980), pp. 498–9.
8   *IT* 24 May 1969, p. 1.
9   *Nationalist* (Carlow) 23 May 1969, p. 1.
10   *Annual Report 1969*, p. 68. The manifesto is given in full in ibid., pp. 68–83.
11   *General Election 1969: Canvasser's Notes* (Dublin: Irish Labour Party, 1969).
12   *Annual Report 1969*, p. 17.
13   *S Ind* 25 May 1969, p. 2.
14   *IT* 2 June 1969, p. 9.
15   See e.g. the assessment in *IT* 31 May 1969, p. 1.
16   *IT* 29 May 1969, p. 14, and 30 May 1969, p. 9: *Evening Herald* 29 May 1969, p. 1.
17   *IT* 16 June 1969, p. 1.
18   *ITGWU Annual Report 1969*, p. 218; *IT* 12 June 1969, p. 7.
19   *Southern Star* 14 June 1969, p. 15.
20   *Kerryman* 14 June 1969, pp. 1, 3, 12.
21   John Ryan, in *Nenagh Guardian* 14 June 1969, p. 7. Holders of medical cards are entitled to free health services, and the claim to be able to procure one for deserving constituents is a traditional campaigning ploy.
22   *IT* 4 June 1969, p. 17.
23   See *Anglo-Celt* 6 June 1969, p. 3.
24   *IT* 28 May 1969, p. 1.
25   Gerard Marry, in *Drogheda Independent* 13 June 1969, p. 9.
26   *Roscommon Herald* 30 May 1969, p. 9.
27   Cf. Conor Cruise O'Brien, *States of Ireland* (London: Panther Books, 1974), pp. 182–3.
28   See, for example, Brian Farrell, *Chairman or Chief?* (Dublin: Gill and

Macmillan, 1971), p. 4.

29   See e.g. its social welfare policy in *IT* 17 June 1969, p. 5.
30   Calculated from figures worked out by Francis X. Carty and published
     in Brian Farrell, 'The Mass Media and the 1977 Campaign', in Howard
     R. Penniman (ed.), *Ireland at the Polls: the Dáil Elections of 1977*
     (Washington: American Enterprise Institute for Public Policy Research,
     1978), p. 114.
31   *SP* 25 May 1969, p. 3.
32   Gerard Marry, in *Drogheda Independent* 13 June 1969, p. 9; Anthony
     Hederman, in *Leinster Express* 31 May 1969, p. 1.
33   *IP* 31 May 1969, p. 4.
34   *IT* 7 June 1969, p. 5.
35   *IT* 9 June 1969, p. 8; *Donegal Democrat* 13 June 1969, p. 15.
36   *IT* 4 June 1969, p. 17. Exactly the same view was expressed by a Labour
     TD in interview, 1977.
37   *IT* 14 June 1969, p. 9.
38   Michael Kitt, in *Tuam Herald* 14 June 1969, p. 3.
39   Mart Bax, *Harpstrings and Confessions* (Assen: Van Gorcum, 1976),
     pp. 124–5.
40   *People* (Wexford) 14 June 1969, p. 8; Joe Dowling, in *IT* 2 June 1969,
     p. 8.
41   *IT* 6 June 1969, p. 9.
42   E.g. *IT* 11 June 1969, p. 7, and 12 June 1969, p. 6.
43   *Southern Star* 31 May 1969, p. 7, and 7 June 1969, p. 7.
44   *Donegal Democrat* 20 June 1969, p. 4.
45   *Munster Express* 30 May 1969, p. 7.
46   *IT* 4 June 1969, p. 17.
47   *IT* 10 June 1969, p. 8; *IP* 16 June 1969, p. 6.
48   *Nationalist* (Carlow) 30 May 1969, p. 8.
49   *IT* 16 June 1969, p. 1.
50   *DD* 241:69, 2 July 1969.
51   *Sligo Champion* 27 June 1969, p. 10.
52   Interviews, 1976–78. Cf. O'Brien, *States of Ireland*, p. 182.
53   O'Brien, *States of Ireland*, p. 181.
54   *Free Press* (Wexford) 23 May 1969, p. 8.
55   *IT* 28 May 1969, p. 14.
56   Patrick O'Brien, in *Tipperary Star* 14 June 1969, p. 13.
57   Niall O'Shea, in *Westmeath-Offaly Independent* 7 June 1969, p. 11.
58   *Roscommon Herald* 13 June 1969, p. 9.
59   Michael Brady, in *Leinster Leader* 14 June 1969, p. 1.
60   *IT* 27 May 1969, p. 8.
61   Conor Cruise O'Brien, 'The Embers of Easter', in Owen Dudley
     Edwards and Fergus Pyle (eds.), *1916: The Easter Rising* (London:
     MacGibbon and Kee, 1968), p. 235.
62   *Free Press* (Wexford) 23 May 1969, p. 8.
63   *IT* 10 May 1969, p. 11.
64   *Roscommon Herald* 13 June 1969, p. 9.
65   *IT* 24 May 1969, p. 1.

66 *Midland Tribune* 31 May 1969, p. 1.
67 John McManamy, in *Nationalist* (Carlow) 13 June 1969, p. 7.
68 Michael Brady, in ibid., p. 6.
69 *IT* 31 May 1969, p. 1.
70 Maeve Gilmartin, in *Donegal Democrat* 6 June 1969, p. 3.
71 Joan Gallagher, in *Sligo Champion* 6 June 1969, p. 7.
72 See Michael Gallagher, 'Disproportionality in a Proportional Representation System: the Irish Experience', *Political Studies* 23:4 (1975), pp. 509–11.
73 All candidates must lodge a £100 deposit, which is returned to candidates whose votes at any stage of the count equal or exceed a third of the quota.
74 *Annual Report 1969*, p. 16.
75 See e.g. *Evening Echo* 20 June 1969, p. 1; *Nationalist* (Carlow) 27 June 1969, p. 17; *Meath Chronicle* 28 June 1969, p. 11; *Tipperary Star* 28 June 1969, p. 1. See also *ITGWU Annual Report 1969*, p. 248.
76 *IT* 1 July 1969, p. 8.
77 *Westmeath-Offaly Independent* 28 June 1969, p. 3.
78 *Longford Leader* 28 June 1969, p. 3.
79 *Mayo News* 28 June 1969, p. 9.
80 *Annual Report 1969*, pp. 17 and 15.
81 *Canvasser's Notes*, p. 3.
82 Cf. *IT* June 1969, p. 4.
83 *Annual Report 1969*, pp. 13–14.
84 *Annual Report 1969*, p. 7.
85 Cf. Gallagher, 'Candidate Selection in Ireland', p. 498.
86 *Annual Report 1969*, p. 15.

Chapter 6

1   After the election the Fianna Fáil Senator Willie Ryan unkindly suggested that it change its slogan from 'Let's Build the New Republic' to 'Let's Build a Labour Party'. *Tipperary Star* 28 June 1969, p. 7.
2   For some reports of the conference see *IT* 31 January 1970, pp. 1, 7; *IP* 31 January 1970, p. 1; *SP* 1 February 1970, p. 4.
3   *IT* 10 July 1969, p. 10, and 12 July 1969, p. 5.
4   *IT* 30 June 1970, p. 1.
5   *IT* 13 April 1970, p. 4.
6   *IT* 18 December 1969, p. 9, and 22 December 1969, p. 13.
7   *I Ind* 17 December 1969, p. 1.
8   *IT* 12 March 1970, p. 1, and 13 March 1970, p. 5.
9   *IT* 18 March 1970, p. 10, and 19 March 1970, p. 1; *Annual Report 1970*, p. 4; *IT* 23 March 1970, p. 5.
10 *SP* 19 April 1970, p. 4. The 1904 campaign had involved some violence and a boycott of businesses owned by Jews, which compelled many of them to leave Limerick. See *Nusight* May 1970, pp. 25–8.
11 *IT* 21 April 1970, p. 13.
12 *IT* 24 April 1970, p. 1, and 25 April 1970, p. 1.

13   *IT* 27 April 1970, p. 1.
14   For accounts of the meeting see *Annual Report 1970*, pp. 4–5; *Hibernia*
     15 May 1970, p. 9; *IT* 1 May 1970, p. 1.
15   Maurice Manning, *The Blueshirts* (Dublin: Gill and Macmillan, 1970),
     pp. 76, 240, concludes that the quasi-fascist Blueshirts cannot be
     considered to have been in any way anti-semitic.
16   J. H. Whyte, *Church and State in Modern Ireland 1923–1979* (Dublin:
     Gill and Macmillan, 1980), pp. 72–3.
17   See speeches of Oliver J. Flanagan quoted in Joseph Carroll, *Ireland in
     the War Years* (Newton Abbot: David and Charles, 1975), p. 137, and
     Midland Tribune 19 June 1943, p. 1.
18   Michael Donnellan, in *DD* 176:23, 23 June 1959.
19   *DD* 246:694, 7 May 1970.
20   *IT* 21 September 1970, p. 13.
21   See *SP* 27 September 1970, p. 21, 4 October 1970, p. 23, and 11 October
     1970, p. 23.
22   *IT* 21 October 1970, p. 5; cf. *Annual Report 1970*, p. 11.
23   *IT* 4 November 1970, p. 1, and 14 November 1970, pp. 1, 9.
24   *IT* 30 November 1970, p. 1.
25   For some reports of the conference see *IT* 1 March 1971, pp. 1, 8 and 9;
     IP 1 March 1971, p. 4.
26   *Annual Report 1971* p. 9.
27   Ibid. It has been suggested by Owen Dudley Edwards that putting this
     question to Dr Thornley thereby became the Irish Labour Party
     equivalent of applying for the Chiltern Hundreds.
28   *IT* 15 March 1971, p. 13.
29   *Annual Report 1971*, p. 9.
30   Ibid., p. 14; *IT* 3 July 1971, p. 8.
31   *IT* 24 April 1971, p. 9. A month later he said that the Church had always
     been, in effect, the most conservative party in the State, and as such
     should be opposed by socialists (*IT* 17 May 1971, p. 9).
32   *IT* 30 April 1971, p. 1.
33   *IT* 3 May 1971, p. 1, 4 May 1971, p. 13, and 11 May 1971, p. 11.
34   *DD* 258:1447–50, 9 February 1972.
35   For some reports of the conference see *IT* 26 February 1972, p. 13, and
     28 February 1972, pp. 8, 9; *IP* 26 February 1972, p. 4; *SP* 27 February
     1972, p. 6.
36   See *IT* 29 February 1972, p. 1, and 6 March 1972, p. 11; *Annual Report
     1972–73*, pp. 42–3.
37   David Thornley once commented sympathetically that Corish had to
     make the transition from the Fethard-on-Sea boycott 'to trying to govern
     people like me'. *Hibernia* 8 July 1977, p. 6.
38   See *DD* 250:760, 10 December 1970.
39   *DD* 246:767, 8 May 1970.
40   *DD* 256:308, 27 October 1971.
41   See *IT* 25 January 1972, p. 1, and 26 January 1972, p. 5.
42   *SP* 26 March 1972, p. 17.
43   Coughlan later claimed that he had been inaccurately reported on the

point; see *IT* 10 April 1972, p. 9.
44 *SP* 2 April 1972, p. 10.
45 *IT* 10 April 1972, p. 9.
46 *IP* 11 April 1972, pp. 3, 6. The *Irish Times* political correspondent suggested (10 April 1972, p. 9) that perhaps 'the recent incredible decisions of Mr Heath and all their repercussions have created a completely new Mr Coughlan'.
47 *IT* 13 April 1972, p. 9, and 14 April 1972, p. 5; *IP* 14 April 1972, p. 1.
48 *IT* 13 April 1972, p. 9; *Annual Report 1972–73*, p. 9.
49 See e.g. the speech of Liam Kavanagh, *DD* 254:712–13, 1 June 1971.
50 For some of the main statements issued by the party see *Annual Report 1971*, pp. 15–17 and *Annual Report 1972–73*, pp. 10–12. See also Andrew Orridge, 'The Irish Labour Party', *Journal of Common Market Studies* 13:4 (1975), pp. 490–1.
51 *Annual Report 1972–73*, p. 11.
52 See Conor Cruise O'Brien, *States of Ireland* (London: Panther Books, 1974), p. 273.
53 The vote in favour was 1,041,890 (83·1 per cent); against, 211,891 (16·9 per cent). Turnout was 70·3 per cent.
54 Tom Garvin and Anthony Parker, 'Party Loyalty and Irish Voters: The EEC Referendum as a Case Study', *Economic and Social Review* 4:1 (1972–73), p. 39.
55 Colm McCarthy and Terence M. Ryan, 'Party Loyalty at Referenda and General Elections: Evidence from recent Irish contests', *Economic and Social Review* 7:3 (1975–76), p. 283.
56 See the contributions of Barry Desmond and David Thornley, *IT* 8 August 1972, p. 9, and 9 August 1972, p. 11.
57 *IT* 2 December 1972, p. 1.
58 *IT* 23 September 1969, p. 1, and 9 October 1969, p. 4.
59 See *DD* 248:1653, 22 July 1970.
60 Dun Laoghaire Constituency Council, secretary's annual report, 1972.
61 The figures on Article 44 were: for, 721,003 (84·4 per cent); against, 133,430 (15·6 per cent). Turnout was only 47·9 per cent.
62 *IT* 18 November 1971, p. 1, 27 June 1972, p. 9, and 12 December 1972, p. 1; *IP* 18 November 1971, p. 1.
63 *IT* 20 September 1971, p. 1.
64 *IT* 24 October 1970, p. 1, and 26 October 1970, p. 1.
65 *I Ind* 8 December 1969, pp. 1, 20.
66 *S Ind* 7 May 1972, pp. 1, 11.
67 See *IT* 22 May 1972, pp. 1, 6, 26 May 1972, p. 11, and 1 June 1972, p. 13.
68 See J. Bowyer Bell, *The Secret Army*, 2nd edition (Dublin: Academy Press, 1979), pp. 366–8; *I Ind* 30 December 1969, p. 8; *IT* 12 January 1970, p. 1.
69 For the full text see Ted Nealon, *Ireland: A Parliamentary Directory 1973–74* (Dublin: Institute of Public Administration, 1974), pp. 68–9.
70 For accounts of the campaign see ibid., pp. 67–70, and James Knight and Nicolas Baxter-Moore, *Republic of Ireland: The General Elections*

of 1969 and 1973 (London: The Arthur McDougall Fund, 1973), pp. 17–21.
71 Jackie Fahey, in *IP* 12 February 1973, p. 4. Similar comments were made by Tom Hussey, quoted in *Connacht Tribune* 23 February 1973, p. 18.
72 *Annual Report 1972–73*, p. 33.
73 Knight and Baxter-Moore, *Republic of Ireland*, pp. 18–19.

Chapter 7

1 K. R. Minogue, *Nationalism* (London: B. T. Batsford, 1967), p. 25.
2 Cf. *Times Literary Supplement* 26 May 1972, as quoted in Tom Nairn, *The Break-up of Britain* (London: NLB, 1977), p. 230.
3 Eamonn Donnelly, *DD* 67:117, 11 May 1937.
4 John Whyte, 'Interpretations of the Northern Ireland Problem: An Appraisal', *Economic and Social Review* 9:4 (1977–78), p. 269. The article is an indispensable review of theories and models advanced to explain 'the Northern Ireland problem'. For an analysis of the Irish left's attempts to cope with the 'national question' see Austen Morgan, 'Socialism in Ireland – Red, Green and Orange', in Austen Morgan and Bob Purdie (eds.), *Ireland: Divided Nation, Divided Class* (London: Ink Links, 1980), pp. 172–225.
5 E.g. his St Patrick's Day address to the United States, quoted in J. H. Whyte, *Church and State in Modern Ireland 1923–1979* (Dublin: Gill and Macmillan, 1980), p. 48, in which he stated: 'Since the coming of St Patrick, fifteen hundred years ago, Ireland has been a Christian and a Catholic nation. All the ruthless attempts made down through the centuries to force her from this allegiance have not shaken her faith. She remains a Catholic nation.'
6 Michael Farrell, *Northern Ireland: The Orange State* (London: Pluto Press, 1980), pp. 184–7. In 1938 the Unionists had made similar use of Bunreacht na hEireann's claim to the north to destroy a threat from a group of Progressive Unionists who criticised the government's record on unemployment and housing. See ibid., pp. 146–7.
7 For a demonstration that pre-1922 nationalists were equally unable either to understand northern Protestants or to work out how to deal with them see Richard Davis, 'Ulster Protestants and the Sinn Féin Press, 1914–22', *Eire-Ireland* 15:4 (1980), pp. 60–85.
8 John Costello, *DD* 147:178, 28 October 1954.
9 Míchaél Mac Gréil, *Prejudice and Tolerance in Ireland* (Dublin: College of Industrial Relations, 1977), pp. 230–33.
10 *DD* 115:814, 10 May 1949, quoted in the Earl of Longford and Thomas P. O'Neill, *Eamon de Valera* (London: Arrow Books, 1974), p. 434.
11 Brian Farrell, 'Labour and the Irish Political Party System: A Suggested Approach to Analysis', *Economic and Social Review* 1:4 (1969–70), pp. 477–502.
12 For an elaboration of this argument see Michael Gallagher, 'Socialism

and the Nationalist Tradition in Ireland 1798–1918', *Eire–Ireland* 12:2 (1977), pp. 99–102.

13   Peter Mair, 'Labour and the Irish Party System Revisited: Party Competition in the 1920s', *Economic and Social Review* 9:1 (1977–78), p. 62.

14   See Michael Gallagher, 'The Pact General Election of 1922', *Irish Historical Studies* Vol. 21, No. 84 (September 1979), pp. 414–16.

15   Dorothy Macardle, *The Irish Republic* (London: Corgi, 1968), p. 748; Arthur Mitchell, *Labour in Irish Politics 1890–1930* (Dublin: Irish University Press, 1974), pp. 177–78.

16   David Thornley, 'The Development of the Irish Labour Movement', *Christus Rex* 18:1 (1964), p. 19. Cf. Mitchell, *Labour in Irish Politics*, p. 292, and Patrick Lynch, 'The Social Revolution that never was', in T. Desmond Williams (ed.), *The Irish Struggle 1916–1926* (London: Routledge and Kegan Paul, 1966), p. 50.

17   Quoted in P. Berresford Ellis, *A History of the Irish Working Class* (London: Victor Gollancz, 1972), p. 262.

18   Gallagher, 'The Pact General Election', Table 5, p. 420.

19   See Peter Pyne, 'The Third Sinn Féin Party: 1923–1926', *Economic and Social Review* 1:1 (1969–70), pp. 29–50 and 1:2 (1969–70), pp. 229–57; Thomas P. O'Neill, 'In Search of a Political Path: Irish Republicanism 1922 to 1927', in G. A. Hayes McCoy (ed.), *Historical Studies 10* (Dublin: Irish Committee of Historical Sciences, 1976), pp. 147–71.

20   Longford and O'Neill, *De Valera*, p. 256. Cf. J. Anthony Gaughan, *Thomas Johnson* (Dublin: Kingdom Books, 1980), pp. 459–60.

21   Mitchell, *Labour in Irish Politics*, p. 177; Gaughan, *Thomas Johnson*, pp. 471–4; Donal O'Sullivan, *The Irish Free State and its Senate* (London: Faber and Faber, 1940), p. 262.

22   *DD* 64:1402, 12 December 1936.

23   *DD* 75:1273, 27 April 1939.

24   *Labour Party Constitution* (Dublin: Irish Labour Party), Section 2, para. 2.

25   *DD* 147:160–250, 28 October 1954.

26   *Irish People* 5 April 1947, p. 4. Cf. Gaughan, *Thomas Johnson*, p. 393, for Labour's support for the Mansion House Committee's activities in 1949.

27   Eamonn McCann, *War and an Irish Town*, 2nd edition (London: Pluto Press, 1980), p. 176.

28   *Irish Communist*, No. 73, January 1972, pp. 16–17.

29   J. Bowyer Bell, *The Secret Army*, 2nd edition (Dublin: Academy Press, 1979), p. 291.

30   *IT* 7 January 1957, p. 1, and 28 January 1957, pp. 1, 3.

31   *Munster Express* 1 February 1957, p. 1; *Cork Examiner* 9 January 1957, p. 7; *Munster Tribune* 11 January 1957, p. 2; *Tipperary Star* 12 January 1957, p. 1.

32   *S Ind* 16 June 1957, p. 11.

33   *DD* 164:156–7, 23 October 1957.

34   *DD* 164:368, 30 October 1957.
35   Ibid., cols. 363–5.
36   Ibid., col. 367.
37   Donal Barrington, *Uniting Ireland* (Dublin: Tuairim Pamphlet No. 1, nd). The paper was also published in *Studies* 46:4 (1957), pp. 379–402.
38   *Uniting Ireland*, p. 1.
39   Ibid., pp. 8–11.
40   Ibid., pp. 2–3.
41   Ibid., p. 7.
42   Ibid., p. 10.
43   Ibid., p. 18.
44   William Norton, *Labour's Way* (Dublin: Irish Labour Party, nd [1958]). The section on the north is printed on pp. 9–10.
45   *National Observer* 1:12 (June 1959), p. 3.
46   *IT* 11 October 1958, p. 9, and 8 October 1960, pp. 1, 5.
47   *DD* 230:1086, 26 July 1967.
48   *IT* 15 January 1965, p. 4, and 31 March 1965, p. 6.
49   Mitchell, *Labour in Irish Politics*, p. 221.
50   *1st Annual Report 1931*, p. 80.
51   For some reports see ibid., pp. 3–4; *3rd Annual Report 1933*, p. 3; *4th Annual Report 1934*, p. 7; J. Harbinson, *A History of the Northern Ireland Labour Party 1891–1949* (Queen's University Belfast: MSc Econ thesis, 1966), pp. 59–60, 62.
52   *7th Annual Report 1938*, p. 203; Harbinson, *History of the NILP*, p. 83.
53   *8th Annual Report 1939*, p. 202.
54   Ibid., pp. 15–16.
55   Ibid., pp. 104–14.
56   *9th Annual Report 1940*, pp. 19–20, 54–6.
57   Harbinson, *History of the NILP*, pp. 201–4.
58   Ibid., pp. 213–8.
59   Ibid., p. 221; Michael Farrell, *Northern Ireland: the Orange State*, 2nd edition (London: Pluto Press, 1980), pp. 192–4.
60   Harbinson, *History of the NILP*, pp. 229–30.
61   Ibid., pp. 231–2; Farrell, *Orange State*, p. 195.
62   Electoral statistics from Sydney Elliott, *Northern Ireland Parliamentary Election Results 1921–1972* (Chichester: Political Reference Publications, 1973).
63   *Annual Report 1957–58*, pp. 5–6; Farrell, *Orange State*, pp. 223–4.
64   *Annual Report 1957–58*, p. 5.
65   J. A. V. Graham, *The Consensus-forming Strategy of the Northern Ireland Labour Party, 1949–1968* (Queen's University Belfast: MSocSc thesis, 1972), pp. 216–7; *IT* 11 April 1966, p. 13; *Annual Report 1966–67*, p. 19.
66   For some reports of the discussions see *Annual Report 1966–67*, p. 19; *Annual Report 1967–68*, p. 13; *IT* 2 February 1967, p. 4, 25 March 1967, p. 1, 28 April 1967, p. 11, 24 July 1967, p. 7, and 4 August 1967, p. 13; Graham, *Consensus-forming Strategy*, pp. 218–31, 243–7.

67 *Annual Report 1967–68*, p. 13.
68 *IT* 31 January 1970, pp. 1, 7; *SP* 1 February 1970, p. 1.
69 *Annual Report 1970*, p. 7; *Annual Report 1972–73*, p. 7.
70 Ibid., pp. 21–2.
71 *Annual Report 1973–74*, p. 7.
72 For Westminster's attitude up to the 1970s see Richard Rose, *Governing without Consensus* (London: Faber and Faber, 1971), pp. 118–23.
73 Ibid., p. 104.
74 *Annual Report 1969*, p. 53. This report, pp. 51–9, gives a full account of Labour's actions with respect to the north in 1969.
75 E.g. *Hibernia* 12 September 1969, p. 4.
76 *IT* 9 November 1968, p. 1, and 14 November 1968, p. 1.
77 *IT* 9 December 1969, pp. 1, 13.
78 *IT* 10 December 1969, p. 1
79 *DD* 241:1430, 22 October 1969; 241:1576, 23 October 1969; 241:1484–96, 22 October 1969.
80 Ibid., col. 1455.
81 *IT* 31 January 1970, pp. 1, 7, and Labour Party conference taped records. Within two years Kemmy had swung around to the 'two nations' interpretation; see *IT* 16 September 1971, p. 11.
82 *ITGWU Annual Report 1969*, p. 265.
83 This was later published as Conor Cruise O'Brien, 'The Embers of Easter 1916–1966', in Owen Dudley Edwards and Fergus Pyle (eds.), *1916: The Easter Rising* (London: MacGibbon and Kee, 1968), pp. 225–40. See especially pp. 233–34.
84 *IT* 5 November 1971, p. 9. The British ambassador to Ireland between 1970 and 1973 has commented that O'Brien is probably 'regarded more as an analyst of the Irish than as a typical representative of them'. See John Peck, *Dublin from Downing Street* (Dublin: Gill and Macmillan, 1978), p. 144.
85 Cf. Barrington, *Uniting Ireland*, pp. 11–12; O'Brien, 'Embers of Easter', p. 234.
86 *ITGWU Annual Report 1970*, pp. 219–24. Cf. O'Brien's account in Conor Cruise O'Brien, *States of Ireland* (London: Panther Books, 1974), pp. 265–7.
87 *IT* 8 September 1971, p. 8. In 1964 Thornley had stated ('The Development of the Irish Labour Movement', p. 15) that in the Rising 'it was the Marxists who got taken for a ride'.
88 *IP* 21 September 1971, p. 1.
89 *DD* 256:41 and 37, 20 October 1971.
90 Ibid., cols. 221–4, 21 October 1971.
91 Ibid., cols. 68–9 and 73, 20 October 1971.
92 Ibid., col. 133.
93 Ibid., cols. 236 and 242, 21 October 1971.
94 Ibid., cols. 185, 186 and 191.
95 Ibid., col. 195.
96 *IT* 3 November 1971, p. 8.

97   *IT* 5 November 1971, p. 9.
98   *IT* 10 December 1971, p. 9. The number of occasions on which O'Brien's spokesmanship was challenged was so great that most TDs asked about the subject in the late 1970s had great difficulty in recalling them separately.
99   See *IT* 13 December 1971, p. 1, and 14 December 1971, p. 1.
100   *IT* 14 December 1971, p. 1.
101   *DD* 257:2486–509, 16 December 1971. Brian Faulkner was then the northern Prime Minister.
102   Ibid., col. 2501.
103   *IP* 17 December 1971, p. 1.
104   *DD* 257:2667, 16 December 1971.
105   *IT* 17 December 1971, p. 1.
106   Analysis carried out at the University of Strathclyde.
107   Ibid.
108   *IT* 22 December 1971, p. 9, and 23 December 1971, p. 1.
109   *IP* 24 December 1971, p. 4.
110   *Annual Report 1971*, p. 29.
111   For its full composition see ibid., p. 30.
112   Ibid., p. 29; *IT* 8 January 1972, p. 8. For the full text of the statement see *Annual Report 1971*, pp. 30–2.
113   O'Brien, *States of Ireland*, p. 264.
114   Ibid., p. 283; *DD* 258:1100, 4 February 1972; ibid., col. 1007, 3 February 1972.
115   Ibid., cols. 937 and 928.
116   Ibid., cols. 1184 and 1183, 4 February 1972.
117   *IT* 19 February 1972, p. 9.
118   *IT* 29 January 1972, p. 9.
119   For reports see *IT* 26 February 1972, p. 13, and 28 February 1972, pp. 8, 9; *IP* 26 February 1972, p. 4; *SP* February 1972, p. 6.
120   According to this theory, the island of Ireland contains two nations, corresponding more or less to the two major religious groups. O'Brien, who has often been accused by his critics of being a proponent or even the originator of the theory, has dissociated himself from it in one of his books (*States of Ireland*, p. 305).
121   Sadlier and Keogh were Irish MPs in the early 1850s who became unpopular by reneging on a party pledge, and who left the Irish group at Westminster at a time when its concern with Catholic interests had earned it the name of 'The Pope's Brass Band'.
122   See *IT* 31 October 1972, p. 1.
123   *IT* 13 March 1972, p. 9.
124   E.g. O'Brien, *States of Ireland*, pp. 286–7.
125   See *IT* 22 March 1972, p. 1, 23 March 1972, p. 1, 19 July 1972, p. 1, and 20 July 1972, p. 8. For a British view of the talks see Joe Haines, *The Politics of Power* (London: Jonathan Cape, 1977), pp. 124–31.
126   *ITGWU Annual Report 1971*, pp. 175, 176, 179–80, 190, 170.
127   *IT* 21 September 1972, p. 1, and 22 September 1972, pp. 1, 8. For one assessment of the document see Ian McAllister, *The Northern Ireland*

Social Democratic and Labour Party (London: Macmillan, 1977), pp. 56–8, where it is described as 'impractical'.
128 *Annual Report 1971*, pp. 18–19; *IT* 8 November 1971, p. 7.
129 *Annual Report 1971*, p. 19; *Annual Report 1972–73*, pp. 14–15.
130 *IT* 3 October 1972, p. 1, and 16 October 1972, pp. 1, 8.
131 See *I Ind* 12 October 1972, p. 1; *S Ind* 22 October 1972, p. 4; *IT* 12 October 1972, p. 17; *SP* 22 October 1972, p. 6; *Annual Report 1972–73*, p. 18.
132 *IT* 12 October 1972, p. 17.
133 For reports see *SP* 22 October 1972, p. 6; *IT* 19 October 1972, p. 8; *S Ind* 22 October 1972, p. 4.
134 *IT* 21 October 1972, p. 9, 26 October 1972, p. 11, and 24 October 1972, p. 13.
135 *IT* 23 October 1972, p. 9.
136 Ibid., and *IT* 7 November 1972, p. 1.
137 *IT* 26 October 1972, p. 1.
138 *IT* 27 November 1972, p. 1.
139 *DD* 264:598, 30 November 1972.
140 *IT* 12 February 1973, p. 8.
141 The suggestion of a TD who supported the two communities approach, in interview, 1977.

Chapter 8

1 See *Annual Report 1932–33*, p. 10; *Annual Report 1933–34*, pp. 8–9; *Annual Report 1938*, p. 118; Brian Farrell, *Chairman or Chief?* (Dublin: Gill and Macmillan, 1971), p. 36; The Earl of Longford and Thomas P. O'Neill, *Eamon de Valera* (London: Arrow Books, 1974), p. 332.
2 *Annual Report 1931–32*, p. 7.
3 Michael Gallagher, 'Party Solidarity, Exclusivity and Inter-party Relationships in Ireland 1922–1977: The Evidence of Transfers', *Economic and Social Review* 10:1 (1978–79), p. 15.
4 *IT* 10 June 1944, p. 1.
5 See *I Ind* 16 May 1945, p. 3, and 17 May 1945, p. 3.
6 Gallagher, 'Party Solidarity', pp. 16–17.
7 See *Irish People* 8 November 1947 to 17 January 1948, *passim*, and 31 January 1948, p. 7.
8 Seán Casey, in *Cork Examiner* 21 January 1948, p. 7.
9 For the fullest account of the formation of this government see Farrell, *Chairman or Chief?*, pp. 42–4.
10 See *IT* 16 February 1948, p. 1.
11 See *CIU: Fourth Annual Meeting 1948*, pp. 14–17, 40–3, 68–77.
12 *IT* 31 May 1954, p. 1, and 3 June 1954, p. 1.
13 The best examples are probably Abram de Swaan, *Coalition Theories and Cabinet Formations* (Amsterdam: Elsevier Scientific Publishing Company, 1973) and Sven Groennings *et al.* (eds.), *The Study of Coalition Behaviour* (New York: Holt, Rinehart and Winston, 1970).

14   *IT* 19 February 1973, p. 8. Cf. Peter Mair, 'The Autonomy of the Political', *Comparative Politics* 11:4 (1979), pp. 453–4.
15   *I Ind* 5 March 1957, p. 8.
16   *IT* 25 February 1957, p. 1. Cf. *IP* 6 February 1957, p. 5.
17   *I Ind* 31 July 1956, p. 8; *IT* 29 January 1957, p. 1.
18   *IT* 12 February 1957, p. 1.
19   *IT* 11 February 1957, p. 1.
20   See *IT* 9 February 1957, p. 1; *Limerick Leader* 18 October 1952, p. 2.
21   *IT* 21 February 1957, p. 1.
22   See *IT* 18 February 1957, pp. 1, 3 and *Leinster Leader* 23 February 1957, p. 5.
23   A phrase used during the 1965 election campaign by P. A. O. Síocháin, Labour candidate in Clare. See *Clare Champion* 3 April 1965, p. 14.
24   See Gallagher, 'Party Solidarity', p. 2.
25   *IT* 20 June 1957, p. 1 and 17 June 1957, p. 7.
26   *IT* 12 October 1959, p. 4.
27   *IT* 10 October 1960, p. 4; *Hibernia* December 1960, pp. 11–12; *IT* 12 January 1961, p. 8.
28   E.g. his criticisms of its social welfare policy, in *I Ind* 20 July 1957, p. 10.
29   *S Ind* 11 October 1959, p. 5.
30   *I Ind* 10 October 1960, p. 2.
31   *Hibernia* 1 October 1960, pp. 1–2.
32   Henry Byrne, in *Leinster Express* 16 September 1961, p. 6.
33   *IP* 14 September 1961, p. 5.
34   See *IT* 6 October 1961, p. 1, and 7 October 1961, p. 1.
35   *SP* 23 June 1963, p. 8.
36   *IT* 27 March 1963, p. 9.
37   *IT* 8 February 1964, p. 9.
38   *IT* 26 March 1965, p. 1.
39   *IT* 18 March 1965, p. 11.
40   *IT* 16 October 1967, p. 11. Other reports of the conference used here are *IT* 14 October 1967, pp. 1, 11, and *SP* 15 October 1967, p. 3.
41   David Andrews, quoted in *IP* 29 May 1969, p. 8.
42   See Kurt Steiner, *Politics in Austria* (Boston: Little, Brown and Co., 1972), pp. 412–14.
43   *IT* 11 October 1967, p. 6.
44   *IT* 4 March 1968, p. 1.
45   *IT* 26 January 1968, p. 11.
46   *DD* 233: 1242–8, especially 1246, 27 March 1968; *IT* 14 May 1968, p. 1.
47   E.g. Paddy Donegan, in *IT* 5 March 1968, p. 13; Oliver J. Flanagan, in *IT* 13 May 1968, p. 11.
48   *IT* 31 May 1968, p. 4.
49   *IT* 1 June 1968, p. 1.
50   *IT* 15 June 1968, p. 1.
51   'Coalition – The New Curse to Frighten Labour', in *IT* 20 July 1968, p. 9.

52   See *IP* 20 March 1957, p. 10.
53   *IT* 1 October 1968, p. 8.
54   *IT* 28 October 1968, p. 5.
55   *IT* 11 October 1967, p. 6.
56   *IT* 20 January 1969, p. 11.
57   For the fullest report of the speech see *IT* 25 January 1969, p. 11.
58   *IT* 28 January 1969, p. 13.
59   *IT* 3 February 1969, p. 15.
60   *Annual Report 1969*, pp. 68–9.
61   *IT* 4 June 1969, p. 9.
62   *Westmeath Examiner* 31 May 1969, p. 4; *Drogheda Argus* 13 June 1969, p. 7. See also the speeches of Jack Lynch in *IP* 29 May 1969, p. 1, and Neil Blaney, in *IT* 2 June 1969, p. 9.
63   See above, p. 155, and Fig. 8.1.
64   *DD* 241:41–2, 2 July 1969.
65   Ibid., col. 115.
66   Ibid., col. 58.
67   Ibid., col. 46.
68   *IT* 11 July 1969, p. 11.
69   *IT* 12 July 1969, p. 5.
70   *IT* 8 October 1969, p. 7.
71   For some reports see *Annual Report 1970*, pp. 11–12; *IT* 2 February 1970, p. 1; *IP* 2 February 1970, p. 1.
72   *IP* 14 June 1969, p. 6.
73   *IT* 11 April 1970, p. 14. Cf. *IT* 14 April 1970, p. 1.
74   *IT* 20 April 1970, p. 16.
75   *SP* 4 October 1970, p. 23.
76   *ITGWU Annual Report 1970*, p. 161.
77   Brendan Halligan, in *SP* 11 April 1976, p. 2.
78   Interview, 1977.
79   *Nusight* June 1969, general election supplement, p. 9. D. R. O'Connor Lysaght, *The Republic of Ireland* (Cork: Mercier Press, 1970), p. 149, comments that he was described as being 'so conservative that, if present at the creation of the world, he would have voted against it'. In an appreciation, Garret FitzGerald described him as being 'always very conscious of the dangers of novelty or innovation that might disturb the confidence of a people whom he saw as being themselves conservative in their views'. See *I Ind* 29 January 1970, p. 4.
80   The impact made by FitzGerald was such that a cartoon (*IT* 12 July 1969, p. 10) portrayed the Fine Gael front bench as consisting solely of FitzGeralds, with the backbenches containing several rows of fainter versions of him.
81   See *IT* 9 July 1968, p. 11.
82   *DD* 241:72–3, 2 July 1969.
83   *DD* 249:469, 3 November 1970.
84   Noel Browne, in *SP* 27 September 1970, p. 21.
85   Comment of a rural TD in interview, 1976.
86   Dermot Boucher, in *IT* 5 September 1972, pp. 11, 13.

87   Conor Cruise O'Brien, *States of Ireland* (London: Panther Books, 1974), p. 205. The phrase was used on 4 June 1970.
88   See Warner Moss, *Political Parties in the Irish Free State* (New York: Columbia University Press, 1933), p. 129.
89   See *IT* 7 October 1970, p. 1, 11 May 1970, p. 1, 13 May 1970, p. 8; *DD* 249:635, 4 November 1970; *IT* 1 June 1970, p. 11; *IP* 28 October 1970, p. 4.
90   *IT* 9 November 1970, p. 9; *This Week* 19 November 1970, pp. 10–11.
91   *IT* 14 November 1970, p. 9, and 16 November 1970, p. 5.
92   *IT* 28 October 1970, p. 8; *This Week* 8 May 1970, pp. 8–10; *SP* 27 September 1970, p. 21; *IT* 16 November 1970, p. 5, and 29 October 1970, p. 9.
93   *Annual Report 1970*, p. 11. The AC was at this time less representative of the party than usual, because of the resignation of five of the original members in May 1970 over the Stephen Coughlan affair. Those resigning were mainly anti-coalitionists.
94   See ibid., pp. 12–15.
95   *IT* 24 November 1970, p. 1.
96   *IT* 27 November 1970, p. 1.
97   This account relies mainly on Labour's own taped record of the conference. The conference was conducted in private; for some reports see *Annual Report 1970*, pp. 15–17, and *IT* 14 December 1970, p. 1.
98   See *Annual Report 1970*, pp. 16–17.
99   *IT* 14 December 1970, p. 1.
100   *IT* 14 May 1971, p. 17.
101   *IT* 17 May 1972, p. 13.
102   *IP* 18 May 1972, p. 1; *SP* 21 May 1972, p. 2.
103   The important sections are given in *Annual Report 1972–73*, pp. 16–18.
104   *Annual Report 1972–73*, p. 43.
105   *IT* 22 May 1972, pp. 1, 6; *IP* 22 May 1972, p. 6.
106   *IT* 14 June 1972, pp. 1, 15.
107   See *I Ind* 15 June 1972, p. 1; *SP* 25 June 1972, p. 2; *IT* 29 June 1972, p. 7, and 31 July 1972, p. 7; *IT* 9 August 1972, p. 13.
108   *IT* 5 September 1972, pp. 11, 13.
109   *S Ind* 3 September 1972, p. 4.
110   *IT* 4 October 1972, p. 1, and 5 October 1972, pp. 1, 13; interviews.
111   *Annual Report 1972–73*, pp. 18, 43; *IT* 14 October 1972, p. 8.
112   *DD* 264:295, 29 November 1972.
113   Ibid., col. 299.
114   Much of this section is based on information derived from interviews.
115   *Hibernia* 30 March 1973, p. 5. The article gave no indication as to where, or under what circumstances, the meeting took place, or who had drawn up the document.
116   *Annual Report 1972–73*, p. 31.
117   Ibid., pp. 26–7; *IP* 9 February 1973, p. 1.
118   *Annual Report 1972–73*, pp. 30–1.
119   *IT* 9 February 1973, p. 1; *IP* 9 February 1973, p. 1.

120   *IP* 15 February 1973, p. 7.
121   *IT* 20 February 1973, p. 9; *Annual Report 1972–73*, pp. 20–1.
122   Under Article 28.1 of the Constitution the government cannot have more than fifteen members.
123   Eric C. Browne and Mark N. Franklin, 'Aspects of Coalition Payoffs in European Parliamentary Democracies', *American Political Science Review* 67:2 (1973), pp. 460–2.
124   William H. Riker, *The Theory of Political Coalitions* (New Haven: Yale University Press, 1962), p. 40.
125   See John Throne, *Coalition: The Alternative* (Dublin: Militant pamphlet, nd [1974?]), p. 1.

Chapter 9

1   See *IT* 3 March 1973, p. 1, 5 March 1973, p. 1, 12 March 1973, p. 1, and 17 March 1973, p. 1.
2   *IT* 28 March 1977, p. 1.
3   *Statistical Abstract of Ireland 1977* (Dublin: Stationery Office, 1980), pp. 184, 190. The number of unemployed refers to those on the 'Live Register', which almost certainly underestimates the true level of unemployment.
4   *IT* 7 June 1977, p. 6.
5   For an extended summary of the paper see *IT* 27 September 1976, pp. 6, 7.
6   *Annual Report 1974–75*, pp. 16–17.
7   Ibid., p. 19.
8   See *IT* 19 March 1976, p. 6; *DD* 293:923–7, 3 November 1976.
9   *Statistical Abstract of Ireland 1977*, p. 254.
10   See *IT* 17 December 1975, p. 1, and 18 December 1975, p. 1. In general, the anti-discrimination legislation proved difficult to enforce.
11   See *IT* 31 August 1973, p. 1, 6 January 1974, p. 1, and 27 March 1974, p. 1.
12   See *IT* 26 November 1973, p. 1. Cf. J. H. Whyte, *Church and State in Modern Ireland 1923–1979* (Dublin: Gill and Macmillan, 1980), pp. 407–8.
13   *DD* 274:1269, 16 July 1974.
14   See *Annual Report 1976–78*, pp. 61–2; *IT* 31 March 1977, p. 5.
15   See *SD* 86:801, 5 May 1977.
16   See *IT* 28 February 1974, p. 1, and 16 May 1974, p. 1.
17   *Annual Report 1973–74*, pp. 16–17.
18   See *IT* 23 September 1974, p. 9.
19   See *I Ind* 21 October 1974, p. 8.
20   See *Annual Report 1974–75*, pp. 30–1.
21   See *IT* 19 June 1975, p. 12; *Annual Report 1976–78*, p. 62.
22   *DD* 287:223, 22 January 1976.
23   Browne and Robinson had been elected in 1973 as Independent Senators from Trinity College; Browne remained a Labour member, and Robinson joined the party in 1976.

24   *DD* 292:478–9, 7 September 1976.
25   Ibid., cols. 1074–6, 14 September 1976.
26   Ibid., cols. 734–5, 9 September 1976.
27   Ibid., col. 581, 8 September 1976; John Horgan, 'The Discipline of Labour', *Hibernia* 19 November 1976, p. 7.
28   For a brief discussion of the incident see Michael Gallagher, 'The Presidency of the Republic of Ireland: Implications of the "Donegan Affair" ', *Parliamentary Affairs* 30:4 (1977), pp. 373–84.
29   *DD* 293:600, 28 October 1976.
30   See report in *IT* 23 May 1977, pp. 1, 10, 11.
31   *Western People* 4 June 1977, p. 7.
32   See *IT* 29 April 1976, p. 10, and *DD* 290:646–7, 5 May 1976.
33   For a summary and assessment of the proposals see *Hibernia* 24 September 1976, pp. 9–11.
34   See *IT* 10 December 1973, p. 9.
35   For reports of the case see *IT* 12 January 1974, p. 9, 14 January 1974, p. 1, 17 January 1974, p. 1, 21 February 1974, p. 11 and 23 February 1974, p. 15.
36   *DD* 270:1521–1718, 26 and 27 February 1974.
37   *IT* 21 September 1974, p. 8 and 23 September 1974, pp. 1, 9.
38   *IT* 28 January 1977, pp. 1, 6, 29 January 1977, pp. 1, 5 and 31 January 1977, p. 1.
39   See Basil Chubb, *The Constitution and Constitutional Change in Ireland* (Dublin: Institute of Public Administration, 1978), pp. 98–9. Fianna Fáil reiterated this attitude when the subject of fundamental constitutional reform was discussed in the autumn of 1981.
40   *IT* 1 July 1974, p. 8.
41   *IT* 25 September 1974, p. 1.
42   *IT* 14 January 1974, p. 8.
43   *IT* 14 June 1974, p. 1 and 16 July 1973, p. 1.
44   The polls' conclusions were that 68 per cent of those living in the Republic, 6 per cent of northern Protestants and 39 per cent of northern Catholics regarded a united Ireland solution to the problem as 'most workable and acceptable'. See E. E. Davis and R. Sinnott, *Attitudes in the Republic of Ireland Relevant to the Northern Ireland Problem* (Dublin: Economic and Social Research Institute Paper No. 97, 1979), pp. 61–2.
45   *IT* 28 April 1976, p. 1.
46   *IT* 25 September 1974, p. 9.
47   See Cornelius O'Leary, *Irish Elections 1918–1977* (Dublin: Gill and Macmillan, 1979), pp. 84–5.
48   The fortnightly *Hibernia* chronicled the government's use of patronage, usually, though not always, accurately. See particularly the issues of 1 March 1974, pp. 4–5; 8 November 1974, p. 13; 30 January 1976, p. 4; 7 January 1977, p. 4; 21 January 1977, p. 8.
49   Ibid., 22 July 1977, pp. 4–5.
50   See *I Ind* 8 February 1968, p. 1, and 9 February 1968, p. 1.
51   *IT* 30 March 1976, p. 7.

52 *IT* 2 May 1977, pp. 1, 12.
53 *IT* 8 November 1976, p. 1, and 9 November 1976, p. 1.
54 *Annual Report 1974–75*, p. 18.
55 For an extremely brief report see *IT* 7 September 1976, p. 11. Cf. ibid., 9 September 1976, p. 11.
56 See *Annual Report 1974–75*, pp. 20–1.
57 For the full text of the resolution see *Annual Report 1976–78*, pp. 9–10.
58 For reports see *IT* 22 November 1976, pp. 1, 5, 15.
59 See his article in *Hibernia* 5 October 1973, p. 8.
60 For general accounts of the campaign see Brian Farrell and Maurice Manning, 'The Election', and Richard Sinnott, 'The Electorate', in Howard R. Penniman (ed.), *Ireland at the Polls: The Dáil Elections of 1977* (Washington: American Enterprise Institute for Public Policy Research, 1978).
61 *Annual Report 1976–78*, p. 40.
62 Ibid., p. 11. Browne refused to apply for membership of the PLP.
63 This point was made in interviews, 1980. The rest of this chapter draws heavily on interviews with four Labour and three Fine Gael members of the Coalition administration.
64 The most important was probably the October 1976 vote on the question of whether Fine Gael's Richard Burke or Labour's Justin Keating should be the country's next EEC Commissioner.
65 *Acts of the Oireachtas* (Dublin: Stationery Office, annual).
66 This was stated by the Coalition's Finance Minister, Richie Ryan, as reported in *IT* 27 January 1981, p. 16.
67 The Minister for Finance was also Minister for the Public Service, in which capacity he had to approve of every new appointment or promotion of a civil servant in every Ministry, which some Ministers found even more irritating and humiliating than the power he had over them as Finance Minister.
68 See e.g. Ronan Fanning, *The Irish Department of Finance 1922–58* (Dublin: Institute of Public Administration, 1978), pp. 564–95.
69 Basil Chubb, *Cabinet Government in Ireland* (Dublin: Institute of Public Administration, 1974), p. 50.

Chapter 10

1 The statement is printed in *Annual Report 1976–78*, pp. 62–3.
2 Labour's seventeenth TD, Seán Treacy, remained Ceann Comhairle until the new Dáil met four days later, and was debarred until then from taking part in parliamentary party affairs. He would probably have voted for O'Leary, whose supporters suspected that the leadership change had been effected so soon precisely in order to deprive him of Treacy's crucial vote.
3 Those supporting Cluskey, it seems, were Joe Bermingham, Brendan Corish, Barry Desmond, Eileen Desmond, John Horgan, Ruairi Quinn and John Ryan; O'Leary's supporters were Liam Kavanagh, Pat Kerrigan, Michael Pat Murphy, John O'Connell, Seamus Pattison, Dan

Spring and Jimmy Tully.
4   Joseph O'Malley, in *S Ind* 19 April 1981, p. 4.
5   The elections in Ireland were held under the same electoral system as at Dáil elections, with the country divided into four constituencies: Dublin (four seats), Leinster (three seats), Munster (five seats) and Connacht-Ulster (three seats).
6   The four elected European MPs retained their Dáil seats.
7   *Annual Report 1976–78*, pp. 14–15, 11; *Labour Party Constitution*, Section 3.
8   See *IT* 10 October 1977, p. 5.
9   *IT* 30 September 1977, p. 10.
10 *IT* 27 July 1978, p. 1, and 28 July 1978, p. 4.
11 *S Ind* 8 February 1981, p. 1.
12 *DD* 312:335, 28 February 1979.
13 Barry Desmond admitted in the Dáil that the party was divided in its attitude to the Bill. See *DD* 313:1182, 4 April 1979.
14 *IT* 28 October 1980, p. 11.
15 *DD* 323:1086, 29 October 1980.
16 Ibid., col. 1100.
17 Ibid., cols. 1497–8, 4 November 1980.
18 For Fine Gael's reaction see *IT* 1 May 1981, p. 5; for Fianna Fáil's ibid., and *IT* 15 May 1981, p. 1; for Labour's *IT* 12 May 1981, p. 8, 14 May 1981, p. 9, and 15 May 1981, p. 1.
19 *IT* 21 August 1980, p. 10.
20 *IT* 13 June 1981, p. 8.
21 *IT* 23 June 1980, p. 1, and 20 October 1980, p. 11.
22 *IT* 23 April 1979, p. 9; *Annual Report 1980*, p. 17.
23 Barry Desmond, in *DD* 312:1605–6, 15 March 1979.
24 *The Party Programme: Labour Party Annual Conference 1980* (Dublin: Irish Labour Party, 1980), pp. 7–9.
25 Ibid., pp. 14, 18.
26 Ibid., pp. 29–32.
27 Ibid., p. 47.
28 Ibid., pp. 25–6.
29 Ibid., p. 11.
30 For a report of the discussion see *IT* 23 April 1979, p. 9.
31 *IT* 20 February 1980, p. 6.
32 See the report of its White Paper in *IT* 6 January 1979.
33 For an assessment of the government's economic record see an article by Paul Tansey, in *IT* 26 May 1981, p. 6.
34 *IT* 21 December 1979, p. 1.
35 *IT* 13 October 1979, p. 4.
36 *IT* 10 March 1980, p. 1.
37 *Argus* (Dundalk) 5 June 1981, p. 1.
38 Speech of Ray Burke, Minister for the Environment, in *IT* 9 June 1981, p. 9. There were many other such speeches by Fianna Fáil candidates.
39 *IT* 3 June 1981, p. 6. Kelly later said that he had meant to use the word 'undiluted' rather than 'uncontaminated'.

40 *IT* 26 May 1981, p. 1.

41 See report of Dr FitzGerald's speech in *IT* 5 June 1981, p. 1.

42 *I Ind* 8 June 1981, p. 12. In December 1979 Parliamentary Secretaries were redesignated Ministers of State.

43 *IT* 1 June 1981, p. 8.

44 *Longford News* 5 June 1981, p. 3.

45 *Longford News* 29 May 1981, p. 13; *IT* 2 June 1981, p. 6.

46 Michael Finneran, in *Roscommon Champion* 29 May 1981, p. 1.

47 *Sligo Champion* 29 May 1981, p. 9; *Limerick Echo* 30 May 1981, p. 18.

48 See an article by Richard Sinnott and Brendan Whelan in *IT* 6 July 1981, p. 13, for an elaboration of this point.

49 *IT* 13 June 1981, p. 9, and 15 June 1981, p. 8.

50 In a letter to the press in *IT* 17 June 1981, p. 9. The Militant Tendency was the Irish section of the organisation which was active in the British Labour Party.

51 *IT* 26 June 1981, p. 9.

52 *IP* 24 June 1981, pp. 1, 4.

53 *IP* 22 June 1981, p. 7.

54 See e.g. the arguments of anti-coalitionists reported in *IT* 17 June 1981, pp. 7, 9, and 25 June 1981, p. 8.

55 E.g. *IT* 20 June 1981, p. 5.

56 Many members, whatever their views on coalition, share the view that Labour's 'identity' is not clear enough in voters' minds, and that the reason the party is not more popular is that voters are not sufficiently aware of what it stands for; the marketing, not the product, is at fault. But it is quite possible, of course, that for most voters the Labour Party does have a clear identity, which they simply do not like.

57 *IT* 17 June 1981, p. 9.

58 Much of the information in the remainder of this section was obtained through the interview process.

59 For some of the discussion see *IT* 20 June 1981, p. 5, 23 June 1981, pp. 1, 8, *IP* 24 June 1981, pp. 1, 4. The FWUI (Federated Workers' Union of Ireland) had been formed from a merger between the Workers' Union of Ireland and the Federation of Rural Workers.

60 The poll's findings were reported in *IT* 26 June 1981, p. 7.

61 Late in 1977, the Department of Industry and Commerce had been renamed Industry, Commerce and Energy; in 1980 Energy became a separate department. O'Leary's Ministry was to be designated Industry and Energy.

62 Under the 1977 European Assembly Elections Act, vacancies in the European Parliament in the Republic of Ireland are filled by appointment by the Dáil. It is obliged to appoint someone nominated by the party to which the vacating member belonged when he or she was elected.

Chapter 11

1 Brian Farrell, 'Dáil Deputies: "The 1969 Generation" ', *Economic and Social Review* 2:3 (1970–71), p. 315.

2   M. A. Marsh, 'European Social Democratic Party Leaders and the Working Class', in Kay Lawson (ed.), *Political Parties and Linkage* (New Haven: Yale University Press, 1980), p. 52.
3   Cf. Anthony Downs, *An Economic Theory of Democracy* (New York: Harper and Row, 1957), Chapter 8, especially pp. 117–27.
4   Cf. pp. 67–8 above.
5   *Annual Report 1980*, pp. 64–5. The total income figure given here is for the first eight months of the year only. There was a possibility of more income accruing from some sources (though not from the unions), which would further reduce the proportion of the party's income arising from union affiliation fees.
6   See Barry Desmond, 'Trade Unions and the Labour Party', *IT* 6 July 1972, p. 12.
7   For full details see *Labour Party Constitution*, Section 5, para. 3.
8   See p. 171 above.
9   For a development of this point see Michael Gallagher, 'Societal change and party adaptation in the Republic of Ireland 1960–1981', *European Journal of Political Research* 9:3 (1981), pp. 277–8.
10 Labour's 1980 programme stresses the merits of 'co-operation' and 'solidarity' and condemns competition and 'selfish individualism'.
11 For a discussion of the lack of impact of the 1960–1981 changes in Irish society on the country's politics see Gallagher, 'Societal change and party adaptation'.
12 See p. 9 above.

Appendix 1 *General election results 1957–81*

	1957	1961	1965	1969	1973	1977	1981
Fianna Fáil							
Votes	592,994	512,073	597,414	602,234	624,528	811,615	777,616
% vote	48·3	43·8	47·7	45·7	46·2	50·6	45·3
Seats	78	70	72	75*	69*	84	78*
Fine Gael							
Votes	326,699	374,099	427,081	449,749	473,781	488,767	626,376
% vote	26·6	32·0	34·1	34·1	35·1	30·5	36·5
Seats	40	47	47	50	54	43	65
Labour							
Votes	111,747	136,111	192,740	224,498	185,117	186,410	169,990
% vote	9·1	11·6	15·4	17·0	13·7	11·6	9·9
Seats	12*	16*	22*	18	19	17*	15
Others							
Votes	195,579	146,121	35,887	42,472	67,111	116,235	144,229
% vote	15·9	12·5	2·9	3·2	5·0	7·3	8·4
Seats	17	11	3	1	2	4	8
Total							
Votes	1,227,019	1,168,404	1,253,122	1,318,953	1,350,537	1,603,027	1,718,211
% vote	100·0	100·0	100·0	100·0	100·0	100·0	100·0
Seats	147*	144*	144*	144*	144*	148*	166*

* Includes outgoing Ceann Comhairle, returned automatically.

Appendix 2 *Performance of Labour in general elections 1957–81, by region*

	1957	1961	1965	1969	1973	1977	1981
Dublin							
Votes	20,058	20,606	55,019	93,430	78,347	74,688	54,845
% vote	8·1	8·4	18·5	28·3	22·3	17·5	12·2
Candidates	7	12	15	35	26	26	29
Seats	1	1	6	10	7	6	3
Rest of Leinster							
Votes	39,439	42,868	52,391	48,608	41,281	47,940	45,701
% vote	14·3	16·5	19·2	17·4	14·4	13·6	11·7
Candidates	11	9	10	19	12	14	14
Seats	3	5	6	4	5	5	5
Munster							
Votes	49,911	67,813	72,912	64,784	57,589	56,485	62,387
% vote	12·6	17·7	18·5	16·0	14·0	11·7	12·0
Candidates	11*	11*	13*	25	13	13*	14
Seats	8*	10*	10*	4	7	6*	6
Connacht-Ulster							
Votes	2,339	4,824	12,418	17,676	7,900	7,297	7,057
% vote	0·8	1·7	4·3	5·8	2·6	2·1	2·0
Candidates	2	3	6	20	5	4	3
Seats	0	0	0	0	0	0	1
Ireland							
Votes	111,747	136,111	192,740	224,498	185,117	186,410	169,990
% votes	9·1	11·6	15·4	17·0	13·7	11·6	9·9
Candidates	31*	35*	44*	99	56	57*	60
Seats	12*	16*	22*	18	19	17*	15

| | Number of branches | | | | | Percentage of total branches | | | |
Year	Total	Dublin	Rest of Leinster	Munster	Connacht and Ulster	Dublin	Rest of Leinster	Munster	Connacht and Ulster
1964	248	29	113	103	3	11·7	45·6	41·5	1·2
1965	289	38	124	124	3	13·1	42·9	42·9	1·0
1966	357	52	158	143	4	14·6	44·3	40·1	1·1
1967	457	67	187	187	16	14·7	40·9	40·9	3·5
1968	477	75	174	207	21	15·7	36·5	43·4	4·4
1969	501	83	183	211	24	16·6	36·5	42·1	4·8
1970	479	105	156	193	25	21·9	32·6	40·3	5·2
1971	450	95	147	187	21	21·1	32·7	41·6	4·7
1972	436	99	140	182	15	22·7	32·1	41·7	3·4
1973	480	97	153	210	20	20·2	31·9	43·7	4·2
1974	499	115	158	203	23	23·0	31·7	40·7	4·6
1975	467	115	152	179	21	24·6	32·5	38·3	4·5
1976	538	136	155	225	22	25·2	28·8	41·8	4·1
1977	549	150	173	206	20	27·3	31·5	37·5	3·6

Note. Until 1974 the party did not have a register of individual members. Instead, members registered with a local branch, which paid an annual affiliation fee to Head Office; the size of the fee did not depend on the size of the branch. Inevitably, some branches, no matter how many members they claimed, were 'paper' branches, more or less inactive between elections. For all these reasons, there is no way of telling how many members the party had during this period, although each branch was supposed, under the constitution, to have a minimum of ten members.

An individual membership scheme was introduced in 1974, under which each member had to pay an annual membership fee of £1 (later raised to £3) to Head Office. Branch figures broken down by province are not readily available for the period since 1977, but the individual membership figures at December of each year since 1973 are: 1974, 4,700; 1975, 5,100; 1976, 5,088; 1977, 3,474; 1978, 5,264; 1979, 4,846; 1980, 6,254.

Minimum branch membership is currently ten in Dublin and five elsewhere; in practice branch membership varies between five and not much more than twenty, with an average of ten. The annual branch affiliation fee is £10, so that the cost of setting up a paper branch of completely inactive members, in order to gain support at a candidate selection conference, is £40 in Dublin and £25 elsewhere, with the consequence that while some such branches still exist, they are less numerous than in the past.

Source: Figures provided by Labour Party Head Office.

Appendix 4 *Occupational backgrounds of Labour candidates 1957–81*

	Manual employee		Trade union official		Non-manual employee		Commercial		Farmer		Professional		Other/ unknown		(Politician)		Total	
	N	%	N	%	N	%	N	%	N	%	N	%	N	%	N	%	N	%
1957	9	29·0	10	32·3	4	12·9	2	6·5	2	6·5	3	9·7	1	3·2	7	22·6	31	100·0
1961	3	8·6	16	45·7	7	20·0	3	8·6	2	5·7	1	2·9	3	8·6	8	22·9	35	100·0
1965	3	6·8	16	36·4	7	15·9	7	15·9	2	4·5	9	20·5	0	0	12	27·3	44	100·0
1969	15	15·2	21	21·2	19	19·2	17	17·2	5	5·1	22	22·2	0	0	9	9·1	99	100·0
1973	4	7·1	17	30·4	14	25·0	7	12·5	0	0	14	25·0	0	0	13	23·2	56	100·0
1977	5	8·8	12	21·1	16	28·1	10	17·5	0	0	13	22·8	1	1·8	15	26·3	56	100·0
1981	10	16·7	12	20·0	16	26·7	6	10·0	1	1·7	14	23·3	1	1·7	13	21·7	57	100·0
Total	49	12·8	104	27·2	83	21·7	52	13·6	12	3·1	76	19·9	6	1·6	77	20·2	382	100·0

Note: For an explanation of the classification and categories used, and the sources, see Table 5.1.

Appendix 5 *Ages and occupational backgrounds of Labour TDs 1957–81*

Year	Average age	Manual employee		Trade union official		Non-manual employee		Commercial		Farmer		Professional (Politician)				Total	
		N	%	N	%	N	%	N	%	N	%	N	%	N	%	N	%
1957	47	0	0	6	50.0	2	16.7	1	8.3	2	16.7	1	8.3	7	58.3	12	100.0
1961	47	1	6.2	7	43.7	3	18.7	2	12.5	2	12.5	1	6.2	8	50.0	16	100.0
1965	46	1	4.5	11	50.0	3	13.6	3	13.6	2	9.1	2	9.1	11	50.0	22	100.0
1969	45	1	5.6	7	38.9	2	11.1	2	11.1	0	0	6	33.3	7	38.9	18	100.0
1973	48	1	5.3	7	36.8	4	21.1	3	15.8	0	0	4	21.1	13	68.4	19	100.0
1977	48	1	5.9	8	47.1	2	11.8	3	17.6	0	0	3	17.6	12	70.6	17	100.0
1981	51	2	13.3	5	33.3	2	13.3	3	20.0	0	0	3	20.0	10	66.7	15	100.0
Total	47	7	5.9	51	42.9	18	15.1	17	14.3	6	5.0	20	16.8	68	57.1	119	100.0

Note: The average age given is that of TDs at the time of the general election. See also note to Appendix 4.

Bibliography

1 Interviews

Joe Bermingham TD; Dr Noel Browne TD; Brendan Corish TD; Stephen Coughlan, former Labour TD; Barry Desmond TD; Brendan Halligan, former general secretary of the Labour Party; Justin Keating, former Labour TD; Tom Kyne, former Labour TD; Con Lehane, former Clann na Poblachta TD; Proinsias Mac Aonghusa, former vice-chairman of the Labour Party; Seán MacBride, former leader of Clann na Poblachta; Matt Merrigan, general secretary of the ATGWU; Donal Nevin, assistant general secretary of ICTU; John O'Connell TD; Michael O'Leary TD; John Ryan TD; Seamus Scally, general secretary of the Labour Party; James Tully TD. In addition, interviews were conducted with three Fine Gael members of the 1973–77 National Coalition administration, with another Fine Gael TD, and with a former Fine Gael Senator. Interviews were conducted between 1976 and 1981. Some of those listed were interviewed more than once, and some information has come from individuals not formally interviewed.

2 Government publications

Acts of the Oireachtas
Bunreacht na hEireann (Constitution of Ireland)
Census of Population 1971
Dáil Eireann Debates
Election Results and Transfer of Votes (published for all elections since that of 1948)
Iris Oifigiúil
Local Elections, 1974: Results and Statistics (Dublin: Department of Local Government, 1975)
Local Elections, 1979: Election Results and Transfer of Votes
Seanad Eireann Debates
Statistical Abstract of Ireland

All published by the Stationery Office, Dublin, unless otherwise indicated.

3 Newspapers and periodicals

The place of publication for all items is Dublin, unless otherwise indicated. *Anglo-Celt* (Cavan), *Business and Finance, Catholic Standard, Clare Champion, Connacht Tribune* (Galway), *Cork Examiner, Donegal Democrat, Drogheda Argus, Drogheda Independent, Dungarvan Leader, Evening Echo* (Cork), *Evening Herald, Evening Mail, Evening Press, Free Press* (Wexford), *Freeman's Journal, Hibernia, Irish Independent, Irish Press, Irish Times, Kerryman, Leinster Express* (Portlaoise), *Leinster Leader* (Naas), *Limerick Leader, Longford Leader, Mayo News, Meath Chronicle, Midland Tribune* (Birr), *Munster Express* (Waterford), *Munster Tribune, Nationalist and Leinster Times* (Carlow), *Nenagh Guardian, Nusight, Offaly Chronicle, People* (Wexford), *Roscommon Champion, Roscommon Herald, Sligo Champion, Southern Star* (Skibbereen), *Sunday Independent, Sunday Press, Sunday Review, This Week, Times* (London), *Tipperary Star, Tuam Herald, Western People* (Ballina), *Westmeath Examiner, Westmeath Independent, Westmeath-Offaly Independent, Wicklow People.* In addition to these newspapers directly referred to in the notes, all other provincial newspapers available in the National Library, Dublin, have been examined for the periods of general election and by-election campaigns since 1957, and have been used to gather information about candidates' backgrounds.

4 Party and trade union publications and other documents

All those listed were published in Dublin by the Irish Labour Party, unless otherwise indicated.

Communist Party of Ireland: Outline History (Dublin: New Books, nd [1973?]).

Congress of Irish Unions. Annual Meetings, 1945–1959.

Dun Laoghaire Constituency Council. Records, 1969–73.

Fine Gael Policy 1965, 1965.

General Election 1969: Canvasser's Notes, 1969.

Irish Communist. Published by the British and Irish Communist Organization, from 1967.

Irish Congress of Trade Unions. Annual Report, published since 1959.

Irish People. Published weekly, 1944–48.

Irish Transport and General Workers' Union. Annual Report. Published since 1918.

Labour. Published monthly, 1967.

Labour News. Published monthly by the Dublin South West Constituency Council of the Labour Party, 1965–66.

Labour Party Constitution.

Labour Party Outline Policy, 1969.

The Labour Party: Report of the Administrative Council and of the Parliamentary Labour Party. (Sometimes entitled simply 'The Labour Party Annual Report'; referred to in the notes as 'Annual Report'.) Published since 1917.

Liberty. Published monthly by the Irish Transport and General Workers' Union since 1952.

National Observer. Published monthly and bi-monthly by 'The Research and Information Company Limited', an unofficial Fine Gael group, 1958–60.

The Party Programme: Labour Party Annual Conference 1980, 1980.

Records of Labour Party conferences since 1969 (tape recordings).

United Irishman. Published monthly by Sinn Féin, from 1948.

Workers' Union of Ireland Bulletin. Published monthly since 1957.

5 Books, articles and pamphlets

Alford, Robert, *Party and Society* (London: John Murray, 1964).

Arensberg, Conrad M., and Kimball, Solon T., *Family and Community in Ireland* (Cambridge, Mass.: Harvard University Press, 1968).

Ayearst, Morley, *The Republic of Ireland* (London: University of London Press, 1971).

Barrington, Donal, *Uniting Ireland* (Dublin: Tuairim Pamphlet No. 1, nd [1957 or 1958]).

Bax, Mart, *Harpstrings and Confessions* (Assen: Van Gorcum, 1976).

Bell, J. Bowyer, *The Secret Army*, 2nd edition (Dublin: Academy Press, 1979).

Blondel, Jean, *An Introduction to Comparative Government* (London: Weidenfeld and Nicolson, 1969).

Boissevain, Jeremy, 'When the Saints go Marching out: Reflections on the Decline of Patronage in Malta', in Ernest Gellner and John Waterbury (eds.), *Patrons and Clients* (London: Duckworth, 1977), pp. 81–96.

Bolster, Evelyn, *The Knights of St. Columbanus* (Dublin: Gill and Macmillan, 1979).

Brody, Hugh, *Inishkillane* (Harmondsworth: Penguin, 1973).

Browne, Eric C. and Franklin, Mark N., 'Aspects of Coalition Payoffs in European Parliamentary Democracies', *American Political Science Review* 67:2 (1973), pp. 453–69.

Buckland, Patrick, *Irish Unionism 1: The Anglo-Irish and the New Ireland 1885–1922* (Dublin: Gill and Macmillan, 1972).

Butler, David, and Stokes, Donald, *Political Change in Britain* (Harmondsworth: Penguin, 1971).

Butler, D. E., and Stokes, Donald, *Political Change in Britain*, 2nd edition (London: Macmillan, 1974).

Carroll, Joseph, *Ireland in the War Years* (Newton Abbot: David & Charles, 1975).

Chubb, Basil, 'Ireland 1957', in D. E. Butler (ed.), *Elections Abroad* (London: Macmillan, 1959), pp. 183–226.

Chubb, Basil, *The Government and Politics of Ireland* (Stanford: Stanford University Press, 1970).

Chubb, Basil, *Cabinet Government in Ireland* (Dublin: Institute of Public Administration, 1974).

Chubb, Basil, *The Constitution and Constitutional Change in Ireland* (Dublin: Institute of Public Administration, 1978).

Clarkson, J. Dunsmore, *Labour and Nationalism in Ireland* (New York: Columbia University Press, 1926).

Coogan, Tim Pat, *Ireland Since the Rising* (London: Pall Mall Press, 1966).

Corish, Brendan, *The New Republic* (Dublin: Irish Labour Party, 1968).

Davis, E. E., and Sinnott, R., *Attitudes in the Republic of Ireland Relevant to the Northern Ireland problem* (Dublin: Economic and Social Research Institute Paper No. 97, 1979).

Davis, Richard, 'Ulster Protestants and the Sinn Féin Press, 1914–22', *Eire–Ireland* 15:4 (1980), pp. 60–85.

De Swaan, Abram, *Coalition Theories and Cabinet Formations* (Amsterdam: Elsevier Scientific Publishing Company, 1973).

Downs, Anthony, *An Economic Theory of Democracy* (New York: Harper and Row, 1957).

Duverger, Maurice, *Political Parties*, 2nd edition (London: Methuen, 1959).

Edwards, Owen Dudley, *The Mind of an Activist* (Dublin: Gill and Macmillan, 1971).

Edwards, Owen Dudley, and Ransom, Bernard (eds.), *James Connolly: Selected Political Writings* (London: Pelican, 1973).

Ellis, P. Berresford, *A History of the Irish Working Class* (London: Victor Gollancz, 1972).

Epstein, Leon D., *Political Parties in Western Democracies* (London: Pall Mall Press, 1967).

Fanning, Ronan, *The Irish Department of Finance 1922–58* (Dublin: Institute of Public Administration, 1978).

Farrell, Brian, 'Labour and the Irish Political Party System: A Suggested Approach to Analysis', *Economic and Social Review* 1:4 (1969–70), pp. 477–502.

Farrell, Brian, 'Dáil Deputies: "The 1969 Generation" ', *Economic and Social Review* 2:3 (1970–71), pp. 309–27.

Farrell, Brian, *Chairman or Chief?* (Dublin: Gill and Macmillan, 1971).

Farrell, Brian, 'The Mass Media and the 1977 Campaign', pp. 97–131, and Farrell, Brian, and Manning, Maurice, 'The Election', pp. 133–64, in Howard R. Penniman (ed.), *Ireland at the Polls: the Dáil Elections of 1977* (Washington: American Enterprise Institute for Public Policy Research, 1978).

Farrell, Michael, *Northern Ireland: The Orange State*, 2nd edition (London: Pluto Press, 1980).

Galenson, Walter, *Labor in Norway* (Cambridge, Mass.: Harvard University Press, 1949).

Gallagher, Michael, 'Disproportionality in a Proportional Representation System: The Irish Experience', *Political Studies* 23:4 (1975), pp. 501–13.

Gallagher, Michael, *Electoral Support for Irish Political Parties 1927–1973* (London: Sage Professional Papers, Contemporary Political Sociology Series, Vol. 2, No. 06-017, 1976).

Gallagher, Michael, 'Socialism and the Nationalist Tradition in Ireland 1798–1918', *Eire–Ireland* 12:2 (1977), pp. 63–102.

Gallagher, Michael, 'The Presidency of the Republic of Ireland: Implications of the "Donegan Affair" ', *Parliamentary Affairs* 30:4 (1977), pp. 373–84.

Gallagher, Michael, 'Party Solidarity, Exclusivity and Inter-party Relationships in Ireland 1922–1977: the Evidence of Transfers', *Economic and Social Review* 10:1 (1978–79), pp. 1–22.

Gallagher, Michael, 'The Pact General Election of 1922', *Irish Historical Studies* 21, No. 84 (1979), pp. 404–421.

Gallagher, Michael, 'Candidate Selection in Ireland: The Impact of Localism and the Electoral System', *British Journal of Political Science* 10:4 (1980), pp. 489–503.

Gallagher, Michael, 'Societal change and party adaptation in the Republic of Ireland 1960–1981', *European Journal of Political Research* 9:3 (1981), pp. 269–85.

Garvin, Tom, and Parker, Anthony, 'Party Loyalty and Irish Voters: The EEC Referendum as a Case Study', *Economic and Social Review* 4:1 (1972–73), pp. 35–9.

Garvin, Tom, 'Nationalist Elites, Irish Voters and Irish Political Development: A Comparative Perspective', *Economic and Social Review* 8:3 (1976–77), pp. 161–86.

Garvin, Tom, 'Belief Systems, Ideological Perspectives and Political Activism: Some Dublin Evidence', *Social Studies* 6:1 (1977), pp. 39–56.

Gaughan, J. Anthony, *Thomas Johnson* (Dublin: Kingdom Books, 1980).

Gibbon, Peter, and Higgins, M. D., 'Patronage, Tradition and Modernization: The Case of the Irish "Gombeenman" ', *Economic and Social Review* 6:1 (1974–75), pp. 27–44.

Graham, J. A. V., *The Consensus-forming Strategy of the Northern Ireland Labour Party, 1949–1968* (Queen's University Belfast: M Soc Sc thesis, 1972).

Greaves, C. Desmond, *The Life and Times of James Connolly* (London: Lawrence and Wishart, 1961).

Groennings, Sven, Kelley, E. W., and Leiserson, Michael (eds.), *The Study of Coalition Behaviour* (New York: Holt, Rinehart and Winston, 1970).

Hannan, Damian, 'Kinship, Neighbourhood and Social Change in Irish Rural Communities', *Economic and Social Review* 3:2 (1971–72), pp. 163–88.

Harbinson, John Fitzsimons, *A History of the Northern Ireland Labour Party 1891–1949* (Queen's University Belfast: MSc (Econ) thesis, 1966).

Hart, Ian, 'Public Opinion on Civil Servants and the Role and Power of the Individual in the Local Community', *Administration* 18:4 (1970), pp. 375–91.

Henig, Stanley, and Pinder, John (eds.), *European Political Parties* (London: George Allen and Unwin, 1969).

Huntington, Samuel P., *Political Order in Changing Societies* (New Haven: Yale University Press, 1968).

Inglehart, Ronald, and Klingemann, Hans D., 'Party Identification, Ideological Preference and the Left-Right Dimension among Western Mass Publics', in Ian Budge, Ivor Crewe and Dennis Farlie (eds.), *Party Identification and Beyond* (London: John Wiley, 1976), pp. 243–73.

Jackson, John, 'Ireland', in M. S. Archer and S. Giner (eds.), *Contemporary Europe: Class, Status and Power* (London: Weidenfeld and Nicolson, 1971), pp. 189–222.

Jacobs, Eric, *European Trade Unionism* (London: Croom Helm, 1973).

Judge, Jerome Joseph Joshua, *The Labour Movement in the Republic of Ireland* (National University of Ireland: PhD thesis in the library of University College Dublin, 1955).

Kavanagh, Dennis, *Political Culture* (London: Macmillan, 1972).

Keane, John B., *Letters of a Successful TD* (Cork: Mercier Press, 1967).

Knight, James, and Baxter-Moore, Nicolas, *Republic of Ireland: The General Elections of 1969 and 1973* (London: The Arthur McDougall Fund, 1973).

Kyle, Keith, 'The Panorama Survey of Irish Opinion', *Political Quarterly* 50:1 (1979), pp. 24–35.

Larkin, Emmet, 'Socialism and Catholicism in Ireland', *Church History* 33:4 (1964), pp. 462–83.

Larkin, Emmet, *James Larkin* (London: Routledge and Kegan Paul, 1965).

Lennon, James, Nic Ghiolla Phadraigh, Máire, and Inglis, Thomas F., 'Religious Practice in Ireland', *Intercom* (Bulletin of the Catholic Communications Institute of Ireland) 6:9 (1975), pp. 2–6.

Levenson, Samuel, *James Connolly* (London: Martin Brian and O'Keeffe, 1973).

Lijphart, Arend, *Class Voting and Religious Voting in the European Democracies* (Glasgow: University of Strathclyde Occasional Paper No. 8, 1971).

Lipset, Seymour M., and Rokkan, Stein (eds.), *Party Systems and Voter Alignments* (New York: Free Press, 1967).

Longford, The Earl of, and O'Neill, Thomas P., *Eamon de Valera* (London: Arrow Books, 1974).

Lynch, Patrick, 'The Social Revolution that never was', in T. Desmond Williams (ed.), *The Irish Struggle 1916–1926* (London: Routledge and Kegan Paul, 1966), pp. 41–54.

Lyons, F. S. L., *Ireland Since the Famine* (London: Weidenfeld and Nicolson, 1971).

Lysaght, D. R. O'Connor, 'Religion and Irish Labour', *International Socialist Journal* 2:10 (1965), pp. 495–502.

Lysaght, D. R. O'Connor, *The Republic of Ireland* (Cork: Mercier Press, 1970).

Mac Aonghusa, Proinsias (ed.), *Corish Speaks* (Dublin: New Century Publications, 1966).

Macardle, Dorothy, *The Irish Republic* (London: Corgi, 1968).

McCann, Eamonn, *War and an Irish Town*, 2nd edition (London: Pluto Press, 1980).

McCarthy, Charles, *Trade Unions in Ireland 1894–1960* (Dublin: Institute of Public Administration, 1977).

McCarthy, Colm, and Ryan, Terence M., 'Party Loyalty at Referenda and General Elections: Evidence from recent Irish contests', *Economic and Social Review* 7:3 (1975–76), pp. 279–88.

McCracken, J. L., *Representative Government in Ireland: A Study of Dáil Eireann 1919–1948* (London: Oxford University Press, 1958).

Mac Gréil, Mícheál, *Prejudice and Tolerance in Ireland* (Dublin: College of Industrial Relations, 1977).

McInerney, Michael, 'Noel Browne: Church and State', *University Review* 5:2 (1968), pp. 171–215.

McKibbin, Ross, *The Evolution of the Labour Party 1910–1924* (London: Oxford University Press, 1974).

MacNamara, Brinsley, *The Valley of the Squinting Windows* (Tralee: Anvil Books, 1964).

Maguire, Maria, 'Pressure Groups in Ireland', *Administration* 25:3 (1977), pp. 349–64.

Mair, Peter, 'Labour and the Irish Party System Revisited: Party Competition in the 1920s', *Economic and Social Review* 9:1 (1977–78), pp. 59–70.

Mair, Peter, 'The Autonomy of the Political', *Comparative Politics* 11:4 (1979), pp. 445–65.

Manning, Maurice, *The Blueshirts* (Dublin: Gill and Macmillan, 1970).

Manning, Maurice, *Irish Political Parties: an introduction* (Dublin: Gill and Macmillan, 1972).

Mansergh, Nicholas, *The Irish Question 1840–1921* (London: George Allen and Unwin, 1965).

Marsh, M. A., 'European Social Democratic Party Leaders and the Working Class', in Kay Lawson (ed.), *Political Parties and Linkage* (New Haven: Yale University Press, 1980), pp. 47–72.

May, John D., 'Opinion Structure of Political Parties: The Special Law of Curvilinear Disparity', *Political Studies* 21:2 (1973), pp. 135–51.

Messenger, John C., *Inis Beag* (New York: Holt, Rinehart and Winston, 1969).

Miller, David W., *Church, State and Nation in Ireland 1898–1921* (Dublin: Gill and Macmillan, 1973).

Minogue, K. R., *Nationalism* (London: B. T. Batsford, 1967).

Mitchell, Arthur, 'The Irish Labour Party', in four parts, *Irish Times* 27 February 1967 to 2 March 1967.

Mitchell, Arthur, *Labour in Irish Politics 1890–1930* (Dublin: Irish University Press, 1974).

Morgan, Austen, 'Socialism in Ireland – Red, Green and Orange', in Austen Morgan and Bob Purdie (eds.), *Ireland: Divided Nation, Divided Class* (London: Ink Links, 1980), pp. 172–225.

Morrell, Frances, *From the Electors of Bristol* (Nottingham: Spokesman Pamphlet No. 57, 1977).

Moss, Warner, *Political Parties in the Irish Free State* (New York: Columbia University Press, 1933).

Murphy, John A., 'The Irish Party System, 1938–1951', in Kevin B. Nowlan and T. Desmond Williams (eds.), *Ireland in the War Years and After, 1939–51* (Dublin: Gill and Macmillan, 1969), pp. 147–66.

Murphy, John A., *Ireland in the Twentieth Century* (Dublin: Gill and Macmillan, 1975).

Nairn, Tom, *The Break-up of Britain* (London: NLB, 1977).

Nealon, Ted, *Ireland: A Parliamentary Directory 1973–74* (Dublin: Institute of Public Administration, 1974).

Nevin, Donal, 'Labour and the Political Revolution', in Francis MacManus (ed.), *The Years of the Great Test, 1926–1936* (Cork: Mercier Press, 1967), pp. 55–68.

Nevin, Donal, 'Industry and Labour', in Kevin B. Nowlan and T. Desmond Williams (eds.), *Ireland in the War Years and After, 1939–51* (Dublin: Gill and Macmillan, 1969), pp. 94–108.

Nevin, Donal (ed.), *Trade Unions and Change in Irish Society* (Dublin: Mercier Press, 1980).

Norton, William, *Labour's Way* (Dublin: Irish Labour Party, nd [1958]).

O'Brien, Conor Cruise, 'The Embers of Easter 1916–1966', in Owen Dudley Edwards and Fergus Pyle (eds.), *1916: The Easter Rising* (London: MacGibbon and Kee, 1968), pp. 225–40.

O'Brien, Conor Cruise, *States of Ireland* (London: Panther Books, 1974).

O'Leary, Cornelius, *The Irish Republic* (Notre Dame: University of Notre Dame Press, 1961).

O'Leary, Cornelius, 'The Catholic and Politics', *Christus Rex* 17:4 (1963), pp. 285–97.

O'Leary, Cornelius, *Irish Elections 1918–1977* (Dublin: Gill and Macmillan, 1979).

O'Neill, Thomas P., 'In Search of a Political Path: Irish Republicanism 1922 to 1927', in G. A. Hayes-McCoy (ed.), *Historical Studies 10* (Dublin: Irish Committee of Historical Sciences, 1976), pp. 147–71.

Orridge, Andrew, 'The Irish Labour Party', *Journal of Common Market Studies* 13:4 (1975), pp. 484–91.

Orridge, Andrew, 'The Irish Labour Party', in William E. Paterson and Alistair H. Thomas (eds.), *Social Democratic Parties in Western Europe* (London: Croom Helm, 1977), pp. 153–75.

O'Sullivan, Donal, *The Irish Free State and its Senate* (London: Faber and Faber, 1940).

Petersen, William, 'A General Typology of Migration', *American Sociological Review* 23:3 (1958), pp. 256–66.

Pyne, Peter, 'The Third Sinn Féin Party: 1923–1926', *Economic and Social Review* 1:1 (1969–70), pp. 29–50 and 1:2 (1969–70), pp. 229–57.

Rae, Douglas, *The Political Consequences of Electoral Laws*, revised edition (New Haven: Yale University Press, 1971).

Raven, John, Whelan, C. T., Pfretzschner, Paul A., and Borock, Donald M., *Political Culture in Ireland* (Dublin: Institute of Public Administration, 1976).

Riker, William H., *The Theory of Political Coalitions* (New Haven: Yale University Press, 1962).

Roberts, Ruaidhri, 'Trade Union Organization in Ireland', *Journal of the Statistical and Social Inquiry Society of Ireland* 20:2 (1958–59), pp. 93–110.

Rose, Richard, and Urwin, Derek, 'Social Cohesion, Political Parties and Strains in Regimes', *Comparative Political Studies* 2:1 (1969–70), pp. 7–67.

Rose, Richard, *Governing without Consensus* (London: Faber and Faber, 1971).

Rumpf, Erhard, and Hepburn, A. C., *Nationalism and Socialism in*

Twentieth Century Ireland (Liverpool: Liverpool University Press, 1977).

Sacks, Paul, *The Donegal Mafia* (New Haven: Yale University Press, 1976).

Sartori, Giovanni, *Parties and Party Systems* (Cambridge University Press, 1976).

Sinnott, Richard, 'The Electorate', in Howard R. Penniman (ed.), *Ireland at the Polls: the Dáil Elections of 1977* (Washington: American Enterprise Institute for Public Policy Research, 1978), pp. 35–67.

Smith, Gordon, *Politics in Western Europe*, 2nd edition (London: Heinemann, 1976).

Steiner, Kurt, *Politics in Austria* (Boston: Little, Brown, 1972).

Thornley, David, 'The Development of the Irish Labour Movement', *Christus Rex* 18:1 (1964), pp. 7–21.

Throne, John, *Coalition: The Alternative* (Dublin: a Militant pamphlet, nd [1974?]).

Valen, Henry, and Rokkan, Stein, 'Norway: Conflict Structure and Mass Politics in a European Periphery', in Richard Rose (ed.), *Electoral Behavior: A Comparative Handbook* (New York: Free Press, 1974), pp. 315–70.

Whyte, John, *Dáil Deputies: Their Work, its Difficulties, Possible Remedies* (Dublin: Tuairim Pamphlet No. 15, 1966).

Whyte, J. H., 'Ireland: Politics without Social Bases', in Richard Rose (ed.), *Electoral Behavior: A Comparative Handbook* (New York: Free Press, 1974), pp. 619–51.

Whyte, John, 'Interpretations of the Northern Ireland Problem: An Appraisal', *Economic and Social Review* 9:4 (1977–78), pp. 257–82.

Whyte, J. H., *Church and State in Modern Ireland 1923–1979* (Dublin: Gill and Macmillan, 1980).

Wolinetz, Steven B., 'The Dutch Labour Party', in William E. Paterson and Alistair H. Thomas (eds.), *Social Democratic Parties in Western Europe* (London: Croom Helm, 1977), pp. 342–88.

Zimmermann, Joseph F., 'Role Perceptions of Dual Office Holders in Ireland', *Administration* 26:1 (1978), pp. 25–48.

Index

abortion 109, 229–30, 238

Administrative Council (of Labour Party), structure of, 272; criticises Inter-Party government, 30; and progressive unity, 42–3; expels party members, 65, 227; decisions on candidates, 102, 216–17, 227–8; in Coughlan disputes, 106–7, 294; resignations from, 107; disciplinary role, 111, 114; on Northern Ireland, 132–5, 143, 150, 210; on coalition, 183–6, 191, 214, 232, 248, 251–2; and 1973–77 government, 199, 204; other references, 59, 69, 216

Aiken, Frank 174

Alford, Robert 21–2

Alliance Party (Northern Ireland) 210

Amalgamated Transport and General Workers' Union 62, 75

Ancient Order of Hibernians 39

Andrews, David 292

Angelus 114

Anschluss 128

anti-apartheid campaigners 106, 190

anti-semitism 106–8, 113

Aontacht Eireann 116, 118, 209

Arms Crisis 108–9, 179, 183

Austria 128, 168

Ayearst, Morley 26

Azda 46

Barnhill, John, murder of 141

Barrett, Stephen D. 274

Barrington, Donal 122, 128–9

Barry, Anthony 159

Bartley, Gerard 276

Bax, Mart 18, 94

Beattie, Jack 133

Belfast Corporation 133, 134

Benn, Tony 146

Bermingham, Joe 119, 246, 297

Blaney, Neil, on Labour extremism, 58, 83, 93, 94; in Arms Crisis, 108; expelled from Fianna Fáil, 116; on Northern Ireland, 136; other references, 179, 252

Blondel, Jean 23, 24

'Bloody Sunday' (1972) 144, 145, 146

Blueshirts 284

Boland, Kevin 93, 108, 116–17, 209

Boucher, Dermot 189, 227, 241, 293

Brady, Michael 282, 283

Brennan, Paudge 108

British and Irish Communist Organisation 127

Brody, Hugh 19

brokerage 16–18, 26

Browne, Dan 137

Browne, Noel, and Mother and Child affair, 15; in 1913 Club, 34; founds NPD, 34; and communism, 35, 51; joins Labour, 52–3; becomes Labour vice-chairman, 68; on Labour's record, 68; attacks Church, 68, 111, 113;